Ravenous Identity

Eating and Eating Distress in the
Life and Work of Virginia Woolf

Allie Glenny

St. Martin's Press
New York

To John Logan

RAVENOUS IDENTITY. Copyright © 1999 Allie Glenny. All rights reserved. Printed in the United States of America. No part of this book may be used or reproduced in any manner whatsoever without written permission except in the case of brief quotations embodied in critical articles or reviews. For information, address St. Martin's Press, 175 Fifth Avenue, New York, N.Y. 10010.

ISBN 0-312-21333-6

Library of Congress Cataloging-in-Publication Data
Glenny, Allie, 1963-
  Ravenous identity : eating and eating distress in the life and work of Virginia Woolf / Allie Glenny.
    p. cm.
  Includes bibliographical references and index.
  ISBN 0-312-21333-6
  1. Woolf, Virginia, 1882–1941—Psychology. 2. Women and literature—England—History—20th century. 3. Women novelists, English—20th century—Psychology. 4. Fiction—Authorship--Psychological aspects. 5. Identity (Psychology) in literature. 6. Eating disorders in literature. 7. Food habits in literature.
    I. Title.
PR6045.072Z646   1999
823'.912—dc21   99–19871
                                                                              CIP

Design by Letra Libre

First edition: January, 2000
10 9 8 7 6 5 4 3 2 1

Contents

Acknowledgments iv
Notes on Quotations and Abbreviations iv
Preface v
Introduction xi

1. Anorexia: A Perspective from the Other Side 1
2. My Food Is Affection 13
3. Entirely My Weight Rests on His Prop 45
4. *The Voyage Out:* A Slave to One's Body in This World 77
5. *Jacob's Room:* Helping Himself to Jam 99
6. *Mrs. Dalloway:* Blackberrying in the Sun 117
7. *To the Lighthouse:* An Instinct Like Artichokes for the Sun 133
8. *The Waves:* Some Fasting and Anguished Spirit 155
9. *The Years:* The Admirable Mutton 175
10. *Between the Acts:* Soles. Filleted 203

Notes 229
Texts Cited in Abbreviation 249
Bibliography 251
Index 262

Acknowledgments

I would like to thank Louise DeSalvo for her long-standing faith in and encouragement with *Ravenous Identity*. Thanks are also due to Isobel Grundy, who supervised the doctoral thesis from which this book developed. I am grateful to Emma Robinson at London University Library (who waived library fees, thus enabling me to complete my research) and to Mary Ferdinand at Digital Type for computer assistance. I would also like to thank Maura Burnett, Kristi Long, and Alan Bradshaw at St. Martin's Press for their help with the production of this book. Finally, I am grateful to all of those who have shared with me their personal experiences of eating distress—I wish you well.

Notes on Quotations and Abbreviations

[Brackets] indicate my own insertion.
{Brackets} indicate a quoted insertion or emendation.
Ellipses indicate my own omission unless noted otherwise.
Abbreviated titles are listed in full on page 249.

Preface

Virginia Woolf was in eating distress at many times in her life. Her husband Leonard Woolf has described how, when this distress was at its most acute, he had to sit with her at almost every meal in order to persuade her to swallow a few mouthfuls of food (1963, 89). Even when she was relatively relaxed about food, he said, it was extremely difficult to induce her to eat a sufficient amount to maintain her health (163), and "Left to herself she ate extraordinarily little" (80). It is not my aim to demonstrate that Virginia Woolf was anorexic according to any one of the several sets of diagnostic criteria in circulation (although it is clear to me that her attitudes to food were perplexed in ways that will be familiar to most anorexic women); my interest lies in understanding Woolf's particular and individual relationship with food and eating, both in her life and in her art. In writing about her own anorexia, Sheila MacLeod notes that anorexia is a form of metaphor, and a particularly apt one; she thus proposes that anorexic women may be read and understood "as a text" (68).[1] When that "text" is a writer of the subtlety, sophistication, and intelligence of Virginia Woolf, the process of unlocking the woman-as-text takes place in a highly complex and symbolically resonant space. Continuing Woolf's own lifelong endeavor to release the meaning of her own text has been a fascinating and richly rewarding process for me.

This book started life as a doctoral thesis that I wrote while anorexic. Reflecting ongoing ontological revisions to myself as text, the voyage from that manuscript to this very different work has been one of shifting perspectives. It is my own experience of ten years of anorexia, of a further five years of other forms of eating distress, and of the ultimate transformation of these experiences that informs my view of Woolf's life and work. My viewpoint is thus not "objective." I have also had the privilege of making links with many eating-disordered women (and a small number of men) through work as a contact person for the Eating Disorders Association (EDA). These connections have enlarged and enriched my understanding of eating distress and have afforded me repeated opportunities to reevaluate both my own and Virginia Woolf's position in relation to anorexia. For this I am grateful.

The intention of this book is very much the vindication of Virginia Woolf as a woman not only of genius but also of eminent sanity. I have been motivated by the desire to speak the words that, as I see it, Woolf was unable to speak herself (at least directly), to raise her unspeakable subtexts into the light of day, as I feel she would have wished her literary daughters to do. Increasingly, thanks to feminist commentators, the undercover, authentic voice of Virginia Woolf is being heard. If by adding my weight to Woolf scholar Jane Marcus's woman-centered "slant"[2] I tilt the balance a few degrees in the favor of a truly woman-centered view, then I will be gratified, and so, I believe, would Virginia Woolf.

As an individual of strength, spirit, integrity, and dangerously trenchant vision (or what I would call *through-sight*—the ability to see through and beyond the patriarchal orthodoxy), Woolf has survived the affixation of a stream of pathologizing labels intended to silence her or at the least to devalue her viewpoint—a process which began in her own lifetime and continues today.

According to Leonard Woolf, Virginia's "disease" was most generally considered to be neurasthenia (1963, 75)—an "illness" that was frequently diagnosed in response to all or any of the psychological "symptoms" presented by women from the mid-nineteenth to the early twentieth centuries (as well as to those of the shellshocked soldiers of World War I). Barbara Ehrenreich and Deirdre English refer to neurasthenia as "that indefinable nervous disorder" (1976, 97), and Hillel Schwartz describes it as the catch-all complaint of its day, pointing out its nebulous diagnostic criteria: "Neurasthenia, explained Dr George Beard in 1869, and again in 1879, 1880 and 1881, was a want of force. Unlike anaemia, it was due not to weak blood but to frayed nerves. Its causes were as numerous as its symptoms. Indeed it would be unavailing to list the symptoms—Beard spent page after page doing just that, always to his own exasperation" (69). Leonard, however, was convinced that Virginia's "illness" was manic-depressive (although when he challenged her doctors, they insisted that this was not the case [1963, 161]). In her letters and diaries, Virginia herself repeatedly records bizarre physiological diagnoses of her psychological/existential/sociocultural distress, such as rheumatism, heart disease, and (frequently) influenza.

Virginia's nephew Quentin Bell opines luridly, "From the outset, Virginia's life was threatened by madness, death and disaster" (vol. 1, 35). He speculates on the possibility that she was subject to some kind of inherent insanity—that there was a "seed of madness within her," a "psychic malady."[3] At the same time, if he is to be believed, in Victorian England, "madness walked the streets" (35). Presumably, then, "madness" was a kind of contagion that Woolf unfortunately caught from encountering a "mad" person at large in Kensington. Both these theories have the virtue, from Bell's point of view, of relieving Woolf's immediate family and their descendants of the responsibility of examining what went on within the walls of Virginia's childhood homes, Talland House and 22 Hyde Park Gate.[4] Other writers who have described Woolf as "mad" include Phyllis Rose (who ascribes to her "an inherited tendency to madness" [xvii]) and Jean Love, in her book, *Virginia Woolf: Sources of Madness and Art*. Love also refers to Woolf's "acute emotional and mental illness," which she believes was triggered by her mother Julia Stephen's death and, more important, by her father Leslie Stephen's exaggerated mourning for Julia. An additional factor, in Love's view, was Virginia's "stage of development and her vulnerability" (2).

Among the foremost critics of Bell's biography is Roger Poole, who writes of the work, "I was puzzled by the failure to offer any evidence for the alleged 'madness' of his subject, and I was offended by the looseness and crudity of the word 'mad' as applied to one of the subtlest writers of this century" (1). He continues, "the words 'mad,' 'insane,' 'lunacy' must be withdrawn, since Virginia's behaviour throughout her life is, given the subjective factor, explicable in terms of cause and effect" (3). First studying Woolf as an undergraduate, I was excited to discover Poole's work, which articulated something that I had myself instinctively felt but had not at that time been able to conceptualize fully. It empowered me to speak my own mind in relation to Woolf, to voice an understanding that was at variance with that of most Woolf scholars.

Thomas Caramagno has argued that "Virginia Woolf's symptoms fulfil the manic-depressive paradigm" (2). Alma Bond, writing from a psychoanalytic viewpoint, also regards Woolf as suffering from manic depression (of the most severe kind). This she sees as being inherited (citing Laura, Leslie, James, and James Fitzjames Stephen as other family sufferers) (21–22). Bond also sees Woolf's dysfunctional family as a contributory factor to her "pathology," although she gives no credence to the fact of Woolf's sexual abuse.[5]

James King accepts that Woolf's sexual abuse had tremendous influence on her psychological development and notes the incidence of bipolar disorders in the Stephen family but sees the most important psychological determinant in her life as the death of Julia Stephen. He concludes, "In my opinion, Virginia Woolf's frequent depressions and rare bouts of psychotic breakdown derive from a mixture of frailties, not a single source" (xvi-xvii).

Michael Rosenthal takes a similarly catholic viewpoint, stating that "Although mental illness can certainly not be traced to any single event in a person's life, it is clear that the death of Virginia's mother and the accompanying collapse of her father short-circuited an already fragile system" (4). In his view, "little is known about the exact nature of her condition" (5).

Hermione Lee writes, "Virginia Woolf was a sane woman who had an illness." For Lee, "Her illness is attributable to genetic, environmental and biological factors . . . It was precipitated, but not indubitably caused, by the things which happened to her" (1996, 175).

In her groundbreaking work on Woolf's childhood sexual abuse, Louise DeSalvo asserts that "Virginia Woolf was a sexually abused child; she was an incest survivor" (1). Since DeSalvo has already stated the case convincingly in this respect, it would be superfluous to re-rehearse her arguments in this book. However, because eating disorders are frequently a response to sexual abuse, it is my feeling that *Ravenous Identity* should be considered alongside DeSalvo's *Virginia Woolf.*

Various writers have considered the possibility that Woolf was anorexic or had some anorexic attitudes. A Japanese psychologist, Miyeko Kamiya, was the first to raise this issue in a letter to Leonard Woolf in 1967. She asked Leonard whether he had ever heard of anorexia nervosa, which she described as an illness affecting young girls who showed *some* similarities to Virginia. In an article that she subsequently wrote for the publication *Confina Psychiatrica,* Kamiya identified strains of manic depression and schizophrenia as well as anorexia in Woolf's psychological "illness."[6]

Shirley Panken describes Woolf's behavior during "breakdown" as "starving herself or anorexia" (48n), but with the qualification that she was "not strictly suffering from anorexia nervosa" (50). Panken's opinion is problematic in that she subscribes to outdated Freudian opinions about anorexia, particularly that "restriction of food intake causes cessation of menses that, in turn, engenders pre-occupation with pregnancy" (51).[7]

Madeline Moore refers to Woolf's "anorexia nervosa" unequivocally, emphasizing that "I am not using the term lightly." For Moore, anorexia is one of "Woolf's ascetic practices," adopted as a last-resort gesture of feminist-political defiance adopted in a situation of disempowerment (21–22).

Jane Dunn writes, "Throughout her life she [Woolf] showed very little interest in food, although she could write about it sublimely. Periodically, as a symptom of her breakdowns, she would punish her body in an anorectic denial of its basic needs" (178). This is another problematic statement in that Woolf was clearly far from uninterested in food. Moreover, that anorexic women are not interested in food is a popular misconception; in fact anorexic women are interested in food more or less to the exclusion of all else.[8]

Stephen Trombley, in his excellent study of Woolf's doctors, is dismissive of anorexia as a feature of Woolf's psychological distress. He writes that "to accept this diagnosis would be to confuse the issue. In Virginia's case, the significance of the problem is existential, sexual, ontological" (60). However, Trombley is apparently under a misapprehension about the nature of anorexia, which is in fact an existential, ontological problem, often with a significant sexual element. For me, his account of Woolf's condition during psychological crisis could stand as a description of anorexic being: "she had a peculiar relationship to her body. She felt that it was sordid; she found eating repulsive; she felt as if her body was not the centre of her 'self'—that she somehow existed at odds with it, or divorced from it" (10). In considering this contribution, one must take into account the fact that Trombley, who argues that sexual abuse was at the root of much of Woolf's dis-ease, was writing before the link between sexual abuse and eating disorders had widely been made. Were he to be publishing in the light of this current understanding, perhaps he might reevaluate his stance on Woolf and anorexia.

Lee—clearly another writer with fundamental misconceptions about anorexia—argues that Woolf was not anorexic because "anorexia arises from an obsession with one's body. That does not seem the case here. She simply could not eat" (1996, 176). While anorexia *is* a state of being in which anxieties are projected onto the body, to reduce the anorexic condition to "an obsession with the body" is a ludicrous simplification of a highly complex behavior.[9] That aside, there is in fact ample evidence, both from Woolf and from those who knew her, that her body *was* a lifelong focus of intense concern. Finally, I would contest Lee's assertion that Woolf "simply could not eat." A considerable amount of evidence suggests, on the contrary, that she *could* eat but *would* not.

Feminist philosopher Mary Daly has written that Virginia Woolf "died of being both brilliant and female" (1986, 195), an observation that succinctly identifies Woolf as a woman of genius struggling to speak with integrity within an abusive patriarchy. Daly's incisive perception stands in stark contrast to Rose's inanely blinkered comment: "I think it unfortunate in more ways than one that some of the women writers of our century—one thinks of [Sylvia] Plath and [Anne] Sexton as well as Woolf—have killed themselves" (xvi). Unfortunate? To lose one woman writer of genius may be regarded as misfortune; to lose three raises suspicions of something more insidious.

Feminist writers have redefined female "madness" as an explicable response to the accommodations that women are forced to make in order to live in a man's world. Beyond this accurate but not necessarily potentiating observation, women have begun to reclaim the numinous power of "madness" as a state of transcendent altered consciousness. We are breaking loose from the ratiocinatory straitjackets that have confined us under men's rule and are seeking to become seers and shape-shifters in both ontological and sociopolitical senses. As feminist writer Kate Millett (who was diagnosed by the medical establishment as "constitutionally psychotic, a manic-depressive bound to suffer recurrent attacks of 'affective illness'"

[310]) writes defiantly, "Why not hear voices?" (315): "If we go mad—so what? We could come back again if not chased away, exiled isolated, confined" (314). To Millett, "madness" is "A certain speed of thought, certain wonderful flights of ideas. Certain states of altered perception" (315).

The flight of Woolf's mind arced high and wide, and although ostensibly she often accepted the pathological definition of her "illness," referring to herself at various times as "mad" and to her condition as "madness," on a deeper, more personal level she too regarded "madness" as a subversive and visionary gift, as a rich silt in which creative inspiration was germinated. As she wrote in her diary for 1930, "I believe these illnesses are in my case . . . partly mystical. Something happens in my mind. It refuses to go on registering impressions. It shuts itself up. It becomes chrysalis. I lie quite torpid . . . Then suddenly something springs." She described the process of breaking through the chrysalis as a birth into a heightened awareness of life and an energized creativity: "a tremendous sense of life beginning . . . & all the doors opening . . . I then begin to make up my story whatever it is . . . before I can control my mind or pen" (*D 3,* 287). Faced with the dichotomous options, to conform or go mad, Woolf discovered a transcending third way.

Introduction

People who ask me about this book are often surprised to learn that its subject is Virginia Woolf and food—for there is no food in Woolf's work, is there? They are, like the poet Stephen Spender, under the impression that "healthy sensual appetites scarcely touch on this world" (Noble, 180). This is not only the popular view of Woolf's work but that generally propounded by Woolf scholars; Harvena Richter, for instance, asserts that "save in *Flush*, there are very few tastes or smells in . . . [Woolf's] novels" (69). And yet Woolf's work is full of concrete, sensual descriptions both of food and of the process of eating it. There are the succeeding sharps and sweets of lunch in the men's college and the bitter taste of the greens at dinner in the women's college (*AROOO*); there are Neville's physical (and ontological) sensations digesting dinner, the butter oozing through Bernard's crumpet, and Susan plunging her hands into the bread dough (*TW*); there is the odd taste of Mrs. Malone's fish and the smell of cabbage in the lodging house where Sara Pargiter lives (*TY*)—and one can go on and on. If Woolf is, as Richter argues (69), engaged in rendering the sensual into the abstract, what are we to make of this passage from an early draft of *The Waves*:

> . . . she would like after this walk to drop into a chair & simply eat . . . And she {thought} felt her teeth must meet in the rather solid wing of a pheasant; & her tongue roll its fibres; & then the delicious hotness & scent of pheasant, & the grey dry bread crumbs; & the heaping up of soft bread sauce, and the {half} pungent, curious taste of brussel sprouts . . . that would be very delicious—her being would subside into that. (*TW:Hol*, 190)[1]

The prevalent belief that Woolf was removed from the sensual, and that food in particular is absent from her work, is all the stranger for the fact that she herself explicitly avowed the importance in literature of what is real, palpable, tactile—especially *of what is eaten*. In *A Room of One's Own* she wondered at the conspiracy of silence that had effectively excluded eating from fictional meals. Novelists, she said, would have us believe that lunch parties are chiefly remarkable for their wit and wisdom rather than for what is on the plates, for it is a convention of fiction to ignore food as if it were completely irrelevant. "I," she avowed, "shall take the liberty to defy that convention" (12).

Time and again she did indeed take the *liberty* of defying that convention, dwelling with intensity not only upon what was eaten but also upon the subtly nuanced sensations of anticipating, tasting, and digesting it. I stress the word "liberty" because this dwelling on food was, as Woolf saw it, an act of female liberation. It was part of the process both of seeing the world through our own, female, lenses and, more actively, of righting a skewed world which had purged the sensual and elevated the rational. As Janis Paul notes of Woolf, "a strong current of materialism . . . runs through her work" (3). She was never distanced from the practical realities of food, as she saw that male writers generally were. Writing was for her a pursuit that took place within the context of domesticity, not in monastic seclusion from the activities of the kitchen. In 1920, for instance, she writes, "I'm [in] the middle of baking a cake, & fly to this page for refuge, to fill in moments of baking & putting in bread" (*D 2,* 53), and in 1923 she laments, "I have ruined my mornings work by baking bread & buns, which require constant voyages to the kitchen" (260). In another moment her pen becomes a culinary utensil as she hovers between pan and paper: "I'm frying sausages for dinner as I write; and have just turned them delicately with the holder of this pen, having left the spoon in the kitchen" (*L 5,* 443).

Woolf's womanly connection with food and the kitchen manifests itself throughout her work. Nonetheless, the idea persists that she was "someone who never prepared the simplest meal herself" and that "she could never have understood or shared . . . [James] Joyce's [enjoyment] in frying a kidney" (Alexander, 95–96). One wonders whether Peter Alexander can have read Woolf's diaries. Her excitement in 1929, for example, at the replacement of the old solid-fuel range at Monk's House hardly indicates a woman who was remote from food and incapable of cooking a simple meal. What interested her most, she recorded, was the new stove, which was cooking her dinner as she wrote—she hoped "without smell, waste or confusion." She noted the glass dishes, the handles that one turned, and the thermometer, commenting "I go over the dishes I shall cook—the rich stews, the sauces. The adventurous strange dishes with dashes of wine in them" (*D 3,* 257). She informed her friend and one-time lover, Vita Sackville-West, that she had cooked veal cutlets and a cake in the stove, with the advent of which, she said, she had but "one passion in life—cooking." This, she assured Sackville-West ironically, was "better than writing these more than idiotic books" (*L 4,* 93). Louie Mayer, for many years the Woolfs' cook, described Virginia's skill at breadmaking,[2] commenting that "this was a job needing practical skill that she was able to do well every time." She herself needed several weeks' practice before she could make bread as good as Virginia's, she said (Noble, 157). In fact, as friend and writer Gerald Brenan noted, Virginia "was practical and could run a house better than most women" (Stape, 48).

Indeed, Woolf was no "disembodied neurasthenic sylph" (Paul, 4), and yet this is how she has often been represented. Those who knew her for the most part remember her as ethereal, remote from her body: Christopher Isherwood called her "a fairy-story princess under a spell" (Noble 178); to David Cecil she was a mermaid, a saint and an angel (124); Alix Strachey thought she was "like somebody belonging to another world" (112); Cyril Connolly saw her as "lovely, shy and virginal" (Stape, 37), and Raymond Mortimer felt that her "refinement" and asceticism were "almost like that of an abbess" (Noble, 168). The stereotypical bloodless images of fairy-tale princess, saint, and angel are cloying and (more seriously) crippling in the extreme, and take no account of the strong and indomitable life-force that one senses in Woolf. We know from "Professions for Women" (*Death of the Moth*, 149–154) what she herself thought about female angels. Moreover, the romanticization of Woolf's "virginal" quality is brutal in the light of the fact that the origins of this paradoxical "virginity" lie in experiences of childhood sexual abuse.

And yet such observations do, even if subject to the cultural distortions that idealize bodilessness in women, contain a grain of truth, pointing to a real dis-ease in Woolf's relationship with her body—one which was reflected in her relationship with food. There was a tension in her between healthy involvement with food and an anorexic response to it which she never wholly resolved. Her refusal to eat during periods of what are generally referred to as mental breakdown (but which can more accurately be viewed as periods of break*through*, considering the submerged material relating to sexual abuse that was attempting to surface at these times) is well documented. Leonard Woolf, for example, wrote that among the most worrying aspects of her "breakdowns" was her "refusal to eat." He noted that at such times she felt (as anorexic women typically do) ashamed of her own supposed "laziness, inanition, gluttony" (1963, 79–80). He also testified to her reluctance to eat an adequate amount at times when she was defined as mentally stable. Even when she seemed quite "recovered," he wrote, it was only with difficulty that she could be persuaded to eat "enough" to keep her "well" (79). Virginia herself observed that she tended to see food as nonessential. Visiting her sister's country house, Charleston, where in 1919 postwar shortages made for spartan meals, she was prompted to note, "I had the rare sensation of its being necessary to eat, in order to support life" (*D 1,* 270).

While it seems probable to me that Woolf did generally eat with a restrictive attitude, it should be recognized that both "enough" and "well" are subjective concepts. We must see this "enough" in the context of the perceived need for her to eat large amounts of food in order to stave off "insanity" (a need which was postulated by a succession of doctors and credited by Virginia's successive caretakers: her sister Vanessa Bell and Leonard Woolf). "Well" was to Vanessa and Leonard the absence of "insanity"; "well" thus defined, however, was also a condition of suppressed memory, anesthetized feeling, and underground pain. Although Virginia never ceased to challenge a patriarchy that she regarded as fundamentally abusive, it was this "well" that muted her dangerously subversive voice whenever she came close to exposing the personal abuses she had suffered within her own patriarchally constituted family.

Woolf herself repeatedly expressed her sense of disgust at what she saw as overeating and bad table manners. She wrote of a friend, Kingsley Martin, "he munches mutton chops, & sweeps up fragments, scraping his knife & fork round in a way I hate" (D 5, 165). At the birthday party of her niece, Angelica Bell (daughter of Vanessa), she was affronted and repelled by the behavior of her brother's children, Ann and Judith Stephen, who, she noted, "don't wipe their mouths & eat so much" (244). The voracious appetite of her friend Ethel Smyth was an aspect of Ethel's characteristic lusty vehemence that Woolf frequently found hard to take: "She guzzled over our very tough jobs [chops?], till I could not sit still. She is a greedy old woman; I don't like greed when it comes to champing & chawing & sweeping up gravy. And she gets red, drinking" (D 4, 284).[3] The intensity of Woolf's response to what she saw as grotesque eating resembles that of an anorexic woman described by Peter Dally, who "felt such intense disgust at the noises her father made when chewing that she almost struck him; instead she ran from the room" (Dally and Gomez 1979, 49). During periods of eating distress Woolf's reaction to the spectacle of public eating was markedly similar also to the anorexic response described by Sheila MacLeod. For both Woolf and MacLeod such a brazen display of naked biology appeared depraved. MacLeod writes, "what really disgusted me was the sight of other people eating. It seemed to me shocking that they should engage in such a crude, almost obscene activity in public, and I would watch them with fascinated repulsion" (100). In 1918 Woolf recorded: "We lunched at Valcheras, & there looked into the lowest pit of human nature; saw flesh still unmoulded to the shape of humanity—Whether it is the act of eating and drinking that degrades, or whether people who lunch at restaurants are naturally degraded, certainly one can hardly face one's own humanity afterwards" (D 1, 199).

As MacLeod makes clear, anorexic disgust at the sight of such unashamed eating is mixed with a voyeuristic fascination. Recorded in Woolf's letters and diaries too are moments—generally when she felt that the fragile ontological scaffolding she had constructed was about to topple—when food and those eating it became a lurid exhibition. In Brighton during World War II, for example, she observed:

> A fat, smart woman . . . consuming rich cakes. Her shabby dependant also stuffing. Hudson's van unloading biscuits opposite. The fat woman had a louche large white muffin face . . . They ate & ate. Talked about Mary . . . I opened the marmalade but John doesn't like it—And we have two pounds of biscuits in the tin upstairs . . . [ellipses in original] Something scented, shoddy, parasitic about them. Then they totted up cakes . . . Where does the money come from to feed these fat white slugs? (*D 5*, 357)

Woolf worked on a short story, "The Watering Place,"[4] based on this episode. Perhaps, however, she recognized in it a dysfunctional response to eating, for the story remained unfinished.

Often in her life Woolf succeeded in constructing a firm working relationship with eating. Her strong anorexic fears and aversions were generally balanced by an equally potent appreciation of the life-enhancing aspects of food. Her diaries are full of positive experiences of eating. In 1919, for example, she writes, "Here I am sitting after Saturday tea, a large warm meal, full of currants & sugar & hot tea cake, after a long cold walk" (*D 1*, 311), and in 1926 "We are very hungry . . . ; Nelly is preparing a nice roast chicken & ices for dinner, which I shall enjoy" (*D 3*, 90). Many observers have commented upon Woolf's enjoyment of good food, particularly in the context of good conversation (which entailed for her intimate human connection as much as intellectual brilliance). As a friend, William Plomer, noted, "She liked good talk, good food, and good coffee" (Stape, 144).

If Woolf was disgusted by excessive eating, she abhorred impoverished meals equally vehemently. According to Louie Mayer, although the Woolfs did not eat big meals, "they lived well and enjoyed good food." They were particularly fond of "grouse and pheasant with well made sauces" and "light . . . newly made" puddings such as crèmes and soufflés (Noble 157–158).[5] Virginia criticized David Cecil for offering a meal which was "meagre; exiguous" (*D 4*, 105). For her, lack of consideration of what was to be eaten was an abuse of food. This sense was not rooted in epicureanism but stemmed, like her anorexic attitudes, from an awareness that food was never just food but carried complex metaphorical meanings. Poverty in food was indicative for her of ontological poverty, of joylessness, and meanness of spirit, as a diary entry for 1925 evinces: "Last night we made a meagre meal with the Sangers, whose mediocrity of comfort & taste saddens me: oh for a little beauty in life" (*D 3*, 18).

Woolf's abiding interest in food in her work derives in large part from her awareness of the power that food held over her and her determination to examine and transform that power-over. As she put it, "I think it is true that one gains a certain hold on sausages & haddock by writing them down" (*D 5,* 358). The gift of her anorexic experiences was a deep sense of the symbolic richness and complexity of food—a sense that always fed her writing. She was acutely sensitized to the tastes, textures, colors, and smells of food, which she rendered in words with tremendous evocative power. States of hunger, ingestion, and repletion were not to her ordinary, unremarked phenomena but significant events with ontological implications that could be explored and exploited in both fiction and in sociopolitical feminist writing.

Implicit for Woolf in the process of gaining a hold on sausages and haddock was that of gaining a hold on her own body. As Ellen Rosenman has noted, a fundamental life challenge for Woolf was "telling the truth about my own experiences as a body" ("Professions for Women," *The Death of the Moth,* 153). Rosenman comments that "female embodiment—the experience of living within one's body, of feeling and asserting one's bodily desires, whether specifically sexual or more generalized—remains one of the central unresolved issues in Woolf's theory of female creativity" (in Hussey and Neverow, 272). Woolf herself regarded this dilemma as one that "I do not think I solved." Indeed, she added, "I doubt that any woman has solved it yet" (*The Death of the Moth,* 153). Nor have women "solved" the problem in the half century since Woolf's death, as the exponential rise in eating distress indicates.[6] And yet this huge amount of suffering around our bodies should not be viewed as a simple negative. I would suggest that at this point in women's history, our embodiment is not a "problem" requiring a "solution" but an issue in which exploration is in itself a form of creative transformation. In this voyage of discovery Woolf is a pioneer.

To me, as I first studied Woolf when I myself was an anorexic woman, the omnipresence of food in her writing was self-evident. That all this food was apparently invisible to Woolf scholars I found baffling. Today, having traveled very far beyond anorexia, I remain baffled. How is it that despite Woolf's overt statements of literary interest in food, and her constant literary use of it, the popular and academic consensus continues to be that food and eating are absent from her work? This difficulty in comprehending *both* Woolf's evident ("masculine") intellectual power *and* her deep ("feminine") sensuality is, of course, a reflection of a patriarchal polarization of mind and body—itself a facet of a larger patriarchal schizophrenia. From a gynecentric perspective, however, we can hope to see the totality of the picture. I am inspired by Woolf's hard-fought refusal to bifurcate herself conveniently, splitting off and denying dimensions of selfhood in order to fit the phallic bill. For me, Woolf is not only a consummate artist but also an originating Mother in the journey towards a way of being in which we re-become whole.

Chapter 1

Anorexia:
A Perspective from the Other Side

Anorexia is commonly described as an "illness" or "disease" requiring "treatment" so that the anorexic woman will "recover."[1] This is a particularly invidious form of mislabeling because it obscures the powerfully subversive personal and politico-cultural messages that anorexia encodes. Anorexia is not caught like measles; the anorexic stance is, initially at least, a chosen response to a set of ontological difficulties produced by the particular version of the patriarchal paradigm operant in industrialized Western nations in the twentieth century.[2]

Although the medical literature abounds with diagnostic criteria for anorexia, there is, as Roger Slade notes, "no universally accepted definition" (15). Something of my own sense of what anorexia is is expressed in images of a containing space: a cage, a prison, a fortress within a moat, but also a safe-house, a room of one's own. Many words have, with justice, been devoted to the suffering and despair of the woman who occupies this space. However, it is important also to acknowledge the *value* of anorexia as this kind of holding environment. While I would wish neither to deny the potential dangers of self-starvation[3] nor to suggest that it is a course of action that feminists should either adopt or promulgate, anorexia can, at its most positive, function as a bell-jar in which personal and political change is fermented on the profoundest level.[4] Failing that, it can still serve women by providing a set of stop-gap boundaries against social, sexual, ideological, and other incursions. Such boundaries are, of course, no substitute for an authentic sense of coalescent and unbreachable selfhood, but they are an effective emergency measure, without which the alternative would seem to be disintegration.

The roots of anorexia lie in Judeo-Christianity, of which modern capitalism is a refined product.[5] Anorexia is the ultimate logical conclusion of a patriarchal theology in which being is dichotomized into spirit and body, virtuous and vicious, and the devotee gains religious credibility—becomes more "spiritual"—by chastising the "depraved" body and thereby, supposedly, subduing the sensual nature. The particular association of women with the demonized body has been convincingly described as a political tactic, adopted as part of a Jahwehist bid to stamp out older theacentric religions in the Middle East and disempower women generally.[6] Because of women's supposed physical nature, in Judeo-Christianity we are considered to be in particular need of "purification" and have practiced extreme asceticism in the name of the Lord throughout the patriarchal millennia in a futile attempt to exorcise the reviled body.[7] Anorexia can be seen as a new take on this well-rehearsed patriarchal theme.

The anorexic daughters of Judeo-Christianity, whether they identify themselves with these faiths or not, are indoctrinated with their misogynistic dogma. They have espoused the desirability of incorporeity, endeavoring to slough off the body (and with it their humanity), allying themselves with the strained and separated, sublimated essences of mind and soul. They have entered into a fractured state of ontological and biological nonentity in which to starve the body is to nourish a spirit considered better able to flourish devoid of corporeal parts. They believe that, as Italian psychiatrist Mara Selvini-Palazzoli puts it, "one has only to crush the one (the strong body) to enhance the other (the weak spirit), thus magically reversing their respective roles" (74).

The obsession with food is thus, as formerly anorexic writer Kim Chernin points out, a "spiritual struggle," and a heart-wrenching one, because it is harnessed to "an effort to control or eliminate the passionate aspects of the self" (1983, 187). The anorexic experiences of Gertrude and Eleanor illustrate this kind of passionate purgation very clearly:

> I felt I had to do something I didn't want to do for a *higher purpose*. That took over my life . . . I created a new image for myself and disciplined myself to a new way of life. My body became the *visual symbol* of pure ascetic [*sic*] and aesthetics, of being sort of untouchable in terms of criticism. Everything became very intense and very intellectual, but absolutely untouchable. (Bruch 1978, 17)

> The idea of emptying myself wholly so that a divine presence could enter me, a purified receptacle, was important . . . it was an emotional, intellectual and experiential emptying . . . my belly seemed full of serpents, full of the chaos of *mater saeva cupidinum*, "unbridled and unbroken nature." I felt like the chaos before creation and sought to be the delineation of order after creation . . . (Woodman 1982, 53–54)

Women such as Gertrude and Eleanor live within the circle of a self-sealed, ultra-masculine belief system—what Jungian analyst Marion Woodman refers to as the "patriarchal . . . Kingdom of Beauty, Purity and Light" (26)—devoid of warmth, spontaneity, care, comfort, and love. Their self-punishing credo runs something like Dorothy's as she thinks about her anorexic stair-climbing routine:

> I have to get it done! I can't live, I don't know how to live without them [the stairs]. If I don't do it I will be a self-indulgent, fat, lazy slob . . . Let me do them, get it over and done with, put it behind me, let it be over for another night. Quickly, quickly, faster and faster. Sometimes I feel so ashamed of myself for doing this—I just close my eyes and focus on how good it will be when it's all over. (Abraham and Llewellyn-Jones, 121)

Or like that of an anorexic client of Woodman's: "When can I get out of this box? I drag my body around as if it's some gross foreign object . . . What am I doing? I keep setting these standards for myself and I just can't do it. I can't do anything. NOTHING. NOTHING. Ugly, filthy, fat slob!" (Woodman 1982, 26). Born into the painful anorexic dichotomies of phallic culture, the authors of such monologues are the anguished products of patriarchy's attempts to alienate women from biophilic principals, in which the spirit is immanent in the body, and the things of the body are sacred. Woodman suggests that a healing gynecentric monologue, one which reunites body with soul in a self-loving, self-nurturing organic holism, would go something like:

> I am tired. I love myself. I love my body. I give myself permission to be nourished. I love my inner woman. What food would be best for her? Is it food I really want? Is it music? Is it dancing? . . . I am trying to release my true feminine body, whatever shape it is. What is the reality here? This is me happening to me. I need to relax, to be quiet. I need a bath. I want to affirm my own life. I can do it; I can do it. (1982, 33)

The anorexic woman understands that her role in patriarchy is self-effacement—literally, *the effacement of her self.* Thus Elsa, an anorexic client of psychiatrist Hilde Bruch, describes a fear of "not being human and ceasing to exist" (1978, 12). Another anorexic woman expresses a sense that "I'm just nowhere. I'm not here and I'm certainly not there" (Woodman 1982, 26), and Eleanor recalls of her anorexia, "I lost 'I' and became a void" (53). Anorexic women strive to be meek, unobtrusive, accommodating, deferent, placatory; to stifle their own dissent, irreverence, wildness, and desire; to tread so lightly that they scarcely leave an imprint on the soil. The elimination of hunger becomes an overarching symbol of all these manifold self-suppressions. "I dream of the perfect day when I will have no appetite, no thought, desire, or temptation for food or to eat," writes one anorexic woman (Abraham and Llewellyn-Jones, 56). To be able to eat nothing at all and remain "healthy" would be, for anorexic Annette, "the answer to my dreams! I feel elated even now just thinking about it . . . I wouldn't eat even if I didn't put weight on. There is nothing I would crave to eat!" (MacSween, 116–117). Such statements are a swingeing indictment of the situation of women within modern American and West European patriarchy, for they bespeak the degree to which, at the far end of the continuum, we have embraced the imperative of denial—not only of our appetite for food but of all our lusts and passions. This, as Chernin explains, is the shape of the contemporary woman's soul: "Hollow, shrivelled up, suffering from a wasting disease, with shrunken eyes and sharply pointed nose, converted from a principle of joy to a doomed conqueror of nature," product of "the hidden demonism of . . . [the] retreat from the female, . . . [the] struggle against the flesh" (1983, 197).

Patriarchy depends for its continuation upon women's annexation of one-half of the range of feeling available to humanity, for thus fractured and fragmented, we are in no position to challenge and change its structures. The anorexic statement, however, is nothing if not complex. One of its many paradoxes is that while on an overt level it bespeaks superlative conformity to androcratic dictates, subtextually it expresses powers of dauntless resistance and ferocious rebellion. Furthermore, as feminist psychotherapist Susie Orbach has pointed out (1986, 30), while initially the anorexic woman appears the very embodiment of patriarchally mandated femininity, in her submission beyond—way beyond—the call of duty she becomes, ultimately, a parody of those injunctions by which patriarchal women are expected to live, her "obedience" an act of mocking insubordination.

Hilde Bruch draws attention to the sense of powerlessness experienced by anorexic women: "Long before the illness [sic] becomes manifest, these girls [sic] have felt helpless and ineffective in conducting their own lives, and the severe discipline over their bodies represents a desperate effort to ward off panic about being completely powerless" (in Garfinkel and Garner 1985, 10). The problem with such analyses is that, while accurate in so far as they go,[8] they would have us believe that the anorexic woman's perception of her disempowerment under male rule is wholly unfounded in reality. In fact, however, patriarchy has worked hard to divest women of our authentic power, both by legally enforced removal of rights and by acculturation. We are taught to regard weakness as our innate and desirable condition, to suspect and suppress the numinous power inherent in our own bodies, until, like Karol, we turn to anorexia in a terrified flight from our natural, physically immanent, female potency: "I did not want what it [the body] stood for—to live like a mature woman. It had been a good body—but it was too much for me and the safest thing was 'to forget about it'" (Bruch 1978, 279).

The anorexic position is a cogently ordered, readily comprehensible response to the impossible set of sociocultural demands that do in fact operate upon women in the androcratic world. Anorexic women find themselves at the thin edge of the patriarchal wedge, those on whom the complex series of compromises and contortions required of women by phallocracy will not sit. "Anorexics," as Bruch observes, "struggle against feeling enslaved, exploited, and not being permitted to live a life of their own. They would rather starve than continue a life of accommodation" (*Eating Disorders,* 1974, 250). Again, I would emphasize, the anorexic woman is not wrong. She perceives accurately that "a life of accommodation" is what is expected of women in patriarchal states; that patriarchy denies authentic "identity and selfhood"; that what the patriarchally defined world has to offer her—dispassion, disempowerment, blinds, binds, and desecration—is wholly inadequate. She recognizes, as Woolf did in 1938, that there is no position within patriarchy which it is comfortable for women to occupy; we are "between the devil and the deep blue sea" (*Three Guineas,* 86).

I do not intend to suggest that the anorexic woman has made a thoroughgoing feminist analysis of her situation. On the contrary, she is rather *unlikely* to have perceived the oppressive dynamics of patriarchy on other than a subliminal level. Anorexia generally expresses *in default of* a conscious gynephilic belief system, whereas the evolution of feminist awareness tends to the authentic empowerment of the individual, and the development of existential and sociopolitical strategies beyond self-starvation.[9] This is not to say that feminism provides a quick fix for anorexia on a personal level, nor that those feminists with a sophisticated knowledge of the mechanics of patriarchy (such as Woolf herself) are necessarily immune to eating distress. Nevertheless, feminism does offer anorexic women a framework for understanding their situation, as well as effective patterns for resistance, thus enabling the abandonment of defensive embattlement in anorexia for alternative, creative, and genuinely self-affirming forms of antipatriarchal action.

Self-evidently, the powerful anger unleashed by such movement is feared by the patriarchal orthodoxy whose status quo it threatens and whose institutions therefore do their best to silence, suppress, or sublimate it. Anne's anorexia was precipitated when her rage was infantilized by a school principal whom she had approached with what she considered to be "a brilliant idea" for an editorial in the school newspaper: "[he] censored my article and told me to 'grow up.' He said it wasn't valid to be angry; it wasn't valid to have instincts like mine, always wanting to do battle" (Woodman 1980, 77). Anne's problem with the prevalent socioculture was defined by the principal as a problem with Anne. "I couldn't grow up into that world," she concluded—which, as she had been forbidden from changing that world, meant not growing up at all. As for her now free-floating anger, she turned it inwards: "Not eating seemed a good way of getting back at myself" (77). Dorothy, the compulsive stair-climber, explains that her ritual is necessitated by internalized rage. For her, the sociocultural distortions to which women's anger is subject effectively preclude a positive expression of anger. Driven by the momentum of her silent fury, she has become like a rat on a treadmill: "I'm so angry. Faster, faster, harder, harder . . . Nobody listens, nobody hears, nobody changes. Everything is so bloody frustrating I can't even scream out my anger because society reads it as a sign of needing help or having totally lost the plot. So what was simple frustration is now multiple compounded frustration and my head is paralysed, despite wanting to be bashed against a brick wall" (Abraham and Llewellyn-Jones, 121).

In mainstream hospital "treatment" programs for eating disorders, the aim is to invalidate and pathologize women's anger. Fourteen-year-old Zelda's is a case in point. Zelda was a very angry young woman who was expressing her rage: "She managed in the outpatient setting to frustrate multiple therapists and her parents. When urged to eat, she threw food and milkshakes on the walls and kicked individuals who tried to help [sic] her to eat" (Andersen, Morse, and Santymer, in Garfinkel and Garner 1985, 313). Anyone who believes that medical treatment is no longer used as a behavioral corrective should consider the response of the Zelda's therapists, who pronounce, "*Her behaviors required hospital treatment more than her weight did*" (my italics). I do not find it surprising, and I do not know why therapists do, that an anorexic woman who is "urged to eat" becomes enraged. When a woman refuses food she is speaking with her body because she is unable to speak in words; to force food upon her is thus not to "help" her but to obliterate her message and mute her voice. Clearly, such repeated inappropriate interventions can only generate cumulative anger and frustration, to which the woman again responds in the only language she knows: the body's. I for one would be interested in exploring with Zelda what (apart from people attempting to stuff food down her throat) she is so angry about and how she wants to use her anger. Anger is a wonderful resource, and I hope that, in one way or another, Zelda is still kicking and throwing things around.

As Rebecca Dresser comments, in an examination of the legal implications of force-feeding anorexic women, "available evidence indicates that unrestricted forcible treatment confers little or no long term benefits upon anorexics, but instead can reduce their chances for full recovery" (374).[10] Why then does the medical profession continue to hospitalize and force-feed anorexic women? The answer surely can only be that it is in the establishment's interest to translate anorexic rage into long-term sickness.[11] This is a fact that some well-intentioned feminist writers have failed to recognize. Feminist psychotherapist Marilyn Lawrence, for example, is apparently perplexed by the infantilizing strategies of mainstream treatment regimes. "If we understand anorexia as a problem which has to do with control," she writes, "and if we see the long-term aims of treatment as enabling the woman to take a proper and reasonable control of her own life, to become an effective agent in her own affairs, then surely any approach which begins by taking away the final vestiges of her attempts to control her life must be at best unhelpful, and at worst, downright dangerous" (1987, 81). While Lawrence is right in thinking that such practices are highly unlikely to empower women, she fails to understand that the "long-term aims of [mainstream] treatment" are in fact *not* to enable the woman "to take . . . control of her own life, to become an effective agent in her own affairs" but quite the reverse.

The degree of degradation legally employed to break anorexic women in hospitals is indicative of the importance attached by patriarchy to the prevention of women's self-realization. Hilary Forrester describes her experiences as an anorexic teenager in Frimley Park Hospital in Britain, where, when she refused to stay in bed because, as she correctly pointed out, she was not ill: "Two nurses grabbed me and put me in a room. At first I screamed and banged on the door, but they had given me an injection and I went to sleep." She could not leave the room because there was no handle on the inside of the door. She says, "I missed my parents, and hated being alone in the room. I walked up and down it for hours. They kept pushing plates of food at me that got bigger and bigger. It made me feel sick and all I thought about was how I would lose the weight they were making me put on" ("Anorexia Nervosa," *Sunday Times,* 5.14.78). June recalls her hospitalization for anorexia: "I was a voluntary patient until I was sectioned [compulsorily detained], because I would not eat meat and wanted to go home . . . It was dreadful. I was fattened up to 8 stone [112 pounds], then released, when they thought I had recovered after I had co-operated, and said what they wanted to hear" (MacSween, 245). Even more disturbing is Paula's experience: "Loss of privileges, eg no clothes, no baths, no visitors unless I ate. Force feeding by nursing staff—very forcefully and aggressively. Insulin injections. The worst treatment of all was ECT [electroconvulsive therapy]. My psychiatrist knew how much I hated this and so if I did not eat, and continued to lose weight I was threatened with further ECT" (245).

Lest these should seem, to those who have no experience of what happens to anorexic women in the hospital, to be the dialogues of madwomen, the following inpatient regime (that of family systems therapist Salvador Minuchin and his colleagues) is typical:

- A woman (often in Minuchin's unit a child) who gains 200g (7 oz.) or more may get up, walk around the unit, make a phone call, and visit the first floor of the hospital if accompanied.
- If she gains only 100g (4 oz.) she remains on bedrest but with "bathroom privileges." She may answer the phone but not make calls, receive visitors and mail, watch TV, and have a bed-bath.
- A woman whose weight remains stable must rest in bed with no "bathroom privileges." She may receive no phone calls but can know who called, and receive visitors and mail. She may watch TV and have a bed-bath.
- A woman who loses 100g (4 oz.) may have no phone calls, no visitors, and may not watch TV. She may receive mail and bathe in bed.
- If she loses 300g (10 oz.) she may have no phone calls, no visitors, no TV, no mail, no bathing at all, and "MAY ONLY EAT." (Minuchin, Rosman, and Baker, 115)

There is something particularly crude and thuggish in Minuchin's capitalization of "may only eat"—revealed as the ultimate sanction in a system that operates on threats. (I am reminded of George Orwell's Room 101, in which acts of social defiance are punished by confrontation with the deviant's ultimate fear.) There is, too, a Newspeakian linguistic distortion in the choice of the term "privilege" to refer to such activities as use of the bathroom and contact with the outside world, which are more accurately described as basic human rights. Clearly, as Orbach comments, such "treatment" regimes are not only "coercive, infantilizing and punitive," but also "questionable on legal and ethical grounds" (1986, 185).

Minuchin, Rosman and Baker are archproponents of a favorite psychiatric myth: Anorexic women are "very manipulative" (115).[12] The choice of this term to describe anorexic women's behavior throws into relief the true nature of patient-staff dynamics on such "treatment" programs, designating as it does the powerless partner in a relationship of dominance—women, children, the poor, and the disadvantaged manipulate; doctors, psychiatrists, and other authority figures assert control. I find such comments offensive and rather amusing when emanating from practitioners of behavioralism, the rationale of which is that psychological responses can be manipulated by a program of conditioning. This dog-training approach to therapy is, of course, ideally suited to producing patriarchal obedience champions.

Peter Dally explains that women on his (similarly constituted) inpatient regime[13] at the Westminster Hospital in London often resist the "treatment":

> They may refuse point blank to co-operate, throw food on the floor or at the nurses supervising them, take tiny amounts and chew each mouthful a hundred

times, or scream and weep every time they are asked to eat. But most patients, however resistant initially, eventually give in and co-operate with relief when they have satisfied themselves that staff are capable of taking control. (Dally and Gomez 1979, 110)

Dally's paternalistic reassurance that most women "eventually give in" to hospital staff is deeply disturbing; furthermore, this description of unconditional surrender is incompatible with the notion that women subsequently "co-operate" with those designated (unlike themselves) as "capable of taking control." Cooperation implies an equal power base; what Dally describes is coercion. (For clearly the anorexic woman is not in a position to prevent Dally from using the lavatory, having a bath, or getting dressed—sanctions that he is empowered to use against her.) As Orbach points out, those doctors and psychiatrists who enforce such punitive regimes are engaged in "what can only be described as a struggle for who is to control the individual woman's body." Their self-professedly benevolent actions represent in practice a "kind of rape *par excellence*" (1986, 25)—a physical and ontological assault upon the anorexic woman, aimed at violating her will and shattering her already fragile integrity.

Given the divide-and-rule tactics employed by patriarchy, we should not be surprised that much energy has been invested in blaming mothers for anorexia.[14] In these approaches women's distress under patriarchal conditions is women's fault. Such fallacious causation theories have become increasingly invidious as eating distress (once considered to be a resort of affluent, young, white, adolescent girls) has broadened its demographic reach. Today the anorexic woman may well herself be a mother, both demon and victim in the eyes of the psychiatric orthodoxy. Nor is it surprising if, at some stage, anorexic women are persuaded to collude in viewing their mothers as the source of all their difficulties, since in the patriarchal system the joyless responsibility for inculcating androcratic sociocultural precepts is assigned to our mothers. As Orbach explains: "the mother who herself lives a circumscribed life in patriarchy, has the unenviable task of directing her daughter to take up the very same position that she has occupied. Explicitly as well as unconsciously she psychologically prepares her daughter to accept the strictures that await her in womanhood. She needs to do this so that her daughter is not cast as a misfit" (43).

What is further evident is the absence of fathers from this picture, for fathering has escaped the wide-scale inculpation that mothering has attracted in relation to anorexia. Given that much eating distress is the result of sexual abuse, and that the majority of abusers are male, this absence is an shameful one.[15] The consensus is that around 30 percent of women with diagnosed eating disorders remember and report sexual abuse. However, as therapist

Margot Maine comments, "such violence is generally under-reported" due to fear, shame, and denial (100). Some studies nevertheless elicit much higher rates of disclosure. Maine herself finds that at least 40 percent of women in her treatment program have experienced "sexual trauma," defined as "rape or molestation" (101). Vanessa Davis, Hilary Andrew, and Carole Pearce report that "At an eating disorders clinic, of 78 women 64 per cent had been sexually abused" (124). Liz Hall and Siobhan Lloyd conclude that "There is growing evidence that between one-third and two-thirds of women with eating disorders have experienced childhood sexual abuse" (75).

Clearly, the sexual abuse of women and children must be seen in the context of the generally abusive nature of patriarchal societies, in which rape of the female is only one manifestation of a much wider tendency to despoliation—environmental, ethnic, cultural, spiritual, and so forth. In this context it is not surprising that "treatment" for eating distress produced by sexual abuse may take the form of further violation. Miss B's is a case in point (reported *Time Out,* January 4, 1995). A twenty-four-year-old survivor of childhood sexual abuse, Miss B had repeatedly starved and mutilated herself. She was sectioned in Warlington Park Hospital, Croydon, in 1993, where she began a legal campaign on the grounds that medical staff were not providing her with any help to overcome the problems they had diagnosed as a personality disorder and depression. At the end of 1994, Croydon Health Authority won an appeal upholding their decision to feed Miss B (then weighing 5 stone [70 pounds]) by nasogastric tube, a decision which she was preparing to petition against in the House of Lords. As far as I can tell, none of the medical authorities in this case has questioned whether inserting foreign objects into the orifices of a woman who has been sexually abused is likely to persuade her to relinquish the self-starvation which, we may reasonably suppose, defends against such invasions, or whether it is likely further to entrench her stance. No one has asked whether such accepted practice is not in fact a form of legally endorsed medical rape. In "civilized" Western nations at the end of the second millennium C.E., we like to believe that we no longer imprison women for sexual "misconduct." But why is Miss B under compulsory detention while the perpetrator of her childhood abuse is not subject to any such sanction?

As therapist Carole Waskett observes, "people in eating distress survey . . . a risky landscape when they seek help" (53). A "therapeutic context" that, in Orbach's words, "honours the symptom, the client and her struggle" (1986, 119) is indeed a rare discovery. Within the feminist movement, therapy has been damned for exculpating patriarchy and blaming its victims, for encouraging women to eschew the sociopolitical content of our dis-ease and redefine it as individual neurosis, for seeking to condition conformity and eradicate dissent. These are valid criticisms of conventional psychiatry and psychoanalysis as well as other forms of mainstream psychotherapy. We should perhaps not, however, throw the baby out with the bathwater. Good therapy regards itself as an enabler in the individual's process of becoming her authentic self. Since the authentic selves of women do not fit the patriarchal prescription for femininity, such therapy is—by definition—socially and politically subversive, providing a safe space in which to bring about inner changes that are prerequisite for effective political action.[16]

In one sense, the truly epidemic proportions that eating distress has attained at the end of the twentieth century is a depressing indication of the degree of real subordination and level of abuse of women within modern Western patriarchy. At the same time, however, I believe there are some grounds for hope in the subliminal political messages that this rising tide of anorexia encodes—messages which bespeak rejection of the patriarchal world and of the lives that women are forced to live within it. If anorexia is, as I believe it may be, a means to authentic individual power, the fruition of that power on a cultural level may be an escalating movement toward genuine female liberation and, ultimately, a radical sociopolitical revolution beneficial to both sexes.

Orbach observes, "I have encountered a formidable strength and determination in individual women which has allowed me to understand how much of the anorexia is both an honorable pursuit and profoundly worthy cause" (1986 Foreword). As a testimony to the integrity inherent in the anorexic stance (rather than an endorsement of anorexia as its own end), this is a statement I would echo. Ultimately, however, (as Orbach also argues) it is not for us to straiten our dimensions, to pare ourselves down and cinch ourselves in so that we may fit the confines of patriarchal culture; it is for us to expand the parameters of the world with the full girth of our bodies and our immanent souls.

Chapter 2

My Food Is Affection

In 1892, at the age of ten, Virginia Stephen wrote two stories that are tremendously important to our understanding of her childhood: "A Cockney's Farming Experiences" and its sequel, "The Experiences of a Pater-familias." Consistent with Woolf's mature works, these early pieces of fiction are full of food and shed much light on events that had already caused her to fear eating and distrust her body. I do not think it is going too far to say that, on some level, she was already attempting to explore and communicate the ways in which her relationship with food had been distorted and her existence in the body crushed. As it would continue to be, however, her message was metaphorical and thus remained buried in the text during her own lifetime.

In "A Cockney's Farming Experiences," the Londoners, Harriet and her (unnamed) husband, go to the countryside to become farmers. While the eponymous cockney is ostensibly identified as an adult man—a husband and later a father—in fact his status is more complex, for, from the point of view of the child-writer, he represents both an inadequate father figure and (for Virginia uses him as her own narrative voice) a child forced to fend for him or herself in a world that he or she is not yet equipped to deal with. Correspondingly, Harriet can be seen on the one hand as a woman justifiably exasperated by her husband's ineptitude, his failure to support her practically or emotionally—or even to realize that he might be expected to do so; on the other hand she appears as an unapproachable, scolding mother who repeatedly sends her child off on baffling tasks that he (a town-dweller in an alien countryside) has neither the knowledge nor the experience to carry out.[1]

The acquisition of food is a central goal in these tasks. As an adult man, the cockney appears merely incompetent in his repeated failure to meet this objective; as a child, however, his failure is disturbing and tragic. The day after the two Londoners arrive at the farm, Harriet asks him to milk the cow. After half an hour's work he has only half an inch of milk in his jug—about what a cow should give, he thinks—but when he produces this pathetic amount for his wife, she laughs at him "spitefully" (*CFE/EPF,* 1). The significance of this picture of milk starvation lies in what it tells us about the experience, if not of feeding per se at least of maternal nurturance, of the child who created it. This is a child who is responsible for procuring even her own milk—a function which she, reasonably, feels impotent to fulfill. Nothing is offered her in the way of assistance; indeed, the adult who might have helped her only laughs at her fruitless efforts. Moreover, the child's expectation of how much milk she will receive is tiny, suggesting formative experiences of physical and/or emotional undernourishment. It seems probable that, as Louise DeSalvo suggests, the emphasis on lack of milk (which recurs in "The Experiences of a Pater-familias") can be related to Virginia's own early weaning (at ten weeks) and to a consequent deficit "of nurturance, of warmth and care" (1989, 141–142). Throughout her life Woolf would continue to write about infants' milk and childhood milk deprivation in her fiction.[2]

If we regard the cockney through our other bifocal lens, as a feckless and irresponsible husband, we can see that Virginia left some clues as to why she might have been weaned so prematurely. As an adult male he is (like most men of his time) utterly incapable of providing his wife with any support whatsoever—especially when, in "The Experiences of a Pater-familias," he is required to look after the new baby, Alphonso. As DeSalvo comments, he does "absolutely nothing for his child that he is not cajoled or harassed into doing" (1989,147); indeed, he regards any form of child care demanded of him as "compulsory tricks" which he is "made to perform" (5), and when he *is* harassed into looking after the baby, he is sadistically negligent. Under his father's "care," Alphonso falls off the back of a pig (on which his father has sat him) into the pigwash; he falls off a donkey (on which his father has also sat him) into a muddy puddle; he is tied to a tree and left dangling, and his bottle of milk smashes so that he cannot be fed (7). It is likely that Virginia created this picture of fathering from her observation of her own father's attitude to the upbringing of his children. Although Leslie Stephen expressed love of his children and was never wantonly cruel to them, nevertheless, he was in a fundamental sense disengaged from their care and ignorant of how to ensure their wellbeing. The practical inadequacy of his professed concern for their welfare is shown up by the fact that it is so often expressed by letter: He was not there. When it came down to the nitty-gritty, like the cockney, he could not be relied upon to assume any responsibility.

Leslie and Julia accounted for Virginia's early weaning in different ways, but both their explanations focus on the fact that Julia's burden of child care was more than she could cope with. According to Leslie, Vanessa's birth was difficult, debilitating Julia so that she was ill or tired throughout her subsequent pregnancies. It was because of this weakness that Julia breast-fed Virginia for only ten weeks (Love 1977, 109). Julia's expressed reason for taking her daughter from the breast was the amount of time that she had to dedicate to Leslie's "idiot" daughter from his first marriage, twelve-year-old Laura (DeSalvo 1989, 21). It is hard to see how Julia could possibly have provided sufficient care to any one child within her rambling composite family—as well as Laura and the newly born Virginia, she was responsible for two infants under three (Thoby and Vanessa Stephen) and three adolescent children by her first marriage (Stella, Gerald, and George Duckworth); besides which she was often called upon to look after her own mother. Thirteen years later she would die of what was fundamentally exhaustion.[3] Perhaps these demands would not have been so overwhelming and Virginia's feeding would not have been compromised if Leslie had provided practical support. For the last six weeks of Julia's difficult pregnancy with Virginia, however, he was away walking (King, 26), and during the period after Virginia's birth he was again often absent from home—on what DeSalvo refers to as "jaunts . . . with his male cohorts" (1989, 22 and 43).[4]

On the evidence of "A Cockney's Farming Experiences" and "The Experiences of a Pater-familias," it was not her mother but her father whom, on a subliminal level, the child Virginia regarded as responsible for her premature weaning. It is the cockney who repeatedly fails to provide the required milk for Alphonso and who, when it has been provided for him, smashes the bottle in a cab. What most worries him about this incident is not that Alphonso will now go hungry but that he has to pay the cab driver five shillings in compensation, a sum he considers "atrocious" (7)—surely a reflection of Leslie Stephen's oft-reiterated fear that he was "shooting Niagara" to bankruptcy (*MOB*, 144).

The cockney is not only reluctant to feed his son himself but astonished and outraged that the child should require feeding at all. When Alphonso starts to cry for his bottle, he protests, "I was not prepared for this." His reaction is to ignore the baby's needs for as long as possible, and he is incensed that "the dreadfull [sic] noise" has "hardly been going on for five minuits [sic]" before he is ordered to fetch the milk (7). Perhaps this tale of aberrant feeding points to a predisposing factor in Woolf's own later eating problems.[5]

The degree of anxiety generated by the uncertain availability of food is reflected in the universalization of starvation in "A Cockney's Farming Experiences." The animals are starving because the cockney has forgotten to give them food and water. When he does remember to feed them, it is with food that they cannot eat: He gives the cow "toast burnt to a cinder" from breakfast (which he himself had found inedible) spread with butter and marmalade (1). She later dies of neglect or malnutrition or both, with the result that there is no milk for anyone.

The tragedy of starvation was balanced in Woolf's childhood by a corresponding fantasy of unlimited food. In her "Notes on Virginia's Childhood," Vanessa Bell recalls a serial story that the children told in bed about their next-door neighbors, the Dilkes. The plot involved the discovery of large amounts of gold under the nursery floor and described "the wonderful things they could buy in consequence, especially the food, which was unlimited, though mostly consisting of the then not very ruinous eggs and bacon—our favourite dish" (Stape, 5). Virginia also remembered this story, recalling that the Dilkes feasted on fried eggs "with plenty of frizzling" (*MOB*, 79), the evocative "frizzling" indicating the sensual enjoyment that she imagined in an abundance of delicious frying eggs. In contrast, the boiled eggs that are prominent in "A Cockney's Farming Experiences" are "as hard as bricks." The cockney's, indeed, is a nest egg, which he is nevertheless forced to make his breakfast, as there is no other food (1). Since he has eaten the nest egg, a future dearth is ensured.

In "The Experiences of a Pater-familias" a more horrifying vision of a feast is played out. The dramatic high point of the story is a dinner at the Robinsons' to which Harriet and the cockney have been invited. The table is laden with ostentatiously opulent food—as Virginia pointedly notes, "*cracking* with cake, wine, fruit and candles" (10, my italics)—but despite this bounty, the atmosphere is ominous. Mr. Robinson, sitting next to Harriet, throughout the meal repeats the refrain, "Oh I know this table will break down soon." Indeed, his sense of impending doom is borne out, for, as dinner ends and the cockney is about to make a toast, the table gives "a tremendous crack" and collapses (10). Harriet, who is raising her leg to scratch it as the table falls, jumps onto her chair where, caught by her train, she is stranded, wanting to get down but not knowing how. Although physically uninjured, she is exposed, Virginia observes, in a position of extreme shame and humiliation in front of "gentlemen." The perceived disgrace of her situation is only pointed up by the tactless attentions of the servant, Annie, who, pointing to Harriet's dress, loudly remarks upon the huge tear and goes on "rummaging about the dress" until the cockney feels "ashamed" of Harriet (10–1).

DeSalvo points out that this story replicates the six-year-old Virginia's experience of sexual abuse on a shelf where plates were stacked outside the dining room at Talland House (1989, 157–159). In both source experience and fictional re-creation, the child/woman is suddenly and unexpectedly pitched onto an exposed ledge; in both she is trapped, helpless, unable to move; in both shameful "rummaging" with clothes takes place. Woolf remembered in

"A Sketch of the Past" that Gerald Duckworth had sat her on the shelf and explored her body. She recalled the feeling of his hand under her clothes, moving inexorably downwards; that she hoped he would stop but that he didn't; that she "stiffened and wriggled" as "his hand explored my private parts too" (*MOB*, 69). That sexual abuse predisposes to eating distress is clearly established.[6] Given that, in Woolf's case, the locus of sexual abuse was a shelf for dinner dishes, it can surely be no surprise that eating difficulties resulted.

As DeSalvo observes, "The Experiences of a Pater-familias" points to the young Virginia's sense that her abuse was the result of unchecked greed for both sex and food. It is notable that the Robinsons' table collapses not at the beginning of the meal, when it would logically be bearing most weight, but at the end, when the food has been consumed. Woolf associated gluttony with Gerald Duckworth. In her diary for 1903 she remarked how seriously he took the question of where and what to eat, recording that at supper at a dance they had attended he dispatched the waiters helter-skelter for quails and champagne as if he were at the Savoy (*APA*, 171–172). She told Violet Dickinson how, on another occasion, he had described to her with passionate vividness lunches eaten twenty years ago, then fallen asleep like, she thought, a prize pig well satisfied (*L 1*, 307). In George Duckworth too (a later abuser), she saw an all-pervasive, all-invasive physical appetite, describing him repeatedly in "22 Hyde Park Gate" as a pig, as tending to fat (*MOB*, 169), and as reputedly the greediest man in London society (168). She remembered that when Judith Blunt turned down his marriage proposal, he sat at the head of the table and wept openly—while continuing to eat (167).

The tragic result of the Duckworth brothers' abuse was that Virginia came to experience the body's normal needs, be they for food or sex, as rampant, dangerously out of control, and thus in need of rigorous externally imposed checks. Her faith in an ontologically healthy body with its own internal regulators was destroyed. The body was pathological. As is frequently the case in sexually abusive situations—in which "A child's feeling of shame and the abuser's denial of responsibility work together to convince her the abuse is her fault" (Women's Research Centre, 113)—the abused, Virginia, was unable to lay blame where it was due. In "The Experiences of a Pater-familias" she recognized that her sexual abuse had been "caused by an excess of appetite" (DeSalvo 1989,158), but the question remained whose appetite. In her own perception the situation was reversed. It was not Gerald, and later George, Duckworth who was greedy and out of control, but she herself.

As an infant, Virginia had a sturdy sense of hunger, as one of Vanessa Bell's earliest memories testifies. She recalls Virginia, aged about two, as "a very rosy chubby baby, with bright green eyes, sitting in a high chair at the nursery table drumming impatiently for her breakfast" (Stape, 3). According to Vanessa, all this changed in April 1888, when Virginia was six. At this time the four Stephen children went down with an attack of whooping cough—Virginia's being the most serious—at the end of which they emerged from the nursery like skeletons. Although the other children recovered rapidly, it seemed to Vanessa that Virginia was permanently affected. "She was never again a plump and rosy child," Vanessa wrote; indeed, it seemed to her that Virginia had "entered into some new layer of consciousness rather abruptly, and was suddenly aware of all sorts of questions and possibilities hitherto closed to her" (5–6). As DeSalvo notes, if Woolf's own dating is correct, her abuse by Gerald Duckworth took place in the summer following this attack, when she was recuperating at St. Ives (1989, 107–108). That the changes Vanessa noticed in her sister were the result of whooping cough (a fairly common childhood illness) therefore seems highly questionable. Much more plausible is the thesis that they were a reaction to her abuse. Unlike the other children, Virginia did not regain weight after 1888, becoming "marked . . . by that thin, fine, angular elegance which she kept all her life" (Q. Bell, vol. 1, 25). The obvious (and unanswerable) question is whether, as a result of her abuse, she had already begun to suffer some form of eating distress.

Prior to her marriage in 1912, Virginia experienced two periods of "breakdown": The first in 1895 after the death of her mother, the second following her father's death in 1904.[7] Quentin Bell refers to the 1895 "breakdown" as "a great interval of nothingness, a kind of positive death which cannot be described and of which Virginia herself probably knew very little—that is to say could recall little," commenting sensationally that from then on "she knew that she had been mad and might be mad again" (vol. 1, 44). It is true that Virginia wrote little about this first "breakdown" (a few lines in "Reminiscences" describe the summer holiday at Freshwater on the Isle of Wight during which it occurred, and there is a later autobiographical fragment in the Monk's House Papers),[8] and yet the mystery is not so opaque. The loss of her mother must be traumatic in any circumstances to a thirteen-year-old girl; that it was particularly so to Virginia is readily explicable in the context of sexual abuse, inadequate or inappropriate family boundaries, and insufficient experiences of mothering.

Virginia remembered her mother with an unfulfillable longing as someone whose rare presence connoted a kind of prenatal bliss. She recalled with rapture her appearance on the balcony at the Stephens' holiday home in Cornwall, Talland House, and the starred passion flowers growing on the wall there (*MOB*, 65–66). Julia was the "whole thing" (83); she was a pattern of red and purple flowers, seen very close by the child on her lap (64), a scratch of beads, a laugh like a sigh, the lights in her opal ring, and the tinkle of her silver bracelets. She was the passport into an Edenic world, and at night Virginia lay in bed longing for her appearance, when she would tell the child to imagine all kinds of lovely things, such as rainbows and bells (81–82).

But these moments of bliss were few and far between. Woolf remembered that she was never with her mother for more than a few minutes before someone interrupted, and with hindsight she could see that, given the manifold domestic responsibilities with which Julia was saddled, she was of necessity an infrequent and short-lived presence (*MOB*, 83). She recalled vividly the acute anxiety that she felt during her mother's long absences, when she would peep secretly through the blinds to look for her coming down the darkened street, sure that an accident had occurred. She remembered that on one occasion her father found her watching and reproved her anxiously for her nervousness (84).[9]

Because Virginia had been shortchanged with regard to the maternal closeness she needed, she had not fully succeeded in separating from her mother. She later wrote that until she was in her forties she was obsessed with her mother's presence (*MOB*, 80). In "A Sketch of the Past" she used the word "central" to refer to a sense of existing so totally within her mother's ambit that she was never able to see her as an individual in her own right (83), a description which suggests that she remained merged with her mother.[10] Marilyn Lawrence has written, "It is as though the [anorexic] daughter believes that she depends for her very survival upon her mother" (1984, 70); Woolf implies something like this when she writes of her sense that her mother was "keeping . . . the panoply of life . . . in being" (*MOB*, 83).[11] Julia's death was thus for Virginia more than just the bereavement of a loved person; it was the loss of a vital part of herself and posed a threat to her own continued existence. It can therefore be no wonder if she experienced her subsequent "breakdown" as, in Bell's terms, a kind of death.

For the rest of her life Woolf would look for relationships that could supply the maternal nurturance she continued to crave. In 1925 she spoke of how Vita Sackville-West gave her "maternal protection," which she said was what she desired from everyone, and what Leonard and Vanessa gave her (*D 3*, 52). In her teens and early twenties she addressed Madge Vaughan in letters as "Mama Vaughan" and "Foster Parent," signing herself "your infant"; similarly, she cast Violet Dickinson as "mother wallaby" and herself as a joey curled up in her pouch, asking Dickinson, was she "soft and tender to her little one"? (*L 1*, 244). In many senses Vanessa, dependably present, consistently accessible, was always a more reliable source of mothering than Julia had ever been. Virginia saw—or liked to see—Vanessa as her primary childhood caretaker, imagining her as the antithesis of the parental figure that, as a ten-year-old, she had created in the cockney: one vigilant for her siblings' welfare and anxious to ensure they were well fed. She described a fictionalized Vanessa caring tenderly for her three younger siblings, giving up her bottle to Thoby, and reminding the nurse to fasten him carefully in his high chair before giving him his porridge (*MOB*, 28).

It seems likely that, as DeSalvo (1989, 69) and James King (79) believe, Virginia and Vanessa were also sexually involved with one another. Certainly the sisters' letters to one another (in which Virginia was William, Billy, Monkey, or Goat to Vanessa's Maria) were amorous and erotically suggestive. "I have just washed my hair and am extremely furry," runs a 1907 letter of Vanessa's. "Would you like to stroke it?" (V. Bell, 57). "Shall you kiss me tomorrow?" wrote Virginia to Vanessa in 1908; "Yes, Yes, Yes. Ah, I cannot bear being without you" (*L 1*, 355). When Vanessa married Clive Bell, Virginia was extremely distressed, describing herself as "numb and dumb" (*L 1*, 279), but telling Violet Dickinson that she realized it was "all over," that she could not be alone with Vanessa any more and must come to terms with the new situation (276). She later became involved in a chaste affair with Clive, the subintention of which was evidently to reinstate by proxy her physical intimacy with Vanessa.[12] When Virginia herself became engaged, Vanessa also suffered great emotional pain, telling Virginia that when she saw her with Leonard "it was somehow so bewildering and upsetting . . . that I didn't know how to say what I felt" (V. Bell, 117). The sexualization of the sisters' relationship is consistent with Woolf's later pattern of involvement. Although, even within lesbian relationships, as a result of her abuse her sexuality remained suppressed, nonetheless throughout her life she would perceive sex as a means of eliciting close maternal attention.

It was, according to DeSalvo, following Julia's death in 1895 that George began to abuse Virginia and perhaps also Vanessa (1989, 67)—as Virginia put it, insisting "upon a closer and more mature friendship with us" (*MOB*, 44). She perceived, correctly, that her half brother's miasmic emotions were a threat to her physical safety, that his unbounded requirements for sympathy and consolation crested a dark undertow of sexual demand. With Julia's death, she saw that a bulwark (if not a wholly effective one) between herself and her abusers had been removed and that in the shifting family constellations that followed the bereavement, she was at great risk. When George became effectively the head of the family, she later wrote, she and Vanessa "had every reason to feel the earth tremble beneath our feet and the heavens darken" (168).

Virginia's description of the atmosphere surrounding Julia's death and her own breakdown is of a pervasive fog of suffocating emotion that numbed and obscured real sources of pain. The bay at Freshwater is full of a smoky vapor that mingles with memories of hot rooms and, significantly, silence (*MOB*, 45). As Waskett points out, silences frequently characterize anorexic women's families, generally serving to suppress an unspeakable family secret, such as alcoholism, suicide, or—as in Woolf's case—sexual abuse (21). If Virginia was complicit in maintaining the Stephen silence, it was because the source of her own distress lay beyond the terrible bereavement (itself barely mentionable) in happenings wholly unutterable. DeSalvo comments that abuse survivors sometimes feel that they are choking (1989, 10–11)—a sense that may contribute to eating distress. Virginia uses the word "choked" twice within a very short passage of writing to describe her existence at this time (*MOB*, 45). On the one hand choking may have connoted for her gagging on the cotton wool of the Duckworths' out-of-control emotions and unleashed sexuality; on the other hand it seems to have represented the gag which was imposed on her, forcing her to swallow down the telling words which were not permitted to be spoken.[13]

Woolf later described the 1895 "breakdown" (herself using quotation marks) as "a state of physical distress" that lasted two years, and during which she lost all desire to write. Her pulse beat quickly, and she became "terrified of people" and furious with her father and with George, at whom she would sit in her room "raging" (quoted in Lee 1996, 178). Stella Duckworth's diary attests to the longevity of this episode. On October 13, 1896, she took Virginia to see the family doctor, David Seton, because she had had an "anxiety attack" eight days previously (King, 63). Seton's prescription, meted out at a later consultation, was for copious meals and large amounts of mindless activity. Virginia was to be out of the house for four hours each day, and her lessons were to be suspended. In other words, she was to abandon the mind and become the thing she most dreaded: a body solely. She was also medicated, as her diary records. This was a "treatment" at which she balked, but which was still in force in 1897, when, on May 14, she told Thoby that Seton had banned her from lessons for the term (*L 1*, 6).

The regimen imposed on Virginia was basically that for female "hysteria," a condition believed by the Victorian medical establishment to result from mental activity vitiating the reproductive system. The "cure"—severe restriction of intellectual activity—was based on the premise that the womb is primary and—in women—the brain expendable. While the expressed aim of treatment was the restoration of optimum functioning of the womb, the tacit agenda was an intellectual disempowerment rendering the patient meek, pliable, and thus not only physically but also psychologically "fit" to bear the patriarchal children in the patriarchally regulated ways. That such demoralizing and disempowering regimes were intended only and expressly for women is evinced by a comparison of Virginia's treatment to her brother Thoby's for a similar episode of suicidal childhood distress. In 1894, during a bout of what was diagnosed as influenza, Thoby became delirious and tried to throw himself out of a window at Clifton College. A month later he became similarly distressed at home. But whereas Virginia was ordered to give up lessons for months after her "anxiety attack," Thoby was immediately sent back to school, according to King so that "his masters could closely supervise him" (62). (That it was under these masters' "supervision" that he had attempted to jump from the window seems not to have disturbed his parents.)

The curtailment of activities that resulted from Virginia's "illness" was to prove disastrous for her personal development. As her diary for 1897 demonstrates, she was viewed as someone henceforth chronically vulnerable to mental illness and who must therefore be "protected" on a long-term basis. Under the prescription of such effectively pathological "care," this prognosis with regard to her future health was likely to become self-fulfilling, for under such conditions it was impossible for her to separate from her family and forge her own sense of identity. She felt later that her inability to assess accurately her own gifts and defects in relation to other people's was due to the fact that she had not been allowed to go to school and had thus missed out on an important opportunity for competition with peers. Even in her late fifties, she wrote, her early isolation continued to contribute to a problem with self-definition (*MOB*, 65).

Virginia's 1897 diary reveals how essentially nugatory and insular her fifteen-year-old life was. She was supervised almost constantly by other family members. Whereas Vanessa had been allowed to start drawing classes, she had no meaningful activity for herself (not even a solitary one, as studying was forbidden). Her life was a round of errands with Stella, walks with her father, bicycling, and occasional trips with her siblings to the Kensington Museums or London Zoo. Occasionally she went to the theater with George. Not surprisingly, she was often bored and irritable—a condition she attributed with some irony to "nerves" (*APA*, 99, 54, 13). Perhaps most crucial of all was the fact that with intellectual work forbidden, she was cast adrift from the forms of endeavor that made life meaningful for her. In 1930 she recalled the desperation of her younger self to write when she was "mad" and writing was prohibited, remembering "how I used to hook a piece of paper to me out of the nurse's eye" (*D 3,* 315).

It was at this time that Virginia reached menarche, according to Stella's diary on October 16, 1896 (King, 57), ten days after the anxiety attack that had taken her to Seton. There is no evidence of Virginia's response to this event, but given that in her adult life she was never able to feel positive about menstruation, it is unlikely that she found it easy to deal with.[14] Nor is this surprising in the context of sexual abuse. If it is the case that George Duckworth had recently begun to abuse Virginia, menstruation may have seemed to her a direct consequence of this event, a result of the pollution of her body—for certainly she did consider herself defiled, asking Violet Dickinson in 1916 whether marriage could "purge one of impurity" or if she was "forever contaminated" (*L 2*, 86).[15] In adolescence her periods were erratic (King, 58n).[16] That she had been traumatized by sex and made ashamed and afraid of her body might in itself have been enough to disrupt her menstrual cycle; however, it is also possible that Virginia was taking action to ensure that menstruation was suppressed by refusing to maintain the body fat needed to sustain it.

Jean O. Love assumes that Virginia only began to refuse food during her second "breakdown" (1977, 312), but this is conjecture; indeed, considering that rejection of food was typical of all Virginia's subsequent periods of distress, it seems rather *un*likely that she ate normally during the 1895 "illness." Trombley's assertion that "there is no mention anywhere of Virginia refusing to eat prior to her marriage" (64) is demonstrably wrong. Virginia herself made repeated reference to her anorexic attitude toward food during the 1904 "breakdown," writing, for example, to Violet Dickinson (with whom she had stayed at the height of her distress), "I don't mean to have any more disgusting scenes over food." A few days later, describing herself as "recovered," she told Dickinson, "I don't mind how much I eat to keep it going." She explained that when very distressed she had heard voices which "I thought . . . came from overeating—but they can't, as I still stuff and they are gone" (*L 1*, 142). Vanessa's letters to Virginia around this time are a litany of pleas that she rest, take care of herself, and above all *eat*. In December 1904 she wrote, "I'm sure you can't have been eating enough. I heard from Madge [Vaughan] and she said that you had eaten very little there . . . you must make yourself eat. Violet [Dickinson] said that the first day at luncheon you had nothing but fish—I mean no meat" (V. Bell, 26–27). "And do you really eat enough?" she worried again in April 1905 (31). In July 1907, just after her marriage, she once more entreated, "don't starve" (52).

This is not to deny that there were times in Woolf's adolescence and young adulthood (as later in life) when she ate with pleasure. In 1897 she described, for example, how she and Vanessa bought two "beautiful . . . shiny" twopenny buns from the post office and ate them, talking, in a field (*APA*, 124). She even had enjoyable experiences of food with her half brothers, for instance eating strawberry ice cream with George at Gunters in 1892 (86). However, this enjoyment was by no means consistently experienced.

It is possible that in opting for self-starvation, a *passive* form of resistance through food, Virginia was responding to what she had observed of the treatment of her half sister, Laura, who used food to *act out* her distress.[17] When Laura was seven she sometimes spat out her meat at the table, and at the age of fourteen she felt as if she was choking when she ate (Love 1977, 162). Noting that Laura's behavior worsened dramatically when the Stephen and Duckworth households came together, DeSalvo speculates as to whether she too was sexually abused (1989, 32–33). Many of her behavioral problems, not least her difficulties with food, suggest this. As a child, Virginia witnessed Laura's eating and was clearly disturbed by it, late in her life remembering with horror that the other children were made to eat their meals together with this (as she saw her) vacant, idiotic, and stammering half sister. She also saw what happened to Laura as a result of her overt rebellion through food—pathologization, isolation, and institutionalization—and was evidently determined to avoid these consequences for herself. Even at the end of her life she apparently needed to deemphasize the relationship between herself and Laura, whom she referred to as "Thackeray's grand-daughter" (*MOB*, 182).

Although it is uncertain exactly when George Duckworth began to abuse Virginia, we know that between 1895 and 1904 sexual abuse took place and was (for Woolf speaks of it in "Old Bloomsbury" in the continuous past tense) for an indefinite period of time a regular event. Vanessa too was a victim of this unwanted attention—George was, Virginia states, the "lover" of the "Stephen *girls*" (*MOB*, 177, my italics). In "22 Hyde Park Gate" Virginia remembered how, as she was falling asleep, the bedroom door would open and George would enter quietly, urging her not to be afraid or turn on the light, and whispering "oh beloved" would throw himself on her bed and embrace her (*MOB*, 177). In her retelling of this or a similar episode in "Old Bloomsbury," she states that George's abuse was still going on in 1903 when Leslie Stephen was dying. George later told Savage that this behavior was intended to comfort Virginia for her father's illness (182).

Like many abusers, George Duckworth was outwardly a model of social respectability and decency.[18] As Virginia observed, he defined his tyrannies as selflessness, behaving like a "brute" while "profoundly believing in the purity of his love" (*MOB*, 58). She described him as worshipping the aristocracy and determined to climb to the apex of society (170). He was, she remarked wryly, a "saint" (167) who always "played with a perfectly straight bat" and believed in the "ideals of a sportsman." The exaggerated correctness of all his behavior was remarkable; he would, she recalled, "run miles" to fetch cushions, open doors and shut windows, send soup to invalids, remember the birthdays of aunts, attend funerals, and read to his half-siblings when they were unwell (166–167).

George's commitment to climbing the social ladder was inextricably connected with the domination and abuse of his two half sisters, for to be the ornament the up-and-coming young man required on his arm was also, in his mind, to take responsibility for assuaging his emotional and sexual needs. Thus when Vanessa refused point blank to go out in society with him any longer, she passed Virginia, her successor, a double-sided baton. When Woolf writes of George's implacable determination to rise in the social world that "Nothing stood in the way of his advancement" (*MOB*, 169), she is also describing how strong a force he was to resist as an abuser. She remembered feeling in relation to him that she *must* obey, because behind him stood "force, of age, of wealth, of tradition" (154). But the weight of authority was not George's only means of coercion; he also used his rampant emotionalism as a cudgel to beat his half sisters into submission. When Vanessa said that she did not wish to go out with him, according to Virginia, he sobbed, went down on his knees, took Vanessa in his arms and begged (170). When she continued to resist, "every battery was turned upon" her, and he called her "selfish, unwomanly, callous and . . . ungrateful" (171). It is no wonder that later in life Vanessa told Roger Fry "she considered being emotional and irrational akin to having a disease" and that she herself tended "to evade, suppress and conceal" (Dunn, 240).

Virginia must have regarded with a certain amount of irony her brother-in-law Jack Hills's assurances that George was completely chaste until marriage (*MOB*, 169). She knew that George's sexual needs were being taken care of, that part and parcel of her role as favored younger sister of this adoring half brother was (in Lee's words), "George helping her to undress, or coming into the bedroom after she was undressed, lying on her bed and fondling her" (1996, 153–154). She writes in "22 Hyde Park Gate" that "as his passions increased and his desires became more vehement," she felt like a minnow shut up in a tank with a whale (*MOB*, 169). When George turned his attention from Vanessa to Virginia, he made a statement which she found sinister. He claimed that by withholding their affections she and Vanessa were driving Gerald to find companionship on the streets, and that if they continued to refuse George their company on his society outings, he too would be compelled to resort to using prostitutes (172). In other words, Virginia and Vanessa were properly responsible for taking care of their half brothers' sexual needs.

Alluding at least in part to her relations with the Duckworth brothers, Woolf states in "Old Bloomsbury" that her 1904 "illness" was the result of "all these emotions and complications." She recorded that still as she wrote in 1922 she felt "suffocated" by her memories of the time (*MOB*, 183). That she continued to feel this way was due, no doubt, largely to the fact that in 1904 her family, friends, and doctor had done all in their power to stifle both her awareness of what had happened to her and her authentic response to those events. What feeling she was able to express was, symbolically, thrust back down her throat. No one was prepared to face the vast repercussions for the Stephen/Duckworth family, and for the hallowed status of the Victorian family as an institution, that allowing Virginia to voice her experiences and to feel her hurt and anger would entail. It was simpler and less threatening to ignore or pathologize those experiences. Eventually, at least on a superficial level, Woolf swallowed the story that was fed to her: She was mad, she heard voices, she was nervous, and (later on) she was sexually and emotionally frigid. But her real experience was submerged rather than effaced. It continued to condition her daily existence at times when she was "well" and periodically, when she was "ill," erupted through the skin of consciousness.

In 1904 Virginia was under the medical supervision of George Savage. The treatment he prescribed was a version of that famously devised by Silas Weir Mitchell and established as the standard "cure" for neurasthenia. Schwartz explains, "[Mitchell] placed his patients in opaque wombs of darkness, sleep, milk, massage, gentle electric currents and sternly enforced boredom. The body, mind and time itself were suspended while the patient lay inches away from trance, a sleep-eater, gaining weight, trusting in a higher power" (72).[19] Savage believed that too much thought caused madness in "the weaker sex," arguing that when an intelligent young woman is permitted to study at home, "the danger of solitary work and want of social friction may be seen in conceit developing into insanity." To him an educated woman was one who had had "useless book learning . . . crammed into her." He saw such a woman as "exposed, like the Strasborough geese, to stuffing of mental food," and believed that "disorder of functions results" (quoted in Trombley, 126). Obviously, when we are talking about eating distress, these are loaded terms. They are also strikingly sexual. On a subintentional level Savage seems to be implying that what a young woman needs stuffing into her is not an education but a penis, that without this generous male input the female functions cannot possibly be healthy. In a context of sexual abuse, this is at the very least a particularly unfortunate image for what are already a nefarious set of premises—premises that render women down to a set of reproductive functions.

Savage's practice in relation to "insanity" was to disconfirm the "mad" person's "delusions." Indeed, he encouraged friends and relations to send the patient letters explaining and reinforcing the untenability of his or her "insane" perceptions (quoted in Trombley, 152). The use of this "treatment" with survivors of sexual abuse such as Virginia is truly tragic. Surely no more cruelly counterproductive approach can be imagined—none more certain to repress the survivor's memory of the event, to reinforce her sense of guilt, to convince her she is crazy or has made it all up, to alienate her from her own perceptions, to isolate her, and finally to drive her to the suicide that Virginia attempted (by jumping from a window) in 1904.

The single voice to speak out against the destructive regime imposed on Virginia in 1904 was that of her cousin, Madge Vaughan, with whom Virginia stayed in November of that year. A letter from Vanessa to Madge reveals that Madge had objected to the "invalid life" that Virginia was being forced to lead. She felt that Virginia "ought to lead her own life" and that "the more independent she can be the better."[20] Vanessa professed to agree with Madge in principle but objected that "up to the time of her illness it was impossible not to interfere a good deal in physical ways because she . . . would have allowed herself to get ill if one had not prevented her" (V. Bell, 25), her comment evincing that self-responsibility had in fact been taken from Virginia before she actually became "ill." One must therefore speculate whether this removal of responsibility might not have been a factor in creating Virginia's 1904 "illness," given that to infantilize a woman who is in eating distress is only to reinforce her sense that she is out of control, thus driving her to seek surrogate forms of self-control through measures that medicine and psychiatry view as symptomatic.[21]

Vanessa was well aware of her sister's sexual abuse, at least by George Duckworth; indeed, she brought it to an end by drawing it to the attention of Savage, who reprimanded George (Love 1977, 200). Nevertheless, Vanessa's consistent aim as her sister's caretaker was to manage her symptoms and thereby repress the real source of her distress. Even though—or perhaps because—she herself had firsthand experience of George's incestuous attentions, she preferred to maintain the family myth and believe that her sister's distress was due to the fact that she was "highly strung" (V. Bell, 25). It is likely that Vanessa was subconsciously motivated by fear of facing the effects that abuse had had upon herself—which acknowledging the source of Virginia's distress would surely have compelled her to do. This fear became a life pattern of avoidance for Vanessa. According to Jane Dunn, "Evasion of the issue for as long as possible, and a determination to continue with daily life as if nothing had changed was her instinctive response" (82). It is clear from Angelica Garnett's memoir,[22] Frances Spalding's and Jane Dunn's biographies, and Louise DeSalvo's work (1989, 93) that, contrary to the widely accepted myth in which Vanessa is monumentally sane and stable, the effects of sexual abuse upon her were great. As Garnett notes, she suffered from long periods of "crippling . . . lethargy" that suggest "severe depression" (32).

Not surprisingly, given her need to resist confronting her own abuse, Vanessa insisted on viewing Virginia's response to sexual abuse not as just that but as a series of symptoms that were caused by her refusal to eat and rest adequately. She assured Virginia, for example, that her back pain was due to insufficient food (V. Bell, 27). Once past the most acute phase of her distress, Virginia professed agreement, telling Violet Dickinson that she was suffering a little from neuralgia but that it was cured by "food and fresh air" and that all she did was "bask and eat" (L 1, 143). In other words, the Weir Mitchell was efficacious in relieving her "symptoms," and she was following the regime to the letter. Virginia also accepted that her "delusions" (which Vanessa had, according to prescription, disconfirmed) were just that:

"voices" that she had "used to hear" in "imagination." and which were now gone (142).

Virginia's real feelings about Savage and the regimen he was compelling her to follow were, however, rather different. Every so often her sense of the reality of the situation boiled over in letters to Violet Dickinson. On October 30, 1904 she told Dickinson that Savage was "tyrannical" and "shortsighted" (*L 1*,147). She said that doctors could only guess at the causes of illnesses and could not cure them, and that once she was allowed charge of her own life she would "throw their silly medicines down the slop pail." She said that she never had and never would believe in "anything any dr says" (148). A month later she described Vanessa as "silly" for lending credence to Savage's ideas. She said she didn't understand how anyone could be stupid enough to believe in doctors and that her life was a constant battle against their idiocies (159).

Nonetheless, it was essential for Virginia to define herself as an apt patient who was recovering rapidly under the excellent treatment of her doctor in order for her to gain some measure of liberty from his constrictive measures. She realized that what was required of her was a conciliatory admission of her own "madness," demonstrations that she was now reformed, and childlike obedience. It is in this context that one must see her repeated avowals of how much and how unproblematically she was eating in the latter part of 1904. On December 8, the birthday of her aunt, Caroline Emilia Stephen, with whom she and her younger brother Adrian were staying, she told Madge Vaughan with ostensible glee that they were celebrating with chocolate, marzipan, and chestnuts, of which they were going to eat as much as they could (*L 1,* 164). A few weeks later she described to Violet Dickinson her Christmas indulgences: a big tea on top of turkey. She said that on Christmas day Sophie (the cook) "never lets us off at all," that the whole household was "soporific" with food, and that when she had finished writing she would have to polish off the leftover turkey legs (168). My sense is that there are other attitudes than sensual gratification and relaxed contentment latent in this description of Christmas Day (which for those with food problems is generally a source of extreme stress). Her joke about Sophie seems to express a real sense of duress; on this day in particular, Virginia really would not be allowed to avoid eating. If she wanted to maintain the "sane" status which she was then only tenuously establishing with family, friends, and Savage, she would "have to" eat the turkey legs—although perhaps her own word, "attack," is a more accurate expression of what she really wanted to do with them.

In 1906 the relationship between willingness to eat and liberty from doctors' crippling rest regimes was further borne in upon Virginia when Vanessa contracted typhoid. Vanessa's convalescence was marked for her sister by the ease with which she gained the recommended amount of weight, as a result rapidly acquiring the right to personal freedoms and responsibilities. What Virginia referred to as Vanessa's "power of taming drs" was directly due to the fact that "she has the weighing machine to bear witness" (*L 1*, 247). Virginia reported that when Vanessa's weight rose from 9 stone (126 pounds) to 9 stone 4 pounds (130 pounds), Savage permitted her to decrease her bedrest by a week, telling her that she would be well again in two (244). Even when Vanessa's weight-gain diet was modified, she continued to put on weight, gaining, Virginia reported to Dickinson, two and a half pounds on "half rations." This to Savage was proof positive of her exemplary sanity, and he announced that her nerves were "beautiful" (249). So complacent was Vanessa's weight gain, so sublime her accord with her body that, according to Virginia, even Savage was finally forced to concede that she should be allowed total charge of her own welfare—"We had better leave it to her" (247).

Virginia's observations of Vanessa's recovery need to be understood in the context of the tendency for her and Vanessa to polarize. As Dunn notes, the sisters' relationship "came to be symbiotic, in the sense that each relied on the other to express abilities and experiences that the other tacitly had taken for herself" (1). By defining Vanessa as someone who was comfortable with her body, who weighed a healthy amount, and could put on weight easily, Virginia was able to affirm, by contrast, her own anorexic identity. Looking back to 1904, she told Dickinson, "after all our chastening interludes . . . I look upon her convalescence but as another chance for defacing—or is it effacing—myself" (*L 1*, 244–245). Whereas she had wrangled with Vanessa and Savage and struggled with herself over the necessity of eating, Virginia needed to believe that Vanessa had a natural affinity with her body and that gaining weight was thus for her not problematic. She reported Savage as saying that Vanessa had an uncommonly "sound body" (249). She herself, as a corollary, had no body at all. Describing Vanessa's three-pound weight gain, she went on to speak of herself as having become totally disembodied, telling Dickinson that when she came to visit she would find Virginia no more than a cold sharp mist (245).

Much as Virginia vaunted what she saw as Vanessa's physicality, her superlative ability to live in the body and to gain the weight that would sustain it, at the same time her subliminal feeling was that there was something shameful in Vanessa's ontological position. As Virginia described it, there was a brazen quality in Vanessa's glee at her increasing body size; when Vanessa tipped 9 stone 4 pounds (130 pounds) Virginia told Dickinson that even the doctor blushed (*L 1*, 244), and that, "We all looked the other way." Significantly, she compared this weight with Gerald Duckworth's, remarking that with a watch-chain and loose change in his pocket he weighed 15 stone

(210 pounds). Evidently the issue of weight was for Virginia bound up with the body of her abuser, part of her fear apparently being of weighing as much as Gerald and of thus becoming a body equally out of control. In her subliminal perception, if not in reality, Vanessa's weight was spiraling dangerously close to this level, and Virginia was anxious to stress that she herself weighed nothing like as much as Vanessa, let alone Gerald; "She weighs 9.4 [130 pounds]: I dont," she wrote (247).

Defining her weight may have been a way for Woolf to define herself as a separate individual within the sprawling family at 22 Hyde Park Gate, for despite the family's composite nature, the sense of group identity was extremely strong. Woolf later described the bricks and mortar of the house as steeped in family history, recalling her sense that it and its inhabitants were knit together by experiences, emotions, and traditions that had seethed for years beneath its roof, and which must, it seemed, persist forever (*MOB*, 183). As a child, she felt that she must inevitably be subsumed into the entity of the family, the weight of whose collective past—evidence of which tumbled out of every cupboard—was crushing to her sense of herself as just that: an individual with a capacity for a different kind of life.[23]

Defining her weight was also a means for Woolf to define her boundaries within a family characterized by poor containment of individual needs, emotions, and roles. The flimsiness of family boundaries is expressed in Woolf's memory of the folding doors so indispensable to family life at 22 Hyde Park Gate (164). These doors, she wrote, controlled the tidal waves of emotion, crises, and tragedies that constantly threatened to overflow in various parts of the house. Yet they were shaky, impermanent partitions, inadequate to maintain any real separation. Emotional spillage was a family pattern. Thus, for example, Virginia was expected to absorb Gerald's and George's sexual energy; Stella was expected to absorb Leslie's need for a wife, housekeeper, and perhaps lover when Julia died; and when Stella also died, Vanessa was, in turn, expected to serve as Leslie's domestic manager and emotional sponge. This kind of family structure is well described by Sálvador Minuchin, Bernice Rosman, and Lester Baker's term, "enmeshed"— a word which evokes Woolf's own description of the Stephens' home as, "tangled and matted with emotion" (*MOB*, 183).[24]

Woolf remembered that the four children of Leslie and Julia Stephen thought of themselves as a unit. They were, she felt in retrospect, "self-sufficient" (*MOB*, 129). Even when she was fifteen, and "us four" had become to some extent separate, each with a room of her or his own, she recognized that they were not as individuated as siblings generally are in their teens (125). In Sheila MacLeod's recipe for anorexia, one of the ingredients is that "the validity of extra-familial friendships should be denied" (174). This kind of self-reliant coalescence was indeed valorized within the Stephen family system. F. E. Halliday recalled the young Stephens at St. Ives as "never mixing with other children" (quoted in Lee 1996, 26), and Woolf herself remembered that they never had friends to stay. She recalled once at St. Ives feeling her parents' approbation when she rejected a girl called Elsie who had been brought to visit, commenting that "They liked us to be independent" (*MOB*, 129). Such "independence" of the outside world, particularly in the case of Virginia who never went to school, was in fact isolating and problematic for identity formation, intensifying the power of received family patterns and impeding identification with outside role models.

According to his biographer Noel Annan, "Leslie Stephen learnt to base his whole ethical system on the family." Leslie wrote that, "The degree to which any ethical theory recognizes and reveals the essential importance of the family relation is, I think, the best test of its approximation to the truth" (Annan, 154). When Leslie referred to "the family relation," he was, of course, designating not just any old family setup but specifically "the patriarchal family," of which, Annan writes, he was "an uncompromising protagonist" (293). This family was to him not merely a social arrangement but a moral imperative, deviance from which implied an essential corruption. The interests of the individual within it were therefore subordinate to the maintenance of an appropriate family identity, and personal needs that risked shaking the family foundations were forced to find expression as less threatening symptomatic responses. Self-starvation was thus for Virginia an obvious means of protesting against and coping with her sexual abuse. She was known as "the Goat" in the family, a nickname which carries many messages about her family role, not least the fact that on some level she was its scapegoat, the one who (with Laura exiled) could be sacrificed for the well-being of the group. The cost of her father's philosophy was ultimately irredeemable to her—years after the nuclear family he headed had dissolved, she took her own life in the process of unearthing those memories that she had tried to bury under symptoms in the interests of preserving the "family relation" intact.

Until the writing of *To the Lighthouse*, Woolf recalled, she had been obsessed by the suppressions and silences that her father demanded. She wrote, "I would find my lips moving, I would be arguing with him; raging against him; saying to myself all that I never said to him." She commented, "How deep they drove themselves into me, the things it was impossible to say aloud" (Add Ms 61973). Had he not died when she was young, she reflected, his presence would have stifled her life and prevented any writing (*D 3*, 208). She described him as having "a godlike, yet childlike standing in the family." Like the typical anorexic father described by MacLeod, he was both "the ultimate authority" and yet could *appear* "weak and vacillating"; he was "indulgent" and yet "tyrannical . . . , each in turn" (176). He was thus a confusing figure to his daughter, one who provoked an intensely ambivalent response: the "alternately loved and hated father" (Add Ms 61973). Maine notes that "Women who struggle with eating and body-image problems often speak of unrequited love when they speak of their fathers. 'I never felt good enough for him,' is a common refrain. Many report having felt their fathers' disappointment throughout their entire lives" (75).[25] Woolf craved her father's unconditional approval but felt that in order to elicit his love she had to measure up to exacting standards. In *To the Lighthouse* Mr. Ramsay, the fictionalized Leslie Stephen, says he will be proud of his son, Andrew, if he wins a scholarship; Mrs. Ramsay counters that she will be just as proud of him if he does not (74). Leslie Stephen's pride in his daughter tended to center not on what she had actually achieved but on what she might; it was therefore both subtly directive and pressurizing. In 1893 when he told Julia that Virginia was certain to become an author, the decision was one *he* had made. He also seemed to think it was up to him to settle the form her writing would take, for he continued, "I cannot make up my mind in what line" (quoted in DeSalvo 1989, 219). Virginia did, however, receive some unqualified praise from her mother. She remembered the deep pleasure she felt when Julia admired a story she had written for the family newspaper; it was, she said, "like being a violin and being played upon" (*MOB*, 95). It was perhaps because she feared her work would not be good enough for her father that she only ever showed him one of her essays (*MOB*, 1st edn, 138). Indeed, when she was writing *The Voyage Out*, she had a nightmare in which she showed him a draft of the novel and "he snorted, and dropped it on to a table" (*L 1*, 325). As an adult, she was aware that his standards were not her own, that she did not aspire to, and thus could never live up to, the masculine Cambridge rationalism that he upheld, and yet she still felt that her own life understanding and thus her own efforts were subtly undermined by his. "But at the same time I am seduced," she said, "and feel that my measure has been proved faulty" (Add Ms 61973).

When in 1932 Woolf was invited to give the Clark Lectures at Trinity College, Cambridge, as Leslie Stephen had done in 1883, she declined but was nevertheless gratified to receive an honor in her father's own terms, a tangible mark of success that he could have recognized. "[I] like to think that father would have blushed with pleasure could I have told him 30 years ago, that his daughter . . . was to be asked to succeed him: the sort of compliment he would have liked," she wrote (*D 4*, 79). Significantly, she felt that he would have considered the honor an indirect accolade for *himself* rather than a tribute to his daughter. Given that Leslie had encouraged Virginia to become an author, and that he was ultimately disappointed in his own—as he judged it—second-rateness as a biographer (*MOB*, 145), it is pertinent to wonder to what extent Woolf saw her own literary achievements as the realization of her father's ambitions.[26]

Minuchin, Rosman, and Baker observe that the anorexic child's goal in undertaking an activity is generally to elicit love and approbation rather than to gain competence (59). It is evident that throughout Woolf's life a significant motivation of her work was such a desire for approval. Leonard Woolf maintained that after finishing a book her emotional turmoil was often so great as to become symptomatic (1963, 55). Of course, much of this turbulence was due to the fact that she was dealing in her novels with intensely painful personal material—material that brought her ever closer to a confrontation with her sexual abuse—however, it was also in part produced by her need to obtain love through her writing. Leonard described Virginia as having a "terrifying hypersensitivity" to reviews and as being "morbidly . . . sensitive to criticism" (57, 56). Such sensitivity is explicable if we understand it as the fear of rejection of an often insufficiently praised and conditionally loved child.

Leslie Stephen was himself a child in search of love and nurturance, his neediness causing the blurring of important role boundaries within the family. Taking "The Experiences of a Pater-familias" as a reflection of Virginia's observations of her own father, DeSalvo writes that the pater-familias is "another child who will demand that his wife become a mother to him at the very time that she must nurture their child" (1989, 147). Leslie was jealous of his children and constantly tried to displace them. Love suspects envy of the child's legitimate intimacy with his mother prompted Leslie to suggest that Julia should wean Adrian, her youngest and favorite son and the child of whom Leslie "had very little good to say," when he was a year old (1977, 139). In a striking inversion of the appropriate parent-child relationship, Leslie stated that "as long as he could surround himself with the children, like 'an animal in a burrow,' nothing could hurt him" (139). If this paternal reversal did not of itself account for some of Virginia's life-long emotional problems, the further consequences of it certainly did, for the father with his head stuck down a burrow is in no position to notice and put a stop to his daughter's sexual abuse.

Leslie frequently addressed Julia as if he were a naughty child. He confessed, for instance, that contrary to her "orders" he had been mountain-climbing and asked if she was angry that he had gone for an eleven-hour walk. He threatened to "disobey" her and do some writing. He sought to exact a nurturing response by supplying her with a constant stream of extremely detailed information about his health—his headaches, his eating and smoking habits, his sleeping, and his bowel movements (89).[27] His use of the sick body as a means of communicating emotional needs and fears, and Julia's corresponding responsiveness to such language, constituted a pattern that often typifies anorexic family systems (Minuchin, Rosman, and Baker, 61).

Leslie's own childhood experience had taught him that physical illness was the most effective means of eliciting the mothering he needed. He was a sickly child, "frail, ... gangling, almost emaciated, asthenic" (Love 1977, 30), and this vulnerability was the basis of a strong—Annan says "excessive" (50)[28]—bond between himself and his mother, Jane, who "pampered" him "to an excessive degree" (King, 16). This bond was cemented by the emotional inaccessibility of his father, James, who clearly wished and repeatedly tried to make contact with his son but whose feeling responses were effectively paralyzed. King describes how "James would propose long walks to Leslie and then become inarticulate and reserved" (16). Leslie continued to undertake marathon walks throughout his life (as Virginia would also do); perhaps he was still waiting for the elusive expression of love.

If James Stephen could offer little emotional sustenance to his son, the larger patriarchal world, with its misshapen mandates for masculinity, presented him with an ethos of brutality in the context of which it is small wonder he cleaved to his mother and maternal values. As a young child he was considered inappropriately dreamy and too fond of poetry for a boy. The doctor called upon to treat this pathology prescribed no more poetry, plenty of fresh air, and a school at which he would "have the sugar taken out of him" (quoted in Annan, 18). He was sent to Eton where, as per doctor's orders, he was "bullied systematically" (19) and himself learned the art of tyranny. Leslie never lost his sensitivity, what he thought of as his thin skin (20), but as a result of his experiences this quality was distorted. It was with considerable insight that he referred to himself as a "brutal wetblanket" (quoted in King, 26).

Leslie's later attitude to the Eton experience was summed up in a letter he wrote to Julia when Thoby went to school: "You have taken my poor To to school today. I saw a calf going on a sledge to the butcher's & To rather reminded me of it. However, I have no doubt he will be fattened" (quoted in King, 34). The image of the calf to the slaughter expresses the violence that Leslie associated with his school days; however, all specific emotion relating to his own childhood experiences has been systematically purged. There is the pitiful picture, there is Thoby, there is Leslie and a memory, but the emotional connection is absent. Eton had done its work; he was essentially dissociated from any feeling response to the cruelty inflicted on him there. (Woolf would later write similarly about her abuse by George Duckworth.) Although he realized the horrors Thoby would go through in the public school system, he, like many other products of that system, was convinced of the necessity for his son to be put through it all the same. Thoby had to be "fattened"; he had to formed to the patriarchal pattern of man. At the same time, Leslie essentially abjured all responsibility for the boy's torture; it was, according to him, Julia who had sent Thoby to school.

He behaved as if he himself were not Thoby's father but merely an onlooker, as he was when the calf went to the butcher's, impotent to influence his son's fate.

When Woolf looked for the source of her sense of shame at physical pleasure, she pinpointed the inheritance of her father and grandfather as an important factor. Because she was unable to give sufficient weight to sexual abuse as a direct cause of her painful relationship with her body, she probably laid too great an emphasis on the hereditary influence of the puritanical Clapham Sect; to a certain extent, however, her etiology was correct, for exactly this ethos of prurience, suspicion, and demonization of the body typically conditions both incestuous and eating-disordered families. The guilt that she attached to her body suggested to Woolf a memory of her grandfather, James, who, she wrote, "once smoked a cigar, liked it, and so threw away his cigar and never smoked another" (*MOB*, 68). Annan tells a similar story of James Stephen and snuff, describing him as "inexorably suspicious of pleasure," as drinking little and as eating "the lightest of meals" (17). His drive to eliminate pleasure and survive on a baseline of need is characteristic of anorexia, as is his self-loathing and his fear and hatred of own body. According to King, "So convinced was he of his ugliness that he could not abide . . . looking in a mirror" (15).

Woolf described Leslie Stephen as "spartan, ascetic, puritanical" (*MOB*, 68). Walking was one of his ascetic practices, as is evinced by the principles on which he founded his walking society, the Sunday Tramps: "20 miles was an average stroll and the rule of the order was high thinking and plain living. Sometimes, however, they would be fêted at a dinner on their way home . . . but Stephen discouraged such sybaritic festivities" (Annan, 97–98). Such walking was a family trait. According to Annan, Leslie's grandfather walked twenty-five miles to breakfast on his seventieth birthday, going on to his office and then back home (97n). To some extent Leslie seems to have regarded vigorous exercise, as many anorexic women do, as a means to control and contain a dangerous body with threatening sensual appetites. Annan records that on Christmas Day 1866 he walked from Cambridge to Newmarket for lunch, then home again for dinner, "to dispel the excesses of Christmas Eve dinner in Hall" (49).

Virginia inherited the walking habit, and held out all her life against Leonard's embargo on it, writing, for instance, in 1917, "I've promised not to walk at all, and I suppose I must abide by it" (*L 2*, 163), and in 1929, "Leonard thinks it is walking that makes me sleep badly; I dont" (*L 4*, 36). To what extent walking was for her an anorexic response is difficult to ascertain. Although she certainly derived a great deal of genuine physical pleasure from this activity, it seems probable that it also carried for her, if not an anorexic, at least an ascetic appeal.

A journey to St. Ives on which the children were accompanied by their father illustrates another aspect of Leslie's asceticism: his extreme reluctance to waste food. Adrian Stephen remembered that a bottle of lemonade had spilled over the lunch packed by Julia and that they were "repelled by the soggy and perfectly disgusting sandwiches" but that (save Vanessa, who pretended travel-sickness) the children were "forced" by Leslie to eat them (Love 1977, 115–116).[29] But although Leslie's insistence that the children eat the soggy sandwiches was experienced as unpleasant, certainly by Adrian (in 1945 he vividly remembered it) and probably by the others too, Woolf was ultimately attracted by the ethic that underlaid it. In *To the Lighthouse* she describes her father's economy as deriving from a true sense of the value of food—a principle that she would herself honor throughout her life.

Leslie's asceticism was complex and somewhat selective. He appears to have adopted particular forms of eating behavior as both a power ploy and a means of eliciting proof of affection. Like an infant, he used food to express rebellion and rage, for example, refusing to eat his favorite cake at tea after a squabble with Julia (Annan, 99). On another occasion he refused a cake baked specially for him because "I like cake with the plums nearer together." The next day a fruitier replacement was accepted (129). Of course, Leslie's refusal of the perfectly adequate cake was at odds with the eat-everything-on-your-plate principle that he propounded to his children. It seems that this moral dictum yielded before his own need to try the love of his feeder—for apparently the rejection of the too-meager cake constituted just such a test and solicitation of richer affection.

That the offering and eating of food carried strong emotional connotations for Leslie is evinced in his letters to Julia, which frequently contain food-related metaphors and the word "delicious" used in reference to his love for her (Love 1977, 95). He saw Julia as a superlative provider both of food and of a quality of emotional harmony that he desired to experience in eating. When she presided over a picnic there was no question of lemonade in the sandwiches and unpleasant scenes; he wrote in the *Mausoleum Book*: "She was an admirable conductor of such expeditions, catering with unimpeachable skill in the department of provisions, and keeping everyone in good temper" (L. Stephen, 63). Whenever Julia went away to nurse her mother, Maria, she took pains to prepare and store all Leslie's favorite foods to compensate for her absence (Love 1977, 123). Nevertheless, when she was staying with Maria in 1887, he became acutely anxious about impending crop failure and world starvation and tried to lure her home with the prediction that he would turn into a bag of bones—although at the same time he was anxious that the Maitlands, acting as temporary housekeepers, were too extravagant in what he called "the dining department" (121).

Like a small child, Leslie was oblivious to the sensitivities of others at the table. Woolf remembered that he said not a word when his friends Stevenson and Gosse came to lunch and recalled him "sitting often dead silent at the head of the head of the family dinner table." He was, she said, irritated by Julia's greater sociability, finding her "guilty of impulsive hospitality" (Add Ms 61973). In *To the Lighthouse,* she suggests that her father resented Julia's food and attention being lavished on anyone other than himself. He dined in public with a show of ill grace that probably spoiled Julia's pleasure, but Woolf thought that on some level he enjoyed these social dinners—or maybe she meant that he enjoyed his ritual complaint: "'I shall be glad when all this dining out is over Jinny,' he said to me . . . ; and I was flattered by his confidence; yet felt sure that he enjoyed it" (Add Ms 61973).

After Julia's death, Leslie's prandial silences could be preferable to his explosions of grief or rage. Woolf remembered terrible meals when he would groan out loud and protest that he too wanted to die (*MOB,* 41). When his stepdaughter Stella also died, it was at lunchtime each Wednesday that, unforgettably, it fell to Vanessa to present the household accounts to her father—a horrific event that lowered over the week. Woolf recalled how he would bang his fist down on the account book, wail, and roar in an extraordinary exhibition of fury, self-pity, and despair. Her own response was a "rage and frustration" the like of which she never experienced at any other time. Even in her fifties, she felt unable adequately to describe his behavior, save to say that it was as "brutal" as physical violence. Vanessa can only have been confirmed in the conclusion she had drawn from George Duckworth's behavior, that emotion was dangerous. In response to her father's demand, "Haven't you a word to say to me?" she remained as silent and fixed as stone (144). This self-abnegating pattern of response—or rather non-response— to those expressions of powerful feeling that terrified her (in herself as well as others) was thus set for the rest of Vanessa's life.[30]

Woolf could not reconcile her father's self-indulgent rages with his intellectual terseness. She wrote that, "This temper he could not control, and that, considering his worship of reason, his hatred of gush, of exaggeration, of all superlatives, seems inconsistent" (Add Ms 61973). The incongruity is, however, according to Mara Selvini-Palazzoli, a not uncommon trait among anorexic women's fathers, who, she writes, have "often blinded themselves with self-pity" and yet at the same time "consider themselves rational and well-balanced persons." Like Leslie, they "regret that they have never succeeded in making these qualities prevail over their wives' irrational behaviour" (213). In the *Mausoleum Book* Leslie humbly conceded that Julia's "instincts were more to be trusted than my ratiocinations" (L. Stephen, 95); more often, however, the contention of supposed masculine logic and female irrationality was a source of friction. In *To the Lighthouse* Mr. Ramsay is so outraged by his wife's irrationality—lies, he calls it—that he damns her (37). Leslie Stephen's tyrannical overexpressiveness coexisted with a family ethos of intense repression. Although no limit could be imposed upon his loud lamentations at his wife's death, yet to speak simply of Julia, her death, and the feelings it evoked was prohibited. When Stella also died, her memory too became subject to a taboo. Woolf recalled how Thoby avoided saying the word "Stella" when a ship of that name foundered. Even as a young woman, she was aware that maintaining this silence—which, she wrote, "was known to cover something"—gave rise to a paralyzing pathologization of and dissociation from emotions. When Thoby died in 1906, she and Adrian made an agreement to break the family pattern of repression and speak openly of him (*MOB*, 125). Nevertheless, the habit of swallowing feelings persisted. Angelica Garnett remembers that Vanessa and Virginia were always "very, very self-controlled" and that this pattern of behavior was communicated to her own generation: "we were all very good-mannered with each other; we didn't step beyond certain limits, and our feelings . . . seethed underneath and didn't come out" (quoted in Spalding, 313).

Like the fathers of many anorexic women,[31] Leslie Stephen emphasized the desirability of meekness and obedience in his children. According to Love, he approved of them when they were serious and respectful, quickly losing patience when they behaved in normally childish ways. He objected to what he called their "transports," "uproariousness," and "fits of wriggles," and when Julia was absent often wrote to her complaining of such conduct (1977, 150). Woolf felt that she and her siblings were forced "to develop one side prematurely," that helpfulness was valued at the expense of wishes and desires, which were discouraged as "irrelevant and possibly expensive" (*MOB*, 30). This ethos of usefulness and self-subordination extended to their eating behavior. When Stella was ill and did not want food, Leslie told her that, "eating wouldn't do any good, but that it was her duty to please her mother by eating anyway" (Love 1977, 177).

One of a series of children's stories by Julia Stephen, "The Mysterious Voice," illustrates the degree to which she also valued unquestioning obedience. It would seem likely on the evidence of this moral tale that she believed withholding food to be an appropriate means of controlling her children's behavior, for in it the naughty child, Jem, considers dry bread for tea a standard sort of punishment (J. Stephen, 90). Like all children, Jem experiments and tests boundaries—in his mother's terms, behaves badly. He is aware from experience that something is wrong with her equation of perfect behavior and happiness: "Mother always says that good children are always happy but I know they aren't" (89). When the Mysterious Voice offers him the chance to be as naughty as he likes without receiving any punishment, he is overjoyed.

According to Julia, Jem has to learn that a child whose misdemeanors go unchastised will derive no satisfaction from any activity. When Jem escapes punishment for accidentally burning his shoes, he is gratified, but he cannot enjoy his Sally Lunn cake like a "good" child; rather, he feels strangely dissociated, eating it "with the odd feeling of being someone else" (91). Neither is he treated as himself any more. His mother talks through him (93), and when he goes to visit his Aunt Lizzie, she asks "Who is this little boy and why haven't you brought Jem?" (103). In Julia's philosophy, apparently, if a child has done something "bad," he is not really a person any more, until he has been purged of his badness by punishment.

The price Jem pays for permission to enact his little anarchy is the withdrawal of *all* adult attention, punitive as well as nurturant. At the end of the story, worn down by his isolation, he tells the Mysterious Voice that he wants to be good, but the Voice assures him, "Oh, that you'll *never* be," and advises him to try hard to get himself punished. Apparently this child is inherently bad, and all he can do is expiate his sins. Reasonably, Jem protests that he wants to be good so that he doesn't need punishment, but the Voice is adamant: "I don't think you'll ever be good" (103). Finally Jem knuckles under and begs for punishment, to which his Aunt Lizzie's sadistic response is, "I shall be delighted to punish you" (105). Julia's implicit message would seem to be that the imperfectly obedient child (and all children are imperfectly obedient) may receive love only by paying for it in deprivation and beatings.

Significantly, given Woolf's lifelong sense of maternal deprivation, "The Mysterious Voice" also evinces a belief that "good" children should be able to reconcile themselves to very limited contact with their parents. One of the "bad" things that Jem does while he can be naughty with impunity is to have breakfast with his parents rather than the other children and the nurses. His stated reason is that his parents always have much nicer things to eat, but he is also looking forward to spending some time alone with his mother and father. He wants their attention as much as their food, and expects that they will be pleased to see him. In fact, however, his parents barely acknowledge his presence—although when, at the appointed time, his siblings arrive to spend the "children's *quarter of an hour*" with their mother and father, their charming questions and bear hugs are greeted warmly (93, my italics). The moral would seem to be that children who claim more than their legitimate allowance of time (fifteen minutes) with their parents will be denied any contact at all.

In Julia Jackson, primed from birth to respond to sickness in others, Leslie in a sense found his ideal mate. Health was a matter of great concern among the women in Julia's family—Love cites two of her aunts, Julia Margaret Cameron and Virginia Pattle, as having a particularly active interest in illness. Julia's mother, Maria Jackson, was, Love writes, "also very much concerned with health, including her own" (1977, 50–51). As a child, Julia nursed Maria through a serious illness and throughout her teenage years continued to take responsibility for her mother's health, frequently accompanying her to spas in search of the elusive cure for the inexplicable ill. King sees health (explicitly Maria's health) as being "the shared enterprise" that bound mother and daughter together, and excluded Julia's father (himself a doctor) (King, 10). Keen to perpetuate the mother-daughter dyad, Maria endeavored to "protect" her notably attractive daughter from the attentions of young men. Later, when Julia was married to her second husband, Leslie Stephen (and overburdened with domestic responsibilities to the point where her own health was failing), Maria would protest illness and insist that she needed her daughter's presence, in an attempt to reinstate their former intimacy.[32]

Julia re-created this almost symbiotic union in her relationship with her own eldest daughter, Stella. Much as Virginia craved intimacy with her mother, she was aware that the closeness of this particular bond was damaging to Stella, referring to it in "Reminiscences" as "morbid" and preclusive of individuation. She recalled that even a short parting from Julia distressed Stella and that she suffered greatly when Julia went abroad. Virginia felt, at this early stage in her life, that Stella was responsible for creating this unwholesome tie and that Julia herself might have preferred "a different sort of care" (*MOB*, 43). Given, however, the pattern of mothering Julia had learned, it is clear that Stella did not acquire this way of relating in a vacuum. Whatever Julia's overt feelings about her daughter's dependence, it seems likely that on an unconscious level she sought to promote extreme closeness with her. Toward the end of her life, in "A Sketch of the Past," Virginia acknowledged implicitly the reciprocity in the relationship. Julia and Stella were, she wrote, "sun and moon *to each other*" (my italics). She recalled that Julia had admitted she felt Stella to be "part of myself" (96), an attitude which cannot but have crippled the daughter.

Julia learned her first lesson disturbingly well, later stating in "Notes from Sick Rooms" that "The ordinary relations between the sick and the well are far easier and pleasanter than between the well and the well" (J. Stephen, 217). She was active in the relief of the sick, poor, and otherwise distressed, work which, even in a state of chronic exhaustion, she was reluctant to give up. On the one hand, this devotion to charitable works undoubtedly stemmed from the fact that, as King notes, her "self-esteem was fragile" and "centred . . . on caring for others" (6). But on the other hand she seems also to have had a genuine vocation for what might now be considered social work. Publicly, she was an antisuffragist who shared her husband's conviction that a woman's place was in the home. She believed in "the sanctity of separate spheres [for the sexes] and the futility of votes, careers, or a university education for women" (quoted in DeSalvo 1989, 45). Subliminally, however, she seems to have desired independence. According to Love, Leslie Stephen felt that she wanted a career and that she looked upon her charitable work in this light (1977, 125). In retrospect, this was also Woolf's impression. In *To the Lighthouse*, the fictional re-creation of her mother, Mrs. Ramsay, wishes that she might cease to be a do-gooder and become a professional social researcher (13).

Leslie Stephen believed that Julia was "a perfect mother, a very ideal type of mother" (L. Stephen, 83). Obviously, this was an image that no woman could live up to, and perhaps owed more to Leslie's personal fantasy of the mothering he himself desired of Julia than to reality; what her daughters received was certainly somewhat less than this perfection. According to Love, Julia was "best with children when they were infants, and it was then, evidently, that Virginia learned to expect more from her mother than she was ever to receive" (1977, 142). Given her avowed preference for relations with the sick, it does indeed seem likely that Julia engaged most fully with her children when they were helpless, dependent, and could be nursed. Virginia remembered that the only time Julia had for her children (with the exception of Adrian, who could always command her attention) was when they were ill or in the throes of a childhood crisis (*MOB*, 83).

It seems probable that her experience with Julia inculcated in Virginia the subliminal sense that illness was a means to elicit mothering. As Shirley Panken suggests, "Possibly, symptomatology was unconsciously resorted to in hope of restoring or appeasing her mother whose greater mobilization when the children were ill, imprinted for Virginia her future role as a patient. The focus on her body became a template for future involvement with physical illness, in hope of enlisting that aspect of her mother, attuned to ministering to others" (38–39). For anorexic women, illness may be on one level this kind of appeal for nurturance. In the case of Faith, one of Bruch's anorexic clients, for example, the subtext ran, "If I'm well, you won't love me any more, you won't pay any attention to me" (1978, 60). However, anorexia carries a simultaneous message of defiance which also characterized Virginia's attitude to carers. While on the one hand she sought a nurturant experience of mothering in which she was a helpless infant, on the other she fiercely resisted all attempts on the carer's part to legislate for her health. As Panken notes, she maintained "a dual involvement with care-takers, relating to them in both childlike and rebellious attitudes" (38). Like the anorexic woman, what the unmothered child in Virginia really needed but never got was an experience of love which was nurturant while honoring and encouraging her right to self-determination. On the contrary, the price she repeatedly paid for nurturance was infantilization. If her behavior was both childlike and rebellious it was because, within the framework of her relationships particularly with Vanessa and Leonard, accepting the proffered love entailed a fight to retain respect for her status as a self-responsible adult.

When Julia died, Leslie took it for granted that Stella would assume the carapace of her life: charitable work, domestic responsibilities, younger children, and husband. His wedding gift to Julia was a chain bearing what might be called his mission statement for the marriage, the less-than-heartening "We will cling together" (DeSalvo 1989, 57). Stella's birthday present in 1895, some months after Julia's death, was the same chain. The implicit message was that with Julia gone, Leslie required Stella to cling to, but what he demanded from her could not reasonably be asked of a wife, let alone a daughter. According to Love he thought of her as his "exclusive possession" and wanted her to say that she loved him. He was perhaps in love with her "romantically, if not sexually," wanting "everything . . . except a conjugal relationship" (1977, 185). DeSalvo goes further, believing that Stella did become, in every sense, her stepfather's "object . . . of desire" and that her relationship with him may well have been incestuous in the fullest sense (1989, 56). Virginia writes in "Reminiscences" that Stella found herself totally "pledged" to Leslie, that he demanded complete "self-surrender" of her and she "had to acquiesce," that since she was unable to provide him with "intellectual companionship" she "must give him the only thing she had" (*MOB*, 48), and that "any comfort, whatever its nature, . . . she offered him" in his grief (45). Whether the nature of that comfort was sexual, we cannot know; certainly Stella's mental state after her mother's death suggests that it may have been, for she was not only close to "despair" but to some degree emotionally dissociated, having "lapsed . . . into . . . snowy numbness" (48). Indeed, Woolf suggests that at this time Stella married Jack Hills not because she loved him but because she felt she had little to live for and no longer cared what happened to her (47).

Whether Leslie's passion for Stella was consummated or not, it was unwanted, obtrusive, and symptomatic of an enmeshed family system. Given that the family operated in this way, it was inevitable that while his children were still grieving for Stella after her tragically premature death in 1897, Leslie was turning his attentions to the eighteen-year-old Vanessa. In "Reminiscences" Virginia saw her father's behavior at this time as vampiric. Stella's death seemed to have infused him with new strength; he was "brisk" (*MOB*, 55) and "vigorous" as he fixed upon Vanessa for his next "victim," a prospect that roused the sisters to "frenzy." The form that this vampirism took was the demand that Vanessa become one with him; in other words, she should abandon her own feelings and participate in his anger and grief (56). She was saved only by Leslie's death seven years later.

Looking back at the distortions, repressions, and abuses of her adolescence, Woolf used a food-related adjective to sum up her existence then: "what an unwholesome life for a girl of 15" (Add Ms 61973). When the family, once "wedged together" (*MOB,* 184), finally fell apart on her father's death, she observed the collapse of the old rigid structures of meals and the institution of more flexible systems of eating with huge relief. In "Old Bloomsbury" she gave reforms and experiments such as doing without table napkins and exchanging tea at nine o'clock for coffee after dinner equal weight to the freedom to write and paint. Both she and Vanessa felt a great need to purify existences that had been sullied; in their new lives they would, Woolf wrote, "have {large supplies} of Bromo" (185). And yet the sisters' lives could not be so easily disinfected; their sexual and other abuse could not be scoured away. As Woolf noted in *The Years,* such experiences were stains that faded over the years but never completely came out in the wash—indeed, they reappeared down generations. Nor could food problems be simply resolved by changing mealtimes. For the time being Virginia relished the space and light of Bloomsbury, enjoyed her newfound liberty, and looked forward with optimism. When marriage forced her to confront her sexuality and implicitly the buried trauma of her abuse, however, her eating problems would manifest themselves again, weight would once more become an issue, and her distress would mount to a crisis of the proportions of those experienced in 1895 and 1904.

Chapter 3

Entirely My Weight Rests on His Prop

Virginia Stephen's marriage to Leonard Woolf in 1912 was a crucial determinant of the pattern that her relationship with food would assume for the rest of her life. In an immediate sense it is true that marriage to Leonard ensured her existence in a way that, as she was aware, a briefly considered marriage to Lytton Strachey could never have done. Virginia often felt that she could not survive without Leonard's care, for instance telling Vita Sackville-West that were it not for him she would have shot herself long ago during one of her illnesses (*L 4*, 17). More fundamentally, however, Leonard's unquestioning assumption of the role of parental caretaker, and the dictatorial attitude that he brought to this function, militated against the deep exploration and honest confrontation with the past that she needed in order to heal herself in the fullest sense. In the long term, therefore, albeit well intended, Leonard's form of care only perpetuated Virginia's "illness."

In 1912 there was scant awareness of anorexia nervosa (although it had been recognized as a clinical condition since 1873 [R. West, 10]), and sexual abuse was largely unacknowledged.[1] Leonard thus had to trust to instinct in responding to Virginia's problems, and unfortunately his response was misconceived. Today the advice of help organizations is that family members "do *not* try to feed or weigh" a woman who is using anorexia as a coping strategy, that "they do not label her as ill or treat her like a helpless child," and that "they encourage her to take responsibility for herself" (The Anorexia Counselling Service,[2] quoted in MacLeod, 181). Leonard, however, became locked into a futile battle to convince or coerce Virginia to eat. He obsessively recorded her weight, menstrual periods, and general state of health. He referred repeatedly to her "illness"—even "insanity." He assumed total and infantilizing responsibility not only for her eating but also for her money, her hours of work, the extent of her social life, and what time she went to bed.

Leonard sedulously gathered data on Virginia's behavior, but he never succeeded in deciphering her problem, for he was unable to make the leap into that symbolic dimension where her beliefs and actions made perfect sense. He saw, correctly, that her reluctance to eat was not due to a fear of fatness but that the real issue lay deeper (1963, 163) and was connected with a sense of guilt (79–80); however, he was perplexed by the origin and precise nature of this guilt, and puzzled at how and why it had become affixed to eating (163).

Leonard's difficulty in understanding may have stemmed from the fact that he had apparently blocked his own sense of guilt, perhaps out of fear that once admitted it would become overwhelming—for it appears from many of his life attitudes that the depth and extent of it was potentially just that. As Alma Bond points out, his background was one of rabbinical asceticism (72)—not dissimilar from the spartanism of the Clapham Sect regarded by Virginia as a source of asceticism in her own family history. In *Sowing*, Leonard reported that his paternal great-grandmother "used to walk to synagogue with hard peas in her boots in the evening of every Day of Atonement until she was well over 70, and she stood upright on the peas in her place in the synagogue for 24 hours without sitting down until sunset of the following day, fasting of course the whole time." He commented, "I feel a faint sneaking agreement with my great grandmother" (15). And yet regret and self-recrimination were impulses that he professed, with a hint of pride, never to have experienced: "I seem to be without a sense of sin and seem to be unable to feel remorse for something which has been done and cannot be undone—I seem to be mentally and morally unable to cry over spilt milk" (157).

Leonard professed little confidence in the specialists' understanding of Virginia's "illness." He described the five experts consulted about it— George Savage, Henry Head, Maurice Craig, Maurice Wright, and T. B. Hyslop—as principled and well-intentioned; they were, he said, "brilliant doctors," and yet it seemed to him that the sum total of their knowledge was practically nil. Despite (or perhaps because of) the diagnosis of neurasthenia, he felt that they had no notion of what was wrong with Virginia, nor any idea of how to treat it. Their advice was simply that if she ate and rested she would eventually recover—as long as she could be prevented from taking her own life in the meantime (1963, 16).

Although he had no confidence in the specialists' understanding of Virginia's distress, Leonard nonetheless placed great faith in their unanimous opinion that eating well and drinking plenty of milk would protect her from further "breakdown." All his observations between 1912 and 1941, he asserted, supported this view (1963, 79–80). Virginia, with a clear grasp of the inanity of lending credence to a professed cure for an incomprehended ill, did not agree (80). Indeed, the idea that food and milk were the solution to her difficulties must have seemed to her an insult to the depth of her distress and a further dismissal of her right to feel that distress.

Leonard was unable to accept that there might be validity in Virginia's perception of her situation and what would help her in it. To him, there was only one version of the truth, and that was his own. In his account of his relationship with Virginia, he sees it as his role to pronounce this truth for her benefit, thereby correcting her own misapprehensions about her state of mind and body. He is an objective judge who has "observed" the symptoms and "confirmed" the diagnosis. Virginia herself can only "*maintain*" that she is not "ill" (my italics). She is to "accept" what she is "told" by Leonard and those doctors consulted by him on her behalf—apparently without any sense that his action was not only inappropriate but also extremely counterproductive (1963, 16).

Leonard was infuriated by Virginia's refusal to recognize the benefits of the food and rest regime that he was convinced of. Indeed, he persisted in the belief that her refusal to do so was but another manifestation of her "madness"—a "symptom" as he termed it. Clearly there was a great deal of good sense in Virginia's contention that "the whole treatment had been wrong," that the life of food and idle retirement that Leonard and her doctors attempted to force upon her was counterproductive; to Leonard, however, this argument was but a mild manifestation of her "delusions" (1963, 80). The bizarre travesty of logic that he applied to the issue of Virginia's "madness" scarcely indicates the presence of those tremendous powers of reasoning for which he was fabled. If not wholly logical, however, it was on a subintentional level extremely clever, for by making her every protest a self-indictment it effectively silenced Virginia. She was in a Catch 22 situation whereby the only way she could prove she was sane was by admitting that she was mad. When she was well, he said, "she would discuss her illness" and "recognize that she had been mad"; at such times she was "obviously well and sane." But even when she agreed that she was mad, she was not *really* sane, according to Leonard. He regarded as a kind of vestigial insanity her refusal absolutely and consistently to disavow the essential meaning of what he termed her "delusions," the "voices that did not exist," and the "frenzy, despair, [and] violence" that during periods of "breakdown" came to dominate her existence. If when she was "well," he noted, some "situation or argument . . . closely connected with her breakdowns or the causes of them" arose, "traces . . . of her madness" would reappear; "deep down," he felt, "she was never completely sane" (79).

Whereas for Virginia truth was always subjective, relative, multidimensional, Leonard believed in *the one* truth, bald, syllogistic, logically derived. He saw himself as the voice of reason pitted against an irrational world, and might have chorused with Mr. Ramsay, "What he said was true. It was always true. He was incapable of untruth; never tampered with a fact . . . facts [were] uncompromising" (*To the Lighthouse*, 8).[3] Within the framework of Leonard's logic it was clear that self-starvation led to organic degeneration and ultimately death, that "to eat well . . . was essential if . . . [Virginia] was to remain well" (1963, 78–79). Obviously Virginia—a highly intelligent woman—understood that Leonard's assertion was in an empirical sense true, but her refusal to eat did not stem from incomprehension of the pragmatic issues.[4] Her primary mode of consciousness, which generally directed her attitude to eating, was what might be called magical, metaphorical, or mythopoeic—a mode of consciousness which is routinely downgraded and invalidated as a significant operant in life decisions within modern patriarchy.[5] For Virginia, however, the metaphorical meanings borne by food and the body carried a far greater weight than did empirical reality or rational proofs. It was on the level of metaphor that Leonard needed to engage with her if a dialogue were to be possible, and this he was unable to do.

Leonard maintained that Virginia's "insanity" resided in "her premises, in her beliefs," that these were "insane because . . . in fact contradicted by reality" (1963, 164). Among these untenable premises was her insistence that she was not ill but ashamed, that there was a fundamental meaning to the voices that she heard and to the birds that spoke to her in Greek outside the window when she was very distressed,[6] that breakfast was not the answer to her problems, that the doctors (whom *Leonard* had consulted, who corresponded with *him* and regarding her treatment, who imposed upon her, unasked, punitive and destructive food and bedrest regimes) and the nurses (whom Leonard had employed against her will to keep her in bed and feed her the unwanted meals) were conspiring against her. To decode the message of the birds, of the voices, and of Virginia's sense of shame required a willingness to enter into mythopoeic, metaphorical consciousness that was not in Leonard's disposition. Other of Virginia's premises, however—that there was a conspiracy against her and that food and rest were a useless cure—were verifiable in empirical terms; Leonard's problem was that he happened to disagree with them.

If Virginia had access to a form of mythopoeic thought from which Leonard was excluded, she was not, as a correlative, unable to think logically. Recalling that Lytton Strachey had used to say she was a poor ratiocinator, she speculated that by instinct she prevented herself from thinking analytically in order to give free rein to her creativity (*D 4*, 303). Indeed, Leonard himself confessed that she had an "extraordinarily clear and logical mind" (1963, 164), and that he, the cool rationalist, was reduced to "gibbering despair" (163) by her ability to build arguments of incontrovertible cogency upon her supposedly misconceived premises. It was, he said, "useless" to argue with her that she should, for instance, eat her breakfast, because she could prove irrefutably that she should not (164). He referred to this ability as "the terrible sanity of the insane" (163–164), but to a certain extent, he seems to have admired and perhaps even envied it. His own rhetorical constructs were no match for Virginia's.

It is evident that Leonard's energy might have been directed more fruitfully into exploring Virginia's problematic premises with her than attempting to convince her of their invalidity. Thus he might have circumvented productively the head-on conflict that inevitably results from trying to persuade an anorexic woman to eat. As Maureen Dunbar, mother of an anorexic daughter, notes, "Only those who have ever tried to argue with an anorectic can understand how futile it is" (45). This was a lesson of "this excruciating business of food" that, on his own admission, Leonard found "very difficult to learn" (1963, 163)—and, unfortunately, never really did. Susie Orbach explains that when a woman is refusing food, the most efficacious intervention is made "on the understanding that she will be continuing to control her own food"; such an open acknowledgment that, in this personal area, she is in charge "avoids the fruitless power struggle that ensues when anyone attempts to seize control of her food intake" (1986, 135, 137). Leonard, however, appreciated neither Virginia's right to self-control nor the workings of this particular power dynamic. The issue of how much of what and how frequently she should eat remained a major source of contention within the Woolfs' marriage. He reported himself as engaged in a "perpetual and only partially successful struggle" to influence her eating, stating that their quarrels were "almost always about eating or resting" (1963, 80).

"It is useless to argue with an insane person," Leonard concluded from his experiences of trying to persuade Virginia to eat (1963, 163). The economist Maynard Keynes once remarked that "it was pointless to argue with Leonard" (Alexander, 94). Leonard's conviction was blind, absolute, and, as George Spater and Ian Parsons observe, "He had a missionary's zeal to destroy the belief of others and to convert them to the Truth: that is, to his way of thinking" (155). Leonard compared trying to convince Virginia that her premises were faulty to attempting to persuade a man who thinks he is Christ that he is not (1963, 164). That there are circumstances where such persuasion is neither productive nor appropriate never occurred to him. Nor did he realize that it was he, rather than Virginia, who resembled this obstinate fanatic.

Leonard was not the only force of "reason" to pit himself against Virginia's version of the truth. The specialists he called in professed themselves, to a man, stern upholders of empirical theoretism. Like Leonard, Savage believed that "to reason with the unreasonable does little good," but nevertheless—again like Leonard—he kept on trying anyway, insisting that "the force of reason" must be brought to bear upon the "insane" (quoted in Trombley, 153). As Trombley observes, "When Savage treats a patient, two points of view come into conflict": that of the "madman" and that of "Reason, of proportion, of common sense and of good"—in other words, Savage's point of view. The "madman's" prognosis is measured by the degree to which he is convertible to the latter; his case is hopeful when "he rejects his own point of view (his self) and comes over to Savage's side" (150–151).

Maurice Craig, first consulted by Leonard in 1913 and thereafter throughout Virginia's life, was amazed and exasperated that some "insane" people "only believe their own opinion to be correct," even when it is "unsupported by evidence and contrary to the ideas of everybody else" (quoted in Trombley, 191). The problem of insanity was for Craig one of "social discord" (192), and the aim in treating an insane person was to lead her or him to a mode of functioning that accorded acceptably with prevalent sociocultural mores. Craig was deeply suspicious of originality—an attitude that rendered him particularly unfitted to consider nonpathologically the trajectories of Virginia's mind. He described the "acutely manic" as ostensibly "brilliant in their conversations" but said that when this brilliance was analyzed, it was revealed to be merely "unconventional" and thus spuriously impressive. He apparently deemed such people to have been restored to health when the threatening incisiveness of their minds had been blunted and their uncomfortably truthful tongues silenced. Their "entertaining" speeches were, in his thinking, due to "loss of control"—words that when "in health" (apparently a state of rigid repression), they would "perhaps think, but forbear to utter" (197).

T. B. Hyslop's theories would seem to have augured an equally unpromising therapeutic alliance. Deeply suspicious of all forms of symbolism, he distrusted art, particularly in innovative forms. In his opinion, to "give to present objective facts a sense of mystery" was a sign of madness. He observed that "lunatics" frequently have a highly developed mystical sense, perceiving "unusual relations amongst phenomena" and regarding "ordinary . . . phenomena" as symbols of "something beyond" (quoted in Trombley, 231). Thus alienated from the numinous in life, perhaps he led a rather sad existence. Even Savage found Hyslop a bit much. On one occasion he read on Hyslop's behalf a paper in which, according to Trombley, "Hyslop charges almost every contemporary artist, composer and writer of note with insanity." Savage commented that he "could not go quite so far as Dr Hyslop, who seemed to think that every artist of distinction had at least 'a bee in his bonnet'; otherwise he feared the author himself might be considered as having more than one" (213).

As an artistic and intellectual community, Bloomsbury was equally ill-disposed toward mythopoeic thought. It is ironic that while Virginia's became arguably the best-known name of the group, her dominant mode of consciousness was very much at odds with the masculine Cambridge-derived rationalism that prevailed within it. Gerald Brenan records that in this intellectual climate, "anyone who held views that could not be justified rationally was regarded as a willful cultivator of illusions and therefore as a person who could not be taken seriously" (quoted in Poole, 62). Although Virginia could justify herself rationally with the best of them, her flexible attitude to truth aroused a great deal of suspicious disapproval among the male minds of Bloomsbury. Clive Bell recalled an evening when Leonard Woolf, reading aloud to friends some extracts from Virginia's diaries, suddenly stopped short: " 'I suspect,' said I, 'you've come upon a passage where she makes a bit too free with the frailties and absurdities of someone here present.' 'Yes,' said he, 'but that's not why I broke off. I shall skip the next few pages because there's not a word of truth in them'" (C. Bell, 97). Clive and Leonard adopt the pejorative tone of a parent reproaching a child for fibbing. However, Virginia was not morally wayward, a habitual liar, as Leonard implied; nor was she simply free with the truth: Her policy with regard to the management of facts was a considered one. In "The New Biography" she explained that "in order that the light of personality may shine through, facts must be manipulated; some must be brightened; others shaded; yet in the process they must never lose their integrity" (*Granite and Rainbow,* 150). In this context, Virginia's own integrity was absolute; she was incapable of writing passages with not a word of truth in them. She was aware, however, as Clive and Leonard were apparently not, that "fact" is not a synonym for "truth."

Divorced from the terse rationalism of the Cambridge men, Angelica Garnett reveled in her aunt's flights of verbal fancy, but she remembered that they elicited a brusque dismissal from Leonard: "We egged her on until Leonard punctured her sallies with a sardonic comment that what she was saying was completely untrue" (Noble, 84). She recalled that he would then "describe the same incident in terms that were factual, forthright and objective" (Garnett, 110). Leonard seems to have regarded the wilder reaches of Virginia's imagination as allied to her "madness."[7] Despite the fact that fiction such as Virginia wrote demands a skillful control of the imagination, he persisted in the belief that she was unable to distinguish the fantastic hyperbole that she created spontaneously, from empirical reality. In his semiautobiographical novel, *The Wise Virgins,* the Vanessa character, Katherine, remarks of the Virginia character, Milla: "I sometimes think there is no dividing line in Milla, between her dreams . . . and her realities. She doesn't pretend. When we were children . . . she never said: 'Let's pretend' . . . And she's just the same now, I'm sure" (103–104). In Katherine's opinion, Milla "simply doesn't know the difference between facts—and . . . her own dreams" (105).

Quentin Bell assumes that when Leonard asked Virginia to marry him, he was unaware of the seriousness of her "illness"; in fact, however, Leonard was far from ignorant on the subject. It may be the case that, as Bell suggests, the Stephen family played down the seriousness of Virginia's past "breakdowns"—for as he rightly observes, "her insanity [sic] was clothed, like some other painful things in that family, in a jest" (vol. 2, 18),[8] but Leonard had taken precautions. As Poole points out, he had, "taken elaborate measures and carried out extensive research into his wife's mental state before they were married. Indeed, he had done more than just make enquiries: he had arrived at a point where, on the question of having children, he could place three medical opinions against one" (125). Initially Leonard consulted Savage, who, with flagrant disregard for confidentiality, entered into a full discussion of Virginia's health. When Leonard subsequently become doubtful of whether Virginia was fit to bear a child, he again, apparently without her knowledge and certainly without her cooperation, consulted Savage, who marred his expert credentials in Leonard's eyes by assuring him that having a child could only benefit her. Given Savage's view on mental illness in women—that it was due to the overdevelopment of the intellect at the expense of the reproductive system—Leonard may well have been right to regard this opinion as suspect. However, there can be no justification for the consultations with Drs. Craig and Hyslop, as well as Jean Thomas (in whose nursing home Virginia had stayed) that he and he alone subsequently embarked upon, apparently in search of endorsement for his own view that Virginia should be prevented from having a baby. According to Leonard, all three agreed that his fears were justified and strongly advised against a child (1963, 82). As King points out, neither Craig nor Hyslop had actually met Virginia when they pronounced her unfit for motherhood (206). Moreover, at the time when she accepted Leonard's offer of marriage, Virginia very much wanted and expected to have a family. In her response to his proposal she stated—with hindsight tragically—that one of the factors in its favor was that he would give her children (*L 1, 496*).

In Leonard's description of this sequence of events (1963, 82), Virginia, whose sanity is in dispute, whose womb is under sentence, upon the course of whose life judgment is to be pronounced, is remarkable by her absence. It is "I"—Leonard—who "went to see . . . ," "I" who "became more and more uneasy," "I" who "began to doubt," "I" who "went and consulted." There are only two points at which Virginia's voice may, obliquely, be heard: "We both wanted to have children"; and—in response to the specialists' veto on this act—a further, rather dubious first-person plural, "We followed their advice." Whereas Leonard's desire for children was apparently slight, and yielded to his subsequent conviction that Virginia was not fit to give birth, she never really accepted that she should not have a baby nor ceased to feel pain that, contrary to her own wishes and best judgment, the experience of motherhood had been denied her. "Never pretend that children . . . can be replaced by other things," she wrote in 1923 (*D 2*, 221). She blamed not Leonard but herself—her supposed lack of self-control—for their childlessness, describing how she awoke wretchedly in the early hours to the knowledge of her failure (107). As time went on she noted that she hardly missed having children any more, that the urge to write was more compelling, and yet she felt that perhaps she had killed her desire for a family out of necessity (*D 3*, 167).

Implicit in the issue of marriage and children was the problem of sex. Julia Buckroyd sees anorexia as a solution to sexual abuse that "abolish[es] all thoughts of sex or interest in it," commenting that, "I have known women spend all the fertile years of their lives in this state, not daring to be sexual because of that original horror and pain with which they first experienced sex" (123). Something like this seems to have happened to Virginia. Since her father's death, the breakup of the family household, and her escape from the Duckworth brothers, sexuality was an issue she had been able to sweep under the carpet. With her engagement to Leonard, however, the quiescent terrors that were, as a result of her abuse, attached to the sexual body were awakened, and—because in the context of repression in which she lived they could not be confronted and addressed—they emerged symptomatically. Although she was generally unable to acknowledge the effects of abuse upon her sexual attitudes, Virginia was very clear that there was a relationship among sex, marriage, and her symptomatology. Many years later she told Ethel Smyth, "I married Leonard Woolf in 1912 . . . and almost immediately was ill for 3 years" (*L 4*, 180), later elaborating, "I was always sexually cowardly . . . My terror of real life has always kept me in a nunnery . . . And then I married, and then my brains went up in a shower of fireworks" (*L 4*, 180). On February 7, 1912, with engagement to Leonard looking increasingly likely, Virginia told her friend Ka Cox that she had been ill in bed for a week with "a touch of my old disease, in the head." That, she was at pains to point out, was "all over," and she was "practically all right," although she was still experiencing what she referred to as "miraculous dreams" (*L 1*, 488–489). By mid-February, however, her distress had increased, and she was compelled to enter Jean Thomas's Twickenham nursing home, Burley, for two weeks' rest and recuperation.

To latterday anorexic women, Burley's regimen of enforced sequestration, large amounts of food, and bedrest may have an unfortunately familiar ring. Virginia loathed the place and the "treatment." On an earlier stay in 1910 she had pleaded with Vanessa, "I really dont think I can stand much more of this," protesting the lack of intelligent conversation, the ugliness of the building, and "all the eating and drinking and being shut up in the dark" (*L 1,* 430–431). She told Clive Bell that she felt dehumanized by the regime (433)—on which, indeed, she was treated like a captive animal. At Burley in 1912 she was, as Quentin Bell notes, "bored to *extinction*" and "near to *complete despair*" (vol. 2, 164, my italics). Although Bell uses these words lightly, they are in fact expressive of extreme distress—an appropriate response in the circumstances. Detained against her will, and forced to eat and rest, Virginia was compelled into a brutal confrontation with the body that she feared. Prohibited from writing, she was also denied a creative means of understanding and transforming her relationship with that body. Thus she dangled on a thin thread over an abyss.

Quentin Bell asserts that Virginia's behavior at Burley in 1912, as at other times when she was in distress, was manipulative. According to Bell, "Savage could be manipulated, so too Miss Thomas . . . , and also Miss Bradbury, . . . a trained nurse." He describes Virginia as "an exceedingly difficult patient," and writes that she "was always adroit enough to use her charm upon her medical advisers so that she might win them over and make them her allies in whatever plot against nature and good sense she might desire" (vol. 1, 164). However, as Waskett emphasizes, the oft-encountered notion that eating-distressed women are "manipulative, deceitful and difficult" is wholly misconceived (1)—the product both of a refusal to interpret the metaphorical messages encoded in the language of eating behavior and of a particular and invidious power relation. Bell's implication that at Burley, imprisoned and denied the exercise of ordinary human rights, Virginia was in a position of power is self-evidently nonsensical; on the contrary, she was, like all eating-distressed women within the orthodox medical system, deliberately *disempowered.*

Virginia and Leonard's engagement finally took place in May, according to Leonard putting emotional pressure on Virginia and causing her a bad headache and sleeplessness (1963, 82). Between May and the marriage in August, he was already acting as her caretaker. In June Virginia wrote speakingly to Violet Dickinson, "I've been rather headachy, and had a bad night, and Leonard made me a comatose idiot" (*L 1,* 502). On one level her message was that Leonard's overprotection was already proving deleterious. On a deeper level the letter meant just what it said: that by defining and treating her as someone with serious mental problems, Leonard was creating in her the symptoms of nervous disorder.

Virginia was as frank as anyone could possibly be about her inability to respond sexually to Leonard. In reply to his letter of proposal, she said that she felt no physical attraction to him, that when he had kissed her she had felt as much as a rock (*L 1,* 496). That Leonard was not discouraged by this admission perhaps owes something to his own attitude toward sex, which was not unproblematic. Although his early letters to Lytton Strachey evince a strong sexual drive,[9] he had been taught an equally strong sexual repression. In *Sowing* he reports that he was a virgin until the age of twenty-five (81), explaining that no adult had ever spoken to him about sex, that "Love and lust, like the functions of the bowels and bladder, were subjects which could not be discussed or even mentioned" (82). Poole believes that Leonard was anesthetized with regard to sex (39, 59), and Peter Alexander notes that "Leonard had sexual fears almost as deep as those of Virginia. Not that he was inexperienced; not at all, but like her, he associated sex with sin and dirt" (62). Indeed, in 1907 Leonard told Lytton Strachey that in his experience being in love with a woman was "unpleasant & filthy." It was mostly, he felt, "the desire to copulate," and "a particular desire to copulate" was "no less degraded than the general." He concluded, "One day I shall fall in love with a prostitute" (1990, 128). On another occasion he told Strachey, "Most women naked . . . are extraordinarily ugly" (quoted in Dunn, 186). A man who considers women's bodies ugly is hardly a delightful prospect as a heterosexual partner. If Leonard's feelings about women and sex had been otherwise, perhaps it might have been easier for Virginia to overcome her own deeply ingrained fears; as things were, he was clearly not someone who could encourage her to regard sex as beautiful, numinous, or fun. If the sexless marriage was in some senses intensely frustrating to Leonard, there seems to have been a part of him that was as relieved as Virginia that their perfect companionship need not be sullied by lust. After her death, he entered into another sexless love relationship with the married Trekkie Parsons. Her feeling was that he was "unsure of his sexual abilities" (Alexander, 203).

Unsurprisingly, the Woolfs' six-week honeymoon, starting in the Quantocks and taking in France, Italy, and Spain, was not, from a sexual point of view, a great success. Years later Gerald Brenan reported Leonard as telling him that "when on their honeymoon he had tried to make love to . . . [Virginia] she had got into such a violent state of excitement that he had to stop" (L. Woolf 1990, 162). In 1926 Virginia had apparently confided this story to Vita Sackville-West, for when Harold Nicolson quizzed Vita on her own sexual relationship with Virginia, she responded, "she has never lived with anyone but Leonard, which was a terrible failure, and was abandoned quite soon" (Sackville-West and Nicolson, 159).[10] At the time, Virginia admitted that sex with Leonard had not proved all it might be, telling Ka Cox that she might as well still be Miss Stephen. She wondered why so much fuss was made about copulation and loss of virginity (which she referred to, oddly, as loss of chastity—possibly in a subliminal attempt to occlude the fact that she had herself lost her virginity, or at least her innocence, in childhood). She reported finding "the climax immensely exaggerated" (*L 2,* 6–7). A letter that Vanessa sent to Leonard during the honeymoon implies that he may have attributed Virginia's sexual fears to her lesbian orientation, and had questioned

Vanessa on the nature of her involvement with her sister. Vanessa's response to his "awful description of a night with the apes" (her nickname for Virginia) was an apparent admission of sexual involvement, couched in terms of malicious humor: "I am happy to say it's years since I spent a night in their company, and I can't conceive anything more wretched than it sounds. It would be bad enough to know they were in the next bed with all their smells and their whines and their wettings, but to have to change beds with them and all the rest of it—a coal hole would be more to my taste. So now you know what I think" (V. Bell, 127).

Given that both Virginia and Vanessa harbored a suppressed jealousy of each other's sexual partners, Vanessa was not the best person to ask for advice on what she referred to as Virginia's "coldness." Vanessa, who had marked herself out as the sensual sister, the one who was a natural at sex, had a great deal of self-esteem invested in her younger sister's sexual "failure"— particularly in the eyes of her own husband, the man in whom Virginia had displayed a sexual interest, Clive Bell. In December 1912, she told Clive that Virginia "still gets no pleasure at all from the act," a state of affairs that she professed to find "curious." She said that the Woolfs had wanted to know when she first had an orgasm, but that she couldn't remember; however, she boasted, "no doubt I sympathized with such things if I didn't have them from the time I was 2." She said she had "annoyed" Virginia but "consoled" Leonard by voicing her opinion that Virginia "never had understood or sympathized with sexual passion in men" (V. Bell, 132). If Leonard was consoled, it must have been cold comfort, but perhaps he got what he deserved. By making Vanessa privy to what went on in his marriage bed, he was playing directly into the incestuous system that had conditioned both sisters' sexual attitudes, a system in which, as DeSalvo puts it, "the children had no chance to internalize . . . a sense that any particular person was 'off limits,' for no one in the family was 'off limits.'" (84). Vanessa's inappropriate and insensitive involvement in the Woolfs' marriage was in some senses not dissimilar to Virginia's flirtation with Clive. Indeed, at one point she wondered if Virginia was "a promising pupil" in sexual matters and suggested, "Perhaps Leonard would like to give me a few lessons" (V. Bell, 125).

In her honeymoon letters Virginia attempted to portray herself as happy in the way that a newly wedded wife should be, but her tone was off key. She harped on the sordidity of all things connected with the body—in Tarragona, for example, describing to Lytton Strachey the contents of the unemptied WC opposite the bedroom and satirizing his life as sexual excess relieved only by gluttony (*L 2*, 4–5). In Madrid—a dismal city, according to Virginia—she noted the immense fatness of the middle-class women, and, when Leonard suffered an attack of malaria, put it down to the sexual activity of microbes excited by the east wind (*Congenial Spirits*, 76).

Leonard tried to convince himself and his friends that he and Virginia were happy and the marriage was going well. From Venice he assured Molly MacCarthy, that neither partner disagreed with or bored the other. He painted a picture of Virginia resting and eating well: lying lazily on a sofa eating chocolates, buttered toast, cakes, and ice cream, and drinking tea, chocolate, and coffee all together. However, in her own postscript to the letter Virginia was ambivalent. She disclaimed Leonard's avowal of connubial bliss with the statement "Like all letters of married people, this is doomed to insincerity," adding "I'm . . . That describes my state of mind. Very well" (*L 2*, 8–9; ellipses in original). Clearly what she really felt about marriage, Leonard, and buttered toast was unspeakable.

By the time the Woolfs returned from their honeymoon in the autumn of 1912, Virginia's psychological well-being was clearly in jeopardy. Leonard was anxious and by 1913 became increasingly worried (1963, 148). In July Savage recommended that Virginia return to Burley. He suggested a bargain whereby if she agreed to stay in the nursing home for two weeks, she would then be allowed to leave for a holiday at the Plough Inn, Holford, where she and Leonard had begun their honeymoon the previous year. This holiday marked the beginning of a period of mental distress from which, despite remissions, Virginia would not finally emerge for several years.

From Burley Virginia addressed Leonard in the voice of a penitent child who has been sent to her room. She repeatedly pleaded her docility and obedience in an effort to elicit release, telling him she was sleeping well and eating all day (*L 2*, 32) and that she was fat and dozy (34). Like most women in eating distress, she was motivated by the desire to get out of institutional care as fast as possible.[11] At the same time, she was riven with a deep and genuine sense of guilt for what she regarded as her failure of Leonard—as a woman who could not have sex, could not have children, could not eat, and required constant nursing. She said that she had disgraced him and, in an apparent allusion to his attempts to make love with her, reassured him that he had never been beastly, that he had always behaved perfectly, that everything was *her* fault (*L 2*, 34).

When Virginia's two weeks at Burley were up, Leonard could see that her distress had not diminished; however, he honored their agreement and took her to Holford. Given that much of her distress was a product of her sexual relationship with Leonard, the return to the Plough, where the honeymoon had started, must have been highly traumatic for her. To add fuel to the fire, the Plough was also associated with large quantities of rich and magnificent food. Writing to Lytton Strachey in 1912, Virginia had praised the cream there (*L 2*, 2), and she had recommended the inn to her former teacher Janet Case as cheap and comfortable, with wonderful food and cream for every meal (4). Speaking of 1913's disastrous return visit, Leonard eulogized the "delicious" food at great length. It was, he said, among "the best cuisine in the world": "Nothing could be better than the bread, butter, cream, and eggs and bacon... The beef, mutton, and lamb were always magnificent and perfectly cooked; enormous hams cured by themselves and hanging from the rafters in the kitchen, were... perfect" (1963, 153). Presumably, in 1913 he hoped that this gastronomic feast would encourage Virginia to eat, but when she was coping by not eating, the omnipresence of such rich food and the insistence that she eat it must in fact have felt extremely threatening. Leonard reported that it was initially "only with the greatest difficulty" that he could induce her to eat, and that her aversion to food increased until "it became impossible to get her to eat" (154).

Virginia consented to return to London to seek medical help, with the proviso that the choice of doctor would be hers. Under this agreement, as Leonard describes it, her health was to become the subject of a bizarre legalistic contention. Her sanity was to be put on trial; she would "put her case" to the doctor (i.e., that she was not ill), "and I would put mine" (that she was). Both parties agreed to abide by the doctor's "verdict" and follow whatever advice he gave. *His* participation in Virginia's consultation about *her* health with *her* doctor apparently presented Leonard with no moral dilemma. Ethics aside, given that the immediate causes of Virginia's distress were located in the marital relationship, Leonard's presence at the consultation must have proved so inhibiting as to render it pointless.

When she opted for Henry Head as her doctor, Virginia was not aware that a few weeks earlier Leonard had taken it upon himself to consult Head on her behalf. It might have been reasonable to suspect that Head's opinion might therefore be prejudiced, but Leonard regarded as a symptom of Virginia's "madness" the fact that if she had known about the consultation, she would have been "influenced... against him." Head was an early Freudian analyst and a friend of the art critic and Bloomsburyite Roger Fry; according to Leonard, Fry felt that he was intelligent both as a doctor and a human being (1963, 155). In choosing him, Virginia must have been hoping for a more enlightened response to her distress than she had received from the old school of mental specialists, but she was under a cruel misapprehension. Head told her she was ill in the same way as if she had a cold or typhoid, and that if she wanted to recover she must rest in bed and eat (156). She was found guilty and sentenced to what was worse to her than death. Crushed by this further disconfirmation and unable to face more of the dreaded food and rest, on the evening of the consultation she attempted suicide by taking an overdose of veronal, one of her prescription drugs. She was thirty-one years old.

Concerned that Virginia might be certified and placed by force in an asylum (a very real danger under the laws of the time), Leonard persuaded the authorities that, helped by nurses, he could take care of her in the country. Urged on by very difficult circumstances, he then made a spectacular misjudgment. Given that he, Virginia, and the nurses could not be accommodated at his and Virginia's own home, Asheham, he accepted George Duckworth's offer of his country house, Dalingridge Place. Leonard referred to George as "an extremely kind man" and as "very fond of Vanessa and Virginia" (1963, 159), and yet it is unlikely that he was wholly unaware of the nature of George's past relationship with his half sisters, given that Savage knew of it, and Leonard had on more than one occasion discussed Virginia's health with Savage in detail. Moreover, he had talked repeatedly to Vanessa about Virginia's health and her inability to respond sexually. In 1967 Gerald Brenan knew of Virginia's "early seduction by her half brother" (whether George or Gerald is unclear), apparently having been told of it by Leonard, who linked it to her fear of sex and her deep distress in 1913 (L. Woolf 1990, 62). Not surprisingly, given the associations that George's house cannot but have had with the abuse that lay at the root of her sexual "failure" of Leonard and of her current distress, Virginia was deeply disturbed at Dalingridge and anxious to return to Asheham; however, she was forced to remain at George's home until November 1913 (L. Woolf 1963, 165).

At Dalingridge Virginia's food problems were severe. In the first few weeks, according to Leonard, the most pressing problem was to get her to eat (L. Woolf 1963, 162–163). He told Clive Bell that her attitude to food was "intractable," and this, Bell reported to Molly MacCarthy, was "the key to the situation so they say" (quoted in Q. Bell, vol. 2, 17). Leonard believed that if she had not been fed, "she would have eaten nothing at all and would have gradually starved to death." Initially, in a state of suicidal depression, she completely ignored the food on her plate, and when the nurses tried to persuade her to eat became "enraged." Leonard himself was usually able to induce her to eat a tiny amount but this was, he said, "a terrible process." Each meal took between one and two hours. He had to sit with her, place a fork in her hand, and every so often touch her arm and gently ask her to eat. About once every five minutes she would distractedly swallow a mouthful of food (1963, 165).

In 1913, as at other times when Virginia was extremely psychologically distressed, Leonard kept detailed notes on her state of mind and physical condition, including her weight and menstrual periods. At times, for secrecy, he wrote in a code composed of Sinhalese and Tamil letters (L. Woolf 1963, 149)—although he insisted that Virginia's allegations of a conspiracy against her were but a symptom of her "madness." There was certainly an obsessive component in Leonard's record keeping—which extended beyond Virginia's health. Bond comments that he "wrote down and catalogued everything he could," and describes him as a "compulsion neurotic" (71). According to Trekkie Parsons, each morning he checked a thermometer by the door at Monk's House and noted the minimum and maximum temperatures for the previous day; he also wrote down on cards that he kept in a box on top of the radiogram when each record had last been played (Alexander, 94). He apparently found the world a very slippery place, in which it was necessary to keep a hold on facts if one was not to lose one's grip entirely.

At Asheham between November 1913 and the summer of 1914, Virginia's distress abated, and the nurses left. Nevertheless, it remained difficult to persuade her to eat what Leonard considered enough (L. Woolf 1963, 165). In June, much against her will, she and Leonard again consulted Craig. He pronounced her "distinctly better" but was "rather concerned about the fixity of her ideas about food" (L. Woolf 1990, 209). By the end of the year she was taking cookery classes, whether to placate Craig and Leonard, out of genuine interest, or as a result of an anorexic need for involvement with food one can only speculate. Whatever her motivation, an incident that took place at one of the classes gave perfect symbolic expression to her feelings in the wake of refeeding by Leonard. She reported to Janet Case, "I distinguished myself by cooking my wedding ring into a suet pudding," commenting that the experience had been "really great fun" (*L 2*, 55).

In fact, Virginia's distress had not in any real sense abated and by 1915 was expressing itself through symptoms as serious as those of the previous year. In April Leonard told Violet Dickinson that she was worse than he had ever seen her. He was surprised, because two weeks previously she had seemed to be improving. This was defined for him by the fact that "She ate so well and put on weight, and even now she is a stone [14 pounds] heavier than she was ever in her life before" (L. Woolf 1990, 212). He did not appreciate that the period following refeeding is highly traumatic for a person whose existence is held together by food restriction. This factor alone, particularly given the unnecessarily high level of weight gain that had been forced on Virginia, would have been sufficient to cause her extreme anxiety. More significantly, however, none of the root causes of her "madness" had been addressed. Her protest had not been heard. Her "treatment" consisted merely of chivvying her into conformity and whitewashing over her anger and distress.

By the early summer of 1915, Virginia's suppressed fury was no longer containable. Vanessa told Roger Fry that she had "taken against all men" (quoted in Q. Bell, vol. 2, 26)—a position that is understandable as a response to the sexual, medical, and sociocultural abuses she had suffered at their hands. Her hostility was focused upon Leonard, whom, according to Vanessa, she was refusing to see at all, a stance that, Quentin Bell reports, she maintained for almost two months. Leonard himself told Violet Dickinson that Virginia had "turned very violently against me . . . and . . . is still very opposed." However, he gave little thought as to why she was so angry, accepting Craig's explanation that "it's very common and will pass away" (L. Woolf 1990, 213). In truth, as Bond points out,

> That the Woolfs' marriage left much to be desired is evident in Virginia's behaviour during her manic episodes. The torment that erupts during psychotic [*sic*] episodes is fuelled by rage that has been repressed during other periods of the individual's life. Virginia's total rejection of Leonard at these times suggests great hostility toward her husband which she managed to squelch during her well periods. (93)[12]

No wonder Virginia was furious with Leonard. By insisting on feeding her at all costs, he rode roughshod over the metaphorical meaning her behavior was attempting to communicate. Every time he forced food upon her against her will, he rejected her message, compelling her to eat her own symbolically encoded words. The weight gain that was imposed upon her between 1913 and 1915 was a measure of the extent to which this crucial message was being ignored—and, as Spater and Parsons note, that gain was one of almost 50 percent. In October 1913, Virginia weighed 8 stone 7 pounds (119 pounds); by October 1915 her weight had been increased to 12 stone 7 pounds (175 pounds) (69). Given that between 9 stone (126 pounds) and 9 stone 7 pounds (133 pounds) seems to have been her normal weight,[13] one must question, as does Poole, "why it was considered necessary to push her up to a weight she had never had before, . . . which would have been in her case a grotesque exaggeration of anything she could carry" (155).

As Poole also points out, the extent of this weight gain gives the lie to Leonard's account of Virginia's being persuaded to swallow only the occasional spoonful of food between 1913 and 1915 (156), tending rather to add substance to his fear that "Leonard . . . allowed a considerable degree of coercion to be brought to bear upon her" in the effort to make her eat, and that if she was not actually force-fed, then "the two nurses' attempts to get Virginia to eat may have been fairly powerful ones" (152–153). Angelica Garnett has pointed out what a very strong force Leonard himself was to resist, describing him as the only family member able to refuse her a thing that she wanted. For her, his "very tone spelt the finality of real authority, against which there was no appeal" (53). She experienced him as mastiff like and as "made of a different material from the rest of us, something which, unlike obsidian, couldn't splinter, and inevitably suggested the rock of ages" (108). Clearly, the wishes of such a man could not be lightly contravened.

Photographs show that in the autumn of 1915 Virginia was plump. She told Lytton Strachey that she weighed 12 stone (168 pounds), and was thus 3 stone (42 pounds) heavier than she had ever been before. As a result, she said, "I can hardly toil uphill," adding with more irony than conviction, "but it's evidently good for the health. I am as happy as the day is long" (*L 2*, 67). To Ka Cox she wrote that at 12 stone (168 pounds) it was difficult to find clothes to fit. Leonard had told her, she said, that Ka weighed 12 stone 10 pounds (178 pounds), but she did not believe him. Again she professed a rather dubious-sounding contentment with her new corpulence: "I'm very well, and enjoy sitting in this mound of flesh" (70). Vituperatively, she took to chiding her friends and relations about their own weight-losses, recommending to them the benefits of milk. She wrote to Vanessa, in what might have been a parody of one of Vanessa's own letters: "I do think you ought to drink more milk. Leonard thought you had grown much thinner—so did someone else. You are always on the trot, if not gallop. Please take 2 glasses, and keep well, for love of me" (109). She told her friend Saxon Sydney-Turner, "Probably I ought to insist upon food and rest at this juncture. If you dont sleep or eat, your feelings will become so much of a puzzle that you'll waste these exquisite days merely scratching your head" (128). And she advised Vanessa's lover, Duncan Grant, to drink two glasses of milk a day, commenting "Its remarkable how all our friends are shedding their flesh until in some cases only an arrangement of bones, loosely covered with skin, and I suppose, an intestine or two remain" (240).

Inevitably, it was impossible for Virginia to maintain her unnaturally high weight once she had been permitted to resume a more normal way of life. She too was shedding her flesh. However, every time her weight fell concern mounted, and Leonard and the doctors imposed a new set of strictures regarding food and activity. By late 1916 her weight had dropped to 11 stone (154 pounds), hardly a dangerously low level, but Craig and Leonard sprang into action. She told Sydney-Turner that she was well but depressed because she had been ordered to rest once more, and protested the difficulty of remaining at the weight Craig considered necessary (*L 2*, 131). By the following July she had lost another stone (14 pounds), causing Leonard to panic, with the result that she had to promise to restrict her social life. Now down to 10 stone (140 pounds) (half a stone [7 pounds] more, she emphasized, than she normally weighed), she complained to Vanessa that it was impossible to maintain permanently a weight which was the product of bedrest and intensive feeding (169–170).

The irony of the situation was that Leonard's own weight in 1917 was only 9 stone 6 pounds (133 pounds); there was far more cause to regard him as seriously underweight than Virginia. In 1914, after he had suffered from influenza, Virginia told Janet Case that he had determined to increase his weight to 11 stone (154 pounds), and that this he would therefore achieve (*L 2*, 45). His target weight was a stone and a half (21 pounds) lower than the one he set for Virginia; however, despite her belief that he would easily succeed where she had failed, he apparently never met it. In 1941 Virginia's doctor, Octavia Wilberforce, commented that Leonard and Virginia "*both* look thin and half-starved, and if anybody ought to benefit from my herd it should be those waifs. Waifs I'm sure *they* are about food" (Jalland, 137, my italics). It is probable that despite his expressed aim, essentially Leonard no more wanted to weigh 11 stone (154 pounds) than Virginia did. Confined to Asheham at the end of 1913—like, she said, an enormous sow with her head on a platter—she imagined him only snatching a bite to eat and sleeping, monastically, on boards (*L 2*, 35). She recognized that his ascetic side was in fact much stronger than her own, asking herself in 1923 whether he was not, through birth or training, too puritan, too disciplinarian, too spartan and self-controlled. She saw in herself a sociability very alien to him, and which she refused to regard as reprehensible. On the contrary, it was, she felt, a gift: "a piece of jewellery I inherit from my mother" (*D 2*, 250).

After the 1913 to 1915 eruption of eating distress, Virginia's weight was eventually allowed to fall to around its natural level; however, the food war between herself and Leonard would never totally cease. Her diaries allude to their sporadic skirmishes over food: "I bicycled back on Wednesday & found L. & we were very happy, until it came to the fat bacon—when, alas!" (*D 1*, 183); and "[I] have written myself into half a headache & had to come to a halt, like a tired horse, & take a little sleeping draught last night: which made our breakfast fiery. I did not finish my egg"(*D 3*, 162). On such occasions, Virginia felt, it was Leonard who was fanatical, impermeable by reason, and she who conciliated: "We quarrelled last night about my jug of cream; & L. was unreasonable, & I was generous" (*D 1*, 135). On the face of it, she would sometimes accept the necessity for food and rest in large amounts, but rarely without an under-current of skepticism. She wrote half facetiously to Vita Sackville-West, "All Friday I was sick without stopping (my own fault—I refused to believe the doctor who said it would stop if I ate a mutton chop—when I did I was cured instantly)" (*L 3*, 218). In a similar vein she told Ethel Smyth that she had been cured by eating a huge plate of saddle of mutton and wondered whether a large amount of plain roast meat might cure Ethel's pains (*L 5*, 4). At other times she was resolutely dismissive of food as a panacea, such as when Leonard forced her to eat a whole cold duck and she was violently sick—"a hideous and awful experience" (*L 3*, 206).

Virginia's social activity was another source of tension between the Woolfs, with Leonard attempting to wrest from her all responsibility for where she should go, when she should leave, and whom she should see.

Indeed, he effectively banned that excitement and frivolity of which he was intensely suspicious. Angelica Garnett recalls that he was unfailingly vigilant, never seeking to conceal his anxiety that Virginia "might drink a glass too much wine or commit some other mild excess." He treated her as something between a well-disciplined child, quelled by the nursery phrase "that's enough," and an obedient dog, trotting along behind his spaniel, Pinka.[14] Not for Virginia the adult social rituals of drinking too much and talking into the early hours. At 11.00 P.M. sharp, no matter how much fun she was having, Leonard would stand up to leave, and she would follow him to the door, Garnett felt, "as though leaving a part of herself behind" (113). Quentin Bell accepts the view that the curtailment of Virginia's social life was necessary for the sake of her health and that Leonard was "cast in the ungrateful role of family dragon" in this respect (vol. 2, 34). If, however, with regard to short-term symptomatic management, there was some validity in Leonard's practice, in a larger sense such parental caretaking, by obstructing confrontation with root causes and the search for a radical solution, was one of the factors that ensured the continuation of Virginia's "illness."

As Alexander notes, Leonard's avowed support for feminism "did not affect his views on which partner should be dominant in marriage" (41). Alix Strachey observes that he attempted to dictate the parameters of *all* Virginia's activities (Noble, 114–115). He also took charge of her income, keeping her "on very short purse-strings" according to Garnett (Noble, 86). His tightness with money, and the drama that exacting it from him entailed, recalls Leslie Stephen (although Leonard's performances were never as flamboyant as Leslie's). Garnett remembered that asking Leonard to write a check was like squeezing water from a stone and that the grim procedure (when, on Virginia's behalf, he paid her dress allowance) "seemed like a test of my endurance" (111–113).

Virginia professed gratitude to Leonard for his undying concern and constant ministrations. She told him that she was repentant for her sins against him and that he had made her happy (*L 2,* 35). Considering how, when she was "ill," he would sit on the edge of her bed judicially considering her symptoms, bring home pineapples, and play the gramophone in her room until he judged her too excited, she thought him "a perfect angel" (*L 4,* 17). Yet often she rankled at this same overzealous attention, writing for instance in June 1923 that she disliked feeling she was always being taken care of (*D 2,* 245). In 1932, after she had suffered from fainting fits, she protested to Ethel Smyth that even though she was now quite well, Leonard insisted on treating her like the princess who felt the pea through thirteen mattresses (*L 5,* 97). Nevertheless, without any voice of support for her sense that such care was counterproductive, it was extremely difficult for her to cast off caution. Moreover, she was trammeled by her concern for *Leonard*'s well-being and her guilt at the crimps and restrictions that she felt her "illness" had caused *him*. In her diary for 1923 she recorded her ambivalence when a disapproving phone call from him forced her to return home early one night: "& so my self reliance being sapped, I had no courage to venture against his will. Then I react. Of course its a difficult question. For undoubtedly I get headaches or the jump in my heart; & then this spoils his pleasure, & if one lives with a person, has one the right—" (*D 2*, 222). Recognizing on a subliminal level that the marriage was a structure too rickety to survive frank appraisal, she avoided close examination of her love for Leonard, acknowledging in her diary this uncharacteristic reluctance to dig deep: "If I dared I would investigate my own sensations with regard to him, but out of laziness, humility, pride, I dont know what reticence—refrain. I who am not reticent" (*D 4*, 18).

Thinking of the Woolfs and on the other hand of Charleston, Angelica Garnett writes, "I felt the austerity of their lives compared with ours—which was much fuller of wine and laughter" (53). She noted that there was a monastic cast to her aunt and uncle's existence, in which their "work allowed them only just time for a frugal meal." Indeed, Virginia was amused to find in 1923 that work had ousted food from all the usual places, telling Vita Sackville-West, "We don't dine so much as picnic, as the [printing] press has got into the larder and into the dining room, and we never dress" (*L 3*, 2). If Virginia worked hard and ate little, she was not, however, the through-and-through ascetic that Leonard was. She was also amusing, lively, and passionately engaged with life. Angelica's compelling picture of tea at Monk's House captures the complexity of this asceticism which was also veined with a rich seam of gaiety. If at the center of such teas Virginia was a greyhound who ate next to nothing of the insubstantial kinds of food she provided, she was also a seductive figure, both elegant and animated, through the haze of her smoke lending a romantic aura even to penny buns as she waved the teapot and talked (110).

Leonard seems to have looked to food to give him an anchor in life. Garnett remembered that always after tea he would offer her a humbug (a traditional candy), one of which he ate, ritualistically, after every meal (53). When the Woolfs holidayed with Vanessa, Quentin, and Angelica in Rome, Vanessa told Clive Bell that Leonard "cant bear trying new & uncertain places." She continued, "Virginia is so difficult to feed that meals become rather an uneasy problem" (quoted in Dunn, 230–231). But in many ways Virginia was far less fixed, less obtrusively demanding than Leonard was. Because he set a limit on what he ate for pleasure, it was very important to him that what he *did* eat was not disappointing. He was extremely exacting and very involved in the quality of food, as is evinced by his running commentaries on the standard of local cuisine when he and Virginia holidayed in Scotland and France (*L 6*, 249, *D 4*, 19, *L 6*, 338).

Virginia often wanted not so much to stop eating altogether as to deemphasize food. She wrote in 1930, "I am more & more attracted by looseness, freedom, & eating one's dinner off a table anywhere, having cooked it previously" (*D 3*, 316). After a visit to Greece in 1932, she fantasized about returning annually with a tent and living primitively off bread, yogurt, butter, and eggs (*D 4*, 97). Right from the start, this kind of rough-and-ready simplicity around food was an association that Vita Sackville-West carried for her. When she first invited Vita to lunch alone, Virginia was in the process of moving out of Tavistock Square, and offered "a complete picnic, among the ruins of books and legs of tables, dirt and dust and only fragments of food" (*L 3*, 44). In June 1926 she again set a tone of romantic austerity, asking, "Will you dine with me off radishes alone in the kitchen?" (278).

One of the attractions of the relationship with Vita was that, unlike that with Leonard, it attached no duress to food. Vita raised no objection to Virginia eating only radishes and fragments of food if that was what she wanted to do. She explained that she felt "protective" of Virginia, but she also had "real affection and respect" (Sackville-West and Nicolson, 158)—sentiments incompatible with coercion. Although she professed to like Leonard, she said she found him "tiresome and wrong-headed" (304), not least, apparently, with regard to his monumental caution where Virginia was concerned. When Virginia fell ill after visiting Vita in Berlin with Leonard, she put her sickness down to influenza and a seasickness draught, "But," she told Vita, "of course the dr and Leonard say it is all the Berlin racketing," conceding that, "I daresay it was" (*L 4*, 13). Vita, however, replied skeptically, "I can't believe it's the 'racketing' of Berlin; really you might have spent every night for a week till 5 in the morning indulging in orgies—to hear you talk—or Leonard talk rather, and the dr" (Sackville-West, 336).

For his part Leonard was, understandably, jealous of the women Virginia loved and had been sexually involved with, Sackville-West[15] and Vanessa Bell.[16] He suspected Vita's careless freedom, which was so antithetical to his own approach to life, seeing in her anything-possible attitude a particular threat to the status quo that he had carefully built up around Virginia's health and which he seems to have needed to preserve for his own security as much as for Virginia's mental stability.

Virginia, on the contrary, was deeply attracted to Vita's daring. Her ability to live life in the raw, an adventurer surviving on sparse expeditionary rations, may have recalled for Virginia her own father, striding off on one of his marathon walks with only some bread and cheese. She tracked Vita in imagination when she traveled across Russia, writing "Now you are nearly at Tehran I make out, motoring across mountains;

stopping at some shed I daresay for lunch, sandwiches, wine" (*L 3,* 326). Whereas Virginia was allowed to go nowhere where a glass of fortifying milk was not readily available, Vita journeyed to wild places living precariously on whatever came to hand. Whereas Virginia must constantly bow to Leonard's opinion that a bicycle ride to Charleston was overly exerting for her,[17] Vita bestrode the world—apparently oblivious to the fact that travel to far-flung and potentially dangerous places was considered inappropriate for English women. How did she manage with "the Bloody Flux"? Virginia wondered (348) (for when she herself menstruated, she was ordered to lie down for two days).[18] At Vita's brazen disregard for such things, she was awestruck.

Virginia rhapsodized about Vita's food in a way that she never did about Leonard's; she admired the food at Holford on her first visit, but it never became transcendent for her in the way that the most humble food could when associated with Vita. The vision of Vita bearing to her breast a bag of soggy fish, for example (*L 3,* 561), became for Virginia archetypical of her romance, part of a private mythology of the lover whose presence was transformational. In that presence even the vision of gluttony—"a fat woman gobbling"—came up rich and strange. Vita catalyzed Virginia's prodigious myth-making powers, inspiring the construction of fabulous love scenarios, such as the mirrored restaurant where "they give you roses" and "one feels one is dangling among octopuses at the bottom of the sea, peering into caves, and plucking pearls in bunches off the rocks" (282). Her present of a goose-liver pie metamorphosed in Virginia's letter of thanks into a kind of fairy gift, "fresh as a dockleaf, pink as mushrooms, pure as first love"; it must have been made, Virginia thought, from "immortal geese." The pie was for her a love potion (which she claimed to have consumed almost all by herself), containing fantastic ingredients and redolent with magical properties. It entranced, she said, the novelist (herself), the poet (T. S. Eliot, dining with the Woolfs), and "even Leonard"; it brought down silence upon meaning, and rendered her able to "forgive any treachery" on the part of the beloved. Where did such pies come from? she wondered. Could they be ordered at will? (*L 4,* 194–195). The answer, of course, was no. They were produced out of a particular and intimate mythos.

The rationing of the two world wars inevitably impacted upon Virginia's relationship with food. In 1918 the Woolfs were well enough provisioned for her to send a food parcel to Charleston (V. Bell, 217), and when they did suffer worse exigencies of rationing, she was to a great extent buffered by Leonard's assiduous efforts to feed her well. Nevertheless, in 1918, she told James and Lytton Strachey to bring their ration cards when they came to stay, as meat, sugar, and butter were in short supply (*L 2,* 226, 227), and she carried on a running correspondence with Vanessa about obtaining milk.

Despite her recent experiences of forced weight gain, as the war drew to a close she looked forward to "a world of food & so on beyond" (*D 1*, 189). Food avoidance is a viable strategy of protest and self-defense only where food is readily available. Selvini-Palazzoli observes increased distress in anorexic women without access to food (22), noting that in situations of shortage they will steal and hoard food, because "The thought of not having free access to food terrifies them, even though they have not the least intention of eating it" (20). Possibly during World War II Virginia felt something of this fear. In 1941 she observed that food had become "an obsession," that "I grudge giving away a spiced bun" (*D 5*, 357). At Christmas 1940, a few months before her suicide, she recorded that the margarine ration was so small she could only make milk pudding, and she had skimmed the cream from the week's milk to make half a pound of butter (although there was scarcely enough milk for the cat). The shops filled briefly at midday, quickly selling out. There was no sugar and only ready-made pastry. The meat ration was to be cut. These things were, she commented, "inconveniences rather than hardships." She and Leonard did not go cold or hungry, although there were no luxuries and nothing left for hospitality. But the threat of real adversity hung over her; she speculated that if rationing increased much more they would experience hunger (*D 5*, 344).

Panken believes that during World War II, "In contrast to her usual anorectic tentativeness about eating, Woolf [was] . . . enormously preoccupied with food" (268). However, an enormous preoccupation with food is by no means at odds with an anorexic tentativeness about eating it; on the contrary, the two go hand in hand. It was the case that, unable to write, Virginia increasingly attempted to lose herself in cooking. After her London house had been bombed, she explained to Ethel Smyth that cooking was part of her effort "to let down a fire proof curtain" against the horror of the war (*L 6*, 433). A few days later she told Ethel that "an hour's cooking" was "a sedative" (434). "How one enjoys food now: I make up imaginary meals," she wrote in 1940 (*D 5*, 347), describing what is on the one hand an understandable response to rationing and on the other a favorite anorexic activity.

Quentin Bell also suggests that in the war time climate of austerity, Virginia's aversion to eating subsided (vol. 2, 222), citing, for example, her rapturous response to Vita's present of butter in 1940 (*L 6*, 447–448). This was another instance of Virginia rendering food into fable; she recompensed Vita for her generosity with a gift of words—here a gloriously hyperbolic paean to butter in mock Victorian style. However, it does not necessarily follow that she was gorging on pounds of it; the "bread and butter" she mentions eating tells us nothing. We cannot assume that, in relation to food, the anorexic woman's words mean what we think they do. Orbach's dialogue with an anorexic client who claims to eat "a bagel in the morning" makes this point: In response to questioning the client reveals that what she actually eats is up to "half of a quarter" of the bagel, and then sometimes only the crust (1986, 135–136). The evidence does not suggest that Virginia was consuming loaves of butter-larded bread; if anything, she was eating less than usual. Octavia Wilberforce, her doctor during this period, wrote in January 1941 that Virginia "looks thinner and thinner" (Jalland, 172). She noted in February that despite her own "milk ministrations," Virginia was "still as thin as a razor" (173), and yet Virginia enthused in letters about these presents—cream, cheese, and milk—and how much she was enjoying eating them, describing herself as feasting magnificently (*L 6,* 474). Thanking Wilberforce on another occasion for "Riding Hood's basket," she asserted, "If I can't write, I can eat" (463), but on Wilberforce's testimony, eating was as problematic as writing had now become.

Those occasions when Virginia did eat more than usual do not seem to me to indicate unequivocally an increased equanimity with regard to food. One experience she describes in a London restaurant is similar in some ways to the binge-eating that is a common correlative of anorexia.[19] Visiting the bomb-blasted city, she observed the "desolate ruins of all my old squares: gashed; dismantled . . . all that completeness ravished & demolished" (*D 5,* 353) and in a mood of desolation at this dereliction decided to eat substantially, in order, as she explained to Ethel Smyth, "to put heart into me" (*L 6,* 466). Such eating is clearly not expressive of contentment but is, as Panken notes, expressly in response to distress, constituting an attempt to assuage "a sense of emotional isolation" and find "succorance" (268n). Profoundly disturbed at the destruction she had witnessed, Virginia wanted comfort, reassurance, and weight (she emphasizes the solidity of the food [*D 5,* 353]) in a world that had become suddenly shifting and unreliable.

Nevertheless, Quentin Bell believes that during World War II Virginia was quietly content (vol. 2, 221). Leonard Woolf also argues that until only a matter of weeks before her suicide she was blithe in her sequestration at Monk's House. He writes in *The Journey not the Arrival Matters,* "I thought at the time and still think that her mind was calmer and more stable, her spirits happier and more serene, than was usual with her," stating that this existence "gave her tranquillity and happiness" (69, 70). Convinced that the life of quiet isolation that, bombed out of London, Virginia had finally been forced to lead was good for her, he was blind to the obvious danger signals that indicated her increasing distress. "This time there were no warning symptoms," he wrote, "The depression struck her like a sudden blow" (79). Yet Virginia's letters and diaries make abundantly clear that far from tranquil and serene she was increasingly desperate. In April 1939 she described the war as bringing a sense of "severance"; she felt that everything had become "meaningless" (*D 5*, 215). In December she spoke of needing to "walk myself calm this afternoon" (250). In June 1940 she wrote, "the war . . . has taken away the outer wall of security. No echo comes back . . . Those familiar circumlocutions—those standards—which have for so many years given back an echo & so thickened my identity are all wide & wild as the desert now . . . We pour to the edge of a precipice . . . & then?" (299; last ellipses in original). She suffered the bereavement of feeling that often overcame her in the face of an event too overwhelming to assimilate, in 1939 telling Vita that with regard to the war she was not "philosophic" but, ominously, "numbed" (*L 6*, 354), and again describing herself as "numb" in the face of a "waste of gloom" when she wrote to Ethel Smyth in May 1940 (399).

Part of the problem, as the war toiled on, was her inability to write. She told Vita that she was trying to write in the morning, but she felt that she was "writing in a vacuum—no one will read it' (*L 6*, 430). To her friend, and partner of Octavia Wilberforce, Elizabeth Robins, she said, "Its difficult, I find, to write. No audience. No private stimulus, only this outer roar" (479). In a letter to Vita, she associated her writer's block with a sense of being "not in the body," of being "completely cut off." She put this feeling down partly to her inability to work: "each word," she said, was "like carrying a coal scuttle to the top of the house" (357). Virginia had always used writing as a means of structuring chaos: "Having got astride my saddle the whole world falls into shape," she wrote in 1930; "it is this writing that gives me my proportions" (*D 3*, 343). In 1937 she determined to save herself through work, explaining that "Directly I am not working, or else see the end in sight, then nothingness begins" (*D 5*, 105). As an ontological life jacket, a tool for survival, this writing was as essential to her as food, and it was failing.

Virginia accounted for her inability to write by her sense of isolation from her audience, if an audience there remained—from her island in Sussex she was not sure. She realized that in the case of invasion there would be no more books, no more Hogarth Press, that suicide would be the only course of action for a Jew and his wife. Meanwhile she saw her erstwhile readership rallying to crassly patriotic banners of war. But although these were serious concerns, it is clear that the real—occluded—reason for Virginia's creative block was located elsewhere, within experiences that during the late 1930s and early 1940s she was attempting to contact and articulate.

In April of 1939, fed up with laboring to write the life of Roger Fry, Virginia turned to her own memoir, "A Sketch of the Past," an undertaking that she compared to psychoanalytical work (*MOB*, 81). It seems likely that, as DeSalvo suggests (1989, 100), it was in the process of writing "A Sketch of the Past" that she uncovered the buried memory of her early abuse by Gerald Duckworth. Indeed, the memoir itself broaches her realization that such traumatic memories can be repressed, that what is actually remembered can be "misleading" because buried memories may in fact be "as important" (*MOB,* 69). There were no foremothers in this particular unearthing of memory; there was no body of survivors' stories. If there had been, Virginia might not have found it so difficult to understand the shame that the abuse had generated in her and to validate her sense that what had happened to her was serious and unacceptable and that her feeling that she had been damaged by it was legitimate. However, she was endowed with what she referred to as her "shock-receiving capacity," that is, the ability to absorb those "sledge-hammer" blows that entailed "a peculiar horror and a physical collapse," and, more than passively to absorb them, to make use of them. They were "particularly valuable," she wrote, because "a shock is at once in my case followed by the desire to explain it" (*MOB,* 72). She was impelled forward by an essential need to know and to make sense of that knowledge.

As she confronted the memory of her abuse, Virginia discussed with Ethel Smyth how women might write honestly about sexual experiences. "As so much of life is sexual . . . it rather limits autobiography if this is blocked out," she put it to Ethel, moving on to speak of "the breaking of the hymen" (which she referred to as "a painful operation") and finally broaching the subject of her abuse by Gerald, at which, she said, she still shivered with shame (*L 6,* 459). Virginia's question was profound. She was exploring how she might expose her experience of abuse in public, an action which in 1941 was pioneering. Perhaps her sense that her readership had vanished owed something to the awareness that there might not be an audience that was able to hear such material and to follow in the direction that her writing needed to take.

Virginia had written and spoken of her abuse by *George* Duckworth several times before. Her accounts of it in "22 Hyde Park Gate" and "Old Bloomsbury" were read to the Memoir Club, and Vita Sackville-West recalled an occasion when Virginia read "Old Bloomsbury" to a party at Ethel Sands and Nan Hudson's house in France—and "didn't shirk a word" (Sackville-West, 205). But Virginia had not invested her real pain in either of these memoirs nor indicated the deep psychological consequences of the abuse. They were amusing, mildly shocking, but not serious. Buckroyd comments that, "I have worked with a number of women who were abused as children and have never forgotten that fact, but who have used eating disorders as a way of keeping the feelings about the abuse away from them. These women can talk about the abuse, but it is as if it happened to someone else" (117). It is this sense of dissociation that one feels in Virginia's retellings of her abuse by George. She distanced herself from her own deep suffering by rendering the episodes comic, thereby also enabling her audience to avoid confrontation with the sharp edge of awful truth. Vita, for instance, described "22 Hyde Park Gate" as "very amusing, and terribly improper," noting that Sands and Hudson "bridled with horrified delight" (Sackville-West, 205). Although in "A Sketch of the Past" as it stands Virginia had not made all the possible emotional connections with her abuse by Gerald, she was treating the episode in a markedly different way than she had her abuse by George in the earlier accounts. She was not sensationalizing or trivializing it but was asking profound personal questions and moving closer to a bedrock of hidden feeling. She clearly wanted to write about the memory of Gerald's abuse in a new, more meaningful, and potentially more genuinely shocking way.

Virginia did have access to some material on incest in the work of Freud, whom she had met in January 1939 and whose books (some of which were published by the Hogarth Press) she was reading while she wrote "A Sketch of the Past." Obviously, to a woman who knew that she had been abused and who was starting to suspect that much of her life had been lived in unconscious response to that event, Freud's theory of infantile sexuality must have been unhelpful. Freud's initial work with hypnosis revealed that all his patients had been abused as children, but when he publicized this finding he was isolated by the psychiatric establishment, and thus recanted in an 1897 paper that redefined his patients' memories as fantasies (Miller, *Banished Knowledge* 1991, 54–55).[20] To Virginia, who was repeatedly, and quite unjustifiably, described as a fantasist, Freudianism must have presented the ultimate condemnation. As DeSalvo suggests, it seems that her reading of Freud "precipitated a crisis" for her, invalidating the explanations for her own "illness" that she was tentatively making between 1939 and 1941: that she was not mad but appropriately angry and distressed (1989, 128).

A further problem was Octavia Wilberforce, whom Virginia met for the first time in 1939. It seems that because Octavia was a woman and a lesbian as well as a doctor, Virginia was disposed to expect something more from her than she had ever looked to receive from her male doctors. She asked Octavia repeatedly about her own childhood as if searching out some standard by which to measure her own, including her experiences of abuse. She began to entrust some of her personal history to Octavia, telling her, for instance, that after Julia's death Leslie Stephen had made "too great emotional claims upon us and that I think has accounted for many of the wrong things in my life. I never remember any enjoyment in my body" (quoted in Jalland, 178). Sadly, Octavia's response to such confidences was unhelpful. She reports that "I said I thought this family business was all nonsense, blood thicker than water—balderdash. Surprised her anyway. I'm sure *she* thinks far to much of it!" Just like Dr. Seton many years before, Wilberforce felt that what Virginia needed was a dose of fresh air and exercise—"to harrow a field or play a game" (180). This, albeit well-meant, disconfirmation of the connections Virginia was making between her childhood and her lifelong distress around food, sex, and her body was critically damaging. If, at this point in her life, she had found a supporter, someone who was prepared to validate the discoveries she was making and encourage her to continue, her sixties might have brought not suicide but rebirth.

Toward the end of her life, Virginia seems to have realized that this friendship was destructive, and refused to see Octavia. However, Leonard contacted Wilberforce and told her that despite Virginia's noncooperation he needed help in coping with her increasing distress. Virginia was thus corralled into a final meeting, which Wilberforce described as "a battle of . . . minds." Understandably, given the response she had thus far received to her confidences, Virginia was reluctant to speak at all at this consultation— "Wouldn't answer my questions frankly . . . and was generally resistive," Octavia noted (Jalland, 180). Virginia did not want to be examined but finally asked Wilberforce, "Will you promise me if I do this not to order me a rest cure?" Wilberforce responded with the promise that "I won't order you anything you won't think it's unreasonable to do" (181). Virginia accepted this guarantee, presumably secure in the knowledge that since she felt that food and rest were totally unreasonable, they would not be prescribed.

Quite unjustifiably (but in line with the practice of Virginia's previous doctors), Wilberforce communicated her professional advice not to Virginia but to Leonard. Her orders were "No writing or criticism for a month. She has been too much nurtured on books. She never gets away from them. Let her be rationed and then she'll come good again" (181–2). Whereas what Virginia needed at this point was encouragement to hold fast to the material that was becoming ever more conscious in her writing, support in carrying on unraveling the threads that she had caught hold of, and assurance that the direction she was taking with "A Sketch of the Past" was valid, Wilberforce issued a prohibition. A finger had, as so many times in the past, been placed on Virginia's lips with regard to her family and what had happened to her within it.[21]

If work was to be rationed, however, food was to be in plentiful supply. Wilberforce was already giving the Woolfs quantities of milk and cream and was "delighted" whenever Virginia was seen to be eating it. Worried by Virginia's "extreme thinness" (161), she told Elizabeth Robins that she wanted to try to "binge her up" (172), a prospect that must have been terrifying to Virginia. In addition, Vanessa was at this time renewing her admonitions with regard to food and rest, telling Virginia one week before her death that she must be "sensible" and that she and Leonard were better able to look after her health than Virginia herself was (V. Bell, 473). In other words, Virginia was a child who could not be responsible for own care and must obey those who could. What she felt was irrelevant. There was no meaning in the series of connections she had been making between past and present; she was simply mad, and if she wished to stave off this madness, she must do as she was told: Eat, sleep, and cease writing. From Leonard, who insists once again in his recollections of this time that "Part of the disease was to deny the disease and to refuse the cure" (1969, 86), there would clearly be no support for Virginia's point of view.

Virginia therefore took her own life, drowning herself in the Ouse on March 28, 1941, the day after her consultation with Wilberforce. In the first draft of a letter[22] left for Leonard she said she was sure she was going mad again, but she did not directly ascribe her suicide to fear of this "madness" but to the fact that "I feel we cant go through another of those terrible times." I believe that what she really meant was that she could not stand a repetition of the "cure" of 1912 to 1917 (and of other periods of psychological distress). In neither version of this letter did she, as she had at other times, attempt to make connections with her abuse, to assert that she was not mad and that she did not need food and rest. On the contrary, she suggested that food and rest had been the correct "treatment" for her "illness" all along, telling Leonard, the arch proponent of this approach, that "If anybody could have saved me it would have been you" (*L 6*, 481). She used those terms she knew he was prepared to hear: "I begin to hear voices," "It is this madness," "this disease" (485). She suppressed her ambivalence about her relationship with him, telling him "You have given me the greatest possible happiness. You have been in every way all that anyone could be. I dont think two people could have been happier" (481). She thus closed her eyes to the whole sexual dimension within the marriage, to the painful question of her nonexistent children, to her infantilization, to her pathologization, to the fact that Leonard could not relate to the most creative dimensions of her being.

Virginia's death was a tragedy—not because her life was tragic (for it was not) but because this death was unnecessary, because if she had found one person to support her in her assertion that she was not ill, that there were fully comprehensible reasons for the "symptoms" she had developed, and that these reasons were located in her family past, then she might have been able to address and resolve every aspect of her very deeply rooted distress.[23] Her death was a tragedy because it was precipitated by her doctors' treatment, her family's fear of honest self-examination, Leonard's misunderstanding and mismanagement, and the general climate of ignorance in which she was seeking to uncover her own history and come to terms with her problems in the present. Virginia believed in living for the joy in life, not wallowing in the misery, making it her philosophy "simply to enjoy what one does enjoy" without dwelling on sources of satisfaction to which she had no access (*D 3*, 107), but she realized that pleasure in life was shallow and inane without an underpinning of that meaning which could come only through personal confrontation with the truth. In 1941, faced with a further explosion of distress and every prospect of a further disconfirmation, she felt she could no longer go on upholding the truth single-handedly against the world and that she had better therefore opt for an absolute death than for a living one. This death was a part of her commitment to a life fully lived. As she herself put it, "I will go down with my colours flying" (*D 5*, 358).

Chapter 4

The Voyage Out:
A Slave to One's Body in This World

In Rachel Vinrace, the protagonist of *The Voyage Out*, Woolf created a character who strikingly evinces the dilemmas basic to anorexia. Like many young women in an anorexic phase, Rachel experiences a recurrent division of mind/spirit from body, retreating finally into an illness which fatally attenuates the already slender link between experiential and physical selves. Her attempts to achieve maturity are perplexed by the absence of a really powerful mother figure from her stringently patriarchal world. Suspended in a prolonged childhood, she is an unawakened character, existing in a state of amorphous consciousness in which her difficulties are vaguely felt but not directly confronted and examined. On her voyage out she begins to emerge tentatively from her infantlike self-absorption to meet the problem of defining herself and negotiating relationships with other individuals in the context of patriarchy, but the psychospiritual mediocrity of patriarchal culture and the existential numbness that afflicts those who live within its parameters repel her, and she is alienated in her own alternately ecstatic and pained responses to life in the androcentric world. Throughout the novel, the issue of how much and what kind of food is allowed Rachel and the problem of the personal and sociopolitical implications of accepting the food on offer are seen as crucial to her physical and spiritual condition.

As opposed to *The Waves*, in which Rhoda's similar state of being is considered predominantly in ontological terms, *The Voyage Out* points to cultural factors as seminal in Rachel's dis-ease. As Lucio Ruotolo observes, her "passivity" is connected with "discomfort over prescribed social roles" (21). Like Rhoda, she often feels divorced from her body, ethereal in a world of palpable obstructions upon which she is impotent to impact. In *The Voyage Out* this kind of estrangement appears to be a particularly female problem. Attempting to convey to Terence Hewet her sense of disembodiment, Rachel asks whether he ever feels that human beings are only "patches of light" in a world made out of solid matter. To the young man, however, this sense of ethereality is absolutely alien; he replies that he feels "immensely solid," as if the legs of the chair he is sitting on were "rooted in the bowels of the earth" (276).[1]

Although an involuntary expression rather than a deliberately adopted gesture of protest and defiance (such as hunger strike, which presupposes a sense of embodiment and of value placed upon the fasting body), Rachel's perceived lack of physical self is inseparable from her conflicted relationship with the society she has been born into. Her sense of corporeal diffusion expresses a feeling of ineffectivity within a cultural framework that allows her no exercise of volition and no means of instigating change—for, devoid of a material self, she is literally impotent to impact upon the world.

When her child's identity becomes untenable and womanhood presses inexorably upon her, Rachel is impelled to put off her adult body at any cost. She seeks refuge in an illness in which self diverges increasingly from body; for long periods she feels that her body is floating on the bed while her mind flits around the bedroom. In this state of personal disjunction she is distressed by the demand implicit in Hewet's presence, which causes her to join mind and body together and thus remember something she would rather forget (327–328). Reminding her of their engagement and imploring her to get well for the sake of it, Hewet only consolidates the rift between Rachel's body and her self, for good health and marriage imply acceptance of a social establishment that is fundamentally *un*acceptable to her, entry into which constitutes a form of annihilation more terrifying than biological death.

Woolf suggests that the prospect of growing up is uninviting to Rachel because the onset of womanhood initiates a strife over the disposal of rights to her body. As the American psychiatrist Thomas Szasz notes, "Addiction, obesity, starvation (anorexia nervosa) are political problems, not psychiatric; each condenses and expresses a contest between the individual and some person or persons in his environment over the control of the individual's body ... To whom does a person's body belong? Does it belong to his parents ... ? Or to the state? Or to the sovereign? Or to God? Or, finally, to himself?" (quoted in MacLeod, 65–66). Szasz uses the male pronoun, but, as is clear in *The Voyage Out*, the question of proprietorial rights to the body is most trenchant for young *women*. Rachel would like to think that her body is her own, but there are other claims upon it: the claim of society, entailing a nugatory and self-destructive conformity; the claim of the conflicted and disempowered patriarchal mother, with its invisible undertow of coercion; the claim of the father, with his insistence that she harness herself to the lumbering wagon of his career.

Ridley Ambrose and William Pepper presume that a woman's body belongs to her father—until through marriage the right of ownership is reallocated to her husband. Discussing the domestic arrangements of a friend who has recently died, Pepper comments that an unmarried daughter acts as his housekeeper, and the two men nod wisely over their apples (9). The cameo of widower and single daughter might also describe Willoughby and Rachel Vinrace. Willoughby designates Rachel as helpmate in the prosecution of his political ambitions, intending to employ her in waiting upon a gluttonous (and in these prewar years exclusively male) electorate. He tells Helen Ambrose that Rachel can be of tremendous help to him as a hostess, because constituents "like to be fed" (77).

Rachel's prospective duties are only an extension of the role she is already expected to fulfill for her father. Awaiting the arrival of her uncle and aunt on board the *Euphrosyne*, she is aware that "as her father's daughter" she must entertain them. The limitations and proscriptions implicit in the responsibility are expressed in her arrangement of the cutlery, which she lays in rigid straight lines (7). Mitchell Leaska describes her setting the table for the Ambroses as "disproportionately anxious at the prospect of acting as a hostess" (1977, 26), but given the implications of playing the role she is cast in, her nervousness is not unjustified. Woolf implies that there is a connection between the death by diminution that assuming the hostess's mantle entails and Rachel's ultimate death, describing the girl as forebodingly as stiff with a kind of rigor—"braced" to receive the guests, as against imminent "physical discomfort" (7).

Susie Orbach observes the deleterious consequences for young women of suppressing their own authentic initiatives in favor of fulfilling the cultural edict to serve others. Such a woman "loses touch with her own needs so that they become not only repressed but unrecognized and undeveloped"; she learns to believe that "needs that do arise from within her are somehow wrong, and she herself is all wrong for having them" (1986, 142). Evidently at the outset of *The Voyage Out* Rachel's volition has been damaged in just this way. Not simply a manifestation of shyness or social gaucherie, her anxiety derives from an essential distortion of that sense of self that enables an individual to operate confidently from an authentic ontological center. It is the product of a subliminal awareness that in jumping obediently through all the patrisocial hoops she is participating voluntarily in the process of her own self-attrition.

Although Rachel's personal dis-ease at her sociocultural situation is exacerbated by her sensitivity, a similar ill-defined unhappiness is seen in the novel to be universal among young women of her class. As a single woman, Susan Warrington feels uncomfortable living in the family home, but the only alternative is scarcely preferable: As traveling companion to her self-centered old aunt, she is expected to assume servant's duties for the price of her ticket. Such, she thinks, are the demands people always make of her (165). It is Susan, at the beck and call of every cantankerous elderly relation and stray male, who is expected to *run* for teacups when the men return from a walk. Woolf depicts her with comic hyperbole, "pouring cascades of water from pot to pot" with great cheerfulness and a competence born out of practice (109), but the joke is a bitter one; in fact (as Woolf would point out again and again in her fiction), there is nothing funny about young women's lives slowly consumed by the never-ending demands of the teapot.

To the hearty young man, Arthur Venning, Susan's life of petty sacrifice is scarcely comprehensible. Used as he is to the satisfaction of all his desires, he cannot seriously entertain the idea of the smallest personal privation. When pressed, he thinks that he would rather do without lunch than tea, but on reconsideration confesses that actually he wants both (108). He pities Susan her life of routine service, telling her that she needs a holiday, that she is always doing things for the benefit of other people. Susan's reply, however, points up the fact that, reductive and unrewarding a role as it is, making the tea at least gives her a purpose in life and the shadow of an identity. Deprived of even this nugatory function, she would be left with nothing at all: "But that's my life," she says as she refills the teapot (109).

Superficially, Susan might be seen as the antithesis of her selfish old aunt; in fact, however, both women are products of a patriarchal system in which women scrabble for scraps and orts—a system in which female community is legislated against and material advantage is gained by cozying up to the male powerholders (loyalty to whom, before other women, is portrayed as normative). Unlike Rachel, who remains tentative regarding the dominant socioculture with its emphasis on female servility, both Susan and Emma have bought unthinkingly into the patriarchal system. The most significant difference between them may lie in their relative skill at playing the patriarchal game: Whereas Susan is a novice, her aunt is an expert.

Indeed, as a woman, Emma Paley is highly unusual in her degree of success in obtaining money and independence within patriculture. She stands alone in *The Voyage Out* as a woman with a limitless supply of good food noncontingent (since her husband's death) upon a man. However, she has paid a price for seeking versions of freedom that are essentially patriarchally constituted. In old age her legs are crippled (106), and she is so immobilized by fat that she can no longer do up her own shoelaces (165). Focus on material wealth has caused her to contract and diminish psychospiritually until her single remaining receptivity is to physical sensations—primarily gustatory. Her empathetic capacity, particularly with regard to other women, has atrophied; she is monumentally selfish with regard to Susan, and when she hears the news of Rachel's death at the end of the novel, she remains preoccupied with a dish of potatoes (341–342).

Mrs. Paley clearly carries the weight of some of Woolf's anorexic fears and aversions in relation to food, weight, and the extinction of mind and soul by a gluttonous body. Nevertheless, the old lady is not a facile personification of appetite; Woolf suggests that her greed is in part a reaction to a hunger in nonphysiological areas which is unfulfillable within the terms laid down for women in patriarchal societies. Her almost total physical immobilization is indicative of an inner constriction that derives from the lack of any intellectual, professional, political, or other such metaphorical space in which she may exercise herself. She is a product of the same checks and curbs that circumscribe Susan and Rachel. Rescued from the sun by her niece, she is described as sitting underneath a wavering pattern of light and shade like a fish in a net (108)—trussed up, unable to move, a prisoner.

Redefined as Venning's fiancée, Susan gains the pseudostatus that goes with belonging to a man. She relishes the unaccustomed respect with which she is now treated by those such as her aunt for whom she was formerly little more than a fetcher-and-carrier, not considered to have needs and desires of her own (165). As a single young woman she runs the risk of never getting enough food for herself, but marriage is a passport into a world of material plenty; through Venning's intervention she finally (literally) obtains a slice of the cake (108). The trembling hand with which she takes it reflects perhaps less the patriarchally prescribed bashfulness of a young woman in love than the fact that to be offered a piece of cake for herself is for her a new and emotive experience. Furthermore, her right to a lifetime's cake ration hangs in the balance, dependent upon her securing for herself this young man with the power to exact cake from the world. For this is what men can do, as Hewet's confident appropriation of the entire cake bears out. Such self-assertion is both inconceivable to and intolerable in a young woman, but engaged to Venning and included in his vigorous "More cake for us!" (133), Susan is allowed, if not her own cake, at least a portion of someone else's.

The cost to Susan, however, is high: the concession of her "I" to the marital "we." Although Susan does not appear to understand what is at stake, Rachel is subliminally aware that what is required of women in patriarchal marriage is nothing less than a subsumation of identity. She strives amorphously toward an objective beyond the "life of greater comfort" that Susan looks forward to as a wife (165), conscious that marriage assures no real freedom, only subservience with a different face. This subservience is seen in *The Voyage Out* to be embodied in women's feeding/servicing roles. Even well-to-do women who can buy labor to produce meals are expected—like Mrs. Elliot with her parcel of chicken and raisins and her expressions of concern—to absorb themselves in the intermediary role of passing the food into their husbands' hands and speaking over it the necessary benediction (104).

No married woman escapes the social injunction to smooth, soothe, and placate her husband—not even the self-professedly nonconformist Helen Ambrose with her determination to deliver her niece from a life of such connubial solicitude—in fact, perhaps she least of all. Hewet accuses Helen of giving in to Ridley Ambrose, of spoiling him, of arranging her life around him, of pandering to his comfort to the point of moral compromise (229).[2] However unconventional she may consider herself, Helen differs not one iota from the hotel wives in making the care of her husband an absolute priority. If she has a life purpose that is authentically her own, it is subsumed into her larger mission: to facilitate Ridley's work.

Whereas Helen's own creative work, her embroidery, is characterized by a wild fecundity, at the villa under her rule a monastic ethos prevails—a reflection of a masculine notion of the conditions that favor creativity: order, silence, and discipline. Significantly, not only punctuality and quiet are named as behaviors that enable Ridley to restore, one by one, the odes of Pindar to the world, but also good cooking—a vicarious virtue in which the scholar is not himself expected to participate, although he reaps the benefits. Such delimited domestic arrangements—not to speak of the woman-hours involved in managing them—are essentially restrictive rather than facilitative of female creative endeavors. Rather than disrupt the labors of the male scholar, however, the women of the Ambrose household abjure self-directed work, preferring to relocate their own creative centers in Ridley's resurrection of the patriarchal classics. Woolf sets up the ostensibly attractive image of Rachel and Helen participating in "the continuity of the scholar's life" (156) only in order to undercut it. Supporting the creative life of a man is not, she suggests, ultimately satisfying for women.

Helen mocks the reliance of more overtly conformist women upon the immutable sequence of meals with their familiar props, seeing in Mrs. Elliot an old lady who would be filled with terror by the notion that dinner might be disregarded or the table shifted an inch (118), but she glosses over the knowledge that she herself, for the sake of her husband and his work, insists upon a similar fixity. Hewet tells the hotel residents that he and Rachel must return to the villa, because Helen, who is "very stern and particular," gets annoyed when they are not punctual for meals (306). In effect, the appealingly enlightened aunt who appears at first to offer her niece a model of iconoclasm presides over the same kind of circumscriptive domestic structure as Rachel's spinster aunts in Richmond.

Recalling that earlier life, Rachel sees mealtimes as four completely immovable "rigid bars" around which the day's events had to arrange themselves (197). The inflexible framework of breakfast at nine, lunch at one, tea at five, and dinner at eight functioned as a cage, a prison, a barrier against the stimulating influx of new ideas, precluding spontaneity, and inhibiting her natural impulse to explore and discover. Although she is not blind to "a sort of beauty" (202) in her Richmond aunts' selfless and unacknowledged devotion to trivial duties, the letter-writing, dog-walking, and sick-visiting with which they fill the interstices between meals suggest most forcibly to her bridles and frustration, provoking the furious urge to destroy their status quo. She recalls how she had raged against them, wanting to shatter the fixity of their closed world, their four meals, and their punctuality (201–202).

Rachel struggles hard to make a space for herself that is not defined and delimited by an unbending tyranny of meals, but when even Helen fails to provide a model for a freer, more permissive structure, her tentative movement forward is quashed, and she retreats into illness. If, however, this sickness is in one sense a form of surrender, an admission of defeat and accession to the passivity and inertia that she sees all around her, paradoxically it is at the same time a means to achieve those goals that she has been unable to realize through more positive means. Through it she is able finally (fatally) to elude and subvert the constrictive system of meals. Illness may be the last resort of the disempowered, but its very real moving potential is frighteningly evident to those who come into contact with it. "Were there no limits to the power of this illness?" Hewet wonders. "Would everything go down before it?" (327).

While, subsisting on a diet of "medicine and milk" (316), the sick Rachel is exempt from participation in the generally strictly upheld meal schedule, initially the other inhabitants of the villa continue to assemble around the dinner table as normal (317). In Rachel's semiconscious perception however, chaos has already set into the household's regular eating pattern. Meals no longer have the power to restrain and compartmentalize her existential experience, her relationship with them having become eccentric and tangential. When she surfaces from sleep, Helen's information that it is lunchtime or teatime seems random. Soon she has slipped through the webbing of mealtimes altogether and floats free of "landmarks" (311). Finally, on the day of her death, her illness creates palpable disruptions. Lunch, forgotten by everybody, happens at teatime. No one is now interested in food, and the housekeeper, Mrs. Chailey, has to assure everybody that it is their duty to eat. The usual patriarchal hierarchy is overturned too. Wearing the wrong clothes for waiting at table, Mrs. Chailey abandons her usual reserve and talks to her social superiors familiarly, as their equal (330).

It is Ridley Ambrose, the hub around whom villa life customarily revolves, who is chiefly discomfited by the disturbance in its usually smooth and predictable pattern. As Rachel's condition deteriorates, he finds himself unable to remain cocooned in his study from the exigencies of real life, and abandons his translations to participate in the general anxiety (330). This reformulation of the patriarchal order that sidelines Ridley and the work from which the household generally derives its identity, instating the young woman in focal position in his stead, is a triumph for Rachel and for the subversive power of her sickness. Her victory, however, is pyrrhic, the coup achieved at the cost of her own life. If a dramatic form of protest, ultimately this illness asserts the vital importance of evolving more empowered means to the revolution that will accord young women a sociocultural space in which to explore their passions and nurture their talents.

Rachel's task of self-realization is perplexed by the absence from her life of female models for fulfilled creativity and meaningful self-direction. Of the women she encounters, only the literary historian, Miss Allan, is engaged in her own work, and that at an emotional and sexual price that Rachel is not herself willing to pay. Miss Allan has eschewed a husband with apparent satisfaction, preferring the loyal companionship of a bottle of crème de menthe, a "gentleman" which she calls Oliver and which has traveled with her for twenty-six years (241). Nor, perhaps, is Rachel prepared to settle for the hard work and relative poverty of women who make their own living. Intellectually challenging as it may be, the life of a female academic is one of intensive labor for small financial return. There is no slice of cake for self-supporting women; Miss Allan's work is "a question of bread and butter" (151), and for the domestic comforts and emotional support that her male counterpart, Ridley Ambrose, relies upon Helen to provide, she must shift for her herself. None of the married women at the hotel is eager to exchange their lot for hers. Mrs. Elliot pities her, and Mrs. Thornbury agrees that the hardest life is that of the single woman earning her own livelihood (104).

Miss Allan, however, clearly regards her independence and her profession as infinitely preferable to the subservience and self-suppressions of marriage, and is genuinely anxious to open to Rachel a view of such an alternative way of living. Encapsulated in the offering of preserved ginger, her sincere desire to give the girl the undefined thing that she really needs stands in stark contrast to the coercive demands and prohibitions that Rachel generally receives in response to her desires. Miss Allan's words as she offers the ginger indicate her awareness that what Rachel requires in order to be able to grow is an openness to new and untried possibilities—a quality that patriarchy demonizes in women. If she has never tried ginger, she must do so, Miss Allan tells Rachel, for she may discover a new pleasure. She points out what a shame it would be to try ginger for the first time on your deathbed and discover that you loved it, adding that for herself, she would be so annoyed she would be spurred to health on account of it (240). For this reason, she says, she always tries everything. Her comment is whimsical but also perceptive. Brought up to suppress rather than investigate her own wants and wishes, Rachel is confused about what she enjoys, unsure whether she is entitled to enjoy it, and frightened to find out. It is indeed, as Miss Allan's words suggest, at least partially on account of her inability to discover the metaphorical sweet that might really fulfill her that Rachel dies.

Rachel's reluctance to try Miss Allan's sweet, her assumption that she won't like it, is on the one hand a reflection of the fear and suspicion of the unknown that a patriarchal upbringing instills in young women. At the same time, however, her instinctive aversion to the ginger suggests a spontaneous recognition that as an alternative to marriage and motherhood, Miss Allan's path is not for her. Ginger is not to everyone's taste. The harshness and asperity of the single professional woman's life in a society organized around woman as man's helpmate and domestic manager can present a viable option only to a few extraordinary and maverick women. When she finally tastes the ginger, she quickly spits it out. Anxious that the girl should not reject her offering out of hand, Miss Allan asks her if she is sure she has really tasted it, but Rachel throws it out the window in response (240).

Rachel's amorphous vision for her future is in a sense far larger and more ambitious than the purposeful but straitened way of life that the older woman represents. Miss Allan's example suggests that for women self-sufficiency and personal challenge entail a negation of femality which is in itself ultimately disempowering. Her surname (she has no forename) is a masculine identifier, and she presents, androgynously, "a square figure in *its* manly coat" (104, my italics). Indicative of her desexualization is the hair which, when she unpins it, reaches only partway down her neck (242). The surrogate male companion, "my Oliver," the crème de menthe, has never been sampled, which, Miss Allen says, proves that she is exceptionally abstemious (241). The closure of the male-gendered bottle may symbolize an unacknowledged desire for a female partner; certainly it is symbolic of those physical pleasures—most notably the pleasure of sexual relationship—that have been renounced in the name of scholarship.[3] As greatly as she desires a deeper and more fulfilling purpose than the vacuous concerns of her Richmond aunts and the women at the hotel, Rachel understands subliminally that that purpose is *inherent in* her problematic femality and cannot be achieved *at the expense of* it. Neither, despite her very real fears of sex, is she disposed to settle for chastity. Beyond intellectual/professional fulfillment, her challenge entails confrontation with sexual experiences that the older woman has perhaps negotiated by evasion.

Considered in the context of feminist history, Rachel's desire both to retain essential femality and to become an actor in the world is sophisticated.

In pre–World War I Britain, women have yet to gain the crudest rights. The establishment position in relation to the fight for female suffrage is voiced by the Conservative politician Richard Dalloway, who denounces on his life the "folly and futility" of the campaign for the vote (35)—an attitude that Rachel's own father supports. Dalloway believes that the role of a wife is to uphold an ideal for her husband, to which end she must be wholly, childishly, preserved from reality. He tells Rachel that he never allows Clarissa to talk politics, attributing his survival of public life to the knowledge that she spends her day visiting, making music, playing with the children, and organizing the household—clearly a highly fantasized version of an upper-class woman's life (56).

The same mixture of ignorance and pejorative paternalism characterizes Dalloway's attitude toward working-class women, whose lot he congratulates himself upon having improved. Although he is, as Rachel recognizes, motivated by a genuine benevolence, the small amelioration in conditions he has won for Lancashire mill girls (the shortening of their working day by an hour—which, he naively believes, they will be able to spend in the sunshine) is a sop to the political empowerment that such women need in order to improve their own lives. Dalloway assumes that Rachel knows nothing about the existences that ordinary women lead, and, indeed, she has rarely visited poor areas, and then only with a chaperone (56). Socially protected and politically ignorant as she is, however, Rachel intuits an oppressive continuity in the conditions of women's lives across patriarchal class boundaries to which Dalloway, as a man, is oblivious. She empathizes passionately with the inner poverty of socially disadvantaged women because it so closely mirrors her own. Evoking an elderly widow in Leeds she challenges Dalloway with his own ignorance, telling him that while he is busy speaking, writing, and getting bills passed, he is missing something central.[4] As a result of his work perhaps a widow finds in her cupboard a bit more sugar and tea, or less tea and a newspaper, but her mind and feelings remain "untouched" (57). Her criticism of Dalloway's politics is twofold. First, for women the tangible benefits churned out by the Westminster machine are unimpressive—a few tea leaves and some lumps of sugar—while men receive the real and metaphorical fat of the land. Second, if politicians profess concern for the material situation of poor women, they fail to acknowledge, let alone address, such women's deeper emotional and intellectual hungers.

Woolf encodes the hunger of the thin black-clad widow staring out of her window (57) in the *Times* article that Hewet reads to the hotel guests about a starving cat similarly fenestrated in Westminster. A woman walking down the street observes the cat in the window of the empty house. Workmen have noticed but ignored it for several days, with the result that it is now famished. When it is finally liberated, it mauls the hand of its male rescuer. Interjected fragments of conversation relating to other news—the decisions of the prime minister and the birth of a son to a Mr. Joshua Harris—suggest the patriarchal context in which this ostensibly inconsequential story must be understood, directing the reader toward its real point: *Women* are shut up in empty houses without any food.[5] The location of the episode in Westminster indicates that such disempowerment is linked with the denial of political franchise. In the newspaper article, men know about the cat's plight but do nothing to rescue it, apparently oblivious to the barbarism of their failure to act. Only when a woman passes the house is an attempt made to help the animal. Hewet is shocked by the ferocity with which the cat turns on its male rescuer. Like Dalloway, who expects the thanks of the widows and mill girls of Britain for his too-little-too-late assistance, he thinks the abandoned cat should be grateful when it is finally rescued. Miss Allan, however, is more sympathetic. As a self-supporting woman, she is aware that "cats are often forgotten" and is unsurprised at the animal's ferocity, she alone realizing that it was ravenous and recognizing the fury that hunger and neglect induce. She comments simply, "Wild with hunger, I suppose" (113).

It takes the sea to effect, temporarily, reversals in the status quo that androcratic politics are unlikely to bring about. The seasickness that it unleashes is subversive, forcing the well-nourished and sociopolitically powerful Dalloway to retreat to the isolation of his cabin, unable to eat. Before the storm he is skeptical of the power of the sea, believing that by exercising the male-identified virtues of self-control and willpower he can defeat its sickness. He asserts that he is never seasick—or, at least, has been only once—explaining that when the sea is choppy it is vital not to miss a meal, even when you feel you cannot possibly eat. He is condescending about Clarissa's inability to suborn her body and break it to food in this way, telling Willoughby that she is a coward (38). But his experience on the *Euphrosyne* is humbling. Once the storm is under way, force of reason is impotent to overcome his repulsion for food. He courageously faces down two meals but is defeated at the third by asparagus "swimming in oil" (61).[6] Seasickness reduces him to a similar state of infantile dependence to that which he generally advocates for women. When he is finally able to return to the table, it is laid with nursery food—yellow cake and bread and butter—for return to health, as Willoughby explains, entails a repetition of the weaning process (64).

The seasickness, with its violent disruption of the usual order of life (61), prefigures the disturbances in the accustomed patterns of eating that are brought about by Rachel's final illness. The normal sequence of meals becomes impossible; indeed, eating is largely replaced by vomiting—or the presence of basins, as Woolf euphemistically puts it (62). Clarissa Dalloway, who had formerly announced that she would rather die than not change for dinner (41), finds herself drinking champagne from a tooth mug (with a toothbrush in it), her underclothes scattered around the floor (62). The cutlery set out by Rachel in rigid geometric patterns breaks rank, the knives veering away from the plates, and the food itself no longer obeys normal rules, appearing to take on a life of its own as the potatoes roll about the dish (61).

One might expect life in a foreign continent—one in which matristic Indian traditions survive—to offer Rachel an opportunity for liberation from the debilitating circumscriptions of patriarchal English society. In fact, however, her experience of South America reinforces her sense that there is no escape from the tentacles of the patriarchal establishment. The English negotiate the foreign country within a sealed bubble of their own culture. They have colonized the Santa Marina hotel, making it over effectively into a microcosm of respectable European middle-class life. Spying through its illuminated windows, Rachel and Helen observe the mechanisms of privilege and subservience characteristic of patriarchal systems operating through the familiar medium of food: In the dining room a servant sweeps the floor; in the kitchen more servants wash up, and cooks dressed in white dip into cauldrons while the waiters make a meal from the wasted food, sopping up gravy with crumbs; meanwhile, in the drawing room affluent Europeans lie back in armchairs, having eaten a good dinner. Among the well-fed ladies and gentlemen, a thin woman playing the piano is suggestive of Rachel herself, her undernourished presence sounding a note of dissonance amid so much self-complacent indulgence (90).

To Hirst, the hotel resembles a zoo, and its guests a carnivorous menagerie gorged into torpor on mutilated carcasses. He compares them to lions holding raw flesh in their paws—although some, he thinks, are more like hippopotami, others like pigs or parrots, and yet others like reptiles wound about the semiputrescent bodies of sheep (162). In Hirst's image, the hotel is a microcosm of a society that operates by predation, in which the culturally disempowered (women, indigenous people, the poor) are destined to feed the maws of the favored (wealthy white men and their associated women). And yet, as the zoo analogy suggests, this is also a society in which even the pampered and wellfed are imprisoned—by the nugatory belief systems and reductive thought processes that keep the hierarchy in being. They are "fat old men" and "cripples" (106), grotesquely deformed and ultimately immobilized, morally and psychospiritually as well as physically, by their gluttony.

Repeatedly in Woolf's work, whereas a good meal energizes and inspires, too much food tamps down the soul, dulling intellect, imagination, and the capacity for empathy. Thus in *The Voyage Out* those wealthy white men at the top of the food chain are gorged into the moral complacency of torpid crocodiles on the hotel's rich and copious meals (168).[7] Excess of food acts spiritually and existentially to obliterate, functioning to extinguish any flicker of "human spirit" that remains in the midday sun. The satiated hotel guests are reduced, horrifyingly, to "bodies without soul" (107), mechanical mouths eating passively at the sound of the gong because it is time to feed (106). For Woolf, this kind of mindless consumption, independent of nutritional need and uninformed by passion or pleasure, is offensive in the face of the endemic starvation at other loci in the patriarchal system. Moreover, the prevalent attitude of disrespect for the food itself is symptomatic of a dereliction inherent in patriarchal values. Stripped of meaningful connection with those who have labored to produce it, with hunger, with the earth, and ultimately with the numinous, the seven-course hotel lunch becomes a lengthy ritual of despoliation and waste, continuing "methodically" until each of the seven courses is a litter of "fragments," and the guests are slicing the fruit like children destroying a daisy, "petal by petal" (107).

The advent of the English has had a major impact on the socioeconomy of Santa Marina, imposing a new, extravagantly wealthy and privileged upper class upon the extant social structure and reducing many of the local population to the status of servants and scavengers. The demands of the English upon the food supply have upset the economic balance, pricing the mass of the population out of the market for basic produce. The Ambroses' servant, Maria, tells Helen that in the high season eggs become an expensive luxury for local people because the English are prepared to pay such exorbitant amounts for them (87).

The incursion of the English is the latest in a series of European invasions and colonizations that have decimated the indigenous Indian culture, erecting over it a greedy and hierarchical patriarchy. Mr. Flushing plies a profitable trade in the clothes and jewelry that carry the religiocultural heritage of the Indian women. Mrs. Flushing tumbles from her wardrobe a stash of shawls, material, embroidery, beads, brooches, earrings, bracelets, and combs, telling Rachel that the native women have worn these things for centuries. She explains gleefully that the women do not know the financial value of these articles, so Mr. Flushing gets them cheap (222). It is somewhat ironic, given the in-comers' proclivity for violence, oppression, and avarice, that in relation to the apparently peaceful ancient culture that he depreciates, Flushing regards the Europeans' lives in Santa Marina as "civilization" (253).

In the space beneath the patriarchal palimpsest, Indian women continue to live—tenuously—in primeval relationship with the Earth, sitting on the ground in the village downriver, plaiting and kneading. In contact with this "soft instinctive people," the tourists feel like "tight-coated soldiers," an image that indicates succinctly the aggressively imperialistic identity of Europeans among Amerindians. Absorbed in the "peaceful . . . beautiful" rhythms of the women's lives (269), Rachel feels an intimation of eternity in the symbiosis of their lives, the trees, and the river (270). She catches a glimpse of a natural and untrammeled way of being in a female body that existence under patriarchy has obscured from her eyes, so that when she turns back to Terence, and the women stop gazing at her, she feels "cold and melancholy" (269).

The attack on the English tourists' picnic by an army of marauding ants alludes satirically to the successive invasions and plunders of South America, suggesting the crucial role that control of the food supply plays in imperial aggression. The tablecloth is made to represent an invaded country and surrounded with barricades of baskets, ramparts of wine bottles, fortifications of bread, and fosses of salt. Whereas, on the face of it, colonialism might seem to indicate an expansive outlook, the response of the picnickers to the ants' incursion—defensive embattlement around the provisions—reveals the real suspicious insularity and determined separatism that characterizes in particular the English on foreign territory. Although Miss Allan's fear that the ants will infest the food (122) is comic, it nevertheless reflects a genuine and presiding national horror of contamination. At home in England, Mrs. Elliot hears, rats have brought plague to the poultry, and it has become dangerous to eat chicken (145).

Throughout the battle with the ants, Rachel lies apart from the others (123), at a distance from the sudden eruption of English tribalism. Observing her separateness, Hewet feels that she might be meditating like him on the ignobility and mediocrity of these people endowed with financial wealth and entrusted with the management of the world. Among such people, he thinks, anyone who really loved "life," loved "beauty" would be crucified for attempting "to share" rather than "to scourge" (123). For Hewet, "someone" is "him"; he does not think far enough to understand that the person he is describing is probably female and that the critique implicit in his words might be a feminist one. In the context of phallic social values, thousands of young women experience their lives as the "agony" and "waste" that Hewet describes. Rachel herself speaks out with anguish against those who hold the power and the purse strings in phallocracy, against their "aimlessness" and "the way they live." People hurt but they do not really feel, she tells Helen; society is "bad," and "living, wanting" is "agony" (249). For Rachel, there is no share on offer; the only option is to scourge. Approaching her on all fours, a piece of bread in his hand, Hewet resembles a person trying to entice a frightened wild animal, or a devotee bearing oblation. If the bread is an offering, however, it is a pitiful one, and as such a reflection of the ontological, intellectual, and other forms of sustenance that are afforded young women within patriarchy.

The South American history of incursion and occupation is encapsulated in the history of the hotel itself. As a monastery of the Catholic Spanish invaders, it was once the setting for a stark ascetic way of life, a past that throws into relief the shallow and decadent existences of the middle-class English who stay there in the present. What was formerly the refectory, "a cold stone room with pots on trestles," is now a luxurious lounge. Surveying it, Signor Rodriguez, the hotel manager, congratulates himself upon the fact that the monks, the naked walls, and the wooden boards have been replaced by gentlemen lying back in their in chairs, couples drinking coffee, and card games under electric light (91). Even the Catholic chapel of the monks, for centuries a place of masses and mystery, of moonlit penances, has been ceded to the Protestantism of the English and filled with their hideous church furniture: shiny yellow benches and claret footstools, a brass lectern in the form of an eagle, bits of carpet, and strips of gold-monogrammed embroidery (213).

To Rachel, the degenerate and hypocritical religion of the English is a contraction of the soul, in comparison with which the simple version of Catholicism practiced by the monks appears to offer something of the spiritual expansion that she desires. Dalloway's jibe that she harbors a secret affinity with Catholicism (48) may not be as facetious as he intends. Within the terms of reference of the novel, Catholicism suggests an alternative to the violent predation that is the modus vivendi of the English Protestants. "Man goeth about to devour me," runs the psalm read by Bax at their service, conjuring God to break teeth and smash jaw bones (214). Catholics, on the other hand, are described as eaters of fish, in the opinion of the *Euphrosyne*'s steward, Grice, a great unrecognized source of nourishment, sufficient alone to sustain Europe. Thinking of the poverty he has seen at soup kitchens in the richest cities in the world, he laments the fact that people do not eat fish, wishing almost for a resurgence of Catholicism, with its (meat) fasts (45).

On the face of it, Grice's fish panegyric is ridiculous—the "tirade" of a fanatic, as Clarissa notes (45); at the same time, however, the paean to fish points up sociocultural issues that are fundamental within *The Voyage Out*. Whereas meat-eating is associated in the novel with gluttony and sloth, fish, as a food for fast days, expresses an aspiration beyond the complacent lethargy that characterizes body, mind, and spirit of the hotel carnivores. As a harvest that (in Grice's eyes) yields itself up mannalike from the sea, fish obviates the bloody slaughter that is a fact of carnivorism and which, within the symbolic terms of the novel, stands as a paradigm for the acculturation of young women in phallocratic societies. In a piscivorous world—one characterized by an equitable social system—no one need starve, for the earth's resources, when not monopolized by privileged minorities, are sufficient to feed everyone.

Although Grice associates fish with Catholic Christianity, as a symbol it arises in fact out of antecedent theacentric cultures.[8] Given Woolf's later preoccupation with matrism, *The Voyage Out*'s expressed nostalgia for the vanished fish-eating past may in fact be a palimpsest covering a sense of grief for a more deeply buried religiocultural loss—one which is of far greater relevance to the young woman struggling to realize herself within patriarchy—of a culture in which godhead is female, and an expansive attitude toward the social, spiritual, and ontological positions of women prevails.

Under patriarchy, *The Voyage Out* argues, women can thrive only by adopting predatory masculine codes of behavior. Motherless, Alice Flushing has been primed from birth for a man's world by a sadistic paternal upbringing. She recalls the—literally—freezing baths administered by her father in the stable-yard, the memory describing a harsh inversion of the maternal experience of immersion in the warm and comforting waters of the womb. If the children refused to get in the water, she remembers, they were whipped. In the father's system, nurturance is absent and jungle law prevails; Mrs. Flushing explains that in her family the strongest children lived and the others died, referring to this method of child rearing as "the survival of the fittest." The extent to which she has acculturated to patriarchalism is indicated by her response to the cruelty of her childhood: If she herself had children, she says, she would treat them in exactly the same way (260).

Alice Flushing is implicated in the patriarchal bloodletting by the red associations that adhere to her: her surname, her florid complexion, and her liking for red meat and red jam. The image of the aristocratic lady "helping herself to cherry jam" points to her gleeful participation in Mr. Flushing's morally dubious but lucrative practice of helping himself to indigenous people's art objects and religious artifacts—her enthusiasm for the trade allying her solidly with the patriarchs and against the older female-identified civilization. Indeed, so superlative is her accommodation to androculture that she has bested her husband in the men's game of submission and domination, having "forced" him into those activities and attitudes that give him the least pleasure (182–183).

If Alice Flushing is a woman with a man's weight in the world, St. John Hirst is in some senses the inverse. Comparing himself to Mrs. Flushing, he bewails his own slightness, telling Helen that, although tall, he has never weighed more than 10 stone (140 pounds) and that since arriving in Santa Marina he has lost weight (187).[9] The nickname "Monk" indicates his greater affinity with the hotel's past identity than its present. His weight loss coincides with the journey away from the monastic environment of collegiate Cambridge where he is an intellectual heavyweight to a South America occupied by the middle-brow English. Academically, he has been cram-fed on the best food available, but physically and emotionally he has been stinted (an artificial polarization that Helen deplores [188]). Rachel's resentment of Hirst owes much to her perception that he has received an intellectual nourishment prohibited to her. She identifies with a fictional sister ordered to make his tea and go and feed the rabbits so that he can have the schoolroom to himself, telling Hewet that she has been feeding rabbits for twenty-four years (197).

Evicted from the schoolroom, Rachel may well feel more affinity with the rabbit fattened for the table than with the consumer of the meal. Indeed, *The Voyage Out* suggests that young women raised for patriarchal marriage are effectively reared as livestock. Rachel is marked out for slaughter by her name, which means in Hebrew "ewe lamb," the central food and sacrificial animal of Judeo-Christian culture. In an earlier manuscript of the novel she is identified as a "spring chicken" (DeSalvo 1980, 55),[10] an analogy that Woolf pursues in the published novel, in which Hewet quizzes Hirst about marriage by asking if there are any "female hens in your circle." The two men's conversation points to the fact that for women marriage is an act of enforced social conformity tantamount to laying one's head on the butcher's block. Hirst berates the hotel residents for their conventionality with the contention that if you drew a circle around them, they would never move outside it; Hewet responds, "You can kill a hen by doing that" (97).[11]

Evelyn Murgatroyd's discussion of marriage initiates Rachel's encounter with the grotesque butchery of the hotel chickens. The kitchen yard upon which she stumbles is a female precinct—one in which the only male presence is a waiter who occasionally comes to throw rubbish on the heap, and even the bushes, draped in wet aprons and towels, appear to be wearing female garb. The yard is occupied by two big women plucking chickens, naked yellow bodies on their knees and bloody tin trays in front of them. This is "the wrong side of hotel life," the secret underbelly of the patriarchal microcosm that Rachel is not supposed to see. As she watches, an ancient wizened woman chases a terrified chicken into the yard, to the laughter and encouragement of the pluckers. She appears furious and is swearing. Confused by the noise and flapping towels, the bird zigzags around the yard and finally runs straight at the old woman, who encloses it in her skirts, drops down over it, and cuts off its head, her face expressive of vindictive triumph (238–239). Rachel is brought into abrupt confrontation with a bitter irony of androculture: that it falls to older women within it to enact the violent subordination of their own sex, the duplicity of woman to woman serving to subvert potential female solidarity. In patriarchal societies the end purpose of maternal nurturance becomes the sacrifice of the daughter into a marriage of submission and restriction. In Woolf's description, the slaughter of the chickens—the naked bodies, the opening of the skirts, the enclosure of the bird, the "blood and . . . ugly wriggling" that both fascinate and repel Rachel (239)—has connotations of a brutal sexual act suggestive of the loss of virginity that lies at the center of the girl's passage from daughter to wife in sexually controlling patriarchal societies.

Rachel is particularly pressurized to meet cultural standards of femininity by the enduring legend of her own late mother's charm. It is made clear to her that Theresa is a touchstone against which, on patriarchal terms, she does not measure up. "She's not like her mother," Ridley Ambrose sighs audibly as she serves him his soup (8). Helen remembers Theresa as a kind of angel, telling Rachel that although not beautiful she inspired love in people, got on with everyone, and made life funny. But Rachel's aunts Lucy and Kate paint a more human picture, describing Theresa as "very good" but also "very sad" (171), suggesting that beneath the veneer of gaiety, she was no more really fulfilled by her role as agent of other people's joy than her daughter promises to be.

Rachel is unlikely to be a nurturer on a par with her mother, given that she remains herself hungry for this kind of care. Unlike Mrs. Flushing, she has not accommodated to maternal deprivation by growing a thick skin, but remains preoccupied with the sustenance she needs in order to grow fully, the milk imagery that surrounds her describing the complexity of her situation in this respect. To Helen, Rachel's involvement with milk points to the arrest of crucial areas of her development in early childhood. Observing that her niece seems like a six-year-old, she connects her aimless spillage of milk with an infant's diffusion of thought, reflecting that Rachel might become interesting if she could learn to "think, feel, laugh and express herself" rather than simply "dropping milk from a height as though to see what kind of drops it made" (18). Sequestrated with her Richmond aunts, Rachel has been offered little as an alternative to the psychological nebulousness produced by their own lack of education. Aunt Lucy's milk slops submerge reason; Rachel remembers how her aunt would kiss her with emotion, spilling the argument "like a bucket of milk." Although Lucy splashes out pails of milky emotion, her love is useless to Rachel because it is indiscriminate; when Rachel asks how fond she is of Aunt Eleanor, Lucy responds with a profession of her love for the dead Theresa, and through Theresa for Rachel herself. Rachel is left suspecting the sincerity of all avowed emotion; nobody really says what they mean or what they feel, she complains (28).

Introduced into the novel as a mother reft from her children, Helen Ambrose appears the obvious maternal surrogate for the girl seeking a means to make up a deficit in nurturance. The name "Ambrose," suggesting ambrosia, points to her as the source of a kind of divine nourishment, and her conscious intention in relation to the younger woman is genuinely benevolent; she thinks that she would like to show her "how to live" (74). Helen is allied with the ancient Indian culture of South America by the embroidery she stitches as she quizzes Rachel aboard the *Euphrosyne* (70), a depiction of feeding and cornucopian fertility: river, rain forest, browsing deer, and fruit—bananas, oranges, pomegranates. However, her design also contains more menacing elements: Among the lush vegetation naked Indians hurl darts (25). The hunting imagery recurs ominously. Bored by the sea voyage and curious to pierce the defenses of her niece, Helen devises "a kind of trap" for Rachel, who appears to her "easy prey" (70). The language of predation suggests that while Helen may be a source of abundant nourishment, within a patriarchal context—in which older women become the agents of acculturation, or metaphorical slaughterers, of their daughters—great risk attends eating her food.

Helen's self-appointed task of enlightening and liberating Rachel is perplexed by the fact that the freedom into which she wishes to initiate her does not exist in any simple sense for women in patriarchy. Paradoxically, her first lesson for Rachel is an exposition of the real restrictions that enmesh her. Her words hew down "great blocks" that have stood at the entrance to Rachel's mind "always," but the shaft of light that they let in is a "cold" one. Introduced to the function of prostitutes in Piccadilly and the ways in which male sexual desire manifests itself within patriarchal structures, Rachel suddenly understands why it is considered unsafe for her to walk alone. She sees the world contract at once around her, her life become darkened and walled in, herself "crippled" (72). And yet there is, as Helen points out, the possibility of a kind of freedom lived between the warp and weft of patriarchy, one rooted in authentic selfhood. Rachel's sense of the trammels and obstacles set to impede her yields transitorily to a new and exciting awareness of discrete selfhood, of herself as an individual, and she declares incredulously, "I can be m-m-myself" (75).

Initially motivated by altruism, Helen's relationship with Rachel becomes increasingly less disinterested and more sexualized. Likewise on Rachel's part, there is every indication, as the novel progresses, that the person whom she really, subliminally, desires is Helen, and that her perceived attraction to Terence is in fact a dislocation of her real erotic center. Ellen Rosenman notes that the echo of the mother's name, Theresa, in the lover's name, Terence, indicates that Rachel "turns to romance as a substitute for mothering" (1986, 24). However, we cannot regard Rachel—at least not by the end of the novel—as seeking simply, neurotically, for a mother surrogate. Her larger, albeit putative, desire is to discover authentic maternal (or gynephilic) sustenance in spiritual and cultural senses. Her encounters with the civilization of the Indian women and with the maternal mythos embodied (albeit largely in a patriarchally reconstituted, Marian form) by her own dead mother point her toward the possibility of a matrism which is personally and politically empowering.

In Helen's behavior the conflicts inherent in the relationship with Rachel become increasingly evident. Swayed by the patriarchal imperative that she prime the younger woman for marriage but moved by her own erotic feeling for the girl, she is unable either to fulfill unambiguously the patriarchal remit or to provide Rachel with the honest and expansive connection she wishes for. When she intuits Rachel's engagement to Terence, her passionate response—flooring her niece and falling on top of her—is expressive of sexual desire and of violent rage. As Helen rolls her over, Rachel sees only the blue of the sky and the green of the grass that whips her face and fills her eyes and ears. When finally she lies still, she is panting, speechless, and senseless. At the same time, however, Helen's action—felling the girl and dropping upon her—recalls that of the old woman butchering the chicken, suggesting her active role in the propagation of the gynecidal patriarchal marriage. When Rachel comes to, the disproportionately large heads of Helen and Terence hang menacingly over her supine body. As if in conspiracy over its fate, they kiss in the air above her and speak of love and marriage (268).

Rachel's own feelings in relation to the love/marriage issue remain perplexed. She tells Terence that she has no doubt she is in love with him but that "It will be a fight," and she is aware that at moments she feels "uncomfortably far apart" from him (266). Her specific response to his (implied) proposal remains a series of questions: Are they to marry? Has he asked her to marry him? (265). Her most authentic sexual feelings continue to be elicited by Helen, contact with whose "soft body" and "strong and hospitable arms" arouses in her an orgasmic emotion: "happiness swelling and breaking in one vast wave" (268). When, on the contrary, she touches Terence she experiences dissociation, an "overpowering sense of unreality" which leads her to feel that not only his body but the whole world is "unreal" (267).

Rachel's profound fear of—in particular—heterosexual sex and subsequent flight from her body cannot, of course, be fully understood outside the biographical context of Woolf's sexual abuse by her half brothers. The bestial forms of "barbarian men" who scuffle down passages and snuffle at the door of Rachel's dreams after Richard Dalloway's kiss recall Woolf's own nightmare of a terrifying animal face following her abuse by Gerald Duckworth (*MOB*, 69). Beyond visceral terror and sexual disgust, however, the imagery of Rachel's nightmare carries an accurate, subliminally conscious body of information about her sociocultural situation. She dreams that she is walking down a long tunnel that becomes progressively narrower—an apposite metaphor for the experience of diminishing opportunity that emergence into adulthood represents for girls in patriarchy. The tunnel opens finally into a vault, in which she finds herself "trapped" in what looks like a horrific image of patriarchal marriage: herself isolated in a small space with a hideous, preverbal, scarcely human man (68).

The long, oozy, narrow tunnel opening into a vault also suggests the womb and the passage to it, the dreamed walk into this space implying the wish of the motherless daughter to return to a prenatal maternal symbiosis. The womb of the dream, however, metamorphoses from a soft, warm comforting place into a hostile environment of clammy unyielding surfaces—the vault is running with damp and made of bricks—and Rachel, inside it, is no longer the sole occupant but is sealed in with a personification of man as animal appetite. The womb proves duplicitous, a closed room in which the girl must eschew all hopes of nurturance and herself assume the role of nurturer of man.

Only through the absolute renunciation of adult womanhood signified by her fatal illness is Rachel able, finally, to regain occupancy of a nurturant womb. Losing consciousness, she thinks that she has fallen into "a deep pool of sticky water," and she feels a kind of profound peace in which she is aware only of rocking, pulsing, and booming sensations reminiscent of those experienced by the unborn child suspended in amniotic water. She thinks that she has finally escaped her "tormentors" and now lies "curled up at the bottom of the sea," washed by first by darkness then light, where every so often she is turned over, neither dead nor quite alive, in a kind of hypnotic trance state (322).

Arthur Venning suggests that Rachel's death is due to her trip up the Amazon—a foolhardy expedition in his opinion. He tells Susan that Englishwomen are not up to "roughing it" like "natives" (341). Although ostensibly ridiculous, Venning's explanation nevertheless contains a grain of unperceived truth. The journey to the Indian village is indeed a crisis point for Rachel, bringing her into simultaneous confrontation with the strange but enticing culture of the indigenous women with its intimations of different ways of being in a female body and with Hewet's love and the concomitant prospect of patriarchal marriage. Venning's ascription of causes points to the true nature of the middle-class English fear of the Amazonian natives, whose fabulous violence is a patriarchal blind. The real threat of Indian culture lies in the subversive potential of really knowing it, for genuine contact with such ways of living connotes openness to alternatives that have been excised from patriarchal organization. It is a nascent awareness of such alternatives, without the personal power to shake the stasis, that generates for Rachel an apparently unresolvable dilemma over how to live—in the teeth of which only death suggests itself to her as a solution.

Wilfrid Flushing's attribution of Rachel's death to eating contaminated food is apparently equally far-fetched; within the symbolic terms of the novel, however, he is right to implicate a problem in the food supply (although wrong in where he locates it). The food offered to young women in patriarchy is poisonous. At the hotel, the patriarchal establishment is anxious to exculpate itself and its food from any role in Rachel's illness; it is ridiculous to imagine that Rachel caught her illness from the English community, Flushing asserts (339). For the hotel residents, the autonomy of the villa from the closed circle of mainstream English society makes its food deeply suspect. William Pepper flees the independent household because he fears infection lurking in its lettuce, which he inspects carefully on the prongs of his fork for germs, certain that it conceals typhoid (84). He informs Flushing that he left the villa because its inhabitants never washed their vegetables properly, telling Mrs. Thornbury he is in no doubt that this carelessness was responsible for Rachel's infection (339).

In truth, Rachel's fatal illness is a reaction against patriarchal conditions rather than a result of the ethos of dissent represented—at least superficially—by the villa. Prompted by an imminent marriage that looks, for all its attractions, like a lethal dart, she is compelled by the carnivorous nature of the patriarchal food chain to relinquish her life. In the context of such a system, in which to be clad in a female body is to be subject to various forms of social predation, divestment of the physical self is for the young woman a last-ditch defense mechanism against a worse form of extinction.

Chapter 5

Jacob's Room: *Helping Himself to Jam*

Jacob's Room, the story, ostensibly, of a young man's rise to glory, hinges on a rumbling peripateia—premature death in war—that lurks always just offstage. A bitter irony is contained in the name Jacob Flanders. The Old Testament relates that Jacob was 147 years old when he died, having fulfilled his destiny as a ruler of men and founder of nations. If the forename "Jacob" promises highly, however, the surname "Flanders," naming the infamous place of World War I carnage, confutes the grandeur of the protagonist's projected destiny. Jacob Flanders is in his early twenties when he is killed, in a war not glorious but ignominious in its pointless waste of young life.

The systemic spasm of death in Europe from 1914 to 1918 is symbolically prefigured in *Jacob's Room* by the potato blight that infects the summer gardens of England. Looking at Mrs. Pascoe's diseased crop, Mrs. Durrant observes that all this year's potatoes are diseased, repeating as if in lamentation "You won't have a potato left." Themes of boys and young men weave through the two women's conversation; Mrs. Durrant reports that she expects her son from Falmouth in a day or two, sailing in a small boat with a friend, thus innocently foreshadowing the future voyage from which neither Timothy Durrant nor Jacob Flanders will return. All the while "the boy Curnow," Mrs. Pascoe's nephew, listens silently (45).

But the obvious tragedy of young men's lives uselessly crushed out in a pointless war is underridden in the novel by another—unacknowledged and routine—wastage: of the lives of young women. These are uniformly lives unfed. They are lives, like Clara's, lived in the etiolated light of drawing rooms, where they are fading before they have begun to bud; they are lives, like Florinda's, sickly straggling in the light of street lamps, characterized by an inner violence no less than that to be found on battlefields; they are lives like Fanny's, spent in a constant struggle to catch up the articles that fall from her like parts of the body she is impotent to hold together, let alone feed effectively.

As the account of a young man's growth and premature death, *Jacob's Room* is in a sense a companion piece to *The Voyage Out*.[1] But if the end of both Jacob's and Rachel's journeys is the same encounter with death, young man and young woman traverse very different territories to meet their fate. Rachel's voyage into womanhood as defined by patriarchal Edwardian society entails a series of contractions, limitations, and prohibitions, the habit of which is inculcated from childhood. Jacob's development, on the contrary, follows a pattern of expansion, exploration, and opportunity. Whereas Rachel must shape herself into the form demanded by society if she is to find a place within it, society shapes itself to Jacob. The granting of the titular room is indicative of the sociocultural space reserved for the young man. Not merely dwelling places, his successive rooms function as outgrowths of self; filled with his clothes, his books, his personal possessions, they concrete and consolidate his identity. When Helen Ambrose entices Rachel to the villa, it is with the promise of just such a room of her own—the kind of personal space that the girl has not heretofore been permitted, in which to "read, think, defy the world, a fortress as well as a sanctuary" (122). On board the *Euphrosyne* her room is only ever temporarily, never by right, her own, and she is forced to make constant shifts and adaptations, compromises in physical space that symbolize the larger and wider-reaching concessions required of young women.[2]

Whereas Jacob is a hero on a quest for his inheritance, Rachel's voyage is neither undertaken on nor guided by her own volition but is directed by others (Willoughby, Helen, Terence). It is in many senses not so much a journey as a retreat, the ultimate manifestation of which is her death, characterized by images of sinking, drowning, and engulfment. The voyage leads her into the darkness and entangled density of a primeval jungle, the complexity of which reflects her confusion as she is thrust into the irresolvable web of contradictions that cleaves to adult women in patriarchal cultures. Jacob's travels, on the contrary, take him upward, the Sky God ascending the mountains of classical Greece, from the summit of which the world is to be unraveled and the patriarchal perspective ("civilization") bestowed. He is, as Carol Ohmann remarks, "the heir of the Western ages" (165),[3] dreaming with Timothy Durrant of worlds ripe for the picking (64). His slaughter at the hands of those same men who promised to hand him the patriarchal crown is thus tragic because of the flagrant betrayal it entails; Rachel's death, on the contrary, is pathetic because she was never vouchsafed anything.

The precedent of the biblical Jacob not only intimates the role of leadership for which Woolf's protagonist is apparently destined; it also suggests duplicity on the part of the patriarchal heir, for, as Isobel Grundy notes, in Hebrew the name Jacob is thought to mean "supplanter" (Clements and Grundy, 214). In Genesis, Jacob gains his preeminence by morally dubious means, buying the birthright from his starving brother Esau for bread and a pottage of red lentils. He obtains his father's benediction ("God give thee of the dew of heaven, and the fatness of the earth, and plenty of corn and wine" [Genesis 27:28]) by a trick involving food, coming to the dying man in the guise of Esau with a dish of two kids. Woolf saw a parallel between the biblical son's manipulation of food and exploitation of hunger, and the readiness of modern-day young men to sell their hungry sisters down the river with a pottage of metaphorical lentils, appropriating the fat of the land for themselves. As *Jacob's Room* makes clear, little has changed between biblical times and the present day, in which domination continues to be enacted through control over the food supply, and subordination effected through starvation.

Repeatedly in her writing Woolf equates hunger with the cultural disinheritance, political disenfranchisement, and educational marginalization which are the particular lot of women in patriarchal cultures. In *Jacob's Room*, education, with all the social advantages it entails, is an exclusive cake consumed by young men in Cambridge rooms. The don Sopwith cuts chocolate cake into slices to dispense, along with the silver stream of his wisdom, to callow undergraduates. As he cuts he reflects romantically that in distant times and places they will recall the rooms and the cake and "refresh themselves again," for a special property of the university cake is that it continues to nourish the eater long after it has been consumed (32). Stenhouse, however, is ambivalent about the cake and all that it represents. An outsider not only because he comes from the provinces but also, it is implied, because of his relative poverty (he will have to scrimp and save to put his own son through university), he suddenly sees the cake and the young men as childish and absurd. Yet at the same time he fully intends to pass on the patriarchal inheritance; he will send his son to Cambridge nevertheless (32–33).

Woolf too was ambivalent about the university cake. On the one hand she doubted profoundly the benefit to be derived from eating it. In *Jacob's Room*, not only does Cambridge dispense an arid, overly intellectualized, and slanted view of the world, but it promulgates values which (as she later made clear in *Three Guineas*) lead to tyranny and war. She ridicules the assumption of the Cambridge establishment (Huxtable who cannot walk in a straight line and Cowan who is still laughing at the same old stories) that it offers a unique recipe for life: "How like a suburb where you go to see a view and eat a special cake! 'We are the sole purveyors of this cake.'" On the other hand, however, she bitterly deplores the refusal to allow women a slice of the special cake. For the daughters of patriarchy, universities equate with a daytrip and a token taste of privilege after which "Back you go to London; for the treat is over" (32).

A Room of One's Own, with its distinctive women's and men's meals, provides a key to the fundamental relationship among food, privilege, and achievement in Woolf's thinking. Lunch at the men's college begins with soles at the bottom of a deep dish, over which is spread a "counterpane" of pure white cream, here and there "branded . . . with brown spots like the spots on the flank of a doe." Soles are followed by partridges—not, Woolf is at pains to point out, two "bald, brown birds on a plate" but fowl "many and various" with a "retinue" of accompaniments: salads, sweet and sour in perfect order; potatoes sliced like coins but tender; and "succulent" sprouts resembling rosebuds (12). Dessert is "wreathed in napkins," a "confection" rising "all sugar from the waves"—to call it "pudding" and thus allude to "rice and tapioca" would be "an insult" (12–13). Meanwhile, the wineglasses have "flushed yellow and flushed crimson," and in the center of the spine, at the seat of the soul has been lit not the "hard electric light" of "brilliance" rather the "rich yellow flame of rational intercourse," which is a "more profound, subtle and subterranean glow." There is no need to rush, no need to display dazzling wit—"no need to be anybody but oneself." Life is good; human society is sweet; the whole company is bound for heaven (13).

This opulent food is sensually gratifying certainly, but its essential quality lies beyond physical pleasure. Such food, for Woolf, is a means of engaging the soul through the body, of uniting the two often polarized aspects of human being in one immanent whole so that neither part can be touched without also affecting the other. The soles that open the meal pun on "souls," the liberation of which is the result of good food and fine wine—consciousness made fluid, free-swimming like a fish out to sea. This kind of meal nourishes the intellect and rubs away the sharp edges of personality, facilitating an easy sense of comradeship and imaginative exchange of ideas. When such community prevails, personal dis-ease is mollified; to be simply oneself is divine.[4]

For the elite company of males who consume it, the meal is also a symbolic affirmation, an edible testament to the strong historical foundations of their privileged position. The sequence of ever more sumptuous courses resembles a ceremonial procession—a Lord Mayor's Show, State Opening of Parliament, or coronation—rituals which reflect in their magnificence the wealth of the ruling class and sex, and in their unchanging formal structure the fixity of the hierarchy. Attending the partridges at the center of the magisterial procession, the coinlike potatoes symbolize munificence, and the roseate sprouts allude to the emblem of English kings. The sweet which emerges Venus-like from a sea of modest white napkins suggests a toothsome kind of femaleness concocted for male consumption. Viewed through the yellow and crimson translucency of the wine, the entire procession appears garbed in the splendid Vandyck colors that distinguish the robes of the power-wielding patriarchal institutions of church, law, and state.[5] This meal transcends function (the satisfaction of hunger); it transcends gluttony or even epicureanism. It unites man with the heroic achievements of his glorious past and assures him of golden plenty secured and to come.

Dinner at the women's college is rather different. The meal begins with "plain gravy soup," in which, Woolf notes, there is "nothing to stir the fancy." Indeed, the soup is so thin as to be almost transparent; had there been a pattern on the plate, one might have seen it (but there is no pattern). After soup comes beef with greens and potatoes, "a homely trinity" suggesting a muddy Monday morning market with its "bargaining and cheapening," its "women with string bags," the backsides of cows, and sprouts with curled and yellowing leaves. But, of course, Woolf acknowledges cynically, there is "no reason to complain of human nature's daily food" for the quantity is sufficient and coalminers may well have less. Prunes follow, "even when mitigated by custard, . . . an uncharitable vegetable" (self-evidently not a fruit), sour and "stringy as a miser's heart." Then come biscuits and cheese, and the water jug is "liberally passed round," for "it is the nature of biscuits to be dry, and these were biscuits to the core." That, then, is all. The meal is finished. Chairs are scraped back; the doors swing "violently to and fro," and the hall is scoured of all traces of food and prepared for next day's breakfast (19).

Here is no pomp and circumstance. Here plenty is replaced by adequacy, and splendor by plain plates, a prosaism that dulls imagination and nullifies any incipient sense of sorority. Crimson and gold have become drab brown and dirty yellow, and the most translucent substance is the watery soup. The spots on the doe's flank have been replaced by mud on the rumps of cattle, and the reassuring chink of coins by the haggling and pennypinching of the marketplace. The only liberality possible at this meager meal is with the water jug, a necessary freedom given the dryness of the biscuits that terminate (rather than culminate) the meal. No one is launched into deep seas of consciousness on the back of such arid wafers. The violence that is done to the spirit by this poverty-stricken experience of eating is evinced by the scraping chairs and the action of the swing doors as the hall is rapidly abandoned and all trace of food expunged.

If the members of the women's college feel bitter, it is not entirely as a result of the acidity of the prunes. They have been allowed sufficiency where their brothers are offered the optimal and inspirational. As a result they are diminished in every aspect of their lives for, Woolf points out, the human body is an organic whole, heart, body, and brain coexisting together; good food is vital not merely to the physical but also to the emotional and intellectual aspects of existence. To "think well, love well, sleep well" requires that one has "dined well," and beef and prunes, far from firing the glow of inspiration, induce a "dubious and qualifying state of mind" against which the eater must struggle to retain a sense of intellectual and creative fluency (20). Nevertheless, women are to feel guilty if they demand truly satisfying food. There is no reason to complain, the authorial voice upbraids herself; "human nature's daily food" was good enough for Wordsworth's "phantom of delight," the eponymous subject of the poem from which this line derives (19).[6] An invidious expectation of gratitude is placed upon the college women, although why, one might ask, and to whom ought they to be grateful for their parsimonious diet, and how are they to argue for the intangible thing—not fine food itself but the physical, spiritual, and mental condition it produces—that they are forbidden?[7]

Jacob is far from grateful for this kind of meal when he lunches with the Cambridge don, Plumer, and his wife: "bloody beastly!" is his verdict upon this dispiriting occasion. He inveighs against Plumer's betrayal of the great academic tradition, deploring the loss of Homer, Shakespeare, and the Elizabethans (32), and the inability of the *parvenu* professor to provide him with the romantic grandeur that he expects of Cambridge (28). Clearly he is right to perceive that something vital is missing from the occasion. The Plumers' food is mediocre, and the failure of inspiring talk at their table is uncomfortably evident, Mr. Plumer stopping the conspicuous holes in the conversation with embarrassing pleasantries (26–27). What Jacob remains blissfully unaware of, however, is the fact that the grand tradition requires a highly enriched soil to flourish and that the Plumers have not been so fortunately nurtured. Neither have they, in the present, the large financial resources necessary to feed four undergraduates the kind of food that sends a heavenly glow down the spine; the "cheese-paring" (27) that Jacob finds so miserable is not mean but essential. Like the students of the women's college, Plumer has struggled to arrive at Cambridge and must continue to struggle against a material dearth to live and work with something more than a sense of duty.[8]

The product of a partial egalitarianization of the education system, Plumer's class origins and his corresponding political orientation are indicated by his proclivity for George Bernard Shaw and H. G. Wells (28).[9] Although he is identified as a progressive and a socialist, however, like the other doubter, Stenhouse, he has not wholly succeeded in prising himself from the grip of the oligarchy. He is aware that lunch with undergraduates is mutual torture, the perpetration of an "outrage upon one hour of human time," but he cannot conceive of a world in which the ritual celebration of academic privilege might not be reenacted. He muses on what would happen if Sundays passed and men graduated without a don giving a luncheon party, but the thought, indicated by a hiatus, is unthinkable (26).

If Plumer's position in academia is not one of ease, the most thoroughgoing disadvantage is suffered by his wife and daughters. Mrs. Plumer, one of Woolf's several female characters with only a husband's name, is a picture of thwarted ambition. A clever woman, her determination to thrust her husband to the top of his socioprofessional tree (27) is the projection of a personal drive almost certainly doomed to frustration in a woman in the rigid patriarchal society of pre–World War I England. For her two daughters the same nugatory vicarious ascent awaits. The bitter irony is that it falls to Mrs. Plumer, as the professor's wife, to feed and pamper the golden boys who are the recipients of all the opportunities from which she is herself debarred.

The lunch that is the object of Jacob's scorn Mrs. Plumer in fact gears throughout to his greatest ease, making a host of invisible shifts and adjustments when he is inconveniently late. It is she who takes a second helping of greens so that he will have time to eat his meat, who anticipates his hunger for more mutton with an inconspicuous nod to the maid, and who tactfully orders in the pudding when it becomes clear that seconds of cabbage will not give him time to finish his first course. Although he tries to restrain himself, Jacob is "infernally hungry"; he cannot resist taking more meat, blissfully unaware that he is polishing off tomorrow's lunch for Mrs. Plumer and her daughters (27). Later he feels "something of pity" for "those wretched little girls," but the notion of a relationship between his own unthinking use of privilege and the wretchedness of their situation eludes him. In fact, his consumption of their lunch is a paradigm for a set of social interactions in which young women's portions—educational, political, material—are as a matter of course eaten up by young men.

Jacob's disapproval of the Plumers in no way inhibits him in eating at their table. On the contrary, he eats their food voraciously and suffers no sense of personal compromise. Whereas a less secure self might fear disintegration through such ambivalent participation, his identity is too secure to be threatened. His defiant reaction, "I am what I am, and intend to be it," contrasts strikingly with the failed sense of self of the women in the novel (as well as of the earlier Rachel Vinrace and the later Sarah Pargiter with her repeated "What's I? . . . I . . ." [ellipses in original]). If anything, he is fortified by the opportunity to define himself against the Plumers and all that they represent. They, he thinks, will attempt to stop him succeeding, but the "shock—horror—discomfort" he feels at their lunch parties and teas is immediately followed by a feeling of "pleasure," of "certainty," of "reassurance from all sides" that grows with every step he takes as he strolls by the Cam (28). The sense of in fact potentiating social opposition that he encounters is very different from the nullifying and erosive series of prohibitions and restrictions that Woolf's young women experience. Rachel Vinrace revolts against conventions that act upon her as crippling shackles. In comparison, Jacob's youthful jibs and refusals appear almost frivolous, for he is the chosen son and all convention seems framed with his well-being in mind. His self-assurance is bolstered by a knowledge that, even at odds with the establishment, he will not be ostracized; his rebelliousness will be indulged and his compliance courted.

Jacob's voyage around the Scilly Isles with Timothy Durrant, and his return from the wilderness to the community symbolized by the dinner table, evinces his ability both to separate from and incorporate in the social body. The dinner jacket that travels with him, hidden among tins of food, represents the option of reintegration into civilized life even at the moment of his greatest divergence from the group, when dinner dress seems irrelevant and incredible. It constitutes a social self that he may put off but need never disown, and which, when the world is once again stable and candlelit, seems to preserve him. This awareness that his social identity may be resumed at any moment liberates Jacob to become an adventurer. He is the possessor of two kinds of food: the refined dinner with its delicate accouterments—fine glasses, elegant silver forks, and cutlets wearing pink frills (46–47), and the unadorned functional nutrition of expedition—tinned meat and pickle, and the sandwiches that he eats while hunting (87).

Jacob's easy ability to satisfy his infernal physical and ontological hungers contrasts with the impotence of the young women in the novel, all of whom are in some sense crucially at odds with food, as they are with their social and existential identities.[10] The suicidal despair of the "thin girl" (100), Fanny Elmer, is connected obliquely with Jacob's unfailing ability to generate a meal for himself. She remembers how he would cadge a meal from his male cohort, Bonamy (in a kind of rehearsal for the old boys' network), and she thinks that at least she can drown herself in the Thames (122). His confidence in both the abundance of food for his consumption and in his own solidity stands in sharp contradistinction to her own ontological experience, in which alienation from food is a reflection of personal disunity. In Evelina's dress shop where she looks at clothes, women's parts are separated. Like Fanny's body, that of the dummy is in a state of multiple schism. Her left hand clutching a skirt is disjoined from her middle—in fact a pole, around which twines a feather boa, her gold and scarlet patent-leather feet rest limply on the carpet, and the hats arranged around her resemble the decapitated heads of criminals (105).

Fanny is in constant danger of losing her self in the multiplicity of the external world; she walks quickly but is constantly distracted (99). Her experience of disintegration and of scanty differentiation of self from environment is expressed in her *Leitmotiv*—she drops items continually from her person: her balled-up black glove (102), her umbrella (103), and Madame Tussaud's program, which falls out of her bag. The bag with a loose clasp (99) is a symbol of Fanny herself; her own body is a faulty container, allowing personal contents to spill out and mingle with the external world. Madame Tussaud's waxworks function as a similar metaphor, for they are, like Fanny, vacant bodies, human frames in appearance only, devoid of inner reality. Her identity is not an essential product but an artificial construct, put on like the fancy dress she assumes for the artist, Nick Bramham. She is attracted to Jacob just because his own identity is, conversely, genuine and immutable. Some people are real, she thinks, and do not try on each other's clothes, like Robertson, who wears her shawl, and she herself, who wears Robertson's waistcoat. This kind of borrowing, she notes, Jacob finds very awkward (106).

Fanny's acquisition of food is, as one might expect of a woman so estranged from her body, fortuitous and unreflectively cumulative. She enters the baker's "abruptly," "adding cakes" to rolls, and moving on again (99). In the Express Dairy shop where she goes for lunch (116), eating is disjunctive and depersonalized. The uninspiring food (pie and greens, eggs on toast, roll and butter) and the vacuous atmosphere are a reflection of a poverty which is both ontological and financial, for the tenpence Fanny can afford to spend on lunch is insufficient to purchase conviviality and spiritual uplift.[11] For tenpence eating is revealed as the tumbling of damp cubes of pastry into triangular baglike orifices, a view in which, reflecting Fanny's essential sense of organic non-entity, the mouth is objectified and detached from the rest of the body as well as from mind and soul.

In the cheap café, eating is reduced to function. The Express Dairy shop is a kind of feeding factory, in which food is inserted into bodies on a conveyor-belt system that ensures the maximum speed and efficiency and entails the minimum human contact. In this process devoid of emotional engagement between feeder and fed, an anonymous waitress barks the order to a faceless cook, and the food issues from an invisible kitchen. Washed up on islets of abstraction and indifference, the café eaters are also divided from one another. The asynchronicity of café meals, indicated by the constantly opening and closing doors, together with the scattered deposition of the many small and separate tables, mitigates against communication, intimacy, and the transcendence of personal preoccupations. Stranded in private thoughts and feelings, each customer anticipates with silent intensity the arrival of her or his own meal (103–104).[12]

Jinny Carslake shares Fanny's ontological insecurity. Her inner diffusion is written in the motelike freckles that dot her body—one the many images of disintegration and dispersal, of disparate pieces without a nexus, that characterize her. Her life becomes a wandering quest for the essential significance that will compose this threatening explosion of fragments. After an affair with an American painter, Lefanu, she becomes involved with Indian philosophy, later moving to a series of Italian pensions, carrying with her a jewelry box filled with pebbles from the road. If you look at them with concentration, she says, "multiplicity becomes unity," which is "the secret of life." Despite this knowledge, however, her hungry eyes continue to pursue the macaroni on its passage around the table (114). For Jinny, devoid of a cohesive sense of self, the unity of multiplicity is more than a tenet of mystical philosophy; it is an ontological life-line which, if she clings to it tightly enough, seems to promise delivery from her own essential disintegrity. Both a homogeneous mass and an agglomeration of many tiny separate pieces, the macaroni apparently exemplifies the inner synthesis she strives for. Her fixation upon it as it moves round the table suggests not only the starvation produced by material poverty (she is a woman with only pebbles in her jewelry case) but also a ravenous hunger for the experience of existential consolidation that the dish represents.

The pigeons that surround Jinny present another image of the reduplication of many identical pieces, of the self disturbingly atomized. "I don't want you right on the table," she says, waving them off. Paradoxically, the pigeons also represent an opposite but equally terrifying vision of solid embodiment, for the individual birds are "swollen" and "waddling"—enlarged but futile existences whose sole purpose is apparently to eat. In the cross-currents of conversation they are thrown up against "those fat women" near the British Museum whom Cruttendon ridicules, the juxtaposition suggesting obliquely that in the pigeons Jinny intuits an appalling reflection of her own ontological experience of being a woman, one of empty physical inflation devoid of purpose or worth. Her apparently throwaway comment, "Everybody feeds them," contains an expression of horror at the propensity of human beings to encourage such vacant engrossment; at the same time, however, it implies the unspoken corollary, "Nobody feeds me," suggesting a subliminal desire for a really nourishing kind of food. The depth of her existential distress is evinced by her unheeded assertion "Sometimes I could kill myself" (113).

Florinda presents a picture of ontological distress—articulated by her reiterated cry, "I'm so frightfully unhappy"—which is at root closely related to Fanny's and Jinny's, although on the surface it may appear to be very different. Whereas Fanny and Jinny are impotent to gather the body consistently about themselves, Florinda is ostensibly sunk in an all-too-consolidated body, in a corporeal existence of which prostitution is the logical end. Less like the romantic stereotypes that inhabit men's fiction and more like the traumatized products of sexual abuse who in fact constitute the majority of workers in the sex industry, she is neither innately carnal nor knowing; rather, she is a guileless ingenue, lost and vulnerable in an exploitative world.

A completely unnurtured child, she has no surname, and for parents only a photograph of a tombstone, which, she says, marks her father's burial place.[13] By a grotesque inversion of nature it is not the child Florinda who grows, but—fatally—her father, who is said to have died of an irreversible bone growth. The only mother she has known is the cynically titled Mother Stuart, the madam whose interest in her is predominantly mercenary. If she clings to the notion of a fictitious virginity (in which childhood is implicit), it is as much in appeal for the love she has never received as for professional reasons (65).

Florinda's greed for sweets is less an aspect of sensuality than of a desire to experience the sweet things absent from both her childhood and her present life. She seeks a substitute for the love and security she has been denied by filling herself with sickly confections—chocolate creams (66) and "pinkish sweet stuff" (148)—patently unnourishing foods physiologically as well as ontologically. In a real sense, she is no less alienated from her body's needs than is Fanny Elmer, for the "good" things she imposes upon it in excess—sex and sweets—are incapable of answering its genuine needs. The difference between the two women lies not in the presence of ontological disintegrity and despair, which both in fact know, but in their response to it; whereas Fanny seems to unshackle self from physical identity, Florinda's attempt at a solution is complete identification with her body.

As a correlative, Florinda often feels overpowered by her body, held in the clutches of the organism that she has, unconsciously, invested with so much authority. She understands her pregnancy as that body once more acting out of her control, tricking and overwhelming her. Her sense of the experience is well described by Mother Stuart's euphemism for her condition, "sunk" (148)—an expression that also describes the failure of her hopes of socioeconomic improvement. An unmarried woman with a child has no such hopes. Herself a child in search of love and nurturance in her various sexual encounters, Florinda is hardly equipped to mother a child, having only her own deprivation to pass on. Her morning sickness, which prevents her from absorbing what little nourishment she does take in, is a symptom not simply of a physiological state but also of the way in which her metaphorical malnutrition has been compounded. It is the sickness of a child who will never now make up her own deficit and of a woman who rejects the miserable hand fate has dealt her in an act of uncomprehending defiance.

The duplicitous nature of the emotional succor she is accustomed to receive—from Mother Stuart and from young men like Jacob who, infatuated by her appearance, engage with her body but do not offer her love—has made Florinda randomly, paranoiacally suspicious of what is taken in. In the ABC shop she sees glass in the sugar bowl and accuses the waitress of trying to poison her. Juxtaposed with the accusation of poisoning is the declaration that young man stare at her, and it is on the table bearing the supposedly lethal sugar that she lays their "love letters" to read—a scenario suggesting that it is this "love," deceptively like sugar, that is the real source of her poison. She props the letters against the milk jug, an indication perhaps that what she would really like from the young men is a milky, nurturing maternal love (65).

The glass in the sugar bowl is one of many images of broken glass or china and food or drink which are motifs of Florinda's, pointing to the emotional violence inherent in her history of failed nurturance and to her own terrible and destructive suppressed anger at her situation. In a restaurant, she and Jacob witness a violent argument between a man and woman at the next table, in which the woman smashes the plates on the floor (68).[14] During the Guy Fawkes dinner at which Jacob is garlanded with roses, Florinda throws a wineglass at a young man. The smashing of the grapelike "purplish globe" is a powerful symbol of the unarticulable rage she suddenly feels at the vast disparity between her own poverty and the position of privilege in which young men (symbolized at the party by the stag's head and the Roman bust) routinely repose. "I'm so frightfully unhappy," she tells the unresponsive Jacob (63).

Dining with Florinda, Jacob doubts that she has a mind (67). Observing her reaction to the argument in the restaurant, he is appalled by what seems to him a revelation of her thorough stupidity, "something horribly brainless" in her face as she sits and stares (68). And yet, Woolf makes clear, Florinda is not stupid, merely "ignorant" (66), a state that is not the result of innate inability but of her general deprivation. She is gifted with a certain amount of instinctive percipience and a naive clear-sightedness (67, 122), and in terms of spontaneous humanity and emotional sensitivity is certainly more evolved than most of the young men who populate the novel. Jacob thinks pejoratively that any implausible lie will suffice to dupe Florinda, for, "Any excuse . . . serves a stupid woman," but in fact his verbal reasoning is transparent to her. "Half-guessing, half-understanding," she painfully perceives in his face and his manner the scorn and rejection that he believes concealed: "I don't like you when you look like that," she says with foreboding (69).

Jacob resents the intellectual compromise that the relationship with Florinda seems to him to entail. Such compromise he regards, however, as an undesirable but inevitable concomitant of the sexual gratification that as a young man he does not expect to deny himself—for he cannot conceive that a beautiful, sexual woman could also be intelligent. There is no answer to the problem, he muses: "The body is harnessed to a brain. Beauty goes hand in hand with stupidity." By the trite formulation of this little dictum Jacob effectively avoids acknowledging Florinda as an individual human being with human feelings and removes from himself any sense of responsibility for his relationship with her. Looking at her, he has grace enough to acknowledge that none of this is "her fault" (69) but not the acuity of insight to recognize himself among those whose fault it really is: those who consume her body but give little in return. Moreover, if the principle that beauty is indisseverable from stupidity is indeed universally true, we are prompted to wonder about the brains of the handsome young Jacob himself. Clearly, however, the beauty/brains equation is gender-specific.

Ostensibly, Florinda has little in common with the well brought up and sheltered young lady Clara Durrant. In fact, however, the two women are as similar as they are different. Humble, apologetic, both exist to serve, Florinda in the bedroom and Clara at the tea table. As much as Florinda, Clara is "at the beck and call of life" (66), and in terms of money for her own disposal she is equally poor. Like Florinda, too, she is an innocent. Her mind uneducated, she dwells upon the dusting while her elders discuss politics (146). Both women idolize the (as he seems to them) morally, intellectually, and practically superior Jacob Flanders. "You're too good," runs Clara's interior dialogue with him (52).

To Jacob, the two women appear, stereotypically, as complementary opposites: Florinda, profane attraction, physical desire; and Clara, idealized, sacralized, bodiless love. He accepts the cultural premise that body and soul, sex and love are unencompassable by a single woman, although in fact, in order to fit this cultural paradigm, both Clara and Florinda have had to deny or discard vast tracts of authentic selfhood. Thus truncated, their ontology contrasts starkly with that of the young man, whose legitimized access to both sensual and sacred is implicit in the attribute of his biblical namesake, the ladder, which in Genesis links the polarized realms of earth and heaven in Jacob's dream.

Picking grapes with Jacob in the greenhouse, Clara stretching up at the top of the ladder apparently occupies this heaven split off and endowed with all the virtues. She radiates a luminescent, angelic beauty surrounded by the leaves of the vines. But her presence among their pendulous plenty, the "yellow and purple bunches" and the tomatoes climbing the walls, is ironic, for none of this plenitude is hers. It is the young man's harvest, even though, as he himself comments as she loads his basket higher, "I have more than I can eat already" (51).

Brought up to efface herself, as an adult Clara is so estranged from the notion of own desire that she can barely recognize a self-initiated want any more, let alone envisage a scenario in which she might fulfill one. It is, of course, this very aptitude for self-subordination that assures her social success within patriarchy. She is an exemplary hostess, handing round the china teacups and gracefully accepting the supreme accolade which is also her condemnation: that she makes the best tea in London (146).

Jacob reveres above all women this angel of the tea table with her "flawless mind" and "candid nature," but he cannot brook the irritatingly restrictive forms of worship imposed upon those who are drawn to the shrine. Seated at the tea table with assorted dowagers and Clara, he thinks it is "an insufferable outrage upon the liberties and decencies of human nature" that he can say no more to her over the bread and butter than a few trite and meaningless phrases. He is morally incensed by the web of circumscriptions woven around the "virgin chained to a rock" in Mayfair, but not for her sake; his indignation is born out of the frustration that *he* experiences at her inaccessibility. That an insufferable outrage is done to Clara's liberties and decencies is beyond the scope of his imagination. He is only a brief visitor at the tea table, while she, it seems, is permanently stationed there, filling the teacups of elderly gentlemen, but it does not occur to Jacob that she must suffer routinely the tedium that he cannot stand for a moment (106–107). As a woman, Clara appears to him an animal of a wholly different species from his own, and one whose biological destiny it is to fill teacups and make small talk. She exists for him as a quasi-religious icon, a position which, while it inspires awed respect, tends to mitigate human empathy.

Clara differs from the other women with whom Jacob is romantically or sexually involved (Florinda, Fanny Elmer, and Sandra Wentworth-Williams) in that they are all, in some sense, motherless: Fanny only by implication (she is seen hurrying past the Foundling Hospital [122]), Florinda and Sandra in fact. In their different ways, the motherless women all suffer a sense of vulnerability to loss of self in a hostile world. As Sandra tells Jacob, she was four when her mother died, "and the park was vast" (128). Clara, on the other hand, is eclipsed by her mother, to whom she retains a paralyzing attachment, the overidentification manifesting in her confusion over the boundaries between their respective feelings: She thinks that *she* should feel happy because *her mother* is well and enjoying herself (146). Those around her attribute Clara's lack of individuation to her mother's overinfluence (135), but clearly, in the context of upper-class Edwardian life, patriarchy must be implicated in this failure of self-separation, its denial of opportunities for the exercise of will and the taking of initiatives designed to ensure that young women remain in a semidependent state.

Despite the various difficulties and impoverishments that adult life delivers them, the young women with whom Jacob is connected are only amorphously dissatisfied with their lot because they have never been led to expect anything better. He, on the contrary, is primed to regard himself as a leader, an achiever, a laureate for whom the prize is more than just a copy of Carlyle; it is a place *in* the Carlylian history of heroes. "Does History consist of the Biographies of Great Men?" his undergraduate essay is entitled (31).[15] Yet this fêted and favored son to whom hereditary wealth and status are pledged is to be disappointed in his expectations. There will be no place for Carlylian heroes in the trenches, and the world that survives World War I will have a new and more subversive attitude toward the former status quo.

The seeds of the modern revolution are evident in Jacob's experience of Greece, the ancient source of his cultural inheritance. He anticipates an encounter with the Parnassian ideal that seems the due of the boy garlanded with paper roses and laden with grapes, and scales Olympus, Pentelicus, and Hymettus in pursuit of the expected apotheosis. His experience, however, is anticlimactic. Aristotle is no longer a philosopher but a dirty and lecherous waiter (121). The classical ideal has become a shoddy and anachronistic hotch-potch of ancient Greek adulterated by modern European, "now . . . suburban; now immortal," a Parisian boulevard and a herd of goats, guns and gramophones and the columns of the Parthenon (129–130).

Nor is the Greek feast quite the superlative that Jacob might have expected. When he eats with the Wentworth-Williamses, dinner is described as "excellent," but excellent here is clearly a relative term. The meal starts promisingly, with a plaited basket of "fresh rolls" and "real butter"—the observation of "fresh" and "real" suggesting that such qualities are not what Jacob has come to expect of Greek dinners. However, the meat which "*scarcely* needed the disguise of innumerable little red and green vegetables glazed in sauce" clearly leaves something to be desired (137, my italics). The fact is that, like Athens itself, little of this food is authentically Greek, and equally little of it resembles the English it emulates. Here too the classical ideal has become a degenerate hybrid, capsicum and butter. Greece has fallen victim to a kind of gastronomic colonialism. Eating their soup in an Olympian inn, the Wentworth-Williamses anticipate quail, goat, and caramel custard: unappetizing Greek food mixed with travesties of Anglo-French dishes so execrable that Sandra abandons her soup half finished and Evan has produced a toothpick before the main course arrives (125). Greece has no ambrosia for Jacob, although it lays before him the best it has to offer. The inadequacy of that best as a banquet for a hero is an intimation of the less-than-glorious fate that awaits such warriors and inheritors in the modern age.

The betrayal implicit in the mediocrity of the Greek feast is symptomatic of a huge and sinister duplicity in the sociocultural food chain that reveals itself increasingly as *Jacob's Room* draws toward a close. In the context of World War I with its unprecedented hunger for young cannon fodder, the invitation of the establishment to the young man to sit at its table is shockingly hypocritical—akin to that offered the fly by the spider. Jacob's real fate, of which he is blissfully ignorant, is to feed the blood-lust of a patriarchy so rampantly bellicose that ultimately it is prepared to consume its own favorite sons.

Suggestions of Jacob's tragic fate are present even in episodes that seem to attest most surely to the security of his position. On the river he and Durrant observe, but choose not to join, Lady Miller's picnic party, enjoying instead their own feast of cherries. The predominant images in the scene at first glance are of bounty: the bag of cherries, the lush grass "juicy and thick" and "gilt with buttercups," and the grazing cows, with their "munch, munch, munch" reinforcing the themes of eating and plenty. But the graveyard and tombstones introduce an ominous death note into the idyll. The fall of the unripe yellow and half-eaten red cherries, which Durrant drops lazily into the water, predicts painfully the premature fall in battle of Jacob and so many others of his generation, scarcely older than the children whose legs he can see in the meadow (29). Sticky, red, and wriggling the cherries go down the wasted victims of an idle appetite, just as, on the battlefield, young life will be casually squandered to satisfy the establishment's gluttony for war.

The butterflies that are ostensibly so gentle and innocuous in this scene in fact recur throughout the novel as symbols of military bloodshed, death, and destruction. As a boy, Jacob collects butterflies, but only in order to consign them to butterfly boxes where they die a death of suffocation by camphor or sulfur suggestive of the mustard gas of the trenches. The butterflies themselves often appear as warriors and warmongers, as their fearsome names indicate: the White Admiral, the Purple Emperor and the Death's-Head Moth (found by Rebecca in the kitchen [17]). On the moor, scavenging butterflies—blues, painted ladies, and peacocks—settle on bones lying on the hot grass and gorge themselves on the "bloody entrails" of prey dropped by a hawk (18). As the novel approaches its end, the brown spaniel has smelt a rat. The scent of some treachery is in the air, the nature of which is indicated by the words of the lepidopterist: "Perhaps the Purple Emperor is feasting . . . upon a mass of putrid carrion at the base of an oak tree" (107). The rulers of oaken-hearted England, who had seemed so completely to promote the good of their sons, now turn upon them in an act of unexpected infanticide.

Ultimately, Jacob, as much as Rachel Vinrace, is the victim of a predatory sociocultural establishment. Its war turns the young men who fed so confidently at its table into meat for consumption. "Now Jimmy feeds crows in Flanders" (83), Woolf tells us, giving a sinister twist to an image that is used throughout the novel, often with intimations of death or crumbling fragments of flesh—Betty Flanders feeding the chickens and thinking of her dead husband (11), Mr. Floyd feeding the ducks on Leg of Mutton Pond (16), and day-trippers feeding the pigeons at the Versailles café where Jinny sits with Jacob and Cruttendon (113). What makes Jacob's death the tragedy in a classical sense that, in a classical sense, Rachel's is not, is the reversal in the course of his destiny. Her sacrifice to a carnivorous society is only the *ne plus ultra* of the personal retrenchments she has made to that society all her life. Following upon so many intimations of glory, Jacob's death is profoundly shocking.

In the end it is, predictably, not the really culpable patriarchal establishment but the innocent and impotent young women of *Jacob's Room* who assume the responsibility for their brothers' deaths. At her dinner party Mrs. Durrant playfully attempts to fasten some kind of undefined guilt onto the old man, Mr. Clutterbuck, telling him that he "ought to be ashamed," but the old man is deaf to the accusation. He goes on imperviously eating his plum tart while an anonymous young woman accepts the blame in his stead: "We are ashamed," she says (48).

Chapter 6

Mrs. Dalloway: *Blackberrying in the Sun*

In *Mrs. Dalloway,* a novel centered on the dinner party as both social and ontological nexus, Woolf seeks, once again, to explicate the relationship between food and sociopolitical power within patriarchy while also considering how food may be used as a medium for self-definition within a patriarchal cultural framework. In this as in her earlier novels, those men who hold the political reins also stand in a privileged position vis-à-vis the food supply while for women access to power, as to food, is only ever vicarious and the physiological, political, and personal sustenance thus received never really nourishing.

Despite—or, perhaps more accurately, because of—the invidious conditionality inherent in her own access to the food supply, Clarissa Dalloway uses food in a deliberate way to shore up an inner disjunction. The social dinner spans for her an existential discrepancy or internal schism. Of all Woolf's characters, she may be said to come closest to an anorexic use of food as a means of mediating between the artificial polarities of spiritual and sensual uneasily cohabiting within her. Beyond the sphere of the individual psyche, the meal touches on the point where the personal meets the communal. The giving of dinner is thus also for Clarissa a means of effecting a secularized communion that connects her essential self on a profound level with other identities (for, as Lady Bruton notes, one feels one is webbed to the friends one has lunched with [123]) and, further, with the ineffable center of existence itself.

Clarissa's passionate engagement with life, her ecstatic moments of heightened consciousness (what Woolf referred to in her own life as "moments of being"), closely resemble the anorexic *"élan vital"* described by

Mara Selvini-Palazzoli as "a passionate though suppressed love of life, a 'sthenic spur' which alone explains . . . [the anorexic woman's] heroic defence mechanisms" (67). This abundant joy is clearly apparent in Clarissa's response to the stimulus of the street, the jaunty swing of whose buses, sandwich boards, brass bands, and barrel organs arouse in her a spontaneous love. Like the anorexic woman, who cannot simply *be* in such a rapturous moment, but needs recourse to an action (starvation) both to engage with and control her response to it, Clarissa is impelled to make some form of consciously imposed connection with this inspirational exterior life: the artistic process of "making it up . . . building it . . . tumbling it . . . creating it . . . afresh" (4). If not assimilated with this kind of deliberation, the rapture of the street carries a dangerous wake for her, for the identification that she makes with the world outside herself, although generally a positive form of universal connectedness (a sense of her self as a mist, extending beyond the bounds of discrete identity to incorporate her past, and people met and unmet [9–10]) may also threaten a complete diffusion in that world (not dissimilar from Fanny Elmer's or Jinny Carslake's).

Consolidation of her dispersed selfhood requires of Clarissa a conscious exertion of will: the pursing of her lips before the mirror in order to form her face into a defined point of identity (40). She feels that the parts of her body are "incompatible" and must be "composed" for the world into an ontological entity which is essentially spurious. Her lack of securely differentiated selfhood and problematic relationship with embodiment bear obvious comparison to the anorexic woman's. Physically slight—"light" like a bird (5), "a narrow pea-stick figure," a "delicate body"—she seems scarcely to exist concretely, an incorporeity that is implicitly connected with the undefined illnesses which require repeated retreat from the world she loves. She experiences her body as superimposed upon, rather than an integral part of, her essential self, speaking of it as something she wears, a vestment put on and taken off like her party dress. She refers to it as "nothing at all" and associates with this bodilessness a sense of herself as invisible, unseen, and unknown (11).[1]

As Ellen Rosenman comments, Clarissa's self-construction encompasses "a need to re-constitute femininity in order to exclude its dangerous emotional and biological contingencies"; for Rosenman, Clarissa's "relationship to sexuality" is thus "an outright problem" (1986, 76). Indeed, as one would expect of a woman at odds with her body, Clarissa's sexual identity is perplexed. Named, apparently, for the eponymous heroine of Richardson's *Clarissa*, who starves herself to death after having lost her virginity by rape, Woolf's protagonist dwells in a present shot through with memories of a sparsely adumbrated anterior sexual duress. In the obvious sense she is asexual, compared to a nun in retreat (celibate), a child (sexually immature) (33), a mermaid (nongenital) (191), and an icicle (frigid) (88). Through the conception and birth of her daughter Elizabeth she has, as she recognizes, preserved a sense of virginity that clings to her like a sheet—perhaps a winding sheet (34). But this aura of sexual coldness characterizes only her heterosexual connections. When she recalls her spontaneous lesbian responses—moments when, she has no doubt, she felt "what men felt" (30)[2]—she is warmed, opened, and spilt. Remembering her love for Sally Seton, she experiences a moment that is both existentially and sexually orgasmic, a sensation like a blush that swells and quivers, endowing the world with a rapturous significance before it splits its skin and pours, alleviating all her pain, and finally softens and withdraws. She names this life-affirming moment of woman-woman female connection with a clitoral/vaginal image: "a match burning in a crocus" (30).[3]

In the cloistration of Clarissa's private order, eroticism is not in fact relinquished but sublimated, processed, and relived in a refined and heightened form. Indeed, this practice of assimilating and sharpening experience is one that she applies to the sensuous and joyous in a general sense. Symptomatic not of a rejection of the sensual, her tendency to exclude and select is the product of a desire to reexperience sensual moments with a kind of reverent intensity. Retreat into the closed and finite environment of her house—like a nun who leaves the world for the comforting familiarity of veils and devotions (31)—enables her to control and thus contain the inrush of pleasurable but potentially overwhelming influences from the world outside, for her love of life is not a Falstaffian all-embrace but is subject to an ordering sensibility that might be seen as essentially artistic.

Jane Marcus suggests that a source for Clarissa's name may be an order of nuns known as the Clarissans who, like Woolf and her protagonist, were married but lived celibately with their husbands. A history of sisterhoods written by Woolf's aunt, Caroline Emilia Stephen, discusses the Clarissans (Marcus, 1984, 10). As Marcus observes, "Female heterosexuality is most often represented in Woolf's fiction as victimization or colonization. Those women who accept the ideology of female submission in patriarchal marriage are silently condemned." Marcus argues that for Woolf sexual abstinence constituted, on the contrary, a form of female stronghold within the patriarchal system, that she understood that "Chastity is power. Chastity is liberty" (1987, 77). "Celibacy," in the particular sense of abstention from *heterosexual* relations, enables women in Woolf's novels, Marcus contends, to evade the circumscriptive social structures and cultural roles evolved for them by patriarchy, thereby gaining a measure of independence and a sense of authentic identity.

Clarissa's chastity within marriage may, however, be more an accommodation than a joyful adoption of lesbian separatism—she remains isolated from the women who elicit her impassioned existential and sexual response. Nevertheless, chastity functions effectively for her as a safeguard against the ontological incursion that poses a particular threat to her fragile sense of selfhood. Firm boundaries within marriage are, she thinks, essential; there must be "independence" between two people who share the same house (8). Her marriage to Richard is sustainable, she realizes, just because he allows her this form of separation which is indispensable to "dignity" and "self-respect" (131). Marriage to Peter Walsh, on the other hand, would have been intolerable because of the complete, intrusive mutuality that he would have demanded, for with him "everything had to be shared; everything had to be gone into" (8). "Gone into" in this context has a specifically sexual connotation, suggesting that, unlike Richard, Peter would not have tolerated celibacy as an ontological bulwark.

And yet while Clarissa in one sense wills the distance between herself and Richard, deriving an essential personal strength from it, at the same time she experiences the mutual separation as imposed upon her against her wishes. It is *Richard* who (reminiscent of Leonard Woolf) daily compels her to retire into the seclusion of the bedroom for one hour after lunch, and will do so until the day he dies (131). It is Richard who *insists* that she *must* sleep without disturbance, in other words, that she must abandon the marital bed. For really she prefers to read alone, "He *knew* it" (34, my italics). If Peter would have denied Clarissa her desire for personal space, Richard, albeit perhaps unwittingly, turns it back upon her, instituting a dependent-caretaker relationship that effectively infantilizes his wife and mitigates against real communication. Clarissa complies with his wishes because they are just that, and because she reads tenderness in his bringing the pillow—but not without a silent undertow of grief; simultaneously she feels, for a reason that she cannot define, "desperately unhappy." The respectful distance between husband and wife that she describes is yawningly wide—"a gulf," she terms it, suggesting a painful isolation (132).

Given her evident lesbian orientation, it is clear that no relationship with a man, however much genuine space it allowed her, could be truly satisfying for Clarissa; her real alienation runs deeper than the gorge that divides her from Richard. Her ecstatic asceticism appears to be in part an attempt to evade that knowledge, and it carries a consequent corollary of sadness and loss. In the midst of her retreat, she feels with regret the emotional deprivation that her sequestration involves; there is "an emptiness about the heart of life," she thinks. The emptiness centers on her attic bedroom, where she lies alone at night reading the memoirs of Baron Marbot, which tell a stringently patriarchal story of brutal hardships, cold, hunger, and death.[4] Her lonely bed, with its shroudlike sheets stretched tight and white in a wide clean band, becomes a coffin. "Narrower and narrower would her bed be,"

Woolf tells us (33–34), describing an increasing diminution and constriction suggestive of that enacted in the anorexic body. Repeatedly throughout Clarissa's day the (mock) funeral dirge for Shakespeare's Imogen, "Fear no more the heat o' the sun," is intoned, suggesting that, like the heroine of *Cymbeline,* Clarissa experiences a living death.

Writing retrospectively of her period of anorexia, Sheila MacLeod sees it as just such a time of death in life, of exile in the cold, of emotional alienation and glacial virginity impermeable to natural heat and light. She speaks of herself as a "pale virgin shrouded in snow . . . cold, untouched and untouchable, and in my grave." Although she wished increasingly to be "warm . . . touched by the sun," she was unable to "arise from the grave," to leave behind the "half-life" in which she had become "imprisoned" for a place in the sun (118). For Clarissa the means of arising from her own grave, of putting off her chilly virginity and joining with life, is the creation of the dinner party: the spark that she will "kindle and illuminate" (5). Meditating in her tomblike room, she defines her problem with wholehearted participation as a form of personal frigidity; what she lacks, she thinks, is a kind of warmness that melts the cold superficies of human life enabling molten contact. Her "failure" of Richard—at Cliveden, at Constantinople, and repeatedly thereafter (34)—is, as Lucio Ruotolo points out, sexual, but more than that, involves "the ability to move out of herself into the existence of others' (111). At her party, however, in the arc of her own artificial light, her hard outer casing expands and softens, enabling connection with those around her; she is touched with tenderness; her rigidity is "warmed through," and she is delivered into human community (191).

Given the evident ontological and artistic dimensions of her party-giving, it seems myopic to condemn Clarissa, as many writers have done,[5] as a superficial society hostess. On the contrary, as Rosenman explains, through her "Woolf redeems the hostess from the realms of the trivial" (1986, 92). Clarissa's party is a means to human synthesis, dissolving barriers and creating community—a state of connectedness which is fundamental to both individual psychic and social well-being. As a creative act it is on a par with any other artistic endeavor (writing or playing the piano, Clarissa herself suggests), involving the skillful molding of amorphous human life into a pattern of meaningful harmony. She brings individual human lives together like threads in a tapestry, her purpose "to combine; to create." This celebratory artistic act, this "offering" for its own sake, is not, Woolf makes clear, one that anyone might effect. To give a dinner party that takes wing requires a form of genius. Acknowledging that she cannot do anything else remotely remarkable, Clarissa insists that party-giving is a challenging and essential human activity for which she is endowed with a special talent; it is "her gift," she says (134).

Clarissa anticipates incomprehension and criticism from other characters of her absorption in such an apparently pointless activity as entertaining—Peter's misapprehension that she is "a snob," or Richard's that she is "foolish" and "childish" to enjoy "excitement"—censure that she deeply resents. Both men criticize her, she thinks, "unfairly . . . unjustly," and both entirely misunderstand her motivation; in fact, she gives her dinner parties simply because she loves life. Although allowing Clarissa a certain "genius" in what she does (84), Hugh Whitbread disparages the field of her endeavor as silly and banal; he thinks her parties are a waste of time and a detriment to her intellect (86) and that she gives them in order to further Richard's career—a notion laughable to Clarissa, for whom the social dinner is a self-fulfilling creation, an end in itself. She realizes, however, that men are incapable of understanding such an essentially motiveless inspiration, reflecting that she cannot imagine Peter or Richard bothering to give a party simply for the sake of it (133).

It is in fact Hugh himself who uses Clarissa's party as a professional stepladder, fawning upon her guest, the prime minister (189). Clarissa is gratified by the prime minister's attendance but less because it redounds upon her own or Richard's social or professional status than because of its symbolic significance for her work of art. The presence within the walls of her own female-identified house of the representative of what is in some senses its masculine counterpart, the House of Commons, functions, albeit superficially, as a mutual rapprochement or reciprocal acknowledgment between the two, patriarchally separated, houses. It thus brings if not a radical integration or step toward gender-political revolution at least a kind of formal balance and aesthetic unity to present, lived reality.

To those at work in the female heartland of the house, the kitchen, the attendance of the figurehead of the male establishment is unimpressive, indeed totally irrelevant. In the basement with its blazing fire and glaring electric lights, the cook, Mrs. Walker, appears to be engaged in some great chthonic generative process. Making dinner is a task involving sweat and hard physical graft. She labors with pots and pans, lemons and basins, which, no matter how furiously the servants wash up in the scullery, continue to proliferate, overflowing the table and covering the chairs. Meanwhile the logistics of setting the table, getting the salmon upstairs on time, and supervising the pudding demand her attention, so that, to her, one prime minister or six is unremarkable (181).

Like Clarissa, Mrs. Walker is an artist, with her own creative concerns and aims within the larger pattern of Clarissa's artistic vision. As anyone creating art, she grapples with familiar weaknesses (getting nervous about the pudding and leaving the fish to Jenny, who underdoes it) (181). Her role is a pivotal one, for she is the coordinator and manager of the kitchen, an exacting responsibility requiring considerable expertise. Other women recognize her technical virtuosity: Was the entrée really made at home? a lady asks at dinner (181–182). If the prime minister crowns the party and gilds it with his golden lace, Mrs. Walker is the juggler and the mythic machine (Woolf's imagery suggests both) who works the stuff of the occasion, spinning plates round and round and pushing dampers in and out.

While Mrs. Walker's skills are indispensable to the creation of the dinner party, Clarissa is not, as a correlative, a class-privileged parasite riding on the back of an occasion really created by the working-class woman. She remains the driving force behind the party as a whole, conceiving it, inviting the guests, overseeing, deciding the menu, choosing the flowers, setting it all in motion, and shining in her mermaid dress. Belonging to the spangled glamour of upstairs, she recognizes the interdependency of her own creation and that of the unseen Mrs. Walker, remaining close to the basement underground. Indeed, she is essentially connected to this female territory in a way that she never is to the male world that Richard inhabits. She is in constant communication with the downstairs women; Mrs. Walker anticipates how, on the morning after, they will go over each dish, appraising. She inspires the respect and affection of the servants, her concern for the success of the dinner uniting her with them across class divides in a uniquely female bond. The message of love that she always sends Mrs. Walker as the ladies go up to dinner is no mere formula courtesy but an expression of genuine affection and sorority in a common work (181).

Through the medium of the party, Clarissa is able to recontact a body which, like the patriarchal kitchen, has been split off and relegated to a generally invisible downstairs. The soul-life that takes flight in the elevated regions of dining and drawing rooms (when the yellow curtain with its birds-of-paradise blows out and Ralph Lyon carries on talking as he beats it back [186]) remains for her inevitably connected with the material proliferation of culinary paraphernalia and ingredients in the kitchen below. The animation of the heavenly birds cannot be brought about without the underpinning of the basement; spiritual joy requires inspired food, and inspired food demands the body's labor. Often seeking identification with the soul through retreat and retraction, Clarissa is saved from corrosive asceticism by her urgent desire for the party, the creation of which compels her to recognize the essential holism of body and spirit, effecting in herself at least a temporary unity.

As a social meal, Clarissa's dinner is counterposed by Lady Bruton's lunch. Whereas Clarissa's occasion is a fundamentally female product, Lady Bruton's has a masculine ethos that reflects the gender orientation of her personality. Described as "strong . . . martial . . . [and] well nourished," a woman who says what she thinks and has scant ability to introspect (119), she is seen in patriarchal terms as a man *manqué*. As her forename, Millicent, suggests, her stance in life is militant (as opposed to Clarissa's tendency toward defensive embattlement), checked only by rigid cultural notions of gender-appropriate behavior. She is by nature a Boudica who, in another time, might have led armies and judiciously ruled her tribe, but who, in patriarchy, is condemned to a life of subordination. For Lady Bruton, England is "this isle of *men*" (198, my italics)—a vision that expresses both her relative estimation of the sexes and her own exclusion from the male-designated pursuits she relishes. Despite a genuinely felt bond of common femality, she is perceived as dismissive of women, resentful of their proclivity for obstructing their husbands' careers with inconvenient illnesses. When, apparently offhandedly, she asks after the wives of those men who surround her, her concern is not convincing; Clarissa is sure that Lady Bruton does not like her (115). However, Lady Bruton is equally disparaging of her own femality in the male-defined and dominated fields in which she wishes to excel. She defers to a kind of inalienable male knowledge of how things should be put, what should be said, and how the universe is ordered. These things, she thinks, women cannot know, and she cedes her right to pass judgment upon men for this reason (120).

Although Clarissa and Lady Bruton are generally "indifferent" verging on "hostile," Clarissa is hurt by her exclusion from the eminent lady's luncheon party (to which Richard, of course, has been invited), for Millicent Bruton's lunches are reputed, she thinks, to be "extraordinarily amusing" (32). Although, on a superficial level, it seems unlikely that the masculine party-political occasion would amuse the mythopoeically oriented and woman-centered Clarissa extraordinarily, in some deep place exclusion from it awakens in her neither disappointment at a good time lost nor resentment of a social snub but a genuine sorrow for the loss of a sphere of (male-designated) experience. As she retreats to her room she feels the parameters of her life contracting around her like her solitary single bed.

Whereas Clarissa's aim as a party-giver is to expand and include, to synthesize the apparently disparate (thus she invites Lady Bruton and the prime minister to her own party), Lady Bruton's principles as a hostess are ones of selection and partiality. Being, it is said, more concerned with "politics than people," a woman who talks "like a man" (115–116), she eschews the female-identified interest in the gathering together of multifarious lives. Her party is not intended to serve social or aesthetic but political purposes. Nor is the, albeit always excellent, quality of the food important to Lady Bruton, except in as much as it is a lure. Hugh and Richard (her own private Cabinet) are invited to eat at her table, she admits, for a reason: to draft a letter to the *Times*, thus helping her out of a political difficulty (114). They are, Peter thinks, her "toadies," working for a payment of lunch (190).

To the men of political influence who are Lady Bruton's guests, the production of a fine lunch is a sort of Pagan miracle conjured up not by hired servants but by priestesses of some esoteric mystery, women who tend not a hearth but a fire magically colored, "undomestic," giving rise to "jocund visions." Unlike the lady who appreciates the skill involved in the preparation of Mrs. Walker's entrée, such men are the willing dupes of an "illusion" (laughable to a woman) about such a lunch: first that no one pays for all this luxury, and second that the table lays itself with silver and glass, mats and saucers of fruit, that without the aid of human labor chickens appear, plucked and headless, floating in casserole dishes, that by sorcery the turbot is baked and filmed with brown cream (114).

The miracle of lunch arouses in Hugh Whitbread, however, a sense not of divine ecstasy but of gluttonous delight (watching him eat, Milly Brush thinks he is one of the greediest men she has ever known [116]) and of satisfaction with his own position in the world. As he rests his fork he feels complacently secure in his own standing (114–115). His greed for food is inseparable from his voracity for the rich taste of worldly success, for the accolades of the establishment and the invitations of the people who matter. For him, Lady Bruton's meal is a mark of his gathering prestige, a homage which, as he dives into the casserole, he is "eager to pay to himself" (116). Cloying generosity, social status, and food inform Peter's impression of Hugh. He thinks of him talking graciously to old ladies about the past, recalling with them (punning) "trifles" and urbanely complimenting the homemade cake, although, as his bearing makes clear, he is in a social position to eat the best cake with duchesses every day of the year—and indeed, Peter thinks, observing Hugh's swelling body, probably does (190).[6]

The name "Whitbread" suggests the white bread which, historically, was a luxury eaten only by the affluent—a group to which Hugh, the archetypical public school product (189), belongs. "Afloat on the *cream* of society" (112, my italics), his prestige is reflected in his girth—Lady Bruton notices that he is getting fat (118). Encountering him, Clarissa always feels herself "skimpy" (6), a recognition not only of her relative physical slightness but also of her smallness in terms of worldly influence; she lacks his sociopolitical clout. Moneyed, respected, powerful, he is a man of substance both literally and metaphorically. In his own mind, indeed, his social status is inextricably entwined with his physical bulk. From the apex of his large and magnificent body, he beholds the world "from a certain eminence," and yet realizes self-importantly the "obligations" attendant upon a man of his "size, wealth, health" (113).

As Woolf points out in *A Room of One's Own,* it is the function of women in patriarchal societies to diminish themselves in order that their husbands, fathers, and sons may see themselves reflected large (37). In *Mrs. Dalloway,*

Evelyn Whitbread has practically ceded her own existence in the subliminal desire, apparently, to magnify the image of Hugh. Disempowered to the point of invisibility, she is, Peter Walsh reflects, "obscure" and "mouse-like," a person practically "negligible" (81). Her ill health (an undefined, invisible sickness) and consequent further withdrawal from the world appear to have increased in direct proportion to Hugh's social and physical burgeoning—a fact that his manner of indicating her illness, by a "pout or swell" of his own remarkably plump, masculine, and extremely well-dressed body, serves to emphasize (6).

The (unnamed) wife of the eminent Harley Street physician, Sir William Bradshaw, has likewise declined in marriage while her husband's status has ascended. In an inversion of Evelyn's apparent physical diminution, however, Lady Bradshaw has grown fat in proportion to the degree that she has knuckled under. Her previous single life is characterized by an image of independence: herself catching salmon "freely," but since marrying she has gone under; apt to serve her husband's "craving" for "dominion" and "power," she has retreated: "cramped, squeezed, pared, pruned, . . . [drawn] back, peeped through" (110). No longer a hunter, she has become a prey to her rapacious spouse, just like his patients when he swoops and devours (112). She is herself a victim of his "conversion" which "feasts . . . on the human will," to which she has surrendered with the expected feminine grace—sweet smiles and swift submission. Her essential self has been consumed. She is reduced to the role of social and professional promoter of her husband, whose reputation she feeds with Harley Street dinner parties of eight or nine courses (110). No wonder she regrets her stoutness (104), for it is symptomatic not of nourishment but of subsumation by years of such extensive meals. Indeed, the charge that Hugh levels at Clarissa—that she gives her parties to advance her husband's career—properly describes Lady Bradshaw's entertaining, which, devoid of the personally fulfilling creativity that inspires Clarissa's party-giving and feeds her soul, is a facet of complete self-effacement.

Food and feeding are also significant to Bradshaw's less distinguished colleague, Dr. Holmes, a big man who sets great store by his size. To Holmes, a hefty weight is a mark of the mental stability that he likes to believe he exemplifies. Big, healthily complexioned, and good-looking, he dismisses the headaches, insomnia, dreams, and fears of his patients as *merely* nervous symptoms. He regards loss of weight as a dangerous concession to the nebulous territory of the unconscious, placing his faith in porridge as a specific to guard against this desperate fate. Like Bradshaw, he expects his wife to ensure that this important weight is sustained; if he finds himself so much as half a pound below 11 stone 6 pounds (160 pounds), he asks his wife for a second bowl of porridge at breakfast (100).

To the shellshocked Septimus Warren Smith, Holmes eating his nutritious porridge exemplifies what he sees as the revolting physicality of human nature (154). Centering as it does around his disgust at and horror of "the sordidity of the mouth and belly" (97), Septimus's distress bears obvious comparison to the anorexic woman's and derives from the intensest phases of Woolf's own anorexic experiences. Like Woolf, Septimus is offered as "treatment" isolation (without friends, books, or communication with the outside world), bedrest, and food, until after six months his 7 stone 6 pounds (104 pounds) are transformed into 12 stone (168 pounds) (89).[7] This is a "cure" which naturally succeeds only in increasing his sense of revulsion and alienation from his body, driving him ultimately to the suicide that Woolf also attempted and finally committed impelled by such unhelpful medical interventions.

Woolf's own bitter experience informs the passion with which *Mrs. Dalloway*'s narrative voice denounces the fictional doctors.[8] She herself explicitly connected her sense of personal outrage with that she constructed for the novel, describing the intensity of feeling that re-creating her own distress evoked. Much more than the "illness" itself, it was the duress imposed upon her as a result of it that aroused her undying fury. "You can't think what a raging furnace it still is to me," she wrote, "madness and doctors and being forced" (*L 3,* 180). " 'Must', 'must', why 'must'?" Septimus asks. What authority, he demands, does Bradshaw have over him, what right to order him, "must"? He feels crushed by the doctors' tyranny of weight, "laden" with their healthy bodies that never fall short of 11 stone 6 pounds (160 pounds) (161).

Septimus's "treatment" also shadows that imposed upon Clarissa as a result of her unspecified illnesses. Whereas, however, his response to compulsory bedrest is one of rage, horror, and despair, Clarissa experiences not only an undertow of anger but also a component of ecstasy in what is—importantly—a partially self-willed retreat. She demonstrates the redeeming ability to construct for herself an authentic ontological space, an asylum, that saves her from the total disintegration that besets Septimus. She shares his distressed aversion to the physical and the biological but is ultimately able to reunite body with self through a creative act, her party. For Woolf, Septimus embodies Clarissa's narrowly averted "mad" identity.[9] Like her, he responds intensely to life, but, unlike her, he possesses no effective means of assimilating the stimulus of the ecstatic; "real things" are "too exciting," he thinks; he must proceed with caution (155).

As Shirley Panken notes, "Both Clarissa and Septimus evidence a mystical enmeshing with the universe" (119), but the agglomeration of her mistily diffused self that Clarissa always (if only with difficulty) achieves is impossible for Septimus. The experience of such universal interconnection is for him not one of rapturous communion but of painful invasion by the environment. He feels his body, like the war corpse (which in a sense it is), "macerated" to the very "nerve fibres," "spread like a veil upon a rock." As he lies, it seems, very high up on a bony ridge of the Earth, the ground seems to thrill underneath him, while red flowers, a grisly emblem of the World War I dead, grow through his body, their leaves rustling next to his head (74–75).[10]

Again like Clarissa, Septimus is alienated within a heterosexual marriage that cannot touch him as his remembered homosexual love for Evans does. War has taken Evans violently from him, and there is no sanctified space in which to mourn this kind of loss. He derives no sustenance from the warmth and earthiness of his wife, Rezia, in whom he had thought to find a refuge from his grief, because to him heterosexual love appears "repulsive," heterosexual sex "filth" (97). Married to Rezia, his grief for his budding love for Evans is only compounded by guilt at his "failure"—like Clarissa's "failure" of Richard—sexually to love his wife.

Rezia herself remembers with nostalgia the sunny, flowering Italy where she was born—a country peopled by women creatively occupied in making hats (an activity that parallels Clarissa's sewing). There she felt a Ceres-like connection with the corn, with nature, and with the energy of growth. She dreams of a time when she ran through cornfields and seems to hear rain falling, the whispering of dry corn, and the sea like a caress (165). Her severed connection with burgeoning fertility echoes Clarissa's, for she too, Peter remembers, walked through stubble fields before marriage, in her lesbian past (169), reminding him now of harvests (168). Just as Clarissa loves Richard after a fashion but is aware that marriage to him has killed something vital in her, Rezia, loving Septimus, sees him as the despoiler of her field, as the hawk or crow that destroys the crops (163), for by denying her a child he has, she feels, destroyed her own harvest. Removed from a vibrant and fertile land, bound to a man who cannot love her physically, and estranged from the natural cycle of life, she has become so thin that her wedding ring slips off her finger (25).

Clarissa's and Rezia's stories of estrangement from an abundantly life-giving female principle are part of a larger picture of the destruction of womanly creativity and fruitfulness by bellicose masculine forces. As later in *Between the Acts,* in *Mrs. Dalloway* contemporary war is bireferential, indicating both a modern conflict and an ancient, pre-androhistorical struggle in which gynecentrism was replaced by patriarchy. In London the icon of the Roman corn goddess, Ceres (who once presided over Rezia's Italian fields), has been smashed and symbolically raped by the "prying and insidious . . . fingers of the European War."[11] The same war has "ploughed" into the flower bed where the plaster cast of Ceres once stood, the agricultural image of fructifying, female-patronized activity designating ironically the brutally destructive act. In Muswell Hill, the modern counterpart of the Corn Goddess as giver of food, Mr. Brewer's cook (now, in modern patriarchy, identified only by the name of her male employer) has also been shattered by the war, which has ruined her nerves (94).

The bodily alienation which (in differing degree) Clarissa and Septimus experience is also felt by Doris Kilman. Whereas, however, Clarissa and Septimus largely succeed in identifying against what they experience as the unpleasant biological aspects of embodiment, Miss Kilman (who loathes the body with an anorexic fervor) is dogged by an inescapable corporeality. She is the body salient, irrepressible, perspiring (12) and swelling (143), the "unlovable body which people could not bear to see" (141). With her reiterated cry, "It is the flesh," she is driven by the always unmet imperative of subordinating this detested body. She chastises herself for not having "mastered the flesh," for, she tells herself, it is "the flesh she must control." Although she despises Clarissa for what she regards as her superficiality, at the same time she envies with intensity her apparent evasion of the binding flesh. In the presence of this otherworldly woman she feels her body "ugly, clumsy," her self full of reinvigorated "fleshly desires," and she owns that it distresses her to appear as she does beside the thin and elegant Clarissa (140–141).

Doris Kilman's desire to subordinate the flesh is bolstered by her faith in a Christianity that dichotomizes body and soul, castigating the one and valorizing the other. She seeks in the "bodiless" light of Westminster Abbey to become, as she transiently but deceptively feels, "a soul cut out of immaterial substance; not a woman, a soul" (147). However, patriarchal religion brings her only the ghost of the genuine spiritual joy, the "divine vitality" (7) experienced by the atheistic Clarissa (not for a second does she believe in God, she says [31]) in her ecstatic "moment." She longs for some missionary function that will enable her to deprive her body for a higher cause; she would, she thinks, do anything for Russia, or starve herself for Austria (12). Weighed down by a monumental sense of grievance, she longs to be united with a people full of righteous indignation, to bear with them a legitimate political grudge against a world that has, she believes, rejected her (141).

But the flip side of such self-loathing asceticism is physical insatiability. Clarissa sees Doris Kilman in vampiric imagery (recalling the doctors, Holmes and Bradshaw) as among the "spectres who stand astride us and suck up half our life-blood, dominators and tyrants" (13). She is the appetite which will, Clarissa fears jealously, consume her daughter Elizabeth, for whom Miss Kilman displays a covetous passion that appears the antithesis of the "completely disinterested" love between Clarissa and Sally Seton at Elizabeth's age, a love that Clarissa remembers as characterized by "purity" and "integrity" (37). Reflecting a suppressed appetite both for nice food and for (homo)sexual love (the unspeakable manifestation of the unmortifiable flesh), the devouring character of Miss Kilman's affection is described by her consumption of the chocolate eclair at tea with Elizabeth, an intrinsically innocuous act which, thus accomplished, becomes disturbingly lubricious (144).[12]

Ostensibly predatory, Miss Kilman's unappealing tendency to possess and consume stems from a real emotional neediness. She seeks in Elizabeth the loveliness and lovableness that she cannot find in herself, and which, consequently, no one else sees in her either. Her hand on the table pulsates with anguish at the thought of parting from the aloof young woman, whom, she thinks, she genuinely loves, but for whom her unrequited passion in fact acts to enforce rather than alleviate her feelings of emotional/sexual deprivation and of personal inadequacy. She uses food to comfort herself for the isolating absence of love, having come to feel, despite her ascetic aspirations, that "food was all that she lived for" (141).[13] Whereas the novel's other cake-eater, Hugh Whitbread, eats cake because he was born to eat cake, Doris Kilman eats cake to make up for all the sweet things that have been denied her. This is something that Elizabeth, from her position of personal advantage and social privilege, cannot understand. She wonders whether Miss Kilman is hungry, observing how her eyes become fixated upon the sugared cakes on the next table. When a child takes the cake that Miss Kilman has been staring at, she wonders, could she really mind? Miss Kilman, however, emphatically does mind; she desires the cake because it represents precisely what she has never had: the pink, the pretty, and the delicate. Now that even this surrogate satisfaction is denied her, she seethes with resentment. Eating is the only pleasure that remains to her, she thinks; that she should be thwarted in even this is unendurable (142).

As a German by ancestry and association (she thinks she has only ever been happy in Germany), Doris Kilman is in an ambivalent position within *Mrs. Dalloway*.[14] In the context of the war that forms a backdrop to the novel, her tendency to invade and tyrannize is on one level implicitly linked to her German identity. In another sense, however, she is, like Septimus, a victim of this war, for she has been turned out of her post at Miss Dolby's school because, having German friends, she refuses to pretend that all Germans are evil. Her integrity (she is unable to lie [135]), and her loyalty to human beings as individuals rather than pawns in the game of international warfare is laudable, and has cost her much, apparently putting an end to her only chance in life. Richard believes that she is really gifted in history (12), but she is prey to practical circumstances beyond her control. If she offends Clarissa's sensibilities with her mackintosh, she has "her reasons," and they are valid ones: The coat is cheap and she is degradingly poor; she is past an age where women are deemed to be attractive or sexual within patriarchy; and she dresses for practicality, not elegance (135).

Even Clarissa has to admit that Miss Kilman has suffered bad treatment (12). Indeed (in an implicit acknowledgment of their shared lesbianism) she admits that "with another throw of the dice, had the black been uppermost and not the white, she would have loved Miss Kilman!" (12–13)—an awareness which is tantamount to, as Susan Squier puts it, "the even more important recognition that with another throw of the dice she would have *been* Mrs. Kilman" (98). She is aware that the poorer, uglier woman functions for her as a scapegoat or shadow-side, the repository of fears and aversions that she harbors in relation to herself. She admits it is not the real Miss Kilman that she hates but an "idea of her," which probably encompasses much that is "not Miss Kilman" (12–13). Contemplating this other woman, she confronts a self that she feels she must at all costs continue to control—as Miss Kilman has not succeeded in controlling it—a self in which the body (and perhaps with it the possibility of lesbian love in the present) is terrifyingly predominant.

In her great love, Sally Seton, Clarissa finds an acceptable model of body and spirit harmoniously united, of the life of the body fully lived without compromise to the life of the soul. Sally is completely unashamed of her body, running along the passage naked when she forgets her sponge (37). She is instinctively in touch with and guiltlessly responsive to her body's appetites: She steals a chicken from the larder in the night because she is hungry (199). Indeed, she is the only character in the novel who eats explicitly and simply for the satisfaction of hunger (as opposed, for example, to Hugh Whitbread, who eats to bolster his status; Holmes, who eats to stave off insanity; or Doris Kilman, who eats to compensate for unmet emotional needs). She eludes, significantly, eating in its structured (and not necessarily hunger-related) forms, making her first appearance at Bourton *after* dinner. Later she attempts to introduce a female life and spontaneity into the brittle formality of such meals, routing the army of stiff little phallic vases from the table and setting all sorts of novel combinations of flowers swimming in saucers in their stead (36).

Sally's creative "gift," her "power" is, Clarissa thinks, "amazing" (31). She herself lacks this revolutionary kind of artistic ability, cannot be, as Sally can, "completely reckless," cannot, as Sally does, "shock people" (37). She requires a traditional construct—the formal dinner-party—as a framework for her own creativity. Nor can she approach Sally's natural ease in her body. Through her own creative endeavor, however, she is able to make some form of synthesis of spirit and body. In the last line of the novel, as her party draws to a close, she is at last totally unified, simply, effortlessly present: "For there she was." Beyond the personal, she has also effected a social synthesis, a moment of community, of concord, of human solidarity. In her party she has built a multidimensional bridge—between past and present, man and woman, private self and external life. Above all, perhaps, she has succeeded in communicating her own sense of the joyous in life. Even Peter, generally so cynical about Clarissa's parties, finds himself, as the evening wears on, sharing in her particular piquant sense of being. What is the source of his sense of terror, ecstasy, excitement? he asks himself, and serendipitously Clarissa herself appears. "It is Clarissa," he realizes (213).

Chapter 7

To the Lighthouse:
An Instinct Like Artichokes for the Sun

To the Lighthouse, as several writers have noted, examines a daughter's ambivalence in relation to mothering as it occurs within a patriarchal framework. Maria DiBattista writes, "Woolf's narrative honors the life-sustaining role of the mother as the foundation of social life; yet it also acknowledges that dependence on the mother is a real threat to the growth and transformation of unreflecting life into autonomous consciousness" (76). And Jane Lilienfeld points out that, "It is Virginia Woolf's genius to have re-created the process that a woman who wishes not to be the archetypal mother and wife must go through in order to separate herself from her almost overwhelming urge to fuse herself with such a mother" (347). Perhaps for no daughter is this push-me-pull-you relationship more seductive and more fraught than for the anorexic woman, who may both long for symbiosis with her mother and yet fear subsumation by her. As psychodynamic art therapist Mary Levens puts it, "the [anorexic woman's] desire to re-merge, to fuse with the mother . . . carries with it the fear of being engulfed, swallowed up, annihilated" (27).

For the daughter who has an involved and accessible second parent, the navigation of this dilemma may be facilitated. Such a third party may mediate her relationship with her mother and provide a bridge to the outside world. This, Woolf suggests, is a useful role of the father in traditional patriarchal families. When, however, as in *To the Lighthouse,* fathering is confusing and semidetached, movement outwards into secure independence—the voyage to the lighthouse—becomes a less certain journey. For Cam, her father is fundamentally elusive. She sees him like a bird, which, when she tries to catch it, flies off and settles on a distant stump (220). Like many anorexic women's fathers, he is for her a loving tyrant who evokes an ambivalent response. She acknowledges that he attracts her more than anybody, that his hands and feet, his voice, his oddity, his passion, and even his temper are beautiful to her, that he is "lovable" and "wise" (206). And yet she feels at the same time pitted against his overbearing authority (178), burdened by a terrible sense of grievance against him (180), and unable to forgive the blindness and tyranny that have "poisoned her childhood" so that she wakes from dreams "trembling with rage" as she recalls his orders and his insolence (185).[1]

To the Lighthouse is oriented around two kinds of meal, mother's and father's: Boeuf en Daube dinner and fishing-boat lunch. Ultimately, the novel suggests, the daughter must integrate both maternal and paternal meal if she is to achieve full selfhood. The mother's dinner provides a model of food as sensually, aesthetically, and emotionally gratifying, as redolent with the qualities necessary for living and working richly. However, it carries a lethal undertow, for the mother's imperative is fidelity to the patriarchal norms and forms that her own life has served. The completeness of her achievement in terms of personal satisfaction and creative living is deceptive. The daughter who wholly and solely identifies herself through the mother's meal accepts a series of self-limiting constraints: that she become a wife/mother before she is an individual, a nurturer before she is an artist, a feeder before she is an eater. Ultimately she risks being consumed by the mother's meal rather than fed by it.

The father's meal offers a model in which work is given primacy—over personal physical pleasure, over the emotional needs and sensitivities of others, over social life and social obligation—a model in which one eats in order to work, and works with single-minded focus, detachment, and integrity, eliminating all that is perceived as non-essential to one's goal. In a sense, such a model has much to offer the potential female artist, who often needs to discover a means of preserving personal space for creativity against those forces that would erode it. Yet in paring away what is perceived as extrinsic, the father's model risks missing the stuff of life itself. Purged of superfluous sensuality, existence becomes dry, juiceless, and thus ultimately, self-defeatingly, void of the inspirational. A life sustained on bread and cheese may produce only a bread-and-cheese creativity. Severed from relational components—the connectivity without which we are the last wo/man aboard a sinking ship—work becomes one-dimensional, delimited by the fact that it encompasses only a part of life, a philosophy that sticks at Q.

In To the Lighthouse, Woolf refracts into a spectrum of identities the person of the daughter who must assimilate the parental figures and through this process find herself. Prue Ramsay apparently accommodates herself almost totally to the mother's model and is extinguished in the process, dying young in childbirth. The fate of Rose Ramsay, the potential artist who creates the arrangement of fruit, is unknown. Cam Ramsay sails ultimately with her father and experiences a sense of positive connection with him—perhaps she will succeed in assimilating both maternal and paternal in a self-nourishing way. It is Lily Briscoe, whose position within the novel is in many senses that of figurative daughter, who ultimately makes a creative resolution of her relationship with father and mother figures, carving out a sense of artistic identity that partakes of the qualities of both "parents." In naming Lily after the flower that symbolizes virginity, Woolf links her directly with her own name: Virginia, the virgin. Whereas the Ramsays' actual daughters experience their parents from within the grip of a child's immediate need, Lily views Mr. and Mrs. Ramsay and her emotions toward them as parental figures from the perspective of an adult and an artist. She is in a sense the voice of the mature Virginia Woolf.

Lily describes herself as "hand to mouth" in comparison with Mrs. Ramsay (57), a statement that defines her against the older woman and the model of femininity she embodies, and with the men in the novel—Mr. Ramsay, Charles Tansley, William Bankes—for whom food is functional, subordinate to work. "Hand to mouth" signals self-sufficiency and freedom from old circumscriptive female roles and yet at the same time carries a paradoxical message, for the kind of eating it describes—immediately gratifying, unsocialized, essentially egotistic—is infantile, identifying a part of Lily that is a small child in need of caretaking. Indeed, she is babylike in appearance, having "little Chinese eyes" and a "puckered up face" (21). This deep and apparently contradictory need both for self-fulfilling freedom and for mothering is one that is central to anorexia.[2] For Lily, as for many anorexic women, the challenge of resolving these polarized needs, although highly fraught, ultimately becomes a source of transcending creative energy.

In a sense, Lily's unspoken dialogue with Mrs. Ramsay is not dissimilar from Mr. Ramsay's, containing both the plea *Feed me!* and the protest *Let me be!* (she *likes* to be alone, she thinks; she likes to be herself, and is not suited to marriage [56]). In qualitative terms, however, it is very different. Whereas Mr. Ramsay's demand for food is unbattened and unboundaried, and his protest a wail, Lily's hunger is concealed and contained—for concealment and containment are expected of women's needs and desires. In a practical sense too, whereas both mothering and freedom are available to Mr. Ramsay (if in a tendentious relationship), Lily, as a woman, is expected to put a lid on her own feelings of maternal deprivation and herself become a nurturer. Any sense of independence will be for her hard won and will entail large sacrifices. Ultimately, however, there is a sense of movement in Lily's life where, at a point, Mr. Ramsay's becomes struck in stone. Whereas his response to the dilemma he finds himself in is to go on bewailing his need for mothering and bemoaning the fact that he is never alone, she embraces the nexus of contradictions and (in this particular sociocultural context) unfulfillable desires within her, interacts with it, and makes it the stuff of her art. Thus, while Mr. Ramsay remains at Q both personally and philosophically, Lily makes an artistic breakthrough and finds a deeper level of self-knowing and understanding in her own being.

The meal table is the locus of Mrs. Ramsay's power. "Formidable" in appearance, around it she coerces her daughters into fidelity to the old model of femininity, and around it too the daughters mutely resist, harboring unutterable questions. Here eating becomes for them part of a process of suppression, for with their mother's food the girls are also compelled to ingest her creed—marry and nurture—to swallow rather than speak their dissent. Only silently, as they look up from their plates, can they frame the heretical notion of a different, freer life than their mother's, in which they are not the eternal servants and nurturers of men (10).[3]

For Lily too, a seat at the table entails a constraint to fulfill the conventional responsibilities of womanhood. Under the eye of Mrs. Ramsay she feels compelled to go to the aid of Charles Tansley, to abide by the unbreachable social code which behooves her as a woman, no matter what she is doing, to attend to the man sitting opposite her, thus stroking his vanity and enabling him to relieve himself of his desire for self-assertion (99). But whereas to Mrs. Ramsay the only honorable course of action for a young woman in such a situation is to succor the young man, to Lily it is unclear whether such a response confirms or compromises her integrity as a woman. For her, standing on the cusp of a female revolution, a radically honorable act would be to flout the young man's needs, to refuse to subordinate herself to them. The offering of the small social kindness that she finally makes to him is a breach of faith with her own sense of equal self-worth. Moreover, as an act of altruism it may not be in the long term really generous. In order to make a space for a new, more rewarding kind of relationship between the sexes, she is aware that these forms of feminine chivalry must be eschewed. In acceding once again to Mrs. Ramsay's imperative, to her enormous power of influence (191), she realizes that she has lost an opportunity; now fixed into the polite formulae of conventional social life, she and Charles Tansley will never really know each other (101).

Lily instinctively desires to be fed and nurtured by Mrs. Ramsay. Comparing the older woman to a hive and herself to a bee, she is drawn to her by a sweet, sharp smell (58). When Mrs. Ramsay is dead, Lily's sense of loss is experienced bodily—as a hunger, a physical void that cannot now be filled. She wonders how these "emotions of the body" can be expressed in words, for her sense of emptiness is "one's body feeling, not one's mind." Separate and alone in the world, she experiences her body as defined by straight lines, like the now emphatically empty drawing-room steps. Momentarily she feels like a baby deprived of the breast, and the "physical sensations" of wanting and being unable to have fill her body with "hardness, . . . hollowness, . . . strain" (194).

However, her desire for a nurturant union with the mother figure is not simply an infantile regression. The hunger she experiences is also a woman's hunger for a form of primordial spiritual nourishment which has been denigrated, diminished, and distorted in the patriarchal world. Neither, in this mythic subtext, is Mrs. Ramsay simply an attractive but potentially overbearing wife, mother, and voluntary social worker but, as the quantities of matristic symbolism attached to her indicate, at the same time she represents the Goddess—with whom, before the Christian era, Mrs. Ramsay's emblem, the fruit tree, was associated throughout the Near and Middle East and across Europe.[4] Another of her central symbols, the bee, was a widely known epiphany of the Goddess in the matristic millennia, and beehive tombs dedicated to her are found throughout Europe.[5] Lilienfeld notes that "Olives, oil and juice," the ingredients of Mrs. Ramsay's meal, "are an ancient festival food often sanctified by dedication to the Great Mother" (357). Lily's sense of grief at what has gone out of the world, making the curved straight, the whole separate, and the full void, is thus not merely an individual expression of loss but is a cultural-spiritual lament for a society that does not contain the numinous Mother, that no longer knows how to feel with the feelings of the body and thus has lost a vital dimension of existence. In any formulation for freer women's lives, she senses, the distillation of such maternal qualities is excluded at women's peril.

The nature of Lily's compositional problem—one of filling a gap and thereby effecting a formal unity—indicates her need to eradicate the space that separates her from Mrs. Ramsay. As Avrom Fleischman observes, "It is a personal emptiness as well as a visual space that must be filled" (130). Despite her conscious orientation toward autonomy, in Mrs. Ramsay's presence Lily instinctively wishes for synthesis. She seeks a way to be merged with the object of her love "like waters poured into one jar"—an image which suggests the baby in the womb and a degree of closeness that physical proximity (leaning her head against Mrs. Ramsay's knee) is inadequate to effect (57). But if, as Lilienfeld comments using Jung's words, she desires "to be caught, sucked in, enveloped and devoured, seeking . . . the protecting, nourishing charmed circle of the mother" (351), she is striving on a deeper level for a more constructive kind of unity than the fetal symbiosis that seduces her. Is there an "art," she asks, to achieve this end?, thereby bringing to birth a more positive solution, for the "art," which in context literally signifies "way," also connotes creative art. By engaging with this personal issue through her painting, Lily starts to move and transform it. Moreover, on a transpersonal level she begins to involve herself in the evolution of a paradigm for female art. As she contemplates her emotions, she sees that the form of "unity" she desires is not simply a ceding of selfhood, but "intimacy . . . which is knowledge," and that this is not a mode of knowing that can be conveyed in "any language known to *men*" (57, my italics).

Lily saves herself from the loss of identity that threatens at Mrs. Ramsay's table by understanding that this crisis is material for her art. She appropriates the implements of the mother's table—table cloth and salt cellar—as tools in her own artistic process, using them as markers of the composition that she suddenly conceives. This is an act of huge and daring subversion, flouting the mother's embargo on independent and self-satisfying activity for women within the precincts of her own temple (the dining room) and with the artifacts of her own most sacred ceremony (dinner). Years later Lily still remembers the inspired moment at which she saw that by transforming the mother's objects she could elude the imperative: marry. She recalls how narrow was her escape and how exulted she felt at it (191). Art enables her to undertake a more complex process than a simple rejection of the mother and her creed. Her painting is revisionist rather than iconoclastic, adapting and reworking Madonna and child rather than dispensing with them. Looking at this revolutionary kind of picture, the old man, William Bankes, realizes with incredulity that the patriarchal genre can be interpreted in new and apparently heretical ways without diminishing the maternal (59).

Lily's inspiration is to move the tree in her picture. She thinks that by placing it closer to the middle she will avoid an awkward compositional space (92). The personal-psychological and female-political implications of this artistic decision are wide-reaching given that the tree is a symbol of Mrs. Ramsay herself. For Lily this change signifies not only a new approach to an artistic problem but also a new way of tackling the issue of her relationship with the mother figure and her own (daughter's) role in the world as a woman and herself a potential mother. The original placing of the tree at the side of the canvas suggests that she had been attempting to navigate a passage around the maternal figure by pushing her aside. The decision to make the tree a focal point indicates an understanding that the mother and all that she stands for cannot simply be sidelined by her daughters. To marginalize the mother is to marginalize the womanly in oneself and thus to become alienated from a vital dimension of being. In order to go beyond (rather than simply get past) this mother, Lily understands, the daughter must centralize her. Only thus can she contain within herself a sense of the metacultural, metahistorical continuity of the experience of being female, and only through containing this knowledge can she make authentically new forms of relationship and a really different kind of art.

Whereas the remit of male creativity tends to be to extrapolate and define, the creative objective of women in *To the Lighthouse* is connection, unification. Not delimited, as men's creative products generally are, Mrs. Ramsay's work of art (the Boeuf en Daube) extends beyond its own apparent boundaries, the focal point in a series of concentric circles. It is impossible to say whether those who eat her dinner are her audience or whether they are themselves an element in her creation—and indeed such distinctions are meaningless when a creative work is construed as such a radial connecting force. Beneath their obvious dissimilarities, Lily and Mrs. Ramsay are akin in their striving for synthesis within the artistic product, both sharing a concern for the compositional coherence of their respective works. The Boeuf en Daube, furthermore, is not only a consummate expression of this kind of harmonious integration but a metaphor for the fundamental experience of being female from which unity evolves as an artistic aim. The big brown pot containing the "soft mass" of beef, wine, bay, and juice suggests a pregnant belly in which one flesh is indistinguishable from another—a "confusion of . . . brown and yellow meats." It is in fact a creation that looks back through our mothers, being a French recipe of Mrs. Ramsay's grandmother's (109).[6]

It has been argued that the real creative force behind the Boeuf en Daube is not Mrs. Ramsay but the cook, Mildred.[7] In fact, however, true to its nature as a symbol of mergence and connection, the dish is the product of a conjoined effort. As in *Mrs. Dalloway* and later in *Between the Acts*, work with food draws women together from loci across the patriarchal class system that normally divides them, allying them in a deep and ancient sense. Whereas the men in the novel—Tansley, Bankes, Mr. Ramsay—regard solitary endeavor as the only means to produce good work, for Mrs. Ramsay and Mildred collaboration is a fruitful creative practice. Although the blueprint for synthesis, the recipe, is from her own maternal line, Mrs. Ramsay herself acknowledges Mildred's role in the making of the dinner, describing the Boeuf en Daube as "Mildred's masterpiece" (87). Rather like Clarissa Dalloway and Mrs. Walker, the two women function in a sense as director and actor. While Mildred brings technical skill and expertise to the creation of the center-stage dish, Mrs. Ramsay's role is to resolve all the elements of the evening into a unified entity. And indeed, later on when Mrs. Ramsay leaves the dining room, the whole dissolves (122).

Mrs. Ramsay's dinner party is the product of a particular power of creative/social manipulation, of an ability to shape and to mold that identifies Mrs. Ramsay mythically with the Goddess as weaver of fates. Whereas the male God enforces his law with fire and brimstone, her power to influence human lives is based on the seductive quality of her love; as DiBattista comments, "The dinner over which Mrs. Ramsay presides is an expression of the total form of love, a secular equivalent of the love feasts of religious communities" (88). The "tender" meat reflects an emotional quality that emanates from the deep brown dish along with the "exquisite scent." This is a love that is emollient, oily and juicy, running over surfaces, smoothing the roughness out of life and softening the sharp edges that divide individual from individual (109).

Like the religious ritual that on one level it is, Mrs. Ramsay's dinner has the capacity to resolve time, to stem the flow of moment into moment, creating a space that seems atemporal. Watching family and friends eat, Mrs. Ramsay feels suddenly stable, convinced that beneath the apparently ephemeral surface of life, something unchanging and immutable resides. This timeless quality is seen to derive from the Boeuf en Daube itself, so that (with the omission of a comma) Mrs. Ramsay dishing up the meat appears to hand William Bankes a slice out of time: a "piece, of eternity" (114). Lucio Ruotolo argues that the dinner scene creates a "disposition for stasis" which must be questioned and opposed (12n). For me, however, while the mother's status quo in the novel—marry and nurture—clearly invites challenge, the place in which her dinner dwells is ultimately beneath the level of sociocultural imperatives. To be centered in such a moment as this, Woolf suggests, is to feel existentially at home—a necessary sense that characteristically and cripplingly eludes her anorexic-type characters (such as Rhoda in *The Waves*) and indeed anorexic women in general.

Mrs. Ramsay is a community-forging force, a Witch brewing unity in her cauldronlike vessel. She derives a physical pleasure—"joy" that fills her body with fullness and sweetness—not from the food itself but from the experience to which it gives rise, of husband, children, and friends eating around her table (114). Her dinner is a self-transcendent experience of participation in the group and acknowledgment of a common human bond, a coming together in which the whole is much more than the sum of its parts, and the parts are enriched by the whole. The Boeuf en Daube with its intermingled meats is itself a symbol of this union of human flesh. Before its appearance disjunctive isolation prevails; everyone sits in her or his own separate sphere and nothing seems to merge (91). Only when the big dish is plumbed and the vapor that rises from its depths is stayed over the table like an ether "holding them safe together" is the assemblage of disparate individuals welded into community (114).

Initially feared and resisted by the novel's individualists, those who seek withdrawal and ascetic solitude in order to work, the communalizing experience that the dinner offers in fact nourishes and expands the individual self, thus ultimately enabling deeper and greater achievement on an individual level. Woolf herself was aware that creative work is a product of creative living, that one truly finds oneself only in the context of harmonious community. She sought juice in social life—what she referred to as "the succulence of our group" (*Congenial Spirits,* 373)[8]—in order to support and feed her writing. Whereas the social body may survive without the old kind of mother figure, it cannot thrive without a sense of the nurturance that she once brought to it. When Mrs. Ramsay is dead, none of the younger generation of women—her daughters, Minta, Lily—has the will or the power to keep the old form of connectedness in being. The Goddess is gone from the world, and the prehistoric sequelae of separation take force in the contemporary social world. "People soon drift apart," as Bankes says (96). Initially, life without the archetypal mother appears bleak; *To the Lighthouse,* however, suggests that sustaining social relations may ultimately be reconstituted to include love without the presence of the maternal stereotype and to allow greater freedom of being for everyone.

Perhaps the ultimate feat of synthesis for Mrs. Ramsay lies in the reluctant presence of William Bankes at the dinner table, eliciting her statement, "I have triumphed tonight." Like Lily, Bankes lodges apart in the village, maintaining for the sake of his work a peripheral relationship to the grouping around the table. His allegiance is to a spartan masculine ethic of dedicated industry. Really he would rather, as Mrs. Ramsay knows, go back to his own lodgings than eat dinner with her family and guests. He distrusts the rich, sensual food of the mother and her female cook—its superfluous olives, wine, and bay leaves and the excessive three days required to produce it, preferring the kind of food provided by "his *man,*" who cooks vegetables "properly" (80, my italics). As a biologist, Bankes is a scientist, not an artist of food. For him, eating is synonymous with nutrition, and he regards the best cooking as that which most efficiently preserves nutrients, abhorring the dreadful practices of English cooks (29): overcooking and peeling off the skins that contain the goodness of vegetables (109). Ostensibly his attitude to food is functional; subliminally, however, food and the way it is cooked and prepared carry for him moral messages, encoding "iniquity" (29) and "virtue" (109). To submit himself to the untried cooking of Mrs. Ramsay's table is thus for Bankes not simply to risk a deficit in his nutritional status but to countenance a probable compromise to his integrity.

Beyond the expected cooking time of the vegetables, Bankes is further deterred from joining the Ramsays for dinner by the excessive length of time that social eating entails—dissipated time in his view, which he would rather expend on working. He meditates (as Lily does) on his work at the dinner table, drumming his fingers on the cloth impatiently as he waits for the food to be served, and thinking what a tedious waste of time such meals are compared with work. If he were in his lodgings, he thinks, he would almost have finished dinner by now and could have gone back to work (96–97), for his primary objective in eating is to process nutrients into his body as quickly as possible and return to the grindstone. It does not occur to him that as a sensually gratifying, socially nourishing, and psychospiritually uplifting experience, a good dinner might enhance his ability to work productively and that monastic application is not necessarily the only or most effective approach to labor.

Yet ultimately it is Bankes who most deeply appreciates Mrs. Ramsay's dinner. Once he has tasted the Boeuf en Daube, he is filled with "love" and "reverence" for her, and she sees it. Indeed, he it is who awards the Boeuf en Daube the supreme accolade, "It is a triumph" (109), praising it on those very points about which he is so dogmatic: The food is "perfectly cooked"; it is "tender," and yet it is not overdone. His choice of "triumph" as praise for the dish concedes Mrs. Ramsay's final victory, for it is the same word that she chooses to refer to her success in bringing him to her table. He is a key convert for her because, unlike the other reluctant male diners, he is a worker in her own medium, food. Although apparently the life ethic of mother/wife and biologist are in many senses diametrically opposed—social/solitary, sensual/ascetic, mergence of the many into one/separation of the one into many—the unifying power of the Boeuf en Daube enables woman and man to recognize that in fact they hold in common many feelings about food, that despite their ostensible differences there are points on which they can agree. Regarding the cooking of vegetables, they are in fact fervent disciples of the same religion, both denouncing the horrors of overboiled cabbage and meat roasted to leather (109). If Bankes suspected Mrs. Ramsay of such sins, he was misled. In fact she shares his concern for cooking times. To make of the Boeuf en Daube a synthesis rather than merely a mish mash requires a scientific precision in length of cooking that Bankes would probably recognize. The dish must be "done to a turn" and served up as soon as it is ready (87).

Bankes is aware that in preferring work to social dining he may offend others, a sensitivity that distinguishes him from the other men who share his reluctance to waste work time eating and talking. He puts aside his objections in order to spare Mrs. Ramsay's feelings, knowing that she would be hurt if he declined her invitation (96)—a consideration alien to the essential egotists, Charles Tansley and Mr. Ramsay. Sitting at the dinner table Tansley yearns to be alone in his room working with his books (94–95). His preference for dissertation over dinner table is compounded by a sense of social inferiority; he is acutely insecure among the Ramsays and their guests, feeling at ease only when he has shut his door on them all. The trenchancy of his discomfort precludes enjoyment of the meal and self-transcending participation in the group. Dinner with the middle classes is a game whose rules are imperfectly known to him and which he feels he cannot play whether he will or no. Lily's attempt at politeness for Mrs. Ramsay's sake is wasted on him. He thinks that she despises him—a conclusion which is partly an aspect of his social paranoia in this particular class setting and partly an accurate observation of her distaste for his chauvinism ("women can't write, women can't paint"). In fact, he deplores as much as she does this kind of etiquette which, far from succoring and including him, only increases his feelings of discomfort and isolation.

Crippled by his own sense of inferiority and delimited by the rigidity of his ideas, Tansley effectively cuts himself off from the experience of community. The female-patronized pleasures of good food and conversation are to him not an essential component of civilization, lubricating its artistic and intellectual mechanisms, but are inimical to it. He thinks that women only talk and eat, and that with their "charm" they explicitly preclude civilization (93), which, in his vision, looks like a Victorian university college: rigorously intellectual, high-minded, spartan, and exclusively male. Known to the Ramsay children as "the atheist" (9), he is a nonbeliever in the Mother's religion, the religion of life—too afraid to embrace it, too constrained to give himself up to the celebration of it. An unwitting eater of what is essentially a communion meal, he is dead to the significance of his act of numinous participation.

Tansley's dismissal of the whole social occasion is expressed in the speed with which he empties his plate, efficiently eliminating the dinner and all that it represents. Setting down his spoon exactly in the center of his plate is an attempt to set a symbolic limit on what he regards as the dinner's libertine sprawl. Paradoxically, however, his gusto in polishing off his dinner also hints at a repressed hunger for such ontological nourishment. Lily observes that he sweeps his plate clean as if wishing to make certain he is fed (93)—which perhaps indeed he does, for he comes from an impoverished working-class family. With no dress clothes (humiliatingly, he has to come down to dinner in old flannel trousers [94]), he can have had little experience of eating to feed the soul.

The Boeuf en Daube, its different colored meats like two bodies mingled, symbolizes the kind of sexual-marital unity in which Mrs. Ramsay places an unflinching faith. For her, the achievement of harmonious community and the defeat of irrelation are connected with the match newly made between Minta Doyle and Paul Rayley, who appear together just as the Boeuf en Daube is about to be brought in. Looking into the great pot, she thinks that the food will be a celebration of their union. Ambivalently she feels rising in her two emotions, the sense of something both "freakish and tender," for despite her absolute fidelity to the notion of patriarchal marriage, she remains aware that the culturally purveyed image of marital bliss is an "illusion," that marriage is a duty as much as a pleasure and carries with it "the seeds of death" (109). In her own experience, marriage has indeed entailed a kind of fatal insemination, the multifarious demands of her husband sapping her until, in an image that is both orgasmic and prefigurative of death, "the whole fabric fell in exhaustion upon itself" (44). She sees the new young lovers as sacrificial victims in a deathly rite, to be garlanded and celebrated, but "with mockery" (109). Her imperative, marry, is clearly predicated not on a belief in marriage as productive of happiness but on a sense that rather than a particular social arrangement marriage is a human inevitability like birth and death.

Years later when she thinks of Mrs. Ramsay's "mania" for match-making, Lily seems to scent a "winy smell" which intoxicates her. With Mrs. Ramsay dead, however, and the compelling aroma of the Boeuf en Daube only a vestigial memory, the seduction of obedience to her commands has evaporated, and the deadly reality of marriage is clearly revealed. Conjuring up an imaginary story of the Rayleys' partnership as a pattern for the narrowly escaped fate planned for her by Mrs. Ramsay, she sees the desire to give oneself in marriage as a compulsive urge for self-immolation. The marital pyre becomes in her mind "Paul's fire," the fire of the husband which will devour his wife, as Mr. Ramsay has devoured Mrs. Ramsay.[9] Imagining herself gobbled up by its greedy flames she is both impressed by its power and appalled at its destructive greed (191).

At forty-four still slight, like many anorexic women Lily apparently wishes to signal with her incorporeity that she is a body unfitted to appease the hunger of the voracious male. Nevertheless she is borne down upon by the bereaved and "greedy" Mr. Ramsay with his demand that she may not work until she has succored him (164). She recoils from his now unbattened "insatiable hunger" for her attention (165), feeling inadequate to respond with the appropriate soothing nurturance, the "glow" of "self-surrender" she has seen on the faces of women such as Mrs. Ramsay, when they "blazed up," offering themselves for consumption in the flames of sympathy (164).

A nurturer trained to derive gratification from self-exhaustive giving, Mrs. Ramsay is a willing martyr to the sacrificial fire. "Giving, giving, giving, she had died," Lily thinks (163). Her adoption of food as a creative medium (one which is literally consumed) is suggestive of this kind of total self-offering. The nature of the Boeuf en Daube, the soft agglomeration of meats in the round-bellied pot, symbolizes the female body itself, alluding to the mother's gift of her own body as food to the fetus and then the suckling infant as a paradigm for all women's directions of self into the feeding of others. Mrs. Ramsay's concern with milk is a further manifestation of this kind of nurturing impulse. She is almost obsessively preoccupied with the quality of milk—appalled by the grubby brown milk delivered to London doorsteps (64) and moved to passionate eloquence by the inability of the English dairy system to supply real butter and clean milk (112). Years later Mrs. McNab still remembers how Mrs. Ramsay would tell the cook to keep for her a plate of milk soup (149).

The most demanding by far of Mrs. Ramsay's sucklers is her husband, who has to a large extent displaced the children appropriately dependent on her for food and nurturance. A baby at the breast, he drinks in her succor until he "drops off satisfied" (44). Lily recalls him repeatedly in images of starvation and oral demand, attempting to regain his wife's favor as like "a famished wolfhound" (216) and, after her death, "a lion seeking whom he could devour" (170). Yet there is a certain culturally endorsed codependency in the relationship of husband and wife; if he is all-devouring, she gives herself up to his hungry mouth, a total nurturer without a sense of the need for boundaries to preserve her own body, her own self from erosion. Her lack of resistance suggests the extent to which she feels bludgeoned and defeated by patriarchal conditioning, disempowered and impotent to preserve herself, let alone enact positive change.[10]

Set against the fatal self-renunciation of the individual woman is the resilience of the mythic archetype that she represents. Like Inanna, Ishtar, Isis, Demeter, Ceres, Mrs. Ramsay is a force for fertility. She is "delicious fecundity, the fountain and spray of life," a "rosy-flowered fruit tree laid with leaves and dancing boughs" (42–43). The plants she touches flourish as if blessed. When Mr. Ramsay compliments some of the flowers, she tells him that these are the ones she put in herself (74). Like the Neolithic Goddess and her divine descendants, who were mythically responsible for agriculture and thus for bringing civilization to the world,[11] she is a force for fruitfulness governed rather than inchoate prolixity. Contemplating her, Bankes feels that the wilderness has been brought under control (54). While nature seems unable to flourish without her presence, equally without her it cannot be contained. She stems the slowly encroaching tide of children's beachcombings and sand from shoes, holds at bay a nature that would infiltrate and overwhelm human habitation without her check. When she has gone, civilization is indeed invaded: The carnation mates with the cabbage, the swallow builds in the drawing room, thistles grow through the larder floor, and a butterfly suns itself on a chintz armchair. Deputed after Mrs. Ramsay's death to assume the function of ordering this nature, Mrs. McNab is a shadow of the Great Matriarch, able to do only what is humanly possible. The task, she feels, is bigger than any one woman (150).

Allied by name with her mother's rosy-flowered tree, Rose Ramsay seems designated to inherit her mother's guardianship of ordered fertility. As the architect of the fruit bowl, a cornucopia of great formal beauty, she has already demonstrated her propensity for some manifestation of this role. The dusky vinous tones and pyramid shapes of the piles of fruit with which she composes replicate the shape and color chosen by Lily for her painted rendering of mother and child, the shadowy purple triangle. Drawn up from the depths of female consciousness, the seabed, like Lily's, Rose's work of art is both a product and a celebration of womanhood. With its lowlands and ridges not so much a still-life as a landscape (105), her creation is distinctively womanly in contour, its hills and valleys resembling the female body and its enigmatic deeps and shades suggesting the remoter recesses of female consciousness.

Mrs. Ramsay is drawn into a kind of creative collaboration with her daughter over the fruit bowl. As the older woman contemplates the arrangement, her eyes traveling over the shapes and shadows of the fruit, she makes her own juxtapositions of colors and combinations of shapes: yellow and purple, curved and round (118). A feast for the eyes (105), Rose's food is, like her mother's, a banquet for several senses. Looking at it is a consciousness-altering experience, inducing in Mrs. Ramsay a sense of tranquility ontologically parallel to physical repletion (118). Like the Boeuf en Daube too, the arrangement of fruit is a catalyst of unity. Musing over the dish of fruit with Carmichael, Mrs. Ramsay feels an affinity of sorts with the generally inscrutable old man, an affinity that transcends their differences. His way of looking is different from her own, she observes, but the act of looking brings them together (106).

Rose's creation also symbolizes the transcendence of sexual differences, describing metaphorically a union of male and female—specifically as embodied by her own parents. The juxtaposed "pink-lined shell" and banana suggest vagina and penis, and sexual connection is implied in the penetration of the landscape by the imagined explorer, a walker like Mr. Ramsay, with his phallic staff enfolded in the fructifying undulations of his wife's body. In such a country one could scale hills and descend valleys, Mrs. Ramsay thinks (105); contemplating Rose's work, she becomes in fantasy like her husband, a footloose and solitary wanderer.

Whereas in *To the Lighthouse* the principle of the mother is the flowering, fruiting tree, the father's essence is in the product of the dead tree: wood, and what can usefully be constructed with it. Whenever Lily thinks of Mr. Ramsay's work she always envisages a scrubbed kitchen table, its "virtue" revealed by "years of muscular integrity." Walking with Bankes in the orchard, she sees this table, upside down, wedged into a fork in a pear tree (28). Mr. Ramsay's table embodies qualities of rigor, simplicity, and honesty, tenets of professionalism that as a painter Lily understands and shares. Unadorned and functional, it is a workbench rather than a place to eat, thus opposing Mrs. Ramsay's dining table with its rich sensual profusion of colors, scents, shapes, tastes, and textures. Whereas her table is a locus of empathic connection and social relationship, his plain boards stand for an austere rationality from which feeling is expunged, for the pursuit of a postulated objectivity that necessitates the separation of the subject from the object and for a work ethic that isolates the philosopher from the rest of human kind.

Lily's mental picture of the ratiocinatory table stuck in the pear tree implies the dilemma of being, as Mr. Ramsay is, a logician alienated from realities which are sensual, instinctive, mythic. In paring away what is emotional, nonempirical, unsubmissible to rational thought he has made himself into dead wood dissevered from the living tree, thus becoming dependent on his wife's fertile branches to supply those qualities annexed from himself. (Paradoxically, the process of obtaining the wood he needs for his table necessitates killing the tree.) Cut off from the living and growing, from what cannot be explained in logical terms, the father's is a deficient understanding of life. Like Mr. Ramsay himself, the table cannot stand on its own feet but lies helplessly on its back in the cradle of the tree, waving its legs in the air.

The plainness of Mr. Ramsay's table evinces his antagonism to the embellishments and rituals of his wife's dinner table. He is unable to appreciate the subtle harmonies of sensual and social pleasure that arise there. His is an undiscerning, omnivorous orality, an overwhelming and immediate infantile demand for mother and food. Eating is, for him, an essentially exclusive, egotistic act; he is absolutely out of sympathy with the communitizing function of his wife's meal, at which he sits unsociably silent (200). When Carmichael asks for a second helping of soup, he resents the affront to his own asceticism that the old man's supposed greed entails, for he is disgusted by people indulging themselves with food; he resents too the prolongation of the meal; and, perhaps most trenchantly of all, he resents Carmichael's appropriation of Mrs. Ramsay's nurturance. That the old man should receive one helping of food from her hand—the hand that should nourish only him—is bad enough, but that he should ask for a second is unconscionable. He cannot bear to see Carmichael eat the food that he does not himself have, and his face takes on the appearance of an angry baby's. His initial inability to put the event in proportion and control his rage is equally infantile, but at the last moment he manages to get a grip on himself and contain the violence that had threatened to explode (103–104).

Mr. Ramsay's covetous desire for mother's food is paradoxical in relation to his deeply rooted ascetic vein. He is both a helpless infant dependent on the breast and an intrepid explorer capable of surviving days in an alien landscape on little more than crusts. He remembers how when he was a boy he used to walk all day in the countryside with only a biscuit in his pocket. Bread and cheese in a pub were once for him, he recalls, a meal (75–76). Whereas at social dinners he is bored to tears, as frustrated and restless as a child (130), walking vigorously he feels in the right proportion to life on a grand scale, to the largeness of nature. Alone in an uncivilized, unsocialized landscape, he feels himself rendered to the essence, his mental faculties honed and clarified, his body pared away, and himself powerfully incisive.

This process of external reduction is mirrored in his ontological landscape: a spit of land that the sea is eroding, on which he stands like a lone seabird. As a philosopher, he has placed himself on "a little ledge" facing "human ignorance," which he figures as the sea that "eats away the ground we stand on." Inherent in the propensity to confront this inexorable erosion is both the strength and the limitation of his philosophy, for, while setting his gaze determinedly out to sea is an act of extraordinary courage, rigor, and tenacity, it also constitutes the exclusion of one-half of life from view. He feels compelled to deprecate the other reality on which he has turned his back—the reality of human connectedness, of wife and children, and his own pleasure in them, for these are, "trifles" set against "the august theme" (the inhuman grandeur of nature) and against the contemplation of the sea which is philosophy (50).

The erosion of land by sea also represents a perceived erosion of male by female—somewhat paradoxically, given that Mrs. Ramsay's body is in very obvious ways eaten away by the voracious mouth of her husband. Wife, children, and the financial responsibilities of fatherhood represent for Mr. Ramsay the consumption of time and energy that might otherwise be directed into great work. As the father of eight he feels that he has no choice but to turn away from the sea of human ignorance, and thus his hopes of drawing a great philosophy from it, to consider his wife reading to his son (50).[12] Ironically, he blames his failure as a philosopher upon the demands of his family, directing a large amount of negative energy into self-separation and self-definition against wife and children, whereas in fact they represent the human dimension of existence that he needs to encompass in order to broaden his narrow and abstracted philosophical picture and move on from Q. Incipiently acknowledged but wholly unembraceable, behind him lies the emotional realm from which, self-defeatingly, he seeks to disidentify (51).

Mr. Ramsay's recollection of the walks of his youth, before the advent of wife and children, is of a large and empty countryside, significantly contrasted with the female landscape of fruit into which as a walker he is symbolically projected. He remembers beaches deserted since time began, sandhills that he could walk all day without encountering a single soul. This is a country devoid of domestic habitation; there is scarcely a house to be seen and not a village for miles. The sole female presence in this one-time "over there" is a nameless old woman who pops in from time to time to see to the fire. Mr. Ramsay thinks that he prefers this kind of minimal, utilitarian female presence who only mends the hearth, to the complex emotional connectedness of a wife who immolates herself in it. He recalls with satisfaction how the old woman did not impinge upon his solitude or curtail his time for work with dinner parties. Then, he remembers, he would work for ten hours in one stretch (76).[13]

In a sense, given his practical and emotional dependence on women, Mr. Ramsay's fantasy is totally anomalous. He is a famished child who cannot escape his need by walking away from his mother. In another sense, however, the unpredictable rage that mars his family life and overfills the domestic interior is indeed accommodated in the vastness of the unpopulated countryside. Wailing Lear-like at the sea, he is in harmony with the wildness of the elements, whereas such turbulence overfills and rebounds destructively within the walls of the house. Lily remembers how he would bang the bedroom door, rush in a tantrum from the table, or throw his plate through the window, filling the whole house with a sense of slamming doors and fluttering blinds as if a high wind were blowing at sea and the hatches must be made fast.

The smashing of the window and the violent shaking of all the apertures of the house express Mr. Ramsay's desire to shatter the encumbering behavioral codes of social life, to break domestic bounds, introducing through the breach his own turbulent storms and winds to oust harmony, stability, and civilization. Incongruously, however, his rage is also a demand for more domesticity, since domesticity is an apparatus to supply the nurturance that he cannot live without. Lily recalls how he flung his breakfast out onto the terrace when he found an earwig in his milk (216). The subtext of this anger is outraged betrayal: Only an unloving mother could be so unforgivably negligent as to allow the contamination of her child's milk.

Silently watching this scene, Prue is "awestruck" (216). As Woolf was well aware from personal experience, the witnessing of such paternal antics has serious repercussions for the daughters of the house. Lily remembers Prue's anxiety at the table in those days, how she was so preoccupied with ensuring equanimity that she almost never spoke. She thinks that Prue must have blamed herself for the earwig in Mr. Ramsay's milk, that she must have paled when he threw his plate out of the window, and remembers that she seemed to droop under the weight of her parents' long silences. Prue absorbs the complicated resentment intended for her mother, silently internalizing her father's expectations—feed and nurture—of women. In this context of dissatisfaction and recrimination, Mrs. Ramsay's promise, that one day "that same [marital] happiness would be hers" (217) must seem like a lowering threat. For Prue, eating and the table might all too readily serve as the arena in which to untangle her nexus of guilt at the imputation of female failure and her desire for a different kind of male-female relationship.

Mrs. Ramsay's death brings down the curtain on domesticity. Without her monitory presence the saucepans and crockery become "furred, tarnished, cracked" (141). When family and friends return after nature's interregnum, the mother's old objects, even cleaned and restored by Mrs. McNab, are disorientatingly unrelated and meaningless, so that the statement "It's not in the cupboard; it's on the landing" sounds to Lily like a question. It seems to her as if the connection between things has been severed, and they float meaninglessly in space. Everything seems "aimless . . .

chaotic . . . unreal" as she stares at her empty coffee cup and recalls that Mrs. Ramsay is dead (160). The table, once the focus of social ritual and community, has become instead a place of uncertainty and isolation. When Lily comes down to breakfast no one is waiting to feed her and fill her coffee cup, and she is not sure how one should behave in such an unfamiliar circumstance. "What does it mean . . . ?" she asks herself, thinking about the meaning of life and the loss of it, but at the same time wondering whether she should go to the kitchen and help herself to more coffee or wait for someone to come.

The oldest child now remaining, Nancy, is confused and disorientated by the demands of the domestic role that her father requires her to assume in her mother's wake. She bursts in and looks around as if stunned or in despair, her question, what to take to the lighthouse, expressing reluctance to undertake, and desperation that she will be able to fulfill, what is demanded of her. Her painful ineptitude in such matters is a sign of the times. The death of those Ramsay children with the potential for conforming to Victorian gender ideals—beautiful Prue, destined for marriage and children, and brilliant Andrew, set to become a great mathematician—has ushered out the old roles and conventions and will throw open the doors to the less conformable gifts of their brothers and sisters.

Even for its figurehead, Mr. Ramsay, the death of the old order carries a dim promise of opportunity, for as long as Mrs. Ramsay lives, he remains dependent upon her ceaseless stream of nurturance. Her death initially leaves him like an infant sucking at a shriveled breast, and with an infant's rage berating the daughters who are unable or unwilling to step into the breach and rescue him from extinction. When Nancy, now surrogate mother, forgets to organize sandwiches for the lighthouse expedition, he loses his temper and slams out of the room (159). He is incensed by her inability to meet his need for feeding and affronted by the roughly tied up parcels of bread, cheese, and boiled eggs that in the event he has to make do with. And yet ultimately this failure of nurturance liberates him to eat once more the food that is really his own—basic, hand to mouth, the remembered food of his boyhood, which renders back to him dimensions of selfhood that he had ceded: courage, endurance, and a kind of tranquility.

For Cam, eating her father's own authentic food is part of a process of understanding and casting off the web of invidious demands and circumscriptions implicit in his behavior toward women while understanding and assimilating his useful directives for living. On board the fishing boat she is able to see clearly those aspects of his personality that are occluded within the ambit of the house. His generally inassimilable storms and rages become natural and proportionate held up against the terrible and often unpredictable rhythms of the sea, and his personality assumes an equivalent simple grandeur. Blunderingly imperceptive within the compass of domesticity, at sea he evinces an unexpected sensitivity. Cam is moved by the gentleness of his rebuke when she goes to throw her sandwich into the sea, and impressed by the wisdom and integrity of the ethic he seeks to impart to her—of the value of food in a world where many people go hungry, how it should not be wasted but conserved. This, she understands him to be saying, is how he would like his children to live. The simplicity with which he communicates this fundamental tenet of his life philosophy impresses her, and she puts her sandwich back into its packet at once. When he hands her a gingernut out of his own parcel, it seems to be this ethic itself that he offers her—graciously, respectfully, without scenes and wailing, in such a way that she does not feel upbraided or bad (222).

Not petty or miserly, Mr. Ramsay's concern about the waste of a sandwich is born out of a real awareness, Cam thinks, of the situation of the fishermen, of their poverty, about which he loses sleep at night. On a profound level, however, he does not so much pity as envy the fishermen their lives of harsh austerity, which are in accord with his deepest personal reality. Watching his father slice bread and cheese with his penknife, James thinks that the old man would like to live like a fisherman, in a cottage by the harbor (222). If he could be in daily contact with the ruthless sea and its eternal threat of death, it seems that his life would fall into place, would find its due measure. Uncomfortable with luxury and plenty, he is at ease with the fishermen's plain and finite food which must be rationed and carefully shared, food which does not (unlike Boeuf en Daube) yield dangerous sensual pleasures or allow for indulgent second helpings to favored eaters. Apportioning the sandwiches, Mr. Ramsay appears in stark contrast with his wife dishing up her dinner. Fishing-boat rations do not permit of selecting only the tastiest parts, of picking and choosing, as she does for William Bankes. Here everything is valuable; down to crusts and rinds, everything must be eaten.

In this crude environment, far from all that is domestic, Mr. Ramsay's need for maternal nurturance is dissipated. No longer an infant powerless before the threatened cataclysm of the absent breast, he becomes an independent actor and leader, the head of a polar expedition, the captain of a foundering ship—a manager of food capable of sustaining the crew of a storm-wracked ship on only "six biscuits and a flask of water" (39). No more the usurper of his children's food, he finally assumes his rightful role as their provider and protector. For Cam his presence is a guarantee of safety, the gift of a safe point of departure from which she can explore the world. "This is right," she says to herself as she shells her hard-boiled egg, and she feels that she can carry on thinking whatever she wants, because as long as he is watching over her no disaster will befall (221).

Whereas Mrs. Ramsay's dinner invites surrender on the part of the eater, the ultimate end of which is retreat into a comfortable dependence upon the feeder, the father's food symbolizes a kind of personal resistance, the resilience of bread, cheese, and boiled eggs contrasting with the tender, sumptuously yielding texture of the mother's Boeuf en Daube. For Cam, half asleep on the fishing boat, her father's "Come then" and his opening of the parcel of sandwiches is synonymous with an invitation to exciting new possibilities for independent action and the expansion of her horizons. "Come where?" she asks herself in anticipation, thinking of all kinds of marvelous adventures (221). For her, Mr. Ramsay's food contains the piquant taste of potentiality, connoting confrontation with danger and challenge. She is excited as they sail quickly along the rocks, at the same time both eating their lunch and escaping, she fantasizes, a great storm and shipwreck. "Would the provisions last?" she wonders (222). Eating thus in the teeth of imagined death brings her close to a sense, often obscured by social dinners and complex dishes, of the necessity of food to the support of life—a relationship which, rather than fearful, seems right and proper in the fishing boat bobbing on the infinite sea.

Cam and James fear a melodramatic outburst from their father when Macalister speaks of the three fishermen who were drowned, and they think they cannot bear another eruption of seething emotion. But on the contrary, Mr. Ramsay remains calm and matter of fact. It is the petty irritations of social living and loss within that context that excite his passion; face to face with life unvarnished, he confronts tragedy with equanimity, recognizing it to be a part of the natural scheme of things. The sprinkling upon the water of the crumbs from his sandwich paper suggests a symbolic propitiation of the sea and remembrance of the dead sea men (whose bodies are now human crumbs), a gesture acknowledging implicitly the insignificance of a single human existence within the vastness of nature (223–224).

The daughter's process of assimilating her ambivalence toward both parents and evolving from it a creative way of living in the world is shadowed by Lily, watching the father's boat pull out for the lighthouse while she recomposes the image of the mother on her canvas. Lily's achievement is of a form of objectivity—a perspective—which rather than distancing her from mother and father figures, brings her closer to their essence, acknowledging both separation and connection. In her painting the child James is united for all time with Mrs. Ramsay, locked into the kind of symbiotic stasis that may be a goal of anorexia; the artist Lily, however, achieves a transcendent form of relatedness, one that allows her independence and a space in which to accomplish her own individual goals. The placing of the central line on the canvas marks her arrival at that point of harmonious balance (226).

From this position of ontological strength, Lily persistently refuses to abjure painting in order to nurture the bereft Mr. Ramsay, despite her real sympathy with his grief. Ultimately, however, by holding to her own sense of purpose she renders to him something greater than acquiescence to his emotional demands could have provided, feeling that finally she has given something she has long wanted to give (225). Her gift is the refusal to reinforce his infant status by entering into a relationship of codependence with him. She eschews the option of becoming herself simply a reproduction of Mrs. Ramsay, choosing rather to realize creatively her vision of the woman (and as a correlative her vision of herself). In concrete terms, it is this vision, in paint and canvas, that is her final gift to Mr. Ramsay.

In forging an identity for herself as a painter, Lily chooses to walk the traditionally male road of independence and personal challenge in preference to the established female path of self-subordination to others' needs for food and nurturance. The process of painting, the single-minded dedication it demands, leads her into the kind of aloneness that characterizes the father: she feels "drawn . . . out of community with people." Like him too she is laid bare by her work, led out onto "some windy pinnacle" where she is "exposed without protection to all the blasts of doubt," flayed into "nakedness," reduced to an essence of selfhood like "a soul reft of body." The strife for an underpinning of immutable verity brings her into confrontation with his old adversary; truth, reality, appearing suddenly from behind the superficies of things, grasps her, demanding that she pay attention, calling her away from the social world when she would rather sit on the lawn and chat to Mr. Carmichael (172–173).

At the same time, however, she refuses to alienate the female in her nature, rather traveling the male road in order more fully to express fundamentally womanly qualities and values. Declining to re-create the mother's meal, she adapts its intangible ingredients—love, unity, sensual richness—to her painting and recognizes that her artistic objectives—synthesis and the creation of a timeless moment of significance—resonate with Mrs. Ramsay's own as a host and a nurturer. As she paints, she reflects upon her debt to the maternal sensibility, remembering how Mrs. Ramsay brought people together, how she stayed the moment, as she herself, in her painting, attempts to do (176). The instant that she senses her exposure, her nakedness before the canvas, she is overtaken by a characteristically female response to vision—intuitive, inspired, impelling her like a dance. In an image central also to Mrs. Ramsay, she experiences this inspiration as like "a fountain spurting" or a squirt of juice that lubricates her creative faculty, and she begins dipping her brush into the colors in time with some external rhythm. The rhythm carries her on its beat, and her hand quivers with the force of life (174–175).

For Woolf the composition of *To the Lighthouse* marked a watershed in an on-going process of review and reassessment of her relationship with her mother and father. On Leslie Stephen's birthday in 1928, she noted that she had used to think of her parents every day but that the writing of *To the Lighthouse* had laid their ghosts (*D 3*, 208). Her own sense of deepened understanding and inner peace is mirrored in the resolution that, at the end of the novel, Lily arrives at with regard to the Ramsays. In a sense Lily becomes herself like Mrs. Ramsay's great earthenware dish, a melting pot in which two meats mingle, in which mother and father, male and female, the opposite and inassimilable, are integrated and transformed into something which is more than simply an amalgam but is a new entity.

Chapter 8

The Waves:
Some Fasting and Anguished Spirit

When, as an adolescent, I first read *The Waves*, I was perplexed by much of the symbolism of the novel, but Rhoda, in "this clumsy this ill-fitting body" (78), was immediately and wholly comprehensible. She was for me the existential voice of anorexia, speaking with clarity of an orientation toward life which was at that time also my own and which I have subsequently recognized in the stories and symbol systems of countless other anorexic women.[1] Still today Rhoda seems to me to evince most strikingly a relationship with self, body, and environment that is characteristic of anorexic ways of being in the world. She might be said to personify what Hilde Bruch describes as the crucial dilemma of anorexic women—"*the basic delusion of not having an identity of their own*, of not even owning their body and its sensations" (*Eating Disorders*, 1974, 50), her account of a central and reiterated, indeed definitive, moment of trauma—when she cannot cross the puddle because identity fails (47)—constituting exactly such an instance of disembodiment and mutinous identity.[2]

In *The Waves* issues of food and ontology are refracted not just through Rhoda but through all of the novel's speaking characters. Rhoda, Susan, Jinny, Bernard, Neville, and Louis exist both as six individuals and in composite, as a spectrum of states of being in which no character, as no color in the spectrum, is totally exclusive of shades of the others. While Rhoda is subject to the most extreme form of psychological insecurity (she is described by Beverly Schlack as "the essence of alienation" [105]), other characters share aspects of her existential despair—although none is so distressed that being becomes for her or him, as it often does for Rhoda, untenable. They at times oppose her tattered ontology, counterposing their own success against her difficulties in being, or they offer strategies by which they override their own problems of existence to formulate viable personae.

Rhoda exists as a dichotomy of body and soul. She deprecates the body, experiencing moments of perceived disembodiment as "alleviation" (175). For her the body is a burden to be borne, an inanimate lump of the meat that recurs in her vision of the hostile street. (She decides against a trip to Hampton Court because she fears that standing in a queue and smelling other people's sweat she will become like them a joint of meat [122].) Because she experiences the physical manifestations of her being not as authentic aspects of selfhood but as an inexplicable appendage, her face, repeatedly bobbing up, startles her, and she has to remind herself that it is hers (30). Terror-stricken rather than reassured by the this confirmation of her physical presence in the world, she seeks to conceal it behind Susan.[3] Her body is at paralyzing variance with her pilot self. She must make a constant conscious effort to maintain the link between the two divergent parts, which repeatedly threaten complete separation—a disaster that does at times occur. (Her inability to cross the puddle is an instance of such a split, necessitating the painful hauling of self back into body.)

Although other characters in *The Waves* can draw distinctions between physical and mental selves, in none is selfhood so radically polarized, and effectivity thus so impeded, as in Rhoda. Those who live rooted in the body, she observes, have impact on the surfaces of things; their world is "real"; their objects are "heavy." As integrated selves they are able to make decisions, to say yes or no, whereas she, weightless and transparent, merely flits over surfaces (31). Exceptionally, Bernard, during the breakdown that inspires his final soliloquy, ultimately experiences the contrariety of selves that she knows. For the greater part of the novel, however, it is his effectiveness that most clearly contrasts with her impotence. He notes that, unlike Rhoda and Louis (here seen as her counterpart), he can obtain rolls from the waiter, a simple act that enables him to feed himself (213).[4] He impresses by his ability not only to make this modest self-assertion but also to pit himself against the world. He characterizes himself as someone who can gather himself together and bang with his spoon on the table in dissent (218), a palpable gesture of defiance that is unavailable to Rhoda, who cannot trust her unstable embodiment to sustain her selfhood, let alone stand in opposition to the solid world. Whereas Bernard adapts the implements of eating to his rebellious stance, she can only cling to them defensively. He reads her fear in the way that she clutches her fork like a weapon (100).[5]

Rhoda's feeling of impotence explains her corollary fantasies of control. She imagines herself a Russian empress defying the hostile mob which in reality terrorizes her (41). In one of her *Leitmotiv*s, rocking petals in a basin, she assumes for herself a divine omnipotence, creating a microcosm over which she holds sway. God-like, she controls the fates of her petal-boats, dropping in a twig-raft for a drowning sailor, making waves that dash the fleet, planting a lighthouse, raising bubbles from the bottom of the sea. Her insistence upon her own incontrovertible choice of the color of the ships in the fantasy is a product of her complete lack of realizable volition in fact. Contrary to this actual ineffectivity, her reiterated "I" as she plays, designates actions that directly impact upon her created world: "I want," "I tip," "I have," "I will drop," "I have picked . . . and made," endowing her with a sense of imagined identity strongly rooted in physical self (12).[6]

One of Bruch's clients, Hazel, describes how she used anorexia to create a similar locus of control within her own body in compensation for what she felt to be her lack of real power: "When you are so unhappy and you don't know how to accomplish anything, . . . to have control over your body becomes a supreme accomplishment. You make out of your body your very own kingdom where you are the tyrant, the absolute dictator" (1978, 62). In that Hazel exists in fact as the repressed body as well as the commanding consciousness, as both oppressed kingdom and tyrannical ruler, her position is crucially ambivalent. Similarly, while Rhoda is the autocrat of the basin-world, she identifies herself simultaneously with the storm-tossed boats, a Goddess/victim duality that she retains in her adult life, when, fantasizing suicide by drowning, she becomes both the plaything of a pitiless divinity and that divinity herself as she throws her own body to its death. The foundering petals, white darkened with water, represent what now becomes explicitly her drowning body, floating a moment, then sinking under the waves (158).

Rhoda imagines drowning as release, as deliverance into a fluid element—the dissolving "shower" of the breaking wave—that conducts consciousness uncontained in a solid vessel, so relieving her of the onus of living the difficult life of the body (158). Wishing for water to disencumber her of her troublesome corporeality, she conjures the waves "consume me" as she throws her garland to the sea (157). As Pamela Transue says, "Rhoda's body both imprisons and frightens her, so that she finds a necessary solace in moments of merging with the universe" (130). And yet one can also say that the reverse is equally true, for dissolution of the body implies not only an assuaging mergence but also the complete disintegration of selfhood in which lies one of Rhoda's greatest fears. Comparing herself on another occasion to spume on the sand, she wishes not for this kind of dissolution but "above all things" for "lodgement" (98). In mortal danger (like Fanny Elmer and Jinny Carslake) of the complete atomization of her insubstantial body, she can be understood to commit in her imagined suicide not a simple act of self-annihilation, nor even of retraction from the perceived sordidity of physical existence; this suicide is rather a bid to *confound* annihilation by ridding herself of the annihilable body.[7]

Rhoda's contradictory desires with regard to corporeality and self-extinction are reflected in her ambivalent relationship with time. While she aspires to a disembodiment which is essentially atemporal (because the bodiless self is not subject to those biological changes enacted by the passing years), she fears simultaneously the prospect of the disseverment from time entailed in refuting the mortal lifespan. In closing the loop of the figure O she voluntarily excludes herself from time, yet this same act fills her with horror and the yearning to be encompassed once more in the delimited circle of human mortality (14–15). Disconnected from the natural cycles of the body, the passage of time is not smooth and sequential but jarringly unpredictable. Thus she experiences each moment as an unassimilable assault, leaping at her like a consuming animal. Her moments are all separate pieces which she longs, but fails, to make into a "whole and indivisible mass" as others do (97–98).[8]

Eating is not for Rhoda the instinctive satisfaction of a biological need but a dangerous recognition and empowerment of the antagonistic body. At a concert after Sunday dinner she thinks, "We have eaten beef and pudding enough to live for a week," and she sees the audience clustering like maggots on the back of a music that they hope will transport them beyond. They are "heavy bodies," "gorged" and "torpid" in their seats, beached walruses too fat to waddle out to sea, waiting for a wave to carry them over the dry shingle to liquefaction (122–123). The stranded walruses recall the fed animals—hideous manifestations of human inertia and intellectual vacuity—that inhabit the hotel of *The Voyage Out*. In *The Waves*, however, the bloated animal is an image not only of the antipathetic other but, ominously, also of the self. Rhoda is herself (or perceives herself to be) a partaker in the debilitating gluttony. She experiences her full stomach as a weight upon her soul, pinioning it in heavy flesh and impeding her intellectually and spiritually. Her "therefore" (122) emphasizes the direct cause-and-effect relationship that exists for her between (over)eating and the loss of creative, humane, and spiritual selfhood. Reliant upon the now-immobilized body for movement, the soul is trapped distressingly on the shore.

Of all Rhoda's utterances, the identification of her fed self with the beached walrus is perhaps the most characteristically anorexic. Women who starve themselves report almost unanimously the—one might say definitive—anorexic experience of mind/spirit trapped in a heavy body. Sheila MacLeod, for example, writes: "When I am fat (as I see it) I simply do not feel myself. I associate fatness in myself . . . with heaviness of both body and mind which slows me up, making me dull-witted, un-selfconfident and, above all, less able to think for myself" (MacLeod, 146).[9] For anorexic women such perceptions are not metaphorical. Likewise for Rhoda, although in pragmatic terms her feeling of engorgement is clearly disproportionate and her statement "we have eaten . . . enough to live for a week" demonstrably not the literal truth, there is no "as if." The image of entrapment in the heavy body describes perceptual reality.

Other characters in *The Waves* are far from disconcerted by the consequences of eating heavily. For Bernard, physical satiation is an enjoyable experience. He describes himself after a meal like Rhoda as "gorged," but without any sense of displeasure, discomfort, or psychospiritual distress. When dinner ends, he—who generally cannot countenance wordlessness—is able to let silence descend around him, dissolving himself pleasurably into its anonymity and yet feeling simultaneously substantiated by his fullness, protected from erosion, and made "solid" with "content." With his stomach filled he can embrace any eventuality. As in *A Room of One's Own,* for Bernard eating well disarms anxiety (152) and, by extinguishing egotism, enables genuine community. The blurring of aggressively defined, competitive individuality entailed in the forging of such communal identity is not threatening to him because he operates from a position of fundamental ontological security. He, the self-professed egotist, can welcome the mitigation of distinctions as a temporary relief from the acuity of selfhood rather than as the permanent extinction that constantly threatens the self-less Rhoda. Community itself is therefore possible for him in a way that it seldom is for Rhoda, whose tenuous boundaries can rarely withstand the rubbing away of edges necessary to achieve it.

Neville, like Bernard, finds fullness a pleasurable sensation. For him the mouth is filled with "finer nerves" that "tremble," changing as he eats and drinks. Although he shares with Rhoda a fundamental fear of random formlessness, recoiling with her from a chaos that seems always about to engulf the fragile order erected upon the skin of the world, this terror elicits in him a response in relation to food diametrically opposed to hers. He enjoys being "weighed down with food," made "solid." For him the fork is "*fitly* piled" (my italics). He understands the concretion of his body as stabilizing, fortifying him against the blows of the world so that he can gaze unflinchingly into "the mill-race that foams beneath." Whereas Rhoda is terrified of being pinned down in her body by weight of food, he welcomes the "gravity"—which is both solemnity and earth-binding heaviness—that he derives from eating. Inverting her perception, he associates this "gravity" with "control." He regards water not as she does, as a potential refuge, but, as his image of the mill-race makes clear, as a threat. It is corporeality, the anchoring of a heavy body, that guards him against the danger of falling into its churning foam. Loss of intellectual trenchancy, of "knowledge of particulars," is not, as it is for Rhoda, a correlative to be feared; on the contrary, he relaxes into a physicality which is unthinking but safely freighted (103–104).[10]

Neville also derives a sense of security from the comfortingly familiar sequences of eating—both the harmonious succession of tastes and sensations ("warmth, weight, sweet and bitter") and the biological passage of the food through each chamber of his body ("past my palate, down my gullet, into my stomach") (103). The fundamental constancy of these sequences creates for him the same buttressing of permanence that he derives from the study of Latin—a language which, fixed in antiquity, cannot change and surprise him. System and method are his defense against worldly chaos in every sphere of life. He describes himself as catlike in his neatness, cutting the pages of books cleanly, tying up letters in green silk ribbons, and sweeping up cinders because such acts fend off "deformity." He arms himself against the unruliness of the world with academic precision, with the tidy formulae of scholarly thought and the rigorousness of Latin authors, in whom he seeks the pristine perfection that he pursues throughout the novel (137).

The university as ontological fortress is, of course, a means of defense unavailable to the female Rhoda. Indeed, her exclusion from it is vital to Neville, for he sees women as implicated in the extracollegiate disorder, his homosexuality encompassing, Woolf implies, an aversion to the biology of the female body. What he describes as the "vulgarity of life" (65) is essentially female: shopgirls and old women, perhaps even Jinny, Susan, or Rhoda. The university, on the contrary, is a bastion of manly intellect, uncontaminated by the femality that sprawls obnoxiously without its walls. This, for Neville is "our territory" ("our" meaning "men's"), a refined and orderly world of which men are "masters" and "inheritors." From inside such an institution, he cannot endure that uneducated working-class women (shopgirls) should even exist, for their triviality offends him, interrupting his "purest exultation" to remind him of human "degradation" (64).

Neville's neatness is opposed by Bernard's constitutional slovenliness. Bernard is heedless of the "pother" he creates, knowing that "Mrs. Moffatt will come and sweep it all up"—a phrase which, as he himself predicts, becomes a life refrain (60), providing him with an ontological label indicating his readiness to embrace life even as a multifarious accumulation of litter, of pieces meaningless and unconnected, of greasy crumbs. Neville, who enjoys eating the kind of formal dinner that upholds order for him, recoils from the sloppy disorder of his friend's eating, as Bernard himself is aware. Neville is repelled by Bernard's messy handling of the food (he eats the buttery entrails of the last crumpet with his fingers and wipes the grease on his handkerchief) (62) and disturbed by the chaos inherent in such eating, which is unstructured in terms of time (it takes place between meals) and space (the plate fails to contain the food). Whereas, moreover, for Neville books and papers form the piers of a structure of pristine clarity superimposed upon a shapeless and undelimited world, Bernard permits his books and papers to partake in that worldly deformity, brazenly countenancing their permeation by spots of butter and pools of carelessly spilt tea (64).

Neville is right to see the essential Bernard in this scene (rather than Byron, whom Bernard likes to think he resembles)[11]—not merely as it characterizes him in a familiar setting and stance but as it captures a distinctive loop in his psychic signature: his fundamental inclusivity. Instinctively desiring intermixture with any and every person, Bernard overflows into others' personalities with affable laxity, just as the tea slops flood into his papers. Whereas Neville's need for the definition of separateness leads him to seek the exclusivity of intimate relationships (137), Bernard proclaims his desire to commune widely, preferring fifty people to a single companion (100).

Symbolized by the excavation of the crumpet's soft inside, Bernard's gregariousness is informed by a drive to extract the hidden essence of his miscellaneous companions' personalities. He is a glutton for people—in an earlier draft of the novel he describes himself as "a man of natural curiosity" and "a natural taster" (*TW:Hol*, 521). In the novel as published he elides the physical sensation of hunger with the ontological desire for a selfhood buttressed by social contact, describing himself as greedy both for food and for the sense of self that community bestows (87). Whether it is the crossing sweeper, the postman, or the waiter with whom he redeems this "I" is unimportant to him. He identifies implicitly with the hospitable restaurant proprietor mixing a bowl of salad personally for a favored guest, for Bernard too is mixing a special bowl—of words—for someone as yet unknown to him. More than just words, it is his own identity that he randomly intermixes when he takes a seat in the restaurant, for that, he says, is the pleasure of conversation. He is fascinated by the special combination identity that this interaction produces, pondering what "I" becomes when shaken up with the "I" of an Italian waiter (88).

Bernard benefits from such social intercourse because his basic sense of self is healthily consolidated. Thus his identity is enriched rather than diluted by the liberal influx of others' personalities. He describes social intercourse as self-elaboration, self-differentiation, realizing that his personality is partially composed of other people's stimuli (100). He contrasts himself in this respect with Rhoda and Louis. Too tenuously individuated to flourish in company, they exist fully when alone, he says, resenting "illumination, reduplication" (87). For Rhoda, encounters with strangers entail not self-substantiation but a "dissolution of the soul" (156). At school she feels her individual self absorbed and expunged by the collective, which, in its uniform of brown serge, overrides discrete identity in a way that she cannot withstand (23–24).

The artistic element in Bernard's communality is suggested by another of his *Leitmotivs*; he forms his bread into "pellets," which he endows with imaginary identity (18). This habit from childhood contains the origins of his phrase-making, his desire for the narratives of others. Later, pondering his friend's irrepressible and indiscriminate sociability, Neville wonders whether he is still telling himself a story that began when, as a child, he formed his bread into people. To Bernard, Neville realizes, all his friends are "pellets," potential "phrases" in an eternally evolving serial story (51).

Whereas Bernard's behavior at this stage is relatively sophisticated, Rhoda's seems regressive. She eats like a baby, sucking a crust soaked in milk as she dreams (17). His embryonic artistic ability to give form to and thus objectify imagination is already clearly contrasted with her impotent self-absorption. As Madeline Moore notes, "Rhoda . . . lives completely in her dreams. She makes little distinction between the world of action and the world of fantasy" (132). She daydreams over her bread but is unable to express her inner vision. Although she later finds solace in listening to music, she never learns how to create art from her own internal world as a technique for psychological survival. Her reveries remain undefined, unvoiced, and so dangerously introspective.

Rhoda, like Bernard, uses a pellet image in connection with people. Whereas, however, Bernard is the creative, thus controlling agent shaping his pellet, in Rhoda's image she is acted upon, a victim of uncontrollable forces. She accuses the crowd on the streets of snatching from her the "white spaces" in time, of rolling them into "dirty pellets" with "greasy paws" and throwing them into the wastepaper basket. The sense of disgust informing Rhoda's image points up the great difference between her view of human beings and Bernard's. Perhaps the recipients of those unwanted aspects of her humanity that she has disowned and projected, human beings are for her not full of congenial promise but alarming and nauseating—"hideous" and "squalid," stinking objects of her hate, by whom she is "stained . . . and corrupted" (156). Her pellet is the vestige of something once pure, now soiled and curled by the rubbing up of the passing human throng who lard her with the secretions of their disturbingly evident bodies—sweat and grease.

In the novel's descriptive interludes, the degraded humanity of Rhoda's "mean streets" is split up and reflected in part in the amorphous organic processes of the kitchen rubbish heap and in part in the life of the air-borne birds. The snails inhabiting the rubbish heap's nebulous regions are also associated with Rhoda herself; one of her earliest observations is of a snail crossing the path (5), and Louis describes her eyes as "the colour of snail's flesh" (154).[12] Like the walrus and the maggot, the snail, similarly flaccid and limblessly oval in form, presents a feared version of selfhood, in which intellect is extinguished in a swollen body. Yet while this body is distressingly dominant, at the same time it is a weak (rather than a self-contained and securely self-containing) vessel. Its fluids leak out—like those of the people on the streets. Rhoda's fear of personal disintegration is reflected in the pervasive decomposition of the snail's environment, its contours molded by the shifting detritus ejected periodically from the kitchen. Decay is energetic, rapidly absorbing the individual who cannot defend the boundaries of her own body and replicating the pattern of apparently meaningless movement and change that Rhoda finds so threatening in life on the street (81–82).

In the rubbish heap, with its wetness, greasy mutton steam, rancid scraps of pastry, rotten fruit, and vegetable peelings, Woolf suggests a putrid parallel with the fulsome textures, tastes, and smells of Susan's kitchen—its meat, sticky sultanas, and yeasty dough—indeed, Susan connects herself with the dung heap, hens, steamy windows, and the smell of the sink (146). In fact, both the wholesome kitchen and the opulently rank and festering rubbish heap are centrally involved in the production of life, the similar richness of both sites pointing to the indisseverability of death and new life—for all food was once life, and all eaters ultimately lose discrete identity to become food themselves. With the movement of the descriptive focus into the dining room, this organic mutability is contrasted with the effectively infinite and changeless existence of the utensils of eating. These objects possess a stability, a permanence of a sort that perhaps Rhoda, with her extrabiological aspirations, would like to emulate. Illuminated by the passage of the sun, they emerge salvagelike into daylight: a glazed white plate like a lake, a knife like a dagger made of light, and tumblers balancing—apparently—on light (82).

"Dry-beaked, ruthless, abrupt," the birds with their sharply defined sense of selfhood are clearly marked out from "the sodden, the damp-spotted, the curled with wetness" of the rubbish heap on which they feast (82). They represent another feared vision, of a kind of hyperefficient self (the antithesis of Rhoda's nonidentity) that can compete in order to gratify appetite but is ruthless in its egotism. Snails and birds suggest a polarization of ways of being into the extremes of total helpless selflessness and of aggressive selfhood pursued to the point where the other ceases to exist except as potential food.

The birds' sudden swoop and attack and the battery of their iron beaks replicates the unassimilable shocks that assail Rhoda in her contact with hostile identities—even to an extent in contact with her friends, of whom, she confesses, she is afraid (97). In fact, Bernard exploring his fellows' souls can be seen at worst to probe and expose their vulnerable centers just as the birds disembowel the snails. Other more resilient identities (such as his own) develop, he observes, a tough protective shell to defend themselves against such attacks (196). Rhoda, however, diffusely embodied, is impotent to compact her outer surface into an armor tough enough to withstand the hammer of this predatory beak.[13]

Whereas Rhoda avoids ordinary people, fearing what she perceives to be their vicious assault upon her, Louis courts the working class, longing to surmount his own sense of rootlessness through participation in their culture. He chooses a woman with a cockney accent for a lover, in order, he says, to feel "at ease" (154). Although his bodily dis-ease resembles Rhoda's (he anticipates the moment when he can "put off this unenviable body . . . and inhabit space" [38]), his identity problem appears to be socially induced rather than predominantly existential as hers is. As an Australian, he is by birth a colonist in a "new" country in whose real (Aboriginal) past he has no share—hence his preoccupation with history. In London too he is an outsider, marked out by his inability to mimic the English that English people speak, eternally identified by native Londoners as Australian or Canadian (70).

Louis's chosen diet expresses his hopeless desire for acceptance by ordinary people. He frequents a cheap café where the glass shelves are full of buns and ham sandwiches, and steam from the tea urn hangs in the air, mingling with the smell of beef and mutton, and sausage and mash (69). Even when he has achieved a certain standing in commerce, he continues to gravitate toward working-class food (liver and bacon) and working-class districts (narrow streets around the river where there are pubs, passing ships, and women fighting). He "thinks" that liver and bacon is his favorite dinner (130), but one who eats the food of her or his own people does not generally reflect upon it in this way. Louis is not really certain that he prefers the food he has chosen to adopt—any more than he is really certain that he belongs among these people. As he eats their food in their pubs, the ships in their landscape are a constant reminder of his immigrant status.[14]

Louis is motivated by the need to unify into a meaningful whole. Set apart by his accent, he sits in eating shops and tries to make himself accepted by the clerks, but all the time he remembers his "solemn and severe convictions and the discrepancies and incoherences that must be resolved" (154). The "discrepancies and incoherences" that he wishes to eradicate are situated first in himself, in his own cultural dislocation; second in working-class culture, which he sees as gyrating around a central void; and third in his own attitude toward the working class, to which he would like to belong but which, ambivalently, he berates at the same time for its essential vacuity. Indicative of this ambivalence is his statement in the café: "I prop my book against a bottle of Worcester sauce and try to look like the rest" (69), for if one wants to look like all the rest in this world of sausage and mash, one does not read a book of poetry. And yet Louis cannot leave the book with its "perfect statements" out of the equation, for he believes that only the poetic word will bring order to the apparently random movement of working-class life (70).

The translator/poet Louis conceives his work as a means to bring about the unification he desires. Artistic form is for him a circle that will contain himself and a community with its history, binding all indissolubly together. In a sense his artistic objective is not dissimilar from Bernard's, for both men use language to create a form of connection with others. Both men too conceive of language as a unificatory ring—but whereas Louis's written statements are "forged rings" (70), strong, permanent metal circles, Bernard's spoken phrases are evanescent smoke rings wreathing off the lips (50). Through this ring of words Bernard easily establishes a genuine spontaneous alliance with working people. Louis observes that his friend can talk easily to horse breeders and plumbers, not only achieving their acceptance but also inspiring their devotion (51). This is something that he himself, although (or perhaps because) he agonizes over his connection with working-class people, palpably fails to achieve. His problem is that, unlike Bernard (who accepts the horse breeder and the plumber for what they are and is therefore accepted by the horse-breeder and the plumber), he is compelled to bring working people to reason, to point out what he sees as the deficit in their culture. He hopes he can redeem working-class life by informing it with poetic significance, but the café populace is not only uninterested in the meaning he wishes to inject into its life but oblivious to the existence of any void. Louis realizes, bleakly, that ordinary people are impervious to formal poetry and will never encompass it in their closed circle; nor can he translate the poet's word so that it touches them with the transforming realization that they are "aimless" and their lives are "cheap and worthless" (70).

Like the kitchen rubbish heap swathed in a pendulous cloud of meaty steam, the café where Louis eats is, viewed through his eyes, another habitat of violent predators and mindless life-forms. He describes the men who frequent it as "prehensile," members of a subhuman genus, guillemots or monkeys. These are people who exist solely and unreflectively in their multiple sensations, entirely in the present moment—this latter a characteristic that is to the history-hungry Louis both culpable and perversely attractive. He thinks disapprovingly that this is "the mean . . . the average," and yet at the same time he is preoccupied with himself appearing an "average Englishman . . . an average clerk" (69).

If Louis thought that the café represented community, his observation of the guillemots' and monkeys' activities disabuses him. What passes for community here is motivated by the desire for financial profit rather than human empathy—"I would take a tenner" is reiterated like a chorus throughout the café scene. Discommunity, as recurrently in Woolf's novels, is associated with uninspirational meals, in which the lack of the emotional sustenance, of the spiritual nourishment, and of the celebratory significance that inform satisfying experiences of eating is as significant as the mediocrity of the food.

Like the café of *Jacob's Room*, the eating house is a site of disjunction and alienation, in which consciousness is shredded and tattered rather than assuaged and enhanced. As in *Jacob's Room*, the constant opening and closing of the door emphasizes the disunity of a social arrangement by which people do not arrive simultaneously to eat together at an appointed hour, but enter and exit haphazardly without making contact, deploying themselves at the many separate little tables that speak of dislocation and loneliness. Surveying this picture of meaningless and disorderly motion, Louis thinks that if it contains the sum total of life, life, then, is "worthless" (69).

All the same, he does perceive a rhythm of sorts in the café as he eats his dinner, one based on circularity. Watching people and traffic pass and repass the window, he feels he is at the pivotal point in the cycle of urban life (62). Inside he observes the same kind of ceaseless circling. Like dancers in a waltz the waitresses swing in and out of the doors with balanced trays, placing the correct plate of greens or apricot and custard before the correct customer as if executing choreography. Their rhythm is encompassed like counterpoint in the rhythm of "the average men," who take their plates of food while continuing to rap out, "I would take a tenner . . ." Unusually in Woolf's work, the rhythm of the dance here expresses not a communalizing force but a mechanical, dehumanized movement. The wheeling waitresses are skillful but robotic. Their performance is an exhibition of dexterity and accuracy, lacking the emotional component that one might connect with feeding (69–70).[15] This kind of perpetually dynamic, unreflective gyration lends a sense of ostensible unity but fails to instill the genuine significance that Louis desires. He searches for the imperfection through which meaning leaks and chaos is glimpsed but sees only an unfractured circle and "common mainspring" which repeatedly expands and contracts. The reason for the failure of coalescence is, he realizes, that he is excluded. At the hub of an incessantly rotating wheel, he—who so ardently wishes to belong—is alien, a stationary observer rather than a participant in the movement (70).

Lawrence points out that a secure (nonanorexic) identity not only has a sense of the efficacy of its own boundaries but also of inclusion in a larger community (1984, 49). Unsure both of who he is and of which group (if any) he belongs to, Louis has to resort to imitation: In the café he watches the other eaters and copies what they do (69). Rhoda too must have constant recourse to this tactic; in order to put on her stockings she has to copy Susan or Jinny, and she speaks as she hears them do (98). In this game of Simon Says she resembles anorexic women such as Karen, who explains that "since I don't have any identity—I keep trying to imitate others, accommodate to them, adjust myself to their mood" (Bruch, *Eating Disorders*, 1974, 374).[16] As Louis notes, however, in Rhoda, imitation as a survival technique is counterposed by a more fundamental *opposition* to the mainstream. He sees her as the one who turns away when the "herd" gallop together across "rich pastures" (155)—a significant image in which the bid for independence from the group is expressed, as in anorexia, by a rejection of its good and plentiful food. Unlike Louis, Rhoda does not really wish to identify with the social corpus but rather to defend herself against the losses of self that she experiences when she is one among many.

For Woolf, community is not an institution, like the school, which abrades rather than supports individuality, but a feeling—a special, spontaneously occurring sense of interconnectedness within which personal as well as group identity is affirmed. Percival's farewell dinner is one of many examples in her fiction of the meal as a catalyst for such an upsurge of self-nourishing communal feeling. At this moment, as Bernard remarks, the company is drawn into unity by a depth of shared emotion, the richness and vividness of the carnation on the dinner table testifying to the special quality of this coming together. The combination of the many separate petals in a single bloom symbolizes the union of the seven individuals at the table; yet at the same time the uniqueness of each person is evinced by the specificity of the seven different views of the flower (as Bernard notes, each diner contributes her or his own vision), so that in effect the carnation is both one and seven (95). In this context of positive, self-enhancing togetherness even Rhoda experiences community as pleasurable, enjoying the thickening and deepening it brings. She perceives a kind of existential ripening in which the atmosphere is colored red and orange, and a bloom lies on all the objects in the room. Melting, the dissolution of those boundaries that generally separate self from self, is not here a threat but an enjoyable sensation. Unlike the traumatic uniformity of school, genuine community is for her here a semi-mystical state in which she is enriched and enraptured (101).

For Neville alone, one figure in the grouping is more significant than any other—the unspeaking cipher Percival, with whom he is in love. Before Percival's arrival, Neville sees not a seven-petaled carnation pregnant with significance but a metal vase containing three red flowers. Until synthesized by this special presence, an unnatural irrelation pervades the restaurant for him. Nothing seems real; nothing has coalesced; the piles of fruit and cold meat are suspended, untouchable, in waiting. Just as in the cheap café, the doors swing constantly like choppers, a symbol of the painfully anonymous plurality that for Neville pertains until the loved one makes his entrance. Everything in the room seems harsh and inhuman; the white table cloth glares and the other diners are hostile and indifferent, their look as cruel as a lash (88–89). In contrast, when Percival is finally present, Neville sees the restaurant as warm, bright, and fluid—diners, cutlery, curtains all run together like paint on water (101).

Whereas Rhoda's experience of meaningful community is of the solid made liquid, Jinny's is, characteristically, of the evanescent made solid—"the air [made] tangible" (101). For her the tangible is always preferable, not only because it can be touched but also because it can be tasted. She prefers rain when it has solidified into snow and is thus "palatable."[17] She does not recoil from the bodily secretions that for Rhoda soil the street. On the contrary, she is drawn to the brown stain with its scent of food (the meat that to Rhoda connotes degradation and depravity) or sex, seeing herself like a little dog, always in pursuit of the one or the other. She expresses her appreciation of her own physical beauty in an image of voracious eating: "I gulp it down entire," for it is not immaterial but "flesh . . . stuff" (169).

Whereas Rhoda is completely alienated from physical being (Louis says, "She has no body as the others have" [15]), Jinny is so identified with the body that it becomes consciousness itself for her. "My body lives a life of its own," she says (46); "my imagination is the body's" (169). Hence she hates the small mirror at school that shows only her head, for the decapitation separates her from that self by which she makes sense of the world. Being invested in the body, she cannot be threatened, as Rhoda is, by the possibility of the engulfment of her "real" self in that body. She knows no rift between conscious goal and physical response, no failure at the puddle. On the contrary, she describes her body, in a sexual image, as in sublime accord with essential desire: "I open my body, I shut my body at will" (47).

Jinny's presence is a force for form and harmony, for one-pointed order. Susan notes that when she enters a room she centers objects around her so that she stands like the focal point of the star in a smashed window (90). Whereas external patterns impinge upon and mold Rhoda's body, Jinny is the possessor of a core self that can reach out, raylike, to what is external without losing its central integrity. She not only resists the impress of the world but impacts her own pattern upon what lies beyond her, schematizing the inchoate with her radial lines. However, if Jinny brings order, she also opposes the stasis that can strike into that order. Never settling anywhere for long (133), she knows that "beauty must be broken daily to remain beautiful." Her star is created by the shattering and setting in motion of glass (a fixed inflexible material), so re-creating the constantly flickering dance of her own movement. As a result of recognition by Jinny, "We change," says Susan (90).

The star is also an image of touch and its radiant pulses of sensation, its apotheosis in the streamer sensations of orgasm. Unlike Rhoda, who fears "embraces" (157), Jinny loves physical contact with its promise of sex, which is for her an ontological solution to the problems and pains of life (169–170). She does not fear the duplicities of time as Rhoda does, because for her time is resolved by orgasm, the body's ultimate moment in which only the present exists. Bernard describes an encounter with Jinny as being without past or future, simply their bodies in the present and "climax . . . ecstasy" (194). Time with its "devouring" mouth is to Jinny a feeble enemy, routed by rouge, powder, and handkerchiefs (175). She does not fear loss of youth because her seductiveness is not predicated on conventional notions of attractiveness. (She knows that she is not really beautiful—certainly not as beautiful as Susan or Rhoda [29–30].) Because she is supremely confident in her real physical identity (rather than in a defined-as-beautiful youth), age cannot diminish, cannot defeat her. Growing thin and gray she remains unafraid (170).

Whereas Jinny achieves coalescent identity by dwelling only in the present moment, Susan attains a sense of selfhood by hitching herself to the shafts of time, by joining with larger forces beyond herself and making her body a channel for the slow passage of nature. She feels buttressed by the landscape, that she is not just a woman but part of a larger organic entity—herself the fields, the barn, the trees, the light on the gate, the seasons, the mud, the mist, and the dawn. While Jinny's febrile sexual encounters are without issue, an end in themselves, Susan's body is yoked to its reproductive function. She compares herself to a crop-bearing field, asserting "My children will carry me on" (99). For her a life is not limited to the single span of its own existence but is constantly renewed by the birth of new generations, and personal mortality is thus insignificant. She resolves time by expanding the present to include the future moments of all her children and her children's children. Looking at her baby she thinks that she will continue beyond her own death because her identity is imprinted in his body.[18]

Susan accepts hunger simply as a part of the pattern of nature and acts upon its signals instinctively. When she is hungry she thinks of bread and butter and returns across the fields (73–74). The kitchen is her territory. She is engaged in its work in a way that none of the other characters is—although all are described eating. Here she has an intense physical involvement with objects, with solid materials, with the palpable substantial things that Rhoda despairs of making contact with: moist rich sultanas, heavy bags of flour, and the scrubbed kitchen table. Her ingredients are emphatically heavy, the manipulation of the dough strenuous. Her labor is described in strong simple verbs: "take," "lift," "knead," "stretch," "pull," "plunge." But if work with food is tiring, it yields huge sensual rewards: the contrast between the sticky sultanas and the hard scoured table, between the cold sharp water fanning through her fingers and the thick clinging dough (74)—sensations which are unavailable to the out-of-body Rhoda.

Susan's domestic work connotes the physical effort of childbirth, and her kitchen is redolent with symbols of pregnancy and labor. The roaring fire and the buzz of the circling flies suggest some form of generative process, a forging of new life. The meat in the uterine shape of the oven stands as a metaphor for the child's flesh in the womb (a wholesome image that counterposes Rhoda's association of meat with degradation and depravity). The bread rising "in a soft dome" under the clean tea towel is another metaphor for the mother's swelling belly (74), the dome recalling the triangle and hive forms used as maternal symbols in *To the Lighthouse*.

As Susan walks to the river, leaving her dough to rise, it seems to her that everything is breeding (74). Her pear-colored and pear-shaped eyes suggest her propensity for child bearing—both through the form of the pear, which resembles the pregnant body, and through the association with fruiting and fertility. Late in life Bernard recalls her special gift (like Mrs. Ramsay's) for fostering growth; under her care, even the vine that was killed by the frost has magically put out new shoots. The owner of fields and hothouses in which cucumbers and tomatoes ripen, she is for him a kind of proprietorial Goddess of fertile vegetation, and he envisages her walking heavily across the fields with the fruit of her own generation, her two sons (211–212).

Susan's jam and pickle making—"Now I measure, I preserve," she says (147)—also stands for preserving on a metaphysical plane, for she is the preserver of her own life, reappearing after her proper season is over in the faces of her children. As superintendent of the fruit both of the tree and the womb, she can structure infinity by holding up to it a measure marked in human life spans—a unit subdivided into phases of growth and decline. At the turn of the year when she weighs and counts the produce garnered and stored against the coming winter, she also measures her children against a window shutter, quantifies the produce of her own body, laid in to confront the march of the seasons (146).

Weighing and preserving are also facets of Susan's need to possess—human beings as well as natural goods. As a young woman she foresees her ownership extending over all aspects of feeding and nourishment, becoming in her daydream (as later in reality) the keeper of the kitchen and its provisions, which she locks in the cupboards. She *has* those who grow the food (farm workers), those who prepare it (kitchen servants), those who consume it (children), and those who consume it and later become it (lambs). Her control over the food is a source of personal power over all who rely upon it (73). At school she fantasizes returning to the countryside to feed her animals (39); those that she nurtures become "*my* doves" and "*my* squirrel." Bernard later thinks of her as a kind of *Urmutter*, feeding and seeding in a single motion, pigeons waddling after her to pick up the grain that drops through her "capable earthy fingers" (212, my italics). The image, although attractive, carries undertones of potential tyranny, suggesting a mother who enthralls by fattening and immobilizing her dependents, engrossing bodies that can no longer run.

As Susan matures into middle age, her natural goods augment until she can declare, "I possess all I see." She has enfolded all her produce, vegetable and human, into her own apron—sewn pears and plums into white bags, netted strawberries, lettuces, and children ("like fruit in their cots") into beds.[19] Once her children have grown and broken free, however, she finds herself woven into her own mesh, planted and fenced in like one of her own trees (146). The well-spring of her contentment finally becomes the source of her entrapment. Sitting by the fire, she is unable to see what lies beyond the domestic circle because the kettle has steamed up the window (131). Unlike Jinny, she has allowed herself to become the inmate of a glass prison; "Life stands around me like a glass round the imprisoned reed," she says (147). The maternal milk is beginning to curdle (131). With her offspring grown up and gone on, life has become a repetition of the same, now ritual, actions: placing the meat and the milk beneath the shade and pressing her hands on the heavy bags of tea and sultanas.

For Susan the achievement of her greatest contentment implies the beginning of recoil. "No more," she protests, feeling herself "glutted with natural happiness" and wishing that her "fullness" would end (132). She begins to contemplate with aversion all that she has accrued, and which continues to reproduce itself: children in cradles, kitchen baskets, ripening hams, shiny onions, beds of lettuces and potatoes (131–132). She describes the satisfaction of her desire for fields, for fruit and vegetables, for maternity, and even the sly ferocity that she has used to gather in these harvests, in terms of physical satiation. Just as the food that is pleasurable in moderation becomes sickening in surfeit, so, for her, the life of the reproductive body, once so pleasurable, ultimately becomes nauseating. She is "sick" of fruit and children growing, of the body and of the maternal cunning with which she has jealously collected around the table her crop of children—a crop always her own (146–147).

Only Bernard includes, finally, in a single life, both the confident coalescent selfhood that Susan and Jinny know and Rhoda's failure of identity. Completely self-assured for the greater part of the novel, off its pages he undergoes late in life an existential crisis which he recounts during the final meal of *The Waves*. The young Bernard could postulate such an ontological failure as Rhoda experiences when she cannot cross the puddle but not project himself into such a state of being. He addresses his self as the one who always responds when he calls, reflecting that it would be dreadful if he called and no one came (57). In the end, however, he suffers just this devastating failure of response; that self which has been his unfailing companion suddenly falls silent (218); thus deserted, he becomes a body only, standing by a gate (219).

Existential collapse is for Bernard a terrible experience, but it is also a watershed in terms of personal identity. Through this temporary revolt of the self, his understanding is deepened and broadened. He rises again transfigured by the revelation of a core of being that renders meaningless the trivial desires, the petty imperatives on which he has always acted, making redundant his posturing, his idle curiosity, his need for someone—anyone—to keep company with and all his verbose phrases. All at once it seems to him that solitude is better, and silence and the sparseness of simple things, in the context of which he finally finds authentic identity (227). For the first time the world is revealed to him in its nakedness. When he looks at himself through his new unshaded eyes, his multiple identities have fallen away, and he recognizes that beneath all the affectations only a few human constancies are really his. Among these he acknowledges his lusts and appetites,[20] and the physical self which it is difficult to control (the animal man who burps and scoffs up brandy and viscera), all of which he observes and accepts without judgment, wishing neither to eradicate nor disguise (223). There is no need for the fear and loathing that Rhoda feels when confronted with evidence of her physical self. Bernard broken and reconstituted recognizes that the body with its demands and desires is not divorceable from total identity but a facet of it. Without this body one is like Rhoda, driven by the winds.

This same body is, he sees, a vessel of hallowed beauty, a cathedral space. Looking down on this body from his head, he is awed by its architecture arching upward toward the eye like Gothic vaulting. He sees a temple filled with music and incense rising, banners and—Christian symbol of the soul—a dove. Regarded from this position of profound and peaceful detachment, his hand is a "fan of bones laced by blue mysterious veins," astounding in its capability to fold and squeeze, its wonderful sensitivity. Even the debris of the meal he has just eaten partakes in the numinousness of ordinary life, the breadcrumbs transformed into sacralized "relics," the horns of bread and pear peelings a series of elegant sculptural structures, hard-glazed, intricately carved, delicately toned (223).

The summation of all his past meals, at which he tells for one more time the story of his life and the lives of all his friends, Bernard's final meal in the novel is also a ritualistic encounter with death. Hanging up his coat is a symbolic sloughing of his mortal body; the cloakroom is the antechamber to death. The silent companion with whom he shares his table assumes the character of a Grim Reaper, on whose exit Bernard is bound to settle his account with life and depart the world (225). In this context his words, "it does not matter whom I meet," are ironic, for they no longer express an eagerness to embrace whatever unknown personality he might encounter but indifference toward the identity of the next face to present itself in the eternal human parade. He has done with the superficies of a life that he is ready to abdicate from; as he tells himself, "All this little matter of 'being' is over" (221).

However, Bernard is not allowed the facilely mystic death of tranquil ascent into bodiless soul. By a glance at the face of his companion, on which he seems to see ridicule, he is jolted out of his position of cosmic acceptance into a renewed sense of distaste for the things of the body. The moment of transcendent consciousness passes, and suddenly life is once again "unutterably disgusting," beauty one of its "dirty tricks." He sees stains on the napkins and grease congealing on the knives, and he thinks that dinner is only slobbering over the corpses of dead birds (225). Yet he is grateful for this "blow" that sends him reeling in "peelings and crumblings and old scraps of meat," for to be human is to engage with the reality of the body and the body's decay as well as with the sublimity of the spirit. "I regain the sense of the complexity and the reality and the struggle, for which I thank you," he says (226).

The elderly Bernard encompasses Rhoda's extracorporeality (the Bernard who has experienced breakdown is "weightless" [219], "thin as a ghost" [220]) and her recoil from the perceived sordidity of human nature and human biology, but never to the degree that such things become for him, as for her, absolute and unremitting conditions of existence. Life for him is not so terrible, people not so depraved. As he himself comments, contemplating Rhoda's horror of human beings, "Cruel and vindictive as we are, we are not bad to that extent" (194). *The Waves* seeks neither to propound Rhoda's perceptions as a complete existential view nor to undermine them as an accurate reconstruction of her personally lived world. If a viable way of being is not Rhoda's, whose alienation from her body is so total as to threaten to drive her from the material world irrevocably, neither is it that of the young Bernard, for whom life is as facile as his phrase is glib. A crisis of selfhood such as Bernard's by the gate is not in fact a personal cataclysm but a necessary revelation of the deeper truths that lie beneath the skin of existence. After his moment of lost identity, Bernard passes through the gateway into a state of enhanced consciousness, "a new world never trodden" where there are different flowers (220). Such psychological suffering, Woolf suggests, is in the end self-expansive.

Chapter 9

The Years:
The Admirable Mutton

For the generations of women who inhabit *The Years,* the sweep of modern history can be measured in terms of society's changing expectations of them in relation to food. In 1880 the Pargiter girls are in thrall to the highly organized rituals of family eating—a pointless slavery, for the table duties that consume their lives are an end in themselves, having nothing to do with the necessary business of feeding oneself. (The food is actually prepared in the basement by servants.) In 1910, their Victorian parents dead, Sara and Maggie have achieved a degree of liberty through relative poverty. They live in cheap lodgings where, Rose observes, they cook their own food (137), eating at times that suit them and inviting whom they choose to share their meals. In the novel's Present Day (the mid-1930s), Delia's hosts her party in an office. Purged of ceremony, social eating has become an informal, hand-to-mouth affair, and the once exclusively female role of offering food has been assumed by young men carrying trays (329).

All the same, it would be wrong to suppose that *The Years* portrays the sociocultural movement of the half century from 1880 to the 1930s as one of unmitigated improvement, of linear progress for women from oppression to liberty. In fact, despite its forward movement in time, the novel is in another sense cyclic, for it moves from a situation of maternal absence and patriarchal authoritarianism in the family to one in which the traditional kind of mother is culturally displaced and phallocratic fascist dictatorships, reminiscent of and potentially far more sinister than the domestic Victorian one, are on the rise.

For Woolf the dilemma inherent in the creation of a new, more flexible culture of eating was one of how to liberate women from the constraint to fulfill a caretaking role in relation to feeding without at the same time expelling the nurturant component that makes a meal a richly satisfying experience. As Ellen Rosenman notes, "*The Years* treats the loss of the maternal legacy as more dangerous than its slavish imitation" (1986, 54). Woolf's ideal, however, was neither to lose the maternal legacy nor slavishly to imitate it. In *The Years* she asks if it is possible to transform the immanence of the mother in the food into a way of being that is psychologically healthier for women and is compatible with self-sufficient living.

In "Professions for Women" Woolf famously argued that if women were to live full lives, they must first destroy the Victorian model of femininity, crystallized for her in Coventry Patmore's poem, "The Angel in the House." She described this domestic paragon as "intensely sympathetic," "immensely charming," and "utterly unselfish": "She excelled in the difficult arts of family life. She sacrificed herself daily. If there was a draught she sat in it—in short she was so constituted that she never had a mind or wish of her own, but preferred to sympathize always with the minds and wishes of others" (*Death of the Moth,* 150). In order to live the way they wanted to live, to write what they wanted to write, she explained, women had to kill this angel, an act of violence justified because it was committed in self-defense—"Had I not killed her she would have killed me." Moreover, its victim was not a real woman but a male construct, a "phantom," a "fictitious nature" (151), her destruction not matricide but the shattering of a false icon.

The high altar of the ministering angel was the tea table. Here she charmed, flattered, made small talk, and attended solicitously to her male companions. In Woolf's analysis, it was this tea table which was the focal point of Victorian family life. She described it in her own childhood home as a kind of sacred tribal totem tended by mother pouring out tea (Add Ms 61973). Like the angel, the tea table, although female-identified, was actually of male composition, created by men for men, rather than an arena in which women could express themselves authentically. Here real womanly qualities had to be either repressed or distorted in favor of the vitiated femininity upon which rested a shallow, safely urbane etiquette.[1] Although mother or daughters presided, it was father who held real authority over tea, and it was on his say-so that the ritual was eternally reproduced. In the "1880" section of *The Years,* it is the arrival of the patriarch, Abel Pargiter, that galvanizes his daughters into rolling out the tablecloth and producing the flowered teacup (12).

Although Abel's manner is bluff and ostensibly benevolent, it conceals a teapot tyrant—who is perhaps himself not fully conscious of the impact of his dictates upon his children. In curtailing tea for Martin and sending him off imperiously to do the homework that he regards as more important for a boy, he acts not only as a killjoy but as a trespasser in an area that is most personal to the child, stopping him in the act of reaching out for more food. Banished from the table, Martin slams the door, an action expressive of an intense but unspeakable resentment of his father (15). Indeed, the legislation on his hunger appears to set up in him a deep well of unfocused hatred that as an elderly man he has still not expelled. In her party in the Present Day Kitty observes that as usual he seems to be hating something. According to her, he has always been "a hater" (335).

In a sense Martin might be glad of the command that releases him from the tea table and consigns him to his books. The daughters bound to remain behind the teapot crave for such a liberation and for the school books that are a privilege reserved for sons. For Eleanor, even in middle age, as long as her father lives afternoon tea is effectively a roll call at which her presence is required. His occasional engagement elsewhere provides a welcome opportunity to eschew the onerous meal and expend her energies in some more rewarding activity (86).

Lives lived around the tea table entail long periods of waiting, of unlived time, of meaningful existence suspended. Crosby clearing the tea things seems to Delia to be moving in slow motion as one by one she places the cups, plates, knives, jam pots, and dishes of bread and butter and cakes onto the tray, each with an irritating *chink,* and then returns to take away the table and the cloth (18). For the Pargiter girls, the daily boiling of the recalcitrant tea kettle is an operation of enervating tedium—carried on despite the fact that the operation is pointless, for, as Crosby suggests, she could boil the water much more quickly in the kitchen (11).[2] Milly, characteristically conservative, refuses to deviate from the tradition, but Delia, the rebel, is eager to sweep aside the redundant ritual, instituting convenience in its place. Her apparently inconsequential question, "Must a kettle boil?" (10) is in fact profoundly subversive in a culture that has endowed domestic ritual with a moral significance. In *The Years* the vast and complex institutions of late nineteenth-century civilization are founded upon such domestic conventions. Should the kettle cease to boil, the whole unwieldy structure of the Victorian establishment must, it seems, topple—a catastrophe which, in Delia's eyes, cannot be brought about too soon.

Delia blames her mother for the protraction of the domestic cult, believing that if only she would finally die, the tea table and all its apparatus could be swept away. She sees her as a (half) living embodiment of the Angel, a hindrance whose death is necessary to her own liberation (20). The kettle to which Delia is a slave, an old brass implement whose engraved decoration of roses is almost now effaced (10), is the mother's object. Its pattern of roses is her insignia (her name is Rose), now, like the woman herself, almost erased. Even its meager flame, once bright now amber, suggests Rose's formerly flame-red hair turned white and egg-yolk yellow (19).

Delia's resentment of her mother is, however, misplaced, for Rose is, like her daughters, a victim of tea table culture. The "borderland" in which she now lingers on the verge of death is only an extension of her previous life of consuming malaise. The girlhood portrait of Rose that hangs over the tea table may be a symbol of continuing maternal vigilance, but it is also a poignant reminder of the mother's own loss of youth in the same pointless occupation as her daughters. Abel's habitual use of the rose-sprigged teacup that does not match the rest but bears the emblem of his wife's name suggests that (like Mr. Ramsay in *To the Lighthouse*) he has drunk his wife dry, in some way fatally depleting her energy. Such, Woolf implies, is the patriarchal tradition, for the mismatched teacup once belonged to Abel's own father (12).

Bitterness at her domestic imprisonment leads Delia to discredit both her own mother and maternal values in general. Watching Rose die, she attempts to recapture a lost sense of her as a vivid, joyful presence, the source of a particularly female warmth and bounty, but her positive memories are eclipsed by her mother's deathly face in the present (20). Although she recognizes some real love among her feelings for her mother, the social context in which the two women are set has alienated her from all affection. When Rose finally dies, she tries desperately but in vain to feel grief—indeed, to feel anything at all—for this woman who has evoked in the past such an intense emotional response in her, but her need to be free eclipses the necessity of feeling (71–72).

Directed by her wish for the downfall of what she misconstrues as a matristic domestic culture, Delia allies herself with her father, imagining that he conspires with her in the desire for Rose's death. When this event seems about to realize itself, she feels that both of them are attempting to contain a rising sense of excitement (39). Indeed, she is in a sense not wrong to identify in her father resentment against Rose (he looks forward to being able to leave London when she is dead [7]), nor wrong to see in him a fellow rebel against the tea table, for although his daily return home is the motive for the boiling of the kettle, he secretly loathes tea (12). He suffers under the dead hand of his own patriarchy, drinking tea in the afternoon because his father drank tea in the afternoon, because all Victorian patriarchs drink tea in the afternoon. At the men's club where he lunches, at temporary liberty from the stifling propriety of the house, he drinks coffee (6), a continental beverage devoid of the taint of domestic respectability. And yet he would risk life and limb for the preservation of the status quo. He has lost his fingers fighting against the Mutiny—an uprising of the oppressed which his daughters (most particularly the militants, Delia and Rose, paradoxically identified with him) would love to enact against domestic tyranny.

If Abel is at heart ambivalent about tea, he comes into his own at dinner, which, as Crosby notes, he always enjoys. Whereas the drawing room, where tea is taken, is feminine in ethos, the dining room is a masculine place, identified by the daggers on the mantelpiece, the "*handsome* sideboard" and the "*solid* objects" it contains (my italics).[3] Like Abel himself, the dining room (dark and smelling of meat during the day) is at its most congenial polished and decked out with silver knives and forks for dinner.[4] When her father is in his easy, charming dinnertime mood, Delia enjoys a sense of special kinship with him and is proud to be thought like him (30). Imperceptive of the subtext of oppression in his reminiscences of army life in India, she enjoys a sense of vicarious participation in a world of mess dinners on hot nights and camaraderie that is closed to her as a woman. She does not see in her father's damaged right hand (as he flicks meat onto the plates with his good left) a reminder of the real violence that underlies such military bonhomie, admiring rather "his decision, his common sense" (31).

News of Rose's fatal relapse interrupts the manly joviality of dinner, coming, it seems, as a reproach or reminder (31–32). When Rose briefly rallies, dinner is resumed, but the sense of good humor is extinguished and the food spoilt (33). Woolf implies that for Delia, and perhaps also for Abel (despite his genuine grief when his wife finally dies), it is Rose herself who has ruined the meal, as, for them, she ruins everything with her lingering reluctance to die. The dried-up meat and crusty potatoes resemble both the sick woman and the atrophied culture of eating that, cruelly, her dying body represents. At the same time, paradoxically, they allude to the absence of a flourishing mother at the Pargiters' table, for when a nurturing figure presides—a Mrs. Ramsay with her Boeuf en Daube—dinner is rich and succulent. But such selfless nurturance has its price. Rose has withered as a result of the unsustainable drain of her life juices into her dependents' bodies—a form of socially mandated care which, by a bitter irony, they do not really want.

For the younger Rose Pargiter, the dinner of 1880 is significant as the frame of a double trauma: her mother's fatal relapse and the encounter with the flasher by the pillar box near Lamley's.[5] Subconsciously she perceives both experiences as punishments for her disobedience in making the forbidden trip—an interpretation of events which initiates in her a lifelong guilt complex centered on her own body as well as, perhaps, a determination to expiate herself by endangering her own life in the cause of women's rights.

In an earlier draft of *The Years*, *The Pargiters*, sexual trauma is involved for Rose, as it was for Woolf herself, with food. Waking in terror from a nightmare of the man by the pillar box, Rose breaks in upon her nurse and Mrs. C eating supper. She can see that the nurse is "very cross" at being interrupted. Rose explains that she has had a bad dream, but rather than ask her about the dream or comfort her, the nurse reproaches her angrily for having caused the nightmare by eating cake: "That's what comes of having that rich cake for tea" (*TP,* 45). This spurious connection together with the sense of blame—that it is all Rose's fault, that she has brought the nightmare, and by extension the exposure, upon herself by something bad that she has done—are enough to induce in the child a sense of shame about eating as well as guilt around sex, implicating enjoyment of the former in bringing about abusive experiences of the latter. Later, when the nurse talks to Eleanor about Rose's nightmare, the child is interrogated by the two women in a way that effectively criminalizes her:

> "Did {she} {you let her} eat a great deal of that rich cake at tea, Miss?" she [Nurse] asked.
> Did you eat rich cake at tea? Eleanor asked. (49).

Eleanor is already concerned that Rose eats much more than is good for a "little girl," observing that she is "sturdy" and well grown (whereas girls are supposed to be fragile and tiny). She links Rose's boyishness directly with the amount she eats, thinking that she "ate enormously; and was a worse tomboy than Bobby" (47). Rose's experience conveys a disturbing message: Girls who eat more than the socioculturally prescribed amount will be punished by sexual violation.

In the published novel, Rose becomes a confident cake eater, but a residue of guilt survives from the earlier draft. In 1908 she eats hunks of cake while describing the violence directed at her as she addressed a by-election meeting, an assault which recapitulates the earlier experience of sexual exposure. That she can now claim to have "enjoyed" the violence is a triumph for her, as is, in the context of the excised details, her ability, almost defiantly, to eat too much cake in its aftermath, forestalling and flouting the anticipated reproach that she is spoiling her dinner. Yet she is not still not without a sense of free-floating shame at her body: "I want a bath . . . I'm dirty," she says (127). Clearly, much of her guilt and suppressed anger at the flasher, and at the society which has inculpated her for suffering this special form of assault, has been sublimated into political action for justice for women—a constructive transformation in one sense, but also one that has enabled her to avoid tackling and resolving her personal sexual traumatization as an individual woman.

On the evening in 1880, it is not only the older Rose Pargiter who dies; a part of the woman in the younger Rose dies too. As the inheritor of her mother's name (as well as of the red hair that makes the naming appropriate), she is apparently also designated to inherit the rose-chased kettle and rose-sprigged cup, even though her masculine orientation makes her the least suitable of all the Pargiter girls to fulfill the role that these vessels entail—she is described as the image of her father (16) and as looking like a man rather than a woman (138). The two-pronged trauma of coming into this unwelcome female inheritance and at the same time encountering a disturbing and violatory manifestation of male sexuality has served for Rose to focus a conflict about her own gender (if she identifies herself as a man, perhaps she can avoid both these unwanted impositions in the future) and to trigger her revolt against patriarchy and the subservient position which, as a woman, she is destined to assume within it.

It is ironic, and perhaps problematic, that Rose adopts the militant stance of the dominant sex in her struggle against it. As Grace Radin notes, she personifies for Woolf such questions as: "How was one to distinguish between the 'heroism' of an Ethel Smyth and the 'heroics' of those who led men into senseless battle? How were women to prevent themselves from adopting the 'masculine point of view' as they struggled to achieve an equal place in society?" (5)[6] Interestingly, Rose's choice of this particular form of resistance does allow her, in a sense, to have her cake and eat it, for the militant feminists' rejection of the pacifist values operant in other sectors of the women's movement and tactical use of violence against patriarchy enable her to succeed to the martial legacy of the male Pargiters which, rather than tea kettles, she intuits to be hers. In 1908, seeing Rose as exactly resembling their Uncle Pargiter of Pargiter's Horse, Eleanor reflects that her sister should have been a soldier (127), not realizing that in a sense that is exactly what Rose has become. Already in 1880, on the way to Lamley's, she imagines herself as Pargiter of Pargiter's Horse "on a desperate mission to a besieged garrison" (24). Perhaps the besieged garrison is an image for her own family, cut off from the world behind its heavy curtains; in later life it will become the political garrison of women disenfranchised within patriarchy. On another level it will become Rose herself, who never, after her sexual traumatization, lets down her ontological defenses again. In the Present Day she continues to move, as Peggy observes, like a military man (288).

It is not entirely surprising that Rose adopts a form of feminism which valorizes traditionally male characteristics, given the maternal model of femaleness that she experiences in her childhood, for she knows her mother only in decline. In her experience, adult womanhood is not a bloom but a wizened stick. The different course that the feminism of her cousins, Maggie and Sara, takes is perhaps explained by their knowledge of a vivid, joyful mother. Significantly, Eugenie is a foreigner, originating from outside the influence of the nullifying English culture. Nor has marriage into it caused her to submit. The antithesis of the typical "pink-and-white pretty Englishwoman," she exudes exoticism with her big dark eyes and warm fluid flesh, appearing to Abel, who may be having an affair with her, attractively voluptuous.

In his attitude toward Eugenie and her household Abel manifests the ambivalence which at heart he feels toward patriarchal English culture in general. He disapproves of her continental servants, whom he thinks of as macaroni-eating "dagoes"—their preference for (to him) foreign food marking them out as suspicious and possibly subversive influences within English culture. And yet he is attracted to Eugenie not in spite but because of her foreignness with its promise of something outside English conventions. She is irreverent toward the tea that secretly he dislikes, habitually allowing it to go cold. In her deserted room he notices with a smile the familiar half empty teacup (96), later observing her take it up again and sip at it with characteristic indolence (99). This Latin languor recalls to his mind the warmth and informality of the women in India, sitting in their doorways in the sun (97). Paradoxically, the suppressed culture seems to the colonist to offer a way of life more satisfying than that which he attempts to impose—a paradigm also for his relationship with patriarchy in England, which in truth is almost as oppressive to those who enforce it as to those who live under its thumb.

Sara craves the presence of her mother, which brings to her, as to Abel, a sense of vibrancy and vitality otherwise lacking in her life. The waltz that she cajoles Eugenie to perform—holding her skirt in one hand and a flower in the other as she circles the chairs and tables—weaves a sense of yearned-for female harmony and erotically charged beauty into the night. Her mother's body flows in the shape of the melody, which, escaping from someone else's party, seems to become louder and clearer as she dances, as if enhanced by the movement (116).[7] Eugenie's physical amplitude contrasts with the spareness of her younger daughter's body (114), and Sara uses her helpless-looking and, still in adolescence, childlike body to elicit her mother's presence—a desperate strategy which is central to anorexia for many young women. However, the adoption of permanent infantile status is also a political tactic, used by Sara with increasing consciousness as a means of avoiding the frustrations and circumscriptions that, she observes, await adult women under patriarchy. In a culture in which womanhood entails self-suppression, maturity is a snare she wishes to avoid at all costs.

Sara has been dropped as a baby; as a result one of her shoulders sits higher than the other (99), a physical deformity caused in a metaphorical sense, or so Woolf implies, by the cultural edicts that a girl is forced to obey under men's rule; her skewed body is a living symbol of the distortions in her own nature that she has had to make in order to survive within a male-ordered, male-dominated society. And yet her ontological position is complex, for she is a "victim" who uses her victim status as a source of strength, gaining a sense of identity by defining herself against the patriarchy that has so deformed her. Because, as a "crippled" and therefore "unattractive" woman, she is unfit to win the standard prize—marriage—that patriarchy offers young women, she has no stake in conventional society, a "disadvantage" that she seizes upon and makes her asset (my quotation marks). In her ringside seat she is ideally placed for her role as a trenchant and chillingly honest commentator. If the prescription of passivity which is handed out to all women in 1907 in Sara's case amounts to one of paralysis—she must lie straight and still, the (male) doctor tells her (114)—it is because with her subversive insight and freedom of speech she is a dangerous enemy to patriarchal society.

Thus supine and motionless, Sara both imitates death and practices Antigonean passive resistance, reenacting in her narrow bed the entombment of the eponymous heroine while she reads Edward Pargiter's translation of Sophocles' play.[8] As she skips through the text, events from *Antigone* are increasingly intermixed with her own dreamy perceptions, so that it becomes hard to know whether she is recounting the narrative of the play or describing her own metaphorical experience of entombment (111). In the Sophoclean context, the "dig" component of Sara's father's name is significant, for in Woolf's novel he is Creon to her Antigone, responsible for the digging of her grave much as Creon is responsible for the entombment of his niece. Flaunting his phallic sword, a symbol of masculine violence, Digby inspires impotent rage in his daughter, his war-dance—"Pirouetting up and down with . . . his sword between his legs"—in sharp contradistinction to her mother's waltz of love and beauty (117).

In the kind of society in which Creon's pronouncement, "We'll have no woman's law here while I live" (Sophocles, 140), is enacted by Parliament, Sara, the dissenter, has little choice but to play Antigone's part. Her ontological dwelling place, "this cave, this little antre, scooped out of mud and dung" (153), resembles the tomb in which Antigone is interred; her physical address in the Present Day, Milton Street,[9] "near the Prison Tower" (249), also implies that her situation within patriarchy is one of punitive incarceration. And yet from her position of extreme marginalization she derives a kind of moral strength. The cave is also an ancient matristic home—connected perhaps with Sara's ecstatic memories of own biological mother—indicating her real spiritual and existential residence to be within a culture that honors women and rejects violence. For true to Antigonean philosophy, "My way is to share my love, not to share my hate" (Sophocles, 140), Sara eschews Rose's aggressive revolt against patriarchy. Rather, living in poverty on the fringes of society, she adopts a position of ascetic separateness which is not dissimilar from that of the anorexic viewed as hunger striker.[10] As Shirley Panken comments, she "accepts her state of privation and loneliness in preference to conformity with social values" (222).

North wonders, naively, why Sara has never married (possibly he once loved her himself), not understanding the social and psychological effects that the distortion of her body has had on her, even though he remembers instantaneously that she is "crooked." Clearly, as both a gesture of acceptance of an adult female body and as an endorsement of the patriarchal system, marriage is a practical and moral impossibility for her. She thus grows into an appealingly twisted specimen of womanhood with her skirt on back to front—like North's apple peel, a broken coil (259). Simultaneously innocent and sage, she is the eternal wise-child, seeing life with naked eyes. Martin observes her in the city chop-house watching people like a child at a pantomime (186). She seems naively wondering, and yet he is not sure that she is not laughing at him, understanding something infinitely deeper than he can himself comprehend.

Sara's frequent and easy surrender to sleep is another reenactment of Antigonean mock death. It is also a mark of the way in which the boundary between dream and reality is creatively diffused for her, fugitive fragments from the one state constantly drifting over into the other. On another level, the propensity for sleep is a means of retracting from the onus of adulthood. Asleep under a tree in Hyde Park, she is identified with Maggie's (also sleeping) baby (197). At the novel's final party sleep relieves her—to Eleanor's amusement—of the obligation to socialize in the way that an adult is expected to (294).

In one sense a further indication of her childlike identity, Sara's apparent tendency to drunkenness on very little alcohol is also connected with a sibylline aspect of her character. Men often assume her to be tipsy and speaking nonsense when in fact the unorthodox pronouncements to which they object are trenchant and farsighted—if framed in flamboyantly poetic terms. It is perhaps the case that her male companions would like to believe her discomfiting words to be the product of inebriation. North, for instance, when he dines at Milton Street, reflects that a tiny amount of wine makes her drunk, but he is discomfited by her "vision" (257). Martin, embarrassed by her antipatriarchal speech in the chop-house, also tries to ascribe her outburst to drunkenness. Stopping the mouth of the wine bottle (as he tells her, patronizingly, that she has drunk enough) is a silent expression of his desire to stop her mouth, for people are listening (187). When she mocks North for enlisting, even the nonconformist Nicholas (moving the bottle out of her reach as if curbing a child) attempts to attribute her disturbingly free and honest speech to alcohol (231).

In a culture in which the range of options available to women is strictly limited, Sara plays the patriarch at his own game. Nicholas asks her: "Can you never act for yourself? . . . Can you never even choose stockings for yourself?" Far from indignant, Sara laughs, replying "Never!" Nicholas ascribes this inability to choose to the fact that Sara lives in a dream world (298), but in fact, like all of her apparently vague and inexplicable behavior, this indecision has a sociopolitical subtext. If she is told that women are not capable of choosing, then, her helplessness implies, she will choose nothing at all, not even the small personal articles that are supposed to preoccupy female minds. In the chop-house with Martin, she is presented with the selection of meats from which the City gentlemen daily take their pick[11] but plumps for the first thing joint she sees, which she designates with a wave of her of her hand as "that" (184). Neither is she interested in the wine list, ordering Martin to choose (185).

The men's good mutton that Sara eats in the City chop-house (187) is very different from that which she usually eats at home. Mutton was for Woolf, in more than simply the nutritional sense, the great staple of Victorian patriarchy. (According to Quentin Bell, her own father ate a mutton chop for lunch every day [vol. 1, 73].) As a food that existed in two classes—prime roast and tough, greasy meat—mutton sustained the social as well as the physical body. Women, being considered lesser limbs of the social corpus, could be fed economically on its cheaper cuts and the remains from men's plates. Like Antigone in her tomb, they were provided "with food enough" to salve the patriarchal conscience (Sophocles, 147), but only that. Repeatedly in *The Years* mutton is an indicator of female disadvantage. The Pargiter patriarch himself, Abel, is named after the Old Testament "keeper of sheep" (Genesis 4:2), whose offering of a sacrificial lamb is preferred by the Judeo-Christian Father-God to Cain's corn (which perhaps smacked too much of Goddess religion to Yahweh). The newspaper editor empowered to publish Sara or silence her is a "mutton-fed man" (274). Rose is sexually traumatized on her way to Lam[b]ley's—where Eleanor later encounters Mrs. Lamley chewing a mouthful of cold mutton. For Eleanor this occasion is connected with a sense of restrictive obligation to her own father's care; Mrs. Lamley reminds her, "she had the Colonel to look after" (84). As she eats the excellent chop-house mutton with Martin, Sara notes that Rose, now an imprisoned suffragette, is being punished for the dissent that was born on the day of her assault on the way to Lam[b]ley's by violent force-feeding with meat, a sanction that is a recapitulation of the assault itself (187).

The mutton that Sara offers North for dinner is stringy (257) and underdone. Accompanied by an unappetizing "slabbed-down mass of cabbage . . . oozing green water" and hard yellow potatoes (256), it is gracelessly served on cheap plates (254) by a clumsy girl (whom North refers to insultingly as "the regular . . . skivvy") (253). The unpalatability of this dinner is in part due to Sara's poverty; having rejected marriage and the access to financial resources that it gives to upper- and middle-class women in patriarchy, she cannot afford a decent joint of meat or the services of working-class women who know how to cook it. Her obliviousness to the evident inadequacy of the food she offers North reflects a refusal to engage with a culinary knowledge geared to the servicing of men—a jib that entails a positive reframing of that form of social disempowerment peculiar to women of her class. As a wealthy man's daughter, she has not been taught how to make her own dinner, has scant practical survival skills, and is, moreover, apparently uninterested in acquiring any more, having not so much resigned herself to the poverty of her lot within patriarchy as decided to flaunt her various deprivations in the patriarch's face. If the meal that she offers North is an inept and sordid affair, it is only, she seems to be saying, a reflection of the fact that she herself is inept and sordid, and it is to this pass that her acculturation in a man's world has brought her.

Sara's mutton is more like a corpse than a joint of meat. Carving it resembles a surgical dissection, incision producing a watery red juice (256). The bloody condition of the joint is a metaphorical indictment of North's decision to participate in the war, of which Sara is scornfully disapproving. As they eat, he reminds her of her angry outburst against him, "Coward; hypocrite, with your switch in your hand; and your cap on your head" (258), her accusation being that by enlisting he made himself no better than her own father and the men of his generation. The switch is a phallic symbol related to Digby's hated sword. (Earlier Sara sees North more explicitly "with his switch between his legs" [230].) North is a coward in her eyes because he has not challenged the patriarchy but has, by espousing violence, conformed with it. The dessert, "ornate . . . , semi-transparent, pink, ornamented with blobs of cream," suggests a further satirical reflection of her cousin's militarism and of patriarchal war in general. Pink and vulnerable underneath its uniform of cream and other ornaments, the "quivering mass" yields gruesomely to the thrust of the metal spoon when he strikes into it (258).

In the Present Day, North appears to have joined the ranks of the Pargiter patriarchs completely. He has moved to Africa, where he is a sheep-farmer, producing the food that sustained Victorian patriarchy. The weight gain noticed by Edward (326) indicates that North has left the camp of the lean and hungry revolutionaries and become a member of the mutton-fed male establishment. At the novel's final party, Peggy inveighs passionately against her brother's essential conformity, predicting that he will ultimately make a complete surrender to social convention: start a patriarchal family of his own and write books to make money rather than "living differently, differently" (314). North himself, however, desires above all things to avoid conformity. He admires the old rebel Pargiters who fought to throw off patriarchal authority; he too wishes " . . . To live differently . . . differently," but he is afraid that he does not have their strength or certainty. Ambivalently, he also seeks a father figure—someone good and wise—to tell him how to live and what to think (340; ellipses in original).

Mutton has one further presence in Sara's house, in the form of the Jewish Abrahamson, who is in the tallow trade (273), for, as Jane Marcus points out, tallow is manufactured from mutton fat (1987, 42). The biblical Abraham is the original Judeo-Christian patriarch, the "father of many nations" (Genesis 17:4), but if Abrahamson can be said to be living, in patriarchal style, literally off the fat of the land, it can only be in the most ironic sense, for tallow is not only an unpleasant by-product of mutton, it is also a very cheap and therefore unprofitable one. Living in the lodging house with Sara, he is clearly equally as impoverished as the young woman and, as a Jew, equally marginalized.

The biblical Abraham is also the husband of Sarah, whom, after her death, he mourns and buries in a cave in the field of Machpelah, an act which, within the terms of reference of *The Years,* both suggests a symbolic complicity between Abrahamson and the latter-day Sara and implicates him in her entombment.[12] In actuality Sara's chief contact with Abrahamson is through the greasy mark that he leaves around the lodging-house bath—another indirect reference to his trade in mutton fat. When Sara describes this to North, his response is "Damn the Jew!" for he is disgusted by the thought of grease from a strange man's body (273). When he learns that Abrahamson also leaves hairs in the bath, he shivers, feeling physically sick. Sara, however, is impassive. If the choice is between sharing a greasy bath with a Jewish man and joining the "servile . . . army of workers," she prefers the sordid communal bathroom. In an allusive condemnation of Nazi anti-Semitism, she mocks the "conspiracy" in which one pledges service to a "master" because of infiltration by dirty Jews (274)—a form of tyranny which was to Woolf, as she made clear in *Three Guineas,* utterly loathsome and scarcely distinguishable from English patriarchalism.[13]

Like Sara, Maggie has opted for social revolution, preferring to entertain without servants in the basement than observe the conventions that pertained to the meals of her parents' generation. However, whereas Sara makes a virtue of squalor, Maggie creates a chaotically romantic ambiance. Although she is bohemian in her silver and gold dress, her meal is characterized by a quality of warmth and nurturance which can best be described as a distillation of motherliness, purified of the idealization and prejudice that distorted the Victorian concept of maternal qualities.

Despite the austerity and adversity of the war, the dinner party given by Maggie and Renny in 1917 is an inspiriting and enjoyably informal occasion. Indeed, blitz conditions are conducive to the abandonment of pointless proprieties. In a sense too the war, which put an end once and for all to what remained of nineteenth-century mores, is a reflection on a grand and violent scale of the annihilation of the old that is being deliberately and systematically carried out within Maggie's domestic circle. Cheerfully, if accidentally, the iconoclasts Maggie and Renny smash piece by piece the dinner service that was kept for best in the drawing-room cabinet at Abercorn Terrace, for, Maggie says, it is silly to keep it shut away. Renny claims that they break a piece every week, but Maggie thinks that the act of destruction will not be complete until the war has worn itself out (229). Maggie and Renny take pride in their dirty forks (228). For Maggie, this happy lack of hygiene indicates a successful rebellion against patriarchal culture with its promotion of cleanliness as a virtue. The open acknowledgment of dirt constitutes for her an honesty which is infinitely preferable to the pretense of salubrity which overlaid the moral squalor of Victorian society. In a personal sense, the embrace of dirt is an act of rebellion against her father, who, in 1891, criticizes his daughters for soiling their best clothes, calling them "grubby little ruffians," his humorous tone undercut with a hint of disapproval (103). When, in 1917, Maggie confesses to dirtiness, she looks at her sister, perhaps in silent complicity, perhaps in accusation, for Sara is still in her day clothes. In a sense the paternal dirt has stuck more tenaciously and damagingly to Sara, who is left with a long-standing sense of sexual shame and—rather than homely dirt—an ineradicable stain. Her lodging-house tablecloth is marked with an ancient yellowing splash of gravy (252), and her bath is ringed with Abrahamson's grease and hairs so that it is metaphorically very difficult for her to get herself clean. Sara and Maggie's experience of besmirchment is not a unique one. Their cousin Rose also retains a sense that she is somehow unclean, initially inculcated (before even her sexual violation) by her father's apparently playful reference to her too as "grubby little ruffian," a comment that causes her immediately to cover a stain on her pinafore with her hand (12).

Once the best dinner plates have been smashed and dirt has been admitted with impunity, tentatively Eleanor, the oldest of the revolutionaries, broaches the question of how life may best be lived after the domestic revolution. Nicholas suggests that progress can be made only by abandoning the family unit and establishing in its place a wider and more elastic kind of community, for the human soul needs expansion and innovation, he says, whereas in 1917 people live "screwed up into one hard little . . . knot" (238). He describes the patriarchal familial arrangement as a series of individual cubicles within which each man has his own holy book, his own hearth, and his own wife (239).

Woolf agreed with this view, but although she was keen to dispose of the patriarchal family in which a woman is one more asset of the dominant male, she was anxious not to banish the essence of the motherly from the new more loosely framed society. Maggie (one of Woolf's Vanessa Bell characters) is written as a woman who has succeeded in both retaining this nurturant aspect and in embracing nonconformity.[14] As the bombs fall, she worries about the children, serves plum pudding, and mends a sock, the kind of essential repair and maintenance tasks that women have undertaken for centuries while men kill each other. Echoing unwittingly the words spoken by Abel Pargiter as Rose lies dying in 1880 ("Now, shall we get on with our dinner?" [33]), she tells her family and friends sheltering in the cellar, "We may as well finish our dinner." Recalling the death of the old kind of mother, this reiteration might be seen to suggest, ominously, a second fatality in which all manifestations of the motherly are expunged for good and all by the war of tyrants that rages in the sky. Indeed, the cellar—in one sense an enclave of peaceful maternity, a womblike place in which the occupants are snugly ensconced in quilts and dressing gowns and fed with pudding— also resembles a crypt, the last resting place of womanly values driven underground by male bellicosity (233).

Like Sara's mutton, Maggie and Renny's roast symbolizes the carnage of armed conflict. Carving it seems to parallel for Renny another traditional duty of the man of the house, military combat. His reluctance to undertake the small domestic task to which he is ordered by Maggie (230–231) is a reflection of his ambivalence about the larger responsibility of participation in war. He carves with a glazed, almost shellshocked refusal of feeling, the same kind of disengagement that informs his attitude to his work, making armaments, for though he believes the war in Europe to be unavoidable, he cannot reconcile himself with the essential horror of manufacturing weapons. Unlike North, who, according to Sara, swaggers in his military uniform, Renny is profoundly disturbed by war, sensing an imperfect morality in either withdrawing from or taking part in it. The patriotic defense of one's nation is for him a necessity, but a shameful one (229).

Like Sara, Kitty Malone is identified with Antigone—compared to the interred heroine with ingenuous romanticism by Edward Pargiter, who is oblivious to the truly Antigonean nature of her life. Entombment for Kitty means confinement within a space that is not large enough to accommodate her. Whereas Sara is twisted and stunted by the circumstances of her life, Kitty has grown to a great height, feeling as a consequence always too big for the world she is forced to inhabit (56). She overflows the little garments that are prescribed for feminine wear, suffering in shoes that are too tight (50), and is defined by the patriarchal standard as too large to be really attractive (51). Ostensibly a sign that she is thriving under patriarchy, in fact her soaring stature is a source of personal dis-ease within a culture in which women are expected to be small and unobtrusive. She fits neither physically nor temperamentally, for her desire for freedom and self-direction is also overlarge for a society in which the only model of female amplitude is a cook named Bigge.

Kitty's Oxford revolves around the university, the exclusive preserve of affluent middle- and upper-class males. Here she is, educationally speaking, starving in the midst of plenty. The daughter of a university professor, living at the heart of one of the world's most prestigious academic institutions and entertaining its leading lights, she is not studying at one of its colleges but making do with a weekly history lesson from Lucy Craddock. Lucy, herself a victim, as a woman, of marginalization by the academic establishment (the dons sneer at her [57]), envies Kitty her social contact with the intellectual elite; however, Kitty is not admitted into their circle for the purpose of erudite conversation. Old Chuffy, the history professor, is more interested in fondling her knee than talking history, an experience which she remembers with distaste (54–55).

Kitty's exclusion from the academic feast is more graphically shown in *The Pargiters*. Here, barred by her sex from eating Sunday dinner in college, she is, however, "as her father's daughter," allowed the dubious "privilege" of watching academia consume huge quantities of food from a gallery. She is revolted by the prospect, feeling that "to see Chuffy eat his ordinary meal was enough for her: to see Chuffy and all the other old gentlemen eat what they ate on great occasions would be more than she could bear." She compares the gastronomic superfluity of the university establishment with the meager amount allowed those impoverished and learned women, such as Lucy Craddock, who live outside its walls, observing that "She would like to feed Chuffy for a term on Lucy's rations and see what he said then about Henry the Eighth" (*TP,* 120). The obese and gynocidal male tyrant is an appropriate ghost to raise in this connection.

In *The Years,* Kitty and her mother are reduced to lean pickings when Mr. Malone dines in college. Reminiscent of the lunch that Mrs. Plumer plans to concoct for herself and her daughters out of the remains of the undergraduates' mutton in *Jacob's Room,* their dinner is an unsavory hotchpotch of leftovers: "dull fish" gone tepid, with miserly squares of stale bread (63). The funny taste that Mrs. Malone notices in the fish suggests the rottenness inherent in a society that can feed its various members so inequitably—although, paradoxically, she herself blames egalitarianism for the inadequacy of her dinner, deploring the effects of education on the so-called servant class. She agrees with the *Times* that compulsory schooling has taught poor children the three Rs at the expense of the rudiments of cooking (64–65). Kitty, who finds the *Times* article "pompous" (65) and sympathizes with working people, perhaps realizes that if the working class is learning to read and write rather than make puddings for the well-to-do, a fairer distribution of the sociocultural food stock may lie in the future.

If Kitty has no appetite for the university's stale leavings (faced with dull fish and stale bread, she does not feel hungry), she greatly enjoys a food that is colorful, frivolous, and expressive of irreverence. She delights in the American Mrs. Fripp's dismissal of that monument to male learning, the Bodleian Library; bored with so much respectable worthiness, Mrs. Fripp prefers the bun shop with its ice cream. Kitty recalls with delighted incredulity that evening how they had been eating ice cream when they should have been at the Bodleian (49). For her, Mrs. Fripp is a breath of fresh air, demonstrating that deference to the dry male-dominated institutions of British patriarchy is by no means universal and that in other places in the world there are other possible ways of living.

Stinted in Oxford of really sustaining food, Kitty looks to a matriarchy to supply her deficiency. In *The Pargiters*, she repeatedly wishes to return to Yorkshire, which she loves "from the depths of her heart" (*TP,* 102), to carry on the farming tradition of the Rigbys, her maternal forebears. It is in the desire to learn the history of her mother's people (99) that she goes to Lucy Craddock, herself a Yorkshire woman. She recalls nostalgically her childhood holidays with Mrs. Carter, her mother's old nurse, at Settle, where, away from Oxford's grinding constraints, she has spent the best days of her life. There she was intimately involved in the production of the really nourishing food with which Mrs. Carter's table was always loaded, having "milked the cows & found the eggs, & seen a {pig killed} {calf born} & learnt how to make real bread . . . & she had eaten huge meals, sitting . . . in the great kitchen, with the hams swinging from the rafters" (104–105).

Leaska points out that this Yorkshire matriarchy—known variously as the Gabbits, Hughes, and Brooks in *The Pargiters* and as the Robsons in *The Years*—was inspired by the family of Joseph Wright, a dialect scholar who rose to eminence from a working-class background. The forming and educating role that the public schools and universities played for the upper classes was filled in Wright's case by his mother. As a result, according to Leaska, "his respect for women had no limit," and his ideas on the status of women were "revolutionary" (*TP,* xii). Prior to his marriage, he wrote to his future wife, "It is my greatest ambition that you shall *live,* not merely exist; and live too in a way that not many women have lived before" (xii). In *The Pargiters,* Woolf describes the wholesome food on which Mrs. Wright fed her children, food which seems to derive directly from the nourishing moral fiber of the woman herself: "first-rate Scotch collops and broth" and "the best bread in the world—with a dash of milk and a trifle of lard in it," while "her Yorkshire pudding, eaten before the meat, served with good gravy, and eaten with three-pronged steel forks, was food for the Gods" (157). Adhering to practices which have been superseded in the male-directed Victorian dinner—serving the Yorkshire pudding before the meat and using three-pronged forks—Mrs. Wright seems to belong to a lost and yearned-for time when a really fortifying maternal food culture prevailed.

In *The Pargiters,* the working-class Hughes family (based on the Wrights) is Kitty's refuge from an oppressively patriarchal Oxford. She thinks that Mrs. Hughes would strongly disapprove of the greed and waste of the college dinner; however, the alternative is not, for Mrs. Hughes, the parsimonious and mean-spirited kind of meal that Kitty and her mother eat; on the contrary, it is "the best food in England," a female plenitude which is delicious and substantial without being excessive. Mrs. Hughes's Sunday dinner with Yorkshire pudding properly cooked (by her daughter Nell) surpasses anything, in her husband's opinion, that an Oxford College can offer (134).

In *The Years,* Kitty is initially shocked at the tea offered her by the Hughes—now renamed the Robsons. The dainty sandwiches and fancy cakes that she expects to see on the tea table are replaced by food—fried fish and potatoes (57)—that her class deems proper to (evening) dinner—a meal which for the working-class northern family does not exist. But this "inappropriate" food has a verve and heartiness which is absent from the "dull fish" eaten at the "correct" time in Kitty's home. The thick round of bread offered on a knife's point (58) connotes a way of living that is unaffected, honest, and unadorned, and to Kitty infinitely preferable to the trite, mannered, and superficial life of stale bread cut into miserly squares—the life of a don's daughter. In the Robsons' house eating is simply that, not, as in Kitty's house, a protracted and onerous social ritual entailing the entertainment either of visiting academics or of her bored and aimless mother. The Robsons take a utilitarian attitude to food, eating with a kind of businesslike thoroughness (57, 59). Devoid of the pretension and ritual that has set into middle-class meals like rigor mortis, tea at the Robsons' is refreshingly quick and unceremonious. With the same pragmatic informality with which they gather, the family disperse, the children scrambling down from the table as soon as the meal is finished (59).

In Woolf's working-class family the cult of the tea table is unknown. Kitty is astounded to find that in the Robsons' house it is not the daughter, Nelly, but the son, Jo, who is deputed to see to the kettle (59). Mr. Robson is proud of his wife and holds her former work as a cook in genuine esteem (58). He respects his mother for having brought up a family and considers his daughter with a wholehearted approbation that is very different from the approval tainted with some hint of stain that Abel and Digby offer their daughters (60). Kitty is startled but pleased to be herself treated by Mr. Robson not as an insignificant appendage of her father but as an intelligent and interesting individual in her own right. Not only does Sam Robson *not* ask after her father, the esteemed professor, but he refers respectfully to Lucy Craddock, considered by the university establishment to be a kind of academic joke. Lucy is not to him, Kitty realizes, an object of ridicule, but a person to be taken seriously; he respects her (57).

For Kitty the solution to the problem of how to eat meaningfully and freely as a woman is found in a family with a strong maternal presence. Her experience suggests that far from the elimination of the motherly from meals, what is needed is an injection of motherly qualities—but those qualities of strength and toughness (as well as love) that real mothers embody rather than the spurious virtues that Victorian patriarchs projected onto them. In a scene cut from *The Years* after the galley proofs were pulled,[15] the elderly Eleanor tries eating in a extrafamilial setting—from which the maternal has been completely excised—as a solution to the nurturance/freedom dilemma. In line with Kitty's, her experience demonstrates that without female input in some form, food is unsustaining, uninspirational, and subject to patriarchal tyrannies. The way forward is not, it seems, to circumvent forms of familial eating altogether if that means replacing emotional warmth and a sense of human connection with the impersonal and mechanistic.

Alone and feeling hungry in Oxford Street, Eleanor decides to dine in one of the new chain restaurants which, just prior to the novel's Present Day, have begun to reduplicate themselves across the city. The magnitude both of the social revolution that has enabled such commercially cloned eating places to proliferate and of the personal revolution that enables Eleanor to decide to eat alone in one of them perhaps needs to be underlined for women today. According to food historian Reay Tannahill, until the 1870s it was considered improper for a lady to be seen in a restaurant at all. "By the 1890s there were quite a few places where a respectable gentleman could take an equally respectable lady to dine of an evening," but "there were very few where a lady might dine alone or in the company of another lady" (328). For a woman of Eleanor's generation, to eat unescorted in a restaurant is thus the exercise of a newfound and exciting, if slightly daunting freedom—a truly groundbreaking act.

The novelty of this situation explains the naive wonder which characterizes Eleanor's experience of the restaurant. She does not respond in this way because she is a timid elderly lady but because in the restaurant as much as in China (which she also visits in her old age) she is an explorer in a foreign land. Her first impression is one of a welcoming conviviality which mitigates her sense of loneliness. The restaurant appears cheerful and opulent and is full of the buzz of voices, for everyone seems to have a companion. She feels as if she has come upon some festival, for red and glass-fringed electric table lamps cast a pinkish light over the diners' faces, and everyone is dressed up. She soon realizes, however, that her pleasure is ill-founded; she has been misled by a surface veneer of brightness and sociability. A closer look reveals that the opulence is in fact gaudy and the customers' animation designed to mask their alienation. Their chatter is an empty noise containing no meaningful words, and the gaiety on their faces merely the reflected glow of the lamps. As she takes her seat, several ominous signs fail to alert her to the unsatisfying nature of the experience she is to be offered: the conveyor-belt occupancy of the tables, the silent harried waitress, the debris of someone else's food, and the coffee-stained menu.

In this neutral public space Eleanor hopes to find an easy, efficient, and emotionally unfreighted way of eating, but it becomes increasingly clear to her that in the chain restaurant anonymity has turned into an uncomfortable combination of self-absorption and indifference. She slowly becomes conscious of the sound in the background of the swing doors—a familiar symbol in Woolf's work of isolation and depersonalization in public eating—as the waitresses file in and out with plates. Mixed up with the bang of the doors is the sound of waltz music coming, apparently, from far away, "a pulse of sound merely that surged up and down beneath the clatter." A reminder of an older, maternally directed kind of dinner, the distant music recalls the earlier scene in Sara's bedroom in which Eugenie waltzes for her daughter to the distant strains of party music. In the restaurant, however, the love and intimacy of the mother have given way to an alienation which her substitute, the uncommunicative and constantly departing waitress, can do nothing to mitigate. As Eleanor becomes increasingly unhappy with the food and the ambiance, the music becomes increasingly dissonant, as if the maternal melody is itself degenerating, until at last there is no tune, only "a scramble of bungled notes." As the musical texture breaks down, the maternal symbols—knives and forks, and flower—also degrade, becoming meaningless, without identity. "That's an odd assembly of objects," Eleanor thinks, her experience recapitulating Lily Briscoe's when, with Mrs. Ramsay dead, domestic items fly apart from their functions.

In contrast to the supreme example of the old kind of maternal meal, Mrs. Ramsay's dinner in *To the Lighthouse,* which is composed of a single consummate dish, the fixed-price restaurant meal consists of a protracted string of equally unsatisfactory courses. The hors d'oeuvre, "little pink strips of fish and a potato salad," is "skimpy food"; there is "not much to it," Eleanor thinks. Perhaps that is a blessing, for it is "salty and slippery and not very agreeable." Beneath a fussy dressing of "pink blobs," the white fish in the next course is "insipid" and "watery and full of bones." Whereas Mrs. Ramsay, who regards dinner as her work of art and feeding as her task in life, insists that the Boeuf en Daube must be served the moment it is perfect, the restaurant waitress, interested neither in food nor customer, forgets the chicken so that it is lukewarm by the time it is "slapped . . . down" on the table. Anyway, it is unappetizing, with "only a rag of flesh on the skinny little bird." The peach melba ice cream arrives at much the same temperature as the chicken, "a greyish-white mound, already half melted, at the bottom of a metal cup," finally defeating Eleanor who, trying "a spoonful of the sweet stuff," thinks it tastes of salt and is quite inedible.

Feeling increasingly dissatisfied with the food that appears on her plate, Eleanor begins to doubt the wisdom of the apparently endless menu of pretentiously named dishes. "It might have been better to order one dish and have done with it," she thinks. She starts to long rather irritably for the single satisfying dish that has been denied her. "We don't want all this," she thinks, surveying the list of courses. "Why not have one dish; and that a good one? That's what we want; then why don't we have it?" Gradually she comes to identify an element of coercion in the set menu that she resents. "Why do they force us to have all this?" she asks herself, wondering who is responsible for this long and incoherent travesty of a dinner with its implicit tyranny and speculating that it is "some company with a rich man on top."

Just like the girlhood meals at Abercorn Terrace, the restaurant dinner is the product of male dictates. In the same way that Abel once stipulated how much Martin could eat at tea, an unseen man now controls the composition of Eleanor's dinner. The father's rule that conditioned eating in Kitty's Oxford has not been ousted from, but adapted to, eating in modern Oxford Street. Now, however, one's own father as patriarch has been replaced by an anonymous corporate version of himself. This, it appears, is a change for the worse, for whereas the domestic patriarch at least took a personal interest in the feeding of his family, the patriarch renascent is motivated solely by commercial objectives. In 1891, although Eleanor is restricted by her father's rigid timetable of meals, she nevertheless enjoys the chicken that she eats with him far more than Poulet Marengo in the restaurant, because with her father, despite his authoritarianism, she feels a companionable human connection (85) totally absent from this new patriarchal relation.

Neither has the social revolution in eating, at least as represented by the chain restaurant, proved as advantageous to working-class women as one might have hoped, the shift from service in the patriarchal family to service in patriarchal capitalism apparently bringing no less work and no more pay. Although the waitress is indifferent and surly, Eleanor is moved all the same (perhaps by the maternal sound of the music) to sympathize with her, realizing that she is a victim of commercial greed. "They oughtn't to make her carry all that," she thinks. "They could easily afford . . . more waitresses. They must make huge profits." At least in the old days Crosby felt a personal affection for her the man who paid her wages. Serving dinner in 1880, she has to wrinkle up her face in order not to laugh at Abel's stories; sometimes she laughs so much that she has to turn her back and pretend to be busy at the sideboard (31). By contrast, in the crowded restaurant the "jaded and harassed" waitress is too overworked to raise more than the ghost of a smile when Eleanor tries to make conversation.

A salutary effect of restaurant eating will be, Eleanor expects, to loosen the tightly woven mesh of emotions that conditions family meals; she comes to realize, however, that it is not exhilarating freedom but apathy that makes up the new emotional texture. Remembering Nicholas's vision of a modern society which is adventurous and expansive, she is disheartened by the sight of the restaurant diners "passively eating, passively waiting," adjuring them "break up this weight, this unreality, the dumb passivity" as she taps impatiently on the table. The bright synthetic plumage of modern dining hides an inner malaise. The diners eat en masse, but any real sense of community eludes them. They stare mutely at their food, in a silence more oppressive than the contrived small talk that seemed so constrained at the Abercorn Terrace tea table. They look, Eleanor thinks, as if they have "ceased to exist" or "come to a blank wall," and she wants to shout aloud, "Speak!"

Once, ostensibly at least, the most conventional of women, the Victorian angel who sacrifices her youth to care for her aging father, Eleanor ardently embraces the modernity that, as much as Abel's death, has brought her the possibility of liberation. Yet she leaves the restaurant disappointed with this progressive way of eating that had seemed to promise so well for the future. She becomes aware that she, like all the other diners, has been duped. She too has acceded to apathy, opting for the fixed-price dinner, because "it saved her the trouble of thinking." The tendency of the modern world to relieve the individual of the onus of thought is, however, as she realizes, a dangerous one. In the restaurant it leads to mediocrity; in 1930s Germany it is leading to something much more sinister. Indeed, she sees an ominous parallel between the multiplication of these huge and dehumanized eating machines in London and the rise of Nazism in Germany and fascism in Italy—which, as Eugenie's native land, was once the site of a warm and vital female culture.

In *The Years* as published, Peggy is shocked by the vehemence of her aunt's outburst against the newspaper's picture of "a fat man gesticulating." But Eleanor is not the sweetly innocent old lady that Peggy would like to believe her. She has personal experience of tyranny, having lived all her young life under the thumb of the fat man, the dictator, and understands the full implications of his political reincarnation in a way that Peggy (who is short-sighted and cannot see the picture clearly) is unable to. The prospect that he may return to oppress her when she has experienced a taste of hard-won freedom is intolerable. "Damned . . . bully!" she explodes with rage, tearing the paper in two and flinging it on the ground (265–266).

Eleanor is a determined survivor of the past. When Abel dies she is already middle aged, but she feels she is only now able to start living. For her the equation is simple: His life has ended; her own can now begin. Wholly without nostalgia, she welcomes the sale of the house in Abercorn Terrace, letting it go with a sense of huge relief (174). She much prefers her little flat with its modern conveniences: the shower and the telephone. Reflecting upon the past at Delia's party in the Present Day, she says that "things have changed for the better," that people are "happier . . . freer" (210). Kitty concurs; "the old days were bad days, wicked days, cruel days," she says (322), and Delia describes life at Abercorn Terrace succinctly as "Hell!" (335).

Having spent her young life marooned in stasis, Eleanor embraces an era of transience in all things. When her father dies she realizes with pleasure that everything passes in the end. The framing of the question "Where are we going?" (172) is for her not threatening but an exhilarating admittance of possibility. For the younger Peggy, however, the present is terrifying in its uncertainty (312), and she imagines the world of Eleanor's youth as an idyll of peace and security. Unaware of the systematic tyranny that underlay its superficial tranquility, of the numbing tedium and pointlessness of young women's lives in the 1880s, of the hypocrisy and the suppressions, she finds solace in the family history that Eleanor would rather forget (267). She cannot understand why Eleanor prefers life under threat from European dictators to life under the domestic version. She does not see that the household tyrants of Victorian England were in their own way as brutal as Nazis and fascists, and that to those who have actually lived under their rule, they are more real and more immediate (312).

Possessed of the political voice, the education, the profession that the older women could only dream of, Peggy remains unhappy. She regards her career as a doctor not as an expansion and expression of her self but as an analgesic against her pain. It is for her—in a disturbing reversal of the question posed by the older generations (how to live better)—a means "not to live; not to feel" (285). Paradoxically she, the doctor, does not love human beings (312). To her, the present seems violent and sterile, and the new freedoms are no compensation. Something is missing in modern society, a warmth, an emotional richness—a maternal quality that she believes she might have found had she been born fifty years earlier. For her, the new freedoms have entailed the death not only of the Victorian ideal of motherhood but of the motherly itself. She equates her profession with a monk's cell (285), an ascetic masculine place from which the joyous and womanly are excluded.

There is a suggestion that Peggy's existential pain, her disgust with human nature, and her fear to live are not simply a product of the age in which she lives but of some calamity that has befallen her—perhaps some echo of Rose's violation—forcing her into punitive exile from her own womanliness. In an earlier draft of the novel, she makes a direct connection between her alienation in the present and undefined abuses she has suffered in childhood. She refers to herself as, "I so suppressed I can feel practically nothing" and is described as being "so sexless, so inhibited, so aware of all the things she mustn't be, so abused from childhood for any breach of the conventions that she could never let herself go in any relation without a sense of guilt" (quoted in King, 513–514).[16] In *The Years* as published, Peggy has apparently conceived a deep sense of guilt as a result of something that happened to her as a child, perhaps when (like Rose without her parents' permission) on a night when an argument took place she went with North to the Roman camp, absconding through a window on a rope (317). The experience has filled her with a permanent sense of guilt (even in the Roman camp she remembers thinking "I shall pay for it") and has led her to believe that North has to marry but that she cannot, that unlike him she will not have children (318). That Woolf frames Peggy's experience of cutting off from her sexuality in the context of the militaristic masculine-oriented Roman culture suggests that she wished to point to patriarchy as the underlying cause of whatever buried trauma the child Peggy has suffered.

The only model of the old kind of maternity present at the party, Milly Gibbs, is a degraded one. She is the desecrated icon of the Victorian mother/saint. In pregnancy she appears at first sight to represent a wholesome ideal of motherhood swaying along the orchard path with a basket on her arm, past the ripe yellow pears. But in fact the maternal ideal is rotten at the core; the pregnant-looking pears are spoilt—wasp-eaten and brokenskinned (73–74). In the Present Day, Milly herself appears fly-blown: North thinks her body must be brown and mushy like the flesh of a bruised pear (302).

In the revolutionary 1930s, Milly and her husband, Hugh, are a testament to the tenacity of the past. They are representatives of the kind of family that refuses to lie down and die (although it now appears more comic than insidious). For North, Milly embodies the essential sickness of family relations (303). He loathes and fears her because her emphasis on the family destroys his genuine personal feeling for people who happen to be his aunts or cousins, making their relations false and dull (300). She and Hugh appear to him a parody of those pillars of the Victorian establishment, mother and father; "gross, obese, shapeless," they are an "excrescence" that has "overgrown the form within" (305). Family life in this context is selfish and proprietorial, each family unit sitting tight on its own nest of socioeconomic privileges, determined to secure the future for its own children and caring little or nothing about the welfare of children in society as a whole. Thus the divisions that prevent freedom and equality are perpetuated. Looking at Milly's fleshy "paws," North thinks that the Gibbses would fight like primeval animals for only *their* children and *their* property. For him, human beings will never be civilized while such passionate insularity rages. Soured and dispirited by his contact with the Gibbses, he believes that even Maggie, talking about her children, is moved by an animal sense of possessiveness, that if her children or her possessions were threatened (304), she would kill like a tiger (305).

For Hugh Gibbs (like his namesake, in *Mrs. Dalloway*, Hugh Whitbread), body size is a measure of status. Asking North what he weighs and "sizing him up" (301), he is really looking for information about the younger man's social standing (which has apparently risen since his sojourn in Africa). But to the novel's revolutionaries the ballast of redundant fat that Hugh and Milly carry is indicative of their obsolescence in the modern world. In the Present Day, Milly is "very stout," "voluminous" in draperies donned to conceal her fatness, her plump arms reminding North of pale asparagus. When she gives him her plump hand, he is revolted by the diamond rings sunk into the flesh of her fingers (300), which bespeak a decadent affluence.

Hugh and Milly belong to that genus of the wealthy and influential that populates the hotel of *The Voyage Out*. Like the hotel guests, they are mindless animals, bodies without soul, their lives absorbed like cattle's in munching straw (301). In the Present Day (two decades after *The Voyage Out*), the Gibbses are anachronisms in the modern world: dinosaurs (304), "prolific, profuse, half-conscious" (301). But if they are the last examples of a species on the brink of extinction, they have not yet completely lost their claws. For North, the past that they represent retains its dangerous propensity to overwhelm and suffocate. With them he feels that he is "falling under their weight," that his own identity is subsumed in theirs. (Indeed, Peggy predicts that North, who lives on the verges of conventionality, will turn into a Gibbs [318].) He feels that he must explode the Gibbses, create a revolution to escape their clutches, but then he remembers that Sara has lectured him on the pointlessness of war, and he wonders if the doctor, Peggy, could slip them a dose of those qualities that he sees as explosive of the excrescences of the past, "common sense; reason," a starry crystal in a glass (302).

At her party in the Present Day, Delia thinks it has always been her aim to break down social barriers, to rout the ridiculous conventions of English respectability; looking at her guests eating, she realizes with satisfaction that she has finally achieved it. She categorizes her guests not by the old measure, social class, but by their readiness to behave pragmatically with regard to the conventions of eating. She distinguishes between those who wait for the missing soup spoons and those who start drinking their soup from mugs. "Her sort of people"—like Kitty (Lady Lasswade) unceremoniously swigging her soup—are marked out by their scorn for spoons. The ability thus to throw out formality and improvise is for her indicative of a flexibility, an openness to change in every area of life. Her "English" are those who cannot dispense with their spoons. Those who are reliant upon such pointless old proprieties are, according to her system, locked into equally pointless old attitudes of mind (320).

Delia's eating arrangements are informal, casual, calculated to enable spontaneity. The large maternal meal table at which every guest was allotted a fixed place has been replaced by many little tables. Gesturing "promiscuously," she instructs her guests to squat on the floor or wherever they like (320). Moreover, the tables prove on close inspection to be not the mother's domestic furniture but office desks, stools, and typewriter tables commandeered from the professional woman's world (319). Whereas in the chain restaurant many tables equate with isolation, at Delia's party they create a network of small, fluid groupings between which traffic is constant. If the party succeeds where the restaurant has failed in creating a looser, more permissive kind of community, it is because of an ambiance of love that breaks up divisions and sets in motion. For, although Delia is not about to play mother in the Victorian sense for her guests, she has gone to a considerable amount of trouble to create an environment in which people feel free to be themselves, to dance, to eat, to mix, to communicate openly—aims which are not wholly opposed to those of the old kind of mother-hostess even if the means are very different.

That it is Delia, the Pargiter daughter most anxious to dispose of her own mother, who re-creates in the Present Day this authentic maternal ambiance is paradoxical. Indeed, even in the novel's present, the subtext of Delia's dialogue is a denunciation of her mother, Rose. Kitty laments her cousin's careless treatment of the flowers, for which she herself demonstrates a loving tenderness. "Poor flowers," she says, worrying that without water they will die, and raising a carnation to her lips. Just as she once seemed not to care about Rose's death, Delia is now indifferent to the death of the flowers. "Roses are cheap today," she tells Kitty. "Twopence a bunch off a barrow in Oxford Street" (320). That, runs the subtext, is the rate at which the old kind of mother is valued in the modern world. Consistently pragmatic in her outlook, Delia takes the view that if roses are cheap they are expendable. It seems, however, that it is exactly this kind of irreverence that is required if the real essence of motherliness is to be extracted from the morass of Victorian sentiment that has accreted to it. In fact, Delia's casual attitude toward the flowers, which she has strewn vaseless across the tables (319–320), is refreshingly natural and, in line with her generally informal approach to the role of hostess, designed to foster the maximum number of possibilities in social life. It is, *The Years* suggests, only in an atmosphere of such freedom, in which there is no need to revere the sacred objects of the past, that women can evolve maternal forms which do not involve inhibition, suppression, and self-sacrifice.

Like her flowers, the mother's music and dance are up for reframing in the Present Day. The gramophone emits a sound that is reminiscent of the old maternal melody, but the waltz is gone, and the new dances have a more disturbing choreography. For Peggy the fox-trot resembles the slow and agonizing death of an animal (309). When the music stops and the couples break apart and push out through the door, she starts to think about the end of civilization (312). Does the deconstruction of the mother's rhythms signify that civilization is ending, or is it really only just beginning? Is the fox-trot the start of a new melody and a new kind of movement that is scarcely understood as yet? The fox-trot for the first time permits partners to hold each other closer than arm's length; as such, perhaps the new dance can be seen to promise a genuinely closer and more relaxed relationship between the sexes. Although it has fixed steps, the fox-trot also allows a previously unknown scope for free expression in social dancing. In this sense it is a liberated dance, one that women (and men too) can dance to their own rhythms.[17] The death throes that it suggests are perhaps those of the old formality that did not permit of such naturalness, that kept the sexes at a "safe" distance from one another, and which thus prevented women and men from communicating honestly and openly.

The final party of the novel, which one might expect to offer some form of resolution, in fact refuses the obvious summing up. "This is not a time for making speeches," Nicholas says, giving up the attempt to make one (337). Kitty feels the lack of concluding words, wishing for "a fillip, a finish." What she wants is "not the past—not memories," but "the present; the future" (339). The future, however, does not open itself to the speech-makers of the present. Nor is the temper of the Present Day one to admit of grand orations. Perhaps loud, confident speeches—the "reverberating megaphones" of dubious leaders (329)—are really always part of the repertoire of tyranny. When, in a way, Nicholas does make his speech, it has become something intimate, quiet, personal, which is in harmony with the impulse toward naturalness and simplicity of the modern age. In the face of rising fascism and Nazism, it is a graceful paean to "the lovers, the creators, the men and women of goodwill" gathered together for the night, a mark of abiding faith in the essential goodness of human nature (342).

It is also a recognition that we are young in our knowledge of ourselves. Nicholas's toast is to a "human race" that is "in its infancy" (342). Eleanor also, from the eminence of her seventy years, realizes that "We know nothing, even about ourselves. We're only just beginning . . . to understand, here and there" (343–344). Like Nicholas, she sees this ignorance as a source of optimism. For her the dawning of human knowledge and the distant hope of wisdom that it contains is a thing of effulgent beauty, pregnant with the possibility of fuller, deeper, richer ways of living. She cups her hands as if to contain in them the past and the present moment, so that they fill and fill until they are deep and luminous with understanding (344).

Bringing down his glass at the close of his "speech," Nicholas crashes it onto the table, shattering it. But it does not matter, Delia tells him, for glasses are not expensive (342). Cheap glass is a necessary convenience in an age that has learnt to embrace breakage, that understands how to release the energies of the present by dashing the old. Perhaps, indeed, Nicholas does not break the glass by accident but as a gesture of his own readiness to shatter fixity and open to change. He—with Maggie, Renny, Delia, and Eleanor—might echo Jinny's philosophy in *The Waves:* "Beauty must be broken daily to remain beautiful."

It is not the young but "the old brothers and sisters" (347), the "old fogies" (348), who group around the window to greet the new dawn at the end of the novel. This and not words, says Renny, will be "the peroration": "the dawn—the new day—" (346). Around them, both strange and prosaic, is the debris of what has passed—emptied glasses, used plates, petals, and crumbs—relics and finished things, rather like the old people themselves (347). In the Present Day, the Pargiter generation of the 1880s has, in a sense, learnt how to live differently in an imperfect world. Eleanor, the oldest, feels simply that she is, "Happy in this world . . . happy with living people" (311). The old malcontents and agitators have not acceded to convention, but they have grown tranquil and serene.

Nor have they entirely lost the maternal in an age in which many women have to behave like men in order to be taken seriously in formerly male preserves, when the womanly is still a surmountable disadvantage rather than an asset where exclusively male values were traditionally the norm. At the end of the party Maggie gathers the mother's roses—white, yellow, violet, and several colored, their soft petals folded vulvalike—into a bowl of water (341). As dawn is breaking, she offers a bunch of roses to Delia. Delia's acceptance and admiration of the roses is a final gesture of reconciliation with and acceptance of her own mother and a symbolic honoring of maternal values in general, the essence of which is now passed to the revolutionary daughter for safekeeping: "'Aren't they lovely?' said Delia, holding out the flowers" (349).

Chapter 10

Between the Acts: *Soles. Filleted*

In *The Years,* Woolf argues that the immanence of the mother in food and in eating structures is necessary not simply so that meals will be truly satisfying but because what we eat and the way we eat it is the foundation of all else that we do in life. A culture that honors the mother in its food (rather than enslaving her in the processes of producing and serving it) is one that respects the womanly in all things and abides by matristic principles. In *Between the Acts,* she suggests that in order to discover how to live in the future, we have first to look back to the past, and that for women to find our real past, the one in which we lived in strength and harmony with our bodies and our appetites, we must look to a time excluded from the history books written by men. *Between the Acts* seeks to find this reverence for the womanly in suppressed prepatriarchal history, in the history that women are not supposed to know about, because within it to be female is to be powerful.[1]

For the Christian Mr. Hardcastle in Miss La Trobe's Victorian cameo, after the body has been satisfied with food, the spirit must be gratified with prayer (101). In matristic times, however, such a separation of physical and spiritual desires was not possible. Soul and body were not divided as in Judaeo-Christianity; the one was immanent in the other. Food was divine, and woman, as Earth, as source of food, was a divinity. To understand this, Woolf argues, is an act of punishable subversion, for the patriarchal policeman wielding his phallic truncheon "insist[s]" that all "obey the laws of *God* and *Man*" (97, my italics). And yet, she suggests, while the patriarchal play runs in our heads (69), we have not really forgotten the past in which God was Female. It lies fallow within the collective memory awaiting rediscovery—"what we must remember; what we would forget" (93).

Some commentators have seen *Between the Acts* as a retreat from the sociopolitical critique in which Woolf engaged in *The Years* and from the reality of World War II, which was raging around her at the time of writing. N. C. Thakur, for instance, expresses surprise at what he sees as the novel's disengagement from world events (141). Susan Kenney defends the book with the argument that it "was not conceived as a novel about the horrors of war, and it did not become one as Virginia Woolf became more and more enclosed by the war's daily incursions." For Kenney the novel is not political but concerns "the country house, Pointz Hall . . . , the hub of life in this small part of England. Here all the characters, father, son, grandson, son's wife and aunt, plus their various friends, neighbours, and employees gather to watch the annual pageant" (278). But *Between the Acts* is far from the gentle rural idyll that Kenney's description might suggest. In fact, it is political in a much larger sense than any of Woolf's former and more overtly sociopolitical novels, for her theme here is the 5,000-year patriarchy itself.[2] The title of the novel invites us to read below the surface texture of its words—to look for meaning *between the acts*. On this level lies a subtext of death, destruction, and violent suppression. If there is little specific detail about the particular war in which Woolf was living at the time of writing, it is because in patriarchal history, wars come and go and all look much the same. In the context of the novel, the threatened German invasion is significant only as a metaphor for the more fundamental kind of occupation that has already taken place, overthrowing and forcing underground a cooperative and nurturant woman-centered culture and erecting in its place a masculine value system which is arid and bellicose. As Eileen Barrett comments, "Encoded between the acts of the novel are signs that speak to a matriarchal past, reenact the slaughter of the goddess, [and] symbolize the experience of women under patriarchy" (20).

The movement from matristic harmony to patriarchal war is evident in the revolution that has taken place in agriculture. Ostensibly nothing has changed in the countryside around Pointz Hall. Figgis's guide book description for 1833 still apparently holds true in 1939. No town nor even house has been built, and the folly still stands on its eminence. Although the horse has been superseded by the tractor, the cow remains, and the land is the same patchwork of fields (34). But Woolf sets up this apparent image of enduring rural idyll largely in order to undermine it. The pattern of the fields is not in fact ancient but the product of the agricultural revolution (antedating 1939 by only some 250 years), an event which destroyed remaining common land systems, causing a vast exodus of the rural working class into the new industrial cities (where conditions rapidly became appalling) and initiating the steady degradation of food sources. Indeed, in the midday sun the fields around Pointz Hall appear not soothingly ancient but harsh and hideous, replicating themselves senselessly in a stupefying checkerboard of yellow, red, and blue (42).

The mechanization of the agricultural system, the substitution of tractor for primitive plow, marks a fundamental change, breaking the link between farmer, land, and food—a change which has not in truth happened between 1833 and 1939, nor even during the agricultural revolution, but in a much more distant time when Earth and Her fertility passed from the hands of women into the ownership of men. According to cultural (pre)historian William Irwin Thompson, "Mesolithic society may have seen the domestication of animals, and Neolithic society may have seen the domestication of plants, but what the age after the Neolithic sees is the domestication of women by men." As he notes, these major shifts in food production were of direct political significance to women: "Women had been at the top of traditional Neolithic society, but with the shift from religious, magical authority to masculine, military power, their influence collapsed and they became private property in the new trading and raiding society" (quoted in Sjöö and Mor, 240). Whereas the workers of the land had once been in direct contact with the earth and with the cycles of nature, they were estranged by the new patriarchal systems—a process of alienation which *Between the Acts* describes as enduring in the present day. As Ellen Rosenman notes, "*Between the Acts* explores a crisis of confidence within a culture" (1986, 114)—but it is a crisis with its roots in pre(patriarchal)history.

However, the matristic past has not wholly been wiped out; some vestigial memory lingers in the collective unconscious. The female-identified cow remains, an ancient embodiment of the Goddess in many places, including ancient Egypt, whose woman-oriented predynastic mythology threads through *Between the Acts*.[3] In 1939, at what seems like the eleventh hour for humanity under patriarchy, Miss La Trobe, the lesbian—thus gynecentric—director/playwright, is determined to awaken the tribal memory through her play. The once-robust song of the Earth is now frail and effaceable, the words of the reconstructed Pagan chorus blown away on the wind, but the song is not dead. Miss La Trobe recalls to the villagers a time of numinous engagement with the Earth as a source of food, a time when they ground roots and corn between stones (49). In apparent reenactment of some long-forgotten ancient ritual, the villagers pass in single file in and out of the trees, chanting their hymn of praise to the Earth, Her soil, Her crops, and the wheel of Her year (76).[4] But the reinstated song is accompanied by the mechanical rhythm of the gramophone. Like a motor-driven corn-cutter, its chuffing noise is a reminder of the incursion of patriarchal technology into the matristic song. Finally, in a replication of the patriarchal invasions of the Bronze Age, the paean to the fertile earth is replaced with a pugnacious anthem of war, a eulogy to the "valiant" Rhoderick, "bold and blatant," phallicly "firm" and "elatant," who with his incoming warriors takes up arms against the peaceful extant culture (49).

An echo of the same incursion is found in Bart's destruction of the child George's symbiotic union with nature. Later Bart himself realizes that he has stamped on the little boy's world (120), an act which clearly reverberates beyond the personal experience of the child, alluding to a time when this land (now England) was, as the pageant has it, "*weak and small/a child*" (49). Digging in the soil, George is completely absorbed in the beauty of tree, flower, and earth and his own hands digging. The yellow velvety membrane of the flower petals blazing between the roots and the smell of leaves and dark earth fill his senses, and he feels himself, the earth, and the flower to be one, complete (9–10).[5] This intensely lived moment of connection is violently disrupted by the assault of the boy's grandfather with his symbols of patriarchal dominion—leaping slavering dog and newspaper (containing a story of rape) formed into a phallic beak. Separation immediately sets into George's relationship with the flower as the dog rushes between him and it. He starts to his feet, then falls in fright before the "terrible . . . monster" grandfather who jumps out from his hiding place behind a tree waving his punning "arms" (10).

The little boy's instinctive sense of the numinous wholeness of a nature in which he too is encompassed suggests that the desire to define oneself against and aggressively dominate nature is not innate in men but is culturally inculcated. Indeed, even Bart does not necessarily terrorize his grandson deliberately (he thinks he is playing a game) but because he does not know how to behave to a child in a way that is not terrifying. His angry reaction to the fear and sense of loss he has provoked—that George is a crybaby (10)—may be the only response to tears in his emotional repertoire rather than an accurate reflection of his subliminal feelings, for he has no capacity to recognize, much less express, remorse and regret.

Bart functions within the novel as an image of the patriarchal Father God—thoughtlessly cruel, ostensibly rational, brutally wasteful of life, and demanding of obedience. Indeed, according to Christian belief, as father Bart *is* a manifestation of God within the microcosm of the family. George sees him in an archetypal child's-eye image of the Christian God as a tall, wrinkled, bald old man (10). His ontological landscape is India under colonial rule, a territory in which he is invader and occupier by force. He dreams of a dry hilly terrain where the corpse of a bullock decomposes in the heat, "savages" hide in the shadows of the rocks, and he is armed with a gun (13). In contrast to George's vivid connectedness with the earth, Bart's relationship with his landscape is characterized by separation, indeed alienation. Whereas the boy is in intimate contact with a strong force for life—root, soil, flower, tree—Bart's existential dwelling place is one of death and destruction, of drought and maggot-eaten meat that can sustain no one. The native people (who might know how to create a sustainable agriculture in the apparently barren land) are subhuman antagonists to be annihilated with guns. In the context of India, in which the cow is sacred, the death of the bullock suggests that the occupiers have committed an act of sacrilege against the indigenous population. Woolf suggests an implicit parallel between the Hindu and prehistoric matristic cultures, both of which revere the Goddess in the Cow, and both of which have been invaded and suppressed by the forces of the Father God.

In families dominated by such a patriarch, the mother-child bond has been all but destroyed. As Miss La Trobe's policeman states, "The ruler of an Empire must keep his eye on the cot" (97). Nurses look after Isa's children—women too intimidated by the patriarchal God, Bart, to defend George against him. Rather than protect the child from, or even comfort him after, his grandfather's violation, the nurse (Mabel) orders him to show proper respect for the old man, to say good morning (10). She is well aware that the boy's primitive communion with the Earth is forbidden, ordering him sharply to stop his digging (9). Well trained in the ways of the patriarchal household, she is perhaps not surprised that George's act of insubordination invokes the full wrath of God in person. Isa sees her children only through a wall of glass, too far removed from them to come to their aid. She is aware of George forlornly trailing after the two nurses and the pram, and taps on the window to attract their attention, but they do not hear (11). The degree to which mother is separated from child is dramatically illustrated in George's life-and-death struggle to reach Isa in the barn between the acts of the play, beating blindly through a sea of enormous legs. Although Isa raises her arm to identify herself to him, Woolf suggests that she hardly knows any more that he is her child: He is her boy "apparently" (65).

Isa's separation from her son also suggests an ancient parallel, linking her with the Babylonian Moon Goddess Ishtar and George with the Goddess's son Tammuz, the personification of vegetation. Annually Ishtar condemned her son to death; annually she mourned his loss and awaited the moment when she would travel to the underworld to reclaim him. One of Ishtar's appellations was the Heavenly Cow (Harding, 162); in *Between the Acts,* Isa's pain at separation from George is refracted onto the "moon-eyed" cow who has lost her calf. The woman's suppressed and muted sorrow is given vent in the cow's bellowed distress, which communicates to all the herd, who mourn the loss together (just as in ancient Babylon all women sang together the hymns of lamentation for Tammuz). As women's voices had once done, now the cows' moans fill the world with their pain. When Isa is briefly and unsatisfactorily reunited with George in the barn, she gives him a mug of milk, as if, transitorily, making the connection with the sound of her dimly perceived loss (84–85).

To view *Between the Acts* in a religio-cultural light is by no means to suggest that the novel is not also personal; on the contrary, closely interwoven with the matristic subtext are underground stories of individual suffering under patriarchy. Throughout the novel, Isa is haunted by a newspaper report of gang rape by soldiers—an event which is on the one hand a reflection of the prehistoric rape of the Goddess by the newer male Sky God, but which also has a particular resonance for her as an individual woman struggling for consciousness on a day in 1939. This rape, she thinks, is "real" (15) in a way that the collected literature of the past (androcentric) millennium—Bart's "great harvest" of the mind (71)—is not for her. She sees the rape scene projected onto the mahogany bookcases that bear the load of men's poetry, men's biographies, men's science, men's paeans to themselves, the cultural palimpsest that overlies women's truth (15).

Louise DeSalvo (1989) argues cogently that while Woolf was writing *Between the Acts,* memories of her own childhood sexual abuse were beginning to surface. The elusive nature of these important new truths can be seen as a factor conditioning the structure of the novel, in which what is important is hidden, ungraspable, submerged in an obfusc pool of consciousness like the fish in the pond at Pointz Hall. As Madeline Moore writes, "*Between the Acts* is the drama of female recollection' (146). Throughout the novel, Isa's search for some half-understood knowledge, some dimly recognized memory ("what we must remember; what we would forget"), intertwined with her preoccupation with the story of rape, reflects Woolf's own absorption in floating memories which never quite break water.

Central to both submerged subtexts, the personal and the political rapes, is the issue of food, for the fruitful ground that Isa seeks in order to heal herself is the ground which is the province of God as Woman and Earth—the God who has been driven underground by the new patriarchal God of War. In reality, in 1939 Isa inhabits a dry infertile region, a "harvestless dim field," the symbolic inner landscape of a self burdened by memories which are too painful or too taboo to be released into conscious mind. This is also the terrain of a patriarchy whose structures enable the wide-scale violation of women, a terrain in whose soil the rose, for Woolf a presiding symbol of the maternal womanly, cannot grow (93).

Isa is identified with the great pear tree whose fruit is hard and green (93). Growing in the stable-yard, home of the male-associated animals, dog and horse,[6] the tree exists in a restrictive environment of chains (for the restraint of animals) and walls. Indeed, the pear tree itself is tied to the wall, against which it is espaliered, its branches forced out of their natural forms and trained to conform to rigid, artificial lines and angles. Its roots are not bedded in soft earth but cased in paving. Weighed down with unripe pears, in the dry summer of 1939 it awaits a deluge of water to soften and sweeten its fruit, but the buckets in the stable-yard are apparently empty. In the context of Woolf's association of the pear with maternity,[7] the tree can be seen as a symbol of the matristic Goddess bound in thrall to the upstart male God—tied to his walls (walls wrongly defined, Woolf suggests, as "civilization" [111]), guarded by his dogs, compelled to adapt herself to the distorted forms that he requires.

Indeed, no fruit tree seems able to flourish at Pointz Hall under patriarchy. The apricot trees are all but barren; Mrs. Sands is lucky if she can make six pots of jam from their fruit, which is always too sour to eat fresh. A paltry three apricots, she ruminates, are good enough to bag in muslin. Only Lucy, the female divine, is able to find some redeeming beauty in the bitter fruit, restoring to them a life-giving function within the food chain. She thinks they are so lovely "naked, with one flushed cheek, one green" that she leaves them as they are, and lets the wasps burrow in their flesh (33–34). Her perception that the fruit is most beautiful in its naked state is linked with her observation that "savages" (people still widely of Goddess-centered, nature-based spirituality) are "beautiful naked" (30). Why tie them, runs her implicit question, into the muslin nets of patriarchy?

Looking at the pear tree and fingering one of the pears, Isa thinks that she is "burdened" with something drawn "from the earth," and she compares herself to the last donkey in the caravanserai carrying across the desert the heavy weight of the past. This weight, she reflects ("what we must remember; what we would forget") was imposed upon her "in the cradle," sung into her ears in the lullabies of women (93). Her burden is perhaps on one level a repressed memory of some traumatic event that happened to her as an infant. DeSalvo suggests a connection with sexual abuse (1989, 201). On another level the burden, passed on to her as a baby through the folk history of women's song, is a female birthright, the product of a past in which something rooted in the Earth was stolen from primeval women. Indeed, the two kinds of burden are not wholly disseverable from each other, for, as former psychoanalyst Alice Miller has pointed out (*Banished Knowledge*, 1991), child abuse can be linked with the cultural prescription set forth in the Bible.[8] Isa's task is one of awakening in conscious mind the subliminal memory of what happened to her both in the literal cradle and in the cradle of "pre" history. If she can accomplish this double task, she has a chance of reconnecting with a time when life was not a long slow trudge across a desert or a stony pear that offers no sustenance but something fruitful and nourishing.

As Judy Little has noted, the *green*house in *Between the Acts* has symbolic value (93). As a place for the nurturance of nature, it is in a sense the temple of the superseded female religion. It is there that Isa goes with William Dodge, seeking refuge from the representatives of patriarchal culture, husband and vicar (68). As she walks down the path to the greenhouse, she recites a verse that reflects the flavor of existence for women who live in the shadow of the androcentric Christian church, "I pluck the bitter herb by the ruined wall, the churchyard wall." Before she enters the greenhouse, she symbolically disposes of the Christian God, throwing away a whisker of old man's beard that she has picked. However, in 1939 on the brink of war even the greenhouse is full of inedible fruit, its grapes unripe; looking up from their seat on a plank she and William see that they are only little green buds among thin, yellow leaves (69).

Isa's sense of entrapment in a hostile culture is reflected in her attraction to Rupert Haines, repeatedly referred to in the novel as a "gentleman farmer." Whereas her own husband, Giles, works in the *City*, Rupert's occupation links him to an agrarian past more satisfying than the present day. Once, at a bazaar, he handed her a cup—a gesture that Isa remembers again and again throughout the novel, for this is the vessel that she needs to assuage her reiterated raging thirst. Paradoxically, however, Giles would love to be a farmer; he loathes stockbroking, a profession that he has taken up only because he assumes that Isa, whom he loves, requires capital, and that as her husband he is obliged to provide it (30–31)—although Isa herself, watching him assume an attitude of martyrdom, feels that he uses his sacrifice as a stick to goad her (68).

Within a culture that can offer him no personally sustaining role, Giles needs a scapegoat. In truth he is cabined and confined because patriarchal culture is a perversion; paradoxically, however, he projects his dis-ease onto William, the homosexual whose "perversion" (61) he cannot bring himself to enunciate—William who, defined as something not quite masculine (a "half-breed" [32]), in fact represents the extrapatriarchal with its unexplored possibilities for different ways of living. Indeed, William is to Giles an object of fear just *because* he has the potential to subvert the culture that Giles loathes, but which has the virtue of inflicting a familiar sting.

Isa craves a water that will not only assuage the throat parched from drinking sweet wine at lunch but will also quench an existential thirst (42). This thirst is an expression of contradictory impulses. On the one hand it symbolizes a desire for death and thus escape—both from her burden of memory and from the hard, dry, misogynistic culture of 1939. Her yearning for a beaker of cold water recalls Keats's "Ode to a Nightingale," in which the poet is "half in love with easeful death." She too desires a fatal draught and fantasizes suicide by drowning, making her wish, as she drops sugar into her tea, that water should cover her (63–64). On the other hand, however, the invocation of water connects her, through her namesake Isis, with a strong force for the continuation of life. At the Egyptian festival of Isis and Osiris (which took place in the month of Hathor, the Holy Cow), a vase of water was carried in procession to symbolize fecundating rain. The flooding of the Nile, bringing fertility to otherwise uncultivable land, was celebrated annually as Isis's gift of new life (her son, Horus) to the world.

In the Isis myth, sexual reunion with the brother-lover Osiris is necessary to bring about revitalizing inundation. If Isis is the force of life that invokes the Nile waters, Osiris has been seen as the fertilizing water itself—as, in Mitchell Leaska's words, "a personification of the Nile in flood" (*PH*, 231). In this mythic context, the drought that fills the souls of the inhabitants of Pointz Hall in the summer of 1939 can be related directly to the failure of the marriage of Isa and Giles, and by extension the endemic failure of female-male relations within androcracy. In this situation of patriarchal impasse, in which neither husband nor heterosexual lover can bring regeneration to Pointz Hall, it will be the lesbian, Miss La Trobe, who finally succeeds in invoking the fecundating water.

If Isa looks to Giles for the essential Osirian sexual receptivity, her memory of their meeting—fishing from two rocks in the same river—describes a quite different, patriarchally defined relationship: one of eroticized female submission. In redolently sexual imagery she recalls how her line had tangled with his and (like Sir William Bradshaw's wife in *Mrs. Dalloway*) she had "given over" to the potent penis—symbolized by the fishing rod, the stream rushing between Giles's legs, and the salmon teased and teased until finally it leaps (31). This modern heterosexual coalition is very different from its mythic source, in which Isis is in clear control of the penis. When Osiris is killed and dismembered by his brother Set, she recovers thirteen parts of the body but cannot find the penis (which was believed to have fallen into the Nile and been eaten by fish). She brings Osiris back to life and constructs and consecrates an image of the missing part. Using this penile substitute, she conceives by Osiris and gives birth to Horus. Clearly, in order for cosmic fertilization to take place, a kind of phallic humility is required of the male sexual partner in the Egyptian myth—a humility which men in the phallus-wielding androcracy of 1939 are ill-fitted to embrace.

Fishing also characterizes Lucy and Bart's relationship. Bart remembers how when he went fishing as a child Lucy would follow him, picking wild flowers and making them into little bunches (15). The memory links Lucy and Bart to Isis/Osiris as sister/brother and suggests that their relationship contains a parallel incestuous element. As Woolf pointedly comments, "brother and sister, flesh and blood was not a barrier" (18). Particularly telling is a detail that Lucy recalls with disgust, of how once Bart had made her take a fish off the hook, forcing her to handle the phallic fish, which unexpectedly discharged a bloody (semenlike) fluid from its gills. She had cried out in shock, and he had growled at her the childhood nickname, "Cindy."[9] Perhaps Lucy has also let her brother off the hook, for, as she remembers the incident, she symbolically shuts it away with Bart's hammer in the cupboard where he still keeps his fishing tackle. She knows that he is extremely particular about her putting his things away like this (15).

A further allusion to sister-brother incest is contained in Bart's variation on a repeated line from Swinburne's "Itylus," "O sister swallow, O sister swallow" (87). As Leaska has pointed out, the line can be read as a punning reference to oral sex (*PH,* 220). In the context of incest, "swallow" is a loaded term, not only because it connotes fellatio but also because as a result of sexual abuse many women protect themselves with eating disorders in which swallowing becomes either a prohibited act or a compulsion. In the "Itylus" story Tereus, King of Thrace, rapes his sister-in-law, Philomela, and cuts out her tongue so that she cannot speak of her violation. However, Philomela communicates the story to her sister, Procne, by embroidering it on a peplos. In a rage, Procne kills Itylus, her son by Tereus, and serves the boy to his father for dinner. She then flees with Philomela, pursued by Tereus. Through divine intervention, Tereus is turned into a hoopoe, Procne into a swallow, and Philomela into a nightingale. Itylus is resurrected and turned into a goldfinch. In Swinburne's telling, the story of rape is clearly intended to titillate, and his poem is full of salacious oral imagery. However, it also conveys a moral message, inveighing against the unnaturalness of women who are enraged to violent action against men in response to sexual violation. The obscenity of such patriarchal "morality" is compounded by the fact that the male poet uses Philomela's as his poetic voice, thus usurping the female point of view, distorting the story in which solidarity to the sister is worth sacrifice of the son, and making Philomela into Procne's accuser. Woolf, of course, reclaims the story for women. In Swinburne's "Itylus" the line "Couldst thou remember and I forget?" is an accusation against the sister who avenges rape. In *Between the Acts,* Woolf recasts the line as "what we must remember; what we would forget' and gives it to Isa as an exhortation to empowering remembrance of past violations.[10]

Fish was a staple food in ancient Egypt. Reay Tannahill tells us: "The Nile marshes and canals contained eel, mullet, carp, perch and tigerfish, as well as many other aquatic species that have not been identified. Fish were, in fact, so plentiful that the Egyptians dried and salted them for export to Syria and Palestine" (53–54). In 1939 the alternative of fish—in theacentric Neolithic religion a symbol of the divine womb and vulva (Gimbutas 1974, 107; 1991, 244)—promises reconnection with an original female principle, with Isis and her promise of healing, reunion, and renewal. Isa, ordering food for lunch, invokes types of fish like a litany—cod, halibut, sole, and plaice (12)—the naming of the fish suggesting her yearning for a sustenance that will redeem the soul of Pointz Hall, whose inhabitants are fed up with the patriarchal meat (14). Her final choice, filleted soles (12), is both an expression of tenacious fidelity to the ancient womanly and a grimly punning comment on the ontological state of the Olivers, whose souls are indeed filleted in androcracy on the brink of war.

Isa's concern that the fish may have gone off (14) is a reflection of her awareness that, subordinated to her Osiris, she may not be able to bring to Pointz Hall the renewal it expects. Lucy remembers a time when she lived so close to the sea that fish was brought to the door in a bucket of water; lobsters came fresh from the lobster pots, and salmon still had lice in their scales (20).[11] But in 1939 Pointz Hall is so far removed from the sea that it seems impossible that the fish—delivered inland by the fishmonger's boy on a motor bike (21)—can arrive with its potential for spiritual sustenance intact. Although Bart insists that, geographically, the house is only thirty-five miles from the coast, the women know that in spiritual terms it is much further. To Isa, stranded in the patriarchal desert of 1939 with its rapes and rumblings of war, it seems that the land goes on forever, and Lucy insists the house is at least one hundred miles from the sea. Even so, she believes that Pointz Hall can be connected to the sea again if rain comes, recalling the local belief that after a storm you can hear the waves break on a quiet night (20).

As Lucy is aware, even patriarchal Pointz Hall has its hidden fishpond, home of the Goddess's most intimate symbol, the fish, to whom the old lady comes each day to offer her devotion. For Lucy, the beloved (cunt) fish are "darlings," which she feeds with breadcrumbs and biscuits (gleaned from another secret Goddess-worshipper, Mrs. Sands) (122). Standing on the bank looking for fish, she sees in the water a spiritual vision, of beauty, goodness, and a sea that nurtures all life in its waters. She believes the fish come to her because they feel her love, that they rise to the surface out of trust, because no one has ever tried to catch them. For her, this loving trust defines religion; the fish have faith, she concludes. But Bart, the patriarch, whose creed is based on the notion that all creatures are motivated by base drives requiring subjugation, tells his sister cynically that the fish come to the surface out of greed and that their brilliant colors are merely a sexual lure (121–122). Bart, the Father God, sees, reductively, only greed and sex; his society, the mirror of his soul, can thus be capable only of that. But Lucy, the numinous Mother, sees the "beauty, power and glory in ourselves" (121); her society may rise to meet her vision.

According to household legend, the pond is also where the Goddess symbolically died at Pointz Hall, the place where "the lady" drowned herself.[12] However, she is not as dead as all that, for the kitchen women continue to see her ghost. When the pond was dredged, the only bone discovered was that of a sheep; however, the lack of material evidence for the lady's existence fails to persuade the servants that she is fictitious. Not only are they convinced of her reality, they are adamant that they must have this kind of loving, emphatically female presence (29). At quiet in moments in their long working day they continue to seek out the pond instinctively, as an oasis of peace and tranquility (28).

At Pointz Hall it is (save perhaps for Lucy) the servants who remain closest to the Old ways. Mrs. Sands preparing the fish by dipping it in egg is engaged on a symbolic level in drawing down the Goddess, whose regenerative powers are symbolized in Neolithic iconography by combined fish and egg forms (Gimbutas 1991, 285). The cook's affinity with the regal kitchen cat—renamed by the servants as the Pagan-sounding Sunny—to whom she offers the first slice of fish like a ritual oblation (22) identifies her as a true disciple of matristic religion, for the cat, best known as Bast, was a manifestation of the divine in predynastic Egypt. In 1939, the cat alone has the power to move Mrs. Sands's pragmatic soul to compassion (62)—a comic but really religious movement. As the play notes, human nature is redeemed by kindness to cats (111).

Buried in her book of prehistory, at patriarchal Pointz Hall in 1939 Lucy continues to live in the Goddess-revering epoch, when human beings were "savages" (i.e., peaceful and matrifocal). Her ancient name identifies her with that theacentric past,[13] for the Swithins date, Woolf tells us, from before "the Conquest" (21), the ambiguously partial reference to the 1066 invasion evoking also the much earlier incursions of patriarchal warriors. Her most famous namesake, St. Swithin, ninth-century Bishop of Winchester, lived in a time when the Christian church was still widely influenced by Pagan beliefs and remains best known for his celebration of nature. The well-known connection of St Swithin's Day with inundation[14] links Lucy with the needed rain that falls on Pointz Hall after the pageant, bringing regeneration and renewed vitality.

Although Lucy's faith appears superficially to conform to patriarchal Christian dictates, it is in fact essentially Pagan. The cross that she strokes as she looks into the fishpond has been appropriated by Christianity but is a pre-Christian religious symbol (Sjöö and Mor, 102). "Seduced" by the pattern of a shadow or a patch of sunlight, she finds it impossible to stick to the prescribed Christian prayer, being drawn instead into worship of nature. This spontaneous delight is far removed from the blinkered obeisance demanded by Christianity, with its punitive requirement for "hours of kneeling" at the crack of dawn (121). When Isa assumes that Lucy is contemplating the authority of God enthroned, the old woman is in fact engaged in a Pagan ritual: watching the sky to forecast the weather (16–17).

Lucy contrasts starkly with the priest of the Christian religion, the Reverend Streatfield, who is the wooden purveyor of dogma and social convention: "an intolerable constriction, contraction and reduction to simplified absurdity," an "incongruous" and "grotesque" sight as he makes his oration at the pageant (112–113). The name "Streatfield," composed of a variation on "street" (with its straight, hard, male associations) and "field" (connoting the soft, the fertile, the female), points to the disparity between the present state of institutional religion and ancient spirituality. A "clod" who has all the same estranged himself from the Earth, the modern representative of the divine is spurned by that nature with which his prehistoric precursors were intimately connected. "Ignored by the cows" and "condemned by the cloud," he is "an irrelevant forked stake" in the fluid numinosity of the natural world (113).

Lucy's real affiliation to the Old Religion is indicated by one of her secret backstairs names, "Old Mother Swithin" (23), linking her to the ancient Corn Mother and thus to Isis, who was, in one of her many aspects, the Egyptian Corn Goddess, the discoverer of wheat and barley, known as "Lady of Bread" and, by the Greeks, who identified her with Demeter, as "the mother of the ears of corn" and "queen of the wheat-field" (Frazer, 504). In this context, the barn, which Lucy claims as her own when she nails her placard to it, is her temple. Many villagers implicitly recognize the religious function of the beloved old structure, those who have visited Greece remarking that it looks like a temple. However, it does not require a tour of the classical world to appreciate the barn's spiritual significance; ordinary, "uncultured" people are instinctively awed by it (18).

Woolf sets up the barn and the church as ancient adversaries, both the same age and built of the same stone. The barn, however, scorns the steeple—the upward-aspiring, phallic symbol of Christianity which is, at the village church, in constant danger of tumbling down—a symbolic intimation that in 1939 patriarchal Christian structures are becoming hard to maintain. This is not surprising, for both symbol and culture are at odds with nature, the former indicating, by its attempt to defy gravity, the latter's preoccupation with triumph over natural forces, with movement away from Mother Earth and the body, toward the incorporeal sky. The barn, on the other hand, with its large, essentially female enfolding space, is a structure so harmonious that, roofed in the weathered orange-red colors of nature, it is scarcely distinguishable from the summer fields whose annual burgeoning it celebrates. Amply lit by sunlight (although containing darkness too) and presided over by a deity, Lucy, whose name means light, it has no need of artificial illumination (18), unlike the church, which, impermeable by the sun, is in serious need of literal and metaphorical enlightenment—the profits of the pageant are to go toward installing electric light there (105).

The barn is constantly open to the in-coming of nature; at harvest time the loads of hay and corn sway straight in from the fields (18). Inside it is a microcosmic ecosystem. "The barn was empty," Woolf states ironically, going on to describe the mice running in and out of holes in the walls, the swallows building their nests in the rafters, the insects burrowing in the wood, the bitch nursing her puppies on sacks in one of the corners, the bluebottle eating a pageant cake, and the butterfly sunbathing in the light reflected on a white plate. Unlike the church, which preaches man's supremacy not only over woman but over all forms of creation, the barn is a place of organic unity and prehistoric potential for all manifestations of new life. It is also a place luxuriant with natural plenty. The air there smells sweet and rich, and the "silence' is full of tiny eating sounds (61–62). Indeed, all life seems to be breeding or eating: sacramental acts in the context of an ancient spirituality which regards birth and the sustenance of the body as the foundation of the sacred.

At the Mother's festival, bodies as well as souls must be nourished; in the temple/barn the whole community comes together for the ritual meal (or "semisacramental tea," as Little calls it [93]). If, in the unfavorable climate of 1939, the cakes are fly-blown and the tea tastes like rust (63), this is less important than that all gather to eat together in affirmation of a social unity that is not yet quite dissolved and in celebration of a religion the memory of which is not yet quite erased. The priestess of the Mother's religion, Lucy Swithin, is not a distant or esoteric figure but is practically involved in the preparation and fetching and carrying of the food. She reaps a rich reward from this participation, growing steadily more tranquil as, cutting and buttering with Mrs. Sands, she sees the pile of odd-shaped sandwiches grow. The co-operative nature of women's work with food (as repeatedly in Woolf's writing) transcends social class, enabling Lucy and Mrs. Sands to experience a satisfying sense of sorority as one cuts ham, the other bread, and they talk and muse (23–24).

Wherever food is kept, prepared, or eaten at Pointz Hall, the Goddess is also present. Like the barn, the larder is a storehouse consecrated to the sustenance of both body and spirit, it too being widely compared with a religious edifice. It is to this "semi-ecclesiastical apartment" that Mrs. Sands entrusts the filleted soles/souls. In fact the larder was once—when religion was different—the household chapel, changing its function and name (like Sunny the cat's, the narrative voice points out) after the Reformation. Bart sometimes brings gentlemen to examine the remains of the former chapel. Oblivious to the palpable icons of the larder's real religion—the hams hanging from hooks, the butter laid on a blue slate, and the meat for the next day's dinner—the men come in pursuit of an invisible passage (a Catholic hiding place) known only known by its hollow ring (22).

Whereas Lucy is honored and indulged in the kitchen (23), Bart, who often arrives at inconvenient times, is regarded as intrusive, even threatening. Indeed, his invasions with parties of men recall more ancient and violent male incursions; often occurring before the cook is dressed, they connote gang rape and night raid. The hammer used to sound the wall is connected both with Bart's implied act of coercive incest with his sister (Lucy borrows the hammer to fix her placard to the barn and replaces it in the cupboard with Bart's fishing tackle) and with the newspaper story of gang rape that preoccupies Isa (whose imaginary reconstruction of the act is interrupted by Lucy's arrival carrying Bart's hammer). However, masculine strong-arm tactics have not engendered respect but resentment and an undertow of resistance. Although in the drawing room the servants humor Bart with his patriarchal title, "the Master," in the kitchen's he is known irreverently as "Bartie" (22).

The kitchen is the true heart of Pointz Hall: the nicest room in the house (better than the androcentric library) according to a female visitor (12). Mrs. Sands's operations with the cooking range—raking, stoking, and damping—send a pulse through all the rooms in the house so that its inhabitants are always in touch with the Hall's deep heart, always aware of their position in the cycle of a day measured in meals (22). Like *Mrs. Dalloway*'s Mrs. Walker, Mrs. Sands resembles a chthonic deity. Gruff in manner, she is all the same a beneficent Goddess, ensuring that the household is well and regularly fed. She is a reliable deity too, fulfilling her responsibilities even when the vagaries of her male employers' lives inconvenience her. She remains transcendently elusive as to her own feelings on this point (23), for her survival is dependent on such unobtrusiveness (a quality that is more important under patriarchy than the creative genius that produces "masterpieces"). In "the old days" the former cook, Jessie Pook, had the audacity to make herself known by dropping hairpins in the soup, moving the enraged Bart to invoke the Thunder God (with whom, as the patriarchal Jupiter, he is associated). It is for this act of subversive presence, Woolf implies, that Jessie's position was lost (22–23).

The dining room too is under the protection of the Goddess. Described as a shell (a vulvic symbol) "singing" of a time before time began, it speaks with the voice of Isa's crooning women. The butler Candish, who loves flowers, tenderly places carnations and roses (Woolf's mother symbol) in bowls there. A drinker and gambler, he is ostensibly an unexpected disciple of the Mother's religion, "queerly" adoring the flowers. In fact, however, such named-as-disreputable behavior as use of intoxicants and cards may characterize the adherents of the ancient faith. The table he sets for lunch resembles an altar prepared for ritual devotion, the sacred objects being those of the Mother Goddess: the implements of eating, silver (the moon metal), and roses (variegated, for all things under the mother's protection are various, many-hued, not black and white as under the father's rule) (24).

The color of the rose—yellow—that Candish places carefully in the bowl points to the identity of the anonymous lady (not an ancestor) whose picture hangs on the dining-room wall. Dressed in a yellow robe with a feather in her hair, she appears to be an image of the Goddess herself, as her ability to draw the observer into contemplation of nature also indicates. Hers is a very different presence from that of the male ancestor, the devoted master of his hounds, the limit of whose relationship with nature is expressed in his brusque command to the painter: "If you want my likeness, dang it sir, take it when the leaves are on the trees" (24).

Unlike Lucy, who enjoys working in the kitchen, Isa loathes domesticity, which for her is not a means to connect with other women but thralldom to men. In this context she identifies with Bart's dog, Sohrab, who refuses to admit the "ties of domesticity"; both servile and irritably aggressive in his subjection, he either cringes or bites. Isa wishes to elude Bart's attempt to pinion her into the role of mother/housekeeper, functions that (as defined and desacralized by patriarchy) rob her of identity. He, however, is bent on fixing her in a pigeonhole that confines and alienates. Although aware of how she hates his reductive labels, he persists in superimposing them upon her—"the old brute," she thinks (14). However, in 1939 it is important to patriarchy that it reinforce this kind of stereotyping, for things are changing in the kitchen. Most of the cakes at the play are bought, not homemade (65). Modern technology—fridges and dishwashers (108–109)—has made traditional women's work less laborious, leaving women with time to consider their position within society and perhaps do something to redeem it.

Descending unexpectedly upon the family grouping at Pointz Hall, Mrs. Manresa and William Dodge make an ancient mendicant appeal, not, however, for food itself (they bring their own) but for society, to eat together rather than to eat alone. Seeking the hospitality that binds the human race beyond family boundaries, they evoke an old sense of community and human connection, once omnipresent, now almost lost. The settled grouping still recognizes the necessity of making this primitive link, but in 1939 affirming the human bond is difficult (25).

Mrs. Manresa and William Dodge are outsiders not only at Pointz Hall but also in conventional society, he a homosexual and she with a disreputable past and a marriage to a Jew. As defined by the prevalent culture, they are truly, as Mrs. Manresa triumphantly admits, "dirty and dissolute" (28), and as such their presence at the table shifts perspectives and challenges the status quo. At Pointz Hall their arrival hangs a question mark over the patriarchal nuclear family, a structure which is generally taken for granted. Bart feels that the identity of the family is dissolved in their presence (31). The outsiders present an equal challenge to the patriarchal class system. Mrs. Manresa is proud to put herself on the same level as the servants. She shares their suppressed religion, supporting the back-stairs belief in the ghost of the drowned lady (29), and sees Candish not, as the Olivers do, as a member of a subgenus but as a human being with whom she can imagine making a sexual connection (27).

Mrs. Manresa is well aware that she has created nothing less than "a minor social crisis" by arriving unannounced to sit at the family table, but she is undaunted, taking pleasure in her easy ability to transform the situation (26). Indeed, she relishes the opportunity to disrupt the well-regulated ceremonies of patriarchy and open up a substratum of more spontaneous eating behavior. She is, she says, not as grown up as the family at Pointz Hall (29), thus defining herself against patriarchal civilization (so-called) and with more primitive cultural frameworks. She styles herself (and is repeatedly so termed by the authorial voice, with varying degrees of irony) a "wild child of nature." That this status is self-conferred, one to which she stakes a claim (27), suggests on the one hand that it is merely a fashionable pose. Within the context of the novel's concealed story of the suppression of the Goddess, however, Mrs. Manresa's insistence upon the wild-child identity can be read as an avowed fidelity to the Old Religion (a fidelity which no other speaking character within the novel feels able openly to own), and thus, despite her ostensible male identification, (her name, "man-raiser" suggests a propensity to arouse men to erection,[15] and she has no personal name) as an overt challenge to patriarchal culture.

Mrs. Manresa's life-loving sensual engagement with life (36), her shameless, playful enjoyment of physical pleasures (food and sex) is essentially non-Christian. For her, such things are the source of an enjoyment which is (a contradiction in terms in patriarchal religious thinking) both sensual and numinous. Paradoxically, however, while her commitment to the life of the body fully lived fundamentally contravenes patriarchal dictates, it is also very attractive to men, who connect through it with a way of being from which they have alienated themselves. Mrs. Manresa is adored by the patriarch Bart, who, under the influence of the champagne she has brought to the Hall, yields temporarily to her older and more liberal ways, feeling himself suddenly boyish and reckless (29). Giles too, although overtly hostile, is at the same time discomfitingly attracted to Mrs. Manresa's sensuality, which buzzes in the air, pricking him as if he were a horse and it a fly on his back (36).

Although cognizant of the patriarchal embargo on women taking what they want, Mrs. Manresa flouts the prohibition, helping herself to cream without invitation, even though, she says, she knows that it is wrong. She compounds this act of subversion by proclaiming the fact that, in a world in which women's bodies are to be confined and controlled, hers has been allowed to attain its natural shape (35), and later that through giving up the attempt to be thin, she has become free (28). This act of personal liberation is directly connected with a sense of (forbidden) attunement with her own will. She has attained the age and the size where she does *what she likes,* she states (35). Age and weight (characteristics intensively pathologized in women by patriarchy) are in fact, it seems, is a goal to be desired, for they entail female empowerment and the rejection of patriarchal dictates.

Mrs. Manresa delights in introducing topics of conversation (lavatories and underwear) which, in speaking of the body and of biological functions, confound the decency of a patriarchal society that has outlawed such realities. To her these prohibitions are ridiculous; the body is simply and gloriously the physical nature that all—men and women—share. Indeed, such is for her the stuff of religion, for, she avers, she has "complete *faith* in flesh and blood" (26, my italics). She enacts the Old Religion's festival practice of celebrating obscenity, appearing to the Pointz Hall family utterly "vulgar." And yet for those used to polite suppression, this in-rush of the denied and forbidden is refreshing and liberating, breaking up the usual decorum and allowing a little invigorating license to enter in (27).

Isa is unsure how to evaluate Mrs. Manresa. Her initial reaction is hostile. The "wild-child" identity seems to her affected, and she despises (perhaps also envies) the rings, the red-polished finger nails, and the cute straw hat (26), which she sees as ornamentation for the benefit of men. Yet at the same time she recognizes in Mrs. Manresa an authentic spontaneity and connection with nature. She reads as "quite genuine" her account of taking off her stays and rolling in the grass (28). If Mrs. Manresa "obviously" prefers men (26), this story gives the lie to a simplistic view of her as a simpering bit of skirt harnessed to the desires of men and in thrall to their stipulations for female behavior. On the contrary, she has liberated her body from control of any kind and thus gained a much larger freedom.

This anecdote leads Isa to recall another clearly genuine aspect of Mrs. Manresa's character, one which allies her with women rather than men. Often she comes to stay in the village without her husband and, exchanging the cute straw hat for an old garden number, teaches the village women to weave straw baskets (28). In her husband-free aspect, she is thus another woman who follows in the footsteps of Isis, who was known as a teacher of women. According to Madeline Moore, it was Isis who taught women to weave (156). As a teacher, Mrs. Manresa is instrumental in inculcating female subversion. She prefers "frivolous" and enjoyable arts (the village women want pleasure she says) to the domestic skills approved of by men, emphatically refusing to teach women the patriarchal lesson, "to pickle and preserve" (28)—that is, to conserve and reserve the same old patriarchal "truths," what once was female fruit now boiled down, jellied and set into androcentric forms. Like Lucy, she is allied to the apricot in its natural state rather than its preserved, making everything seem ripe like apricots when the wasps are burrowing into them (36).

This fruitfulness identifies Mrs. Manresa with the ancient Goddess. Indeed, she is described as "goddess-like" and as bearing an overflowing cornucopia. Hers is a female abundance that has not been thwarted and driven underground even in the prevalent climate of patriarchal repression. On the contrary, it is able to communicate itself to men, who respond with instinctive warmth. She brings fruitfulness into even Bart's barren desert so that, following her, he blesses the body for its ability to fertilize the Earth (72). Isa despises Mrs. Manresa for this, as she sees it, fixation upon men, but perhaps at the same time she also feels her own failure in comparison with the less constrained woman, for Mrs. Manresa, by virtue of her own personal liberation, is able to reach the repressed life-force in male consciousness, thus effecting a release that she, an ineffective Isis, wishes for but fails to achieve.

Mrs. Manresa is also identified with fruit by her belief in the game of telling fortunes by counting cherry stones, a remnant of the ancient practice of scrying with natural objects. Can she possibly believe in all that? a skeptical Bart asks, and she replies that of course she does. Her faith restitutes to hyperrational patriarchal society the much-ridiculed faculty of prophesy—and indeed the cherry stones do tell the truth, for (to Mrs. Manresa's delight) they designate her the plowboy (32), thus identifying her with the Corn Mother and her religion. The stones' pronouncement that he is a thief (33) is proof to Bart of the idiocy of the whole procedure, but, in a deeper sense that he cannot recognize, the stones do not lie, for he is in truth the patriarchal thief, guilty of stealing from women nothing less than civilization itself.

Miss La Trobe is another outsider at Pointz Hall, reputedly not wholly English (perhaps from the Channel Islands or with Russian blood), a person whose origins and present life are mysterious (37).[16] She refers to herself as an "outcast," thinking that "nature" has "set her apart from her kind" (125). On one level the reference to nature as an explanation for her annexation from the social group may be read as a reference to her lesbianism; on another level, however, the invocation of nature also indicates that she is marked out from mainstream society by her allegiance to the old woman-focused religion. As a lesbian—an identity which poses an implicit threat to a patriarchy which structures itself upon the male-headed family as the approved social unit—Miss La Trobe is located on the cultural boundaries, an ideal situation for a female artist committed to the subversion of androcentric history. Connected with the drowned woman in the Pointz Hall pond (she directs her play from among the trees by the lily pond), her endeavor is, implicitly, to reconstruct that woman's, and indeed all submerged women's, histories. This revision of patriarchal history is something that men whose identity is bound up in the patriarchal system find painfully difficult to watch. Compelled to take his place in the audience, Giles feels that he is no longer himself, but a kind of Prometheus chained to a rock and compelled to witness the "indescribable horror" (38) of a different version of reality.

The play opens with a girl standing behind a conch, the shell, an ancient symbol of the vagina as a source of power, announcing the play's subtextual matristic orientation and pointing to the way in which it is intended to be read. The audience are puzzled by the overtly matristic scene and wonder if it is part of the play, for they do not recognize it from the annals of history as approved a true and accurate record by men. Miss La Trobe intends the image of female strength as a prologue to the play itself—a cynical allusion to the distorted perspective of a history that can discard 40,000 years of human being simply because it does not fit into the prevailing ideology. In the background to the matristic scene, the ominous chuffing of the patriarchal machine, the gramophone (which refuses to produce music) constantly threatens, emitting the noise of a machine that has "gone wrong" (48). For something has indeed gone badly wrong, something which is about to sweep the image of the girl and the conch from the stage and wipe her from history.

Routed by a chorus of "*Valiant Rhoderick . . . ,*" primitive England and her digging, sowing villagers are replaced by a woman who takes her identity from a pub, the Royal George, a name which situates her in a hierarchical, masculine context. (Now there is no doubt among the audience that the play has begun.) The woman defines herself by her sexual availability to men, to whom she announces, "I don't want no asking" (49), a statement which, in the context of male incursion, sounds ominously like a (paradoxical) invitation to rape—a theme which is taken up by the "pilgrims" who toss hay on rakes and sing of how they kissed a girl but let her go, then "tumble[d]" another in the hay (50–51). The association of rape with pilgrimage and harvest points to the destruction by patriarchy of the once-harmonious interrelationship of sex, spirituality, and food. Formerly a source of intrinsic female power, sex has become a means for men to assert power-over. That rape takes place in the food store indicates that what is going on here is not simply an act of brutal male self-gratification but sacrilege, the deliberate and violent suppression of a culture through attack on the spiritual belief system that holds it in being.

The reign of Elizabeth I (although by no means *in fact* a matristic age) symbolically reinstates an image of female power. Playing the queen, Eliza Clark from the village shop is awarded status for her enormous size and strength; powerfully regal on her soapbox, she is ruler over ships and men (52). Within the age of Elizabeth, however, Miss La Trobe embeds a paradoxical act of usurpation in which a crone—a Witch-like (i.e., Goddess-oriented) woman—conceals "the rightful heir" (a boy) in a basket, so saving his life. These dramatic events suggest the prehistoric scenario in which the son/lover of the matristic Goddess rose with patriarchy ultimately to take preeminence over Her: At the end of the play, the baby boy is a prince, and the old woman has died. The ancient "beldame" ritualistically counts her beads, but not out of Christian piety, for each bead bespeaks a bloody crime committed in the name of the rising male regime. In retribution for her act of motherly subversion, she is "accosted" by three young men who swagger onto the stage, in order, she thinks, to torture her (56). The pitting of the three young men against the elderly woman points, in the context of modern history, to witch-pricking, rape, and casual violence against vulnerable women; in the context of past millennia, it alludes to the cultural ascendancy of the aggressive young male over the crone.

The play breaks for tea after the age of Elizabeth. Against her will, Miss La Trobe has cut the scene (spoiling it, she thinks) to accommodate the interval, thus truncating the reign of the great queen. After tea, according to her text, will rise the dawning of the Age of Reason, an age of men. Gone is the age of *"crone and lover"* states the verse, thus dispelling the era of Goddess and lover-son (58). A reprise of *"Valiant Rhoderick . . ."* indicates that a new incursion is about to take place.

In the second half of the play, masculine logos is on the ascent. At first the only audible line from the eighteenth century is *"reason holds sway"*—a phrase which elicits loud applause from self-proclaimed rationalist Bart. In this age the "savage" is enslaved in patriarchy's mines and the "reluctant earth" is tortured into the production not of food but of material riches; in the possession of commerce, the cornucopia overflows with metal ores rather than fruit (75). The "night" of female mysticism and intuition has passed; now is the supposed enlightenment of masculine "day" (76). This is the age of the clergyman, Sir Smirking Peace-be-with-you-all (94); Venus/Aphrodite (comically personified by Lady Harpy Harraden) is deposed and ridiculed (77), lamenting her fall from Aurora Borealis to a tar barrel, from Cassiopeia to an ass (88). Flavinda alone remains tacitly aligned with the Goddess. She is to come into her inheritance (and truly into her own, for within patriarchy material wealth will endow her with a measure of self-determination) after *three moons* (82–83). As she and Valentine finally embrace, asserting the principle of love over money, the clock strikes nine, the Goddess's triple triplicity (83). In an age characterized by avarice, such a determination to follow the dictates of the heart evinces a subversive alliance with the principle of Venus/Aphrodite.

The Age of Reason is the age of androcentric capitalism, as the words of the nursery rhyme ("Sing a Song of Sixpence") that introduces it point out: "*The King is in* his *counting house/Counting out* his *money*" (74, my emphasis). Although ostensibly centering around an heiress, Miss La Trobe's Restoration comedy is in fact a parable of female *dis*inheritance, for it parodies a society which has all but extinguished authentic female power, effectively denying women's humanity by redefining girls as legacies. Unless, like Flavinda, a young woman is wily, such legacies pass directly from her late father's into her new husband's hands. Such a young woman is in a situation only marginally different from that of the concubines who are apportioned as material goods in Bob's will (80). Even the obvious predator of the piece, Lady Harpy Harraden, is on closer observation another victim of female disadvantage. She, like most eighteenth-century women, is dependent on a man to secure her material prosperity. If she uses her niece as merchandise, it is because she is middle aged and therefore not a salable commodity herself, as the reaction of Sir Spaniel Lilyliver to her final, desperate proposal of marriage evinces.

In Woolf's view, patriarchy reached its apogee with the Victorian age, the age of the policeman with his pronouncement, "*Obey the Rule of my truncheon*"—an instrument that he waves, points, and flourishes about (96–97). The rule of the phallic truncheon indicates a society governed by brutal sexual duress and points to Woolf's personal experience of sexual abuse within it. Victorian England is a police state in which phallic strictures on "thought . . . [;] religion; drink; dress; manners; [and] marriage" are enforced by violence. The policeman has infiltrated the most intimate sanctuary of the Goddess and disrupted the primal relationship of woman with food, recognizing that in order to destroy women's authentic power, it is necessary to oust the Goddess from her hiding place. "The ruler of an Empire,' he says, "must . . . spy . . . in the kitchen" (97).

The empire-builders have forgotten that human being and Earth are in reciprocal relationship and that if She is to sustain human life, She too must be nurtured. In patriarchal consciousness, Earth is simply a mine to be exploited for infinite material gain. Likewise, those people who formerly worked in harmony with her, digging and delving, supplying the needs of the community and not taking more, are to be enslaved to the greed of the ruling elite, to be used, like Her, until they are used up, for that, says the policeman, is the price that empire exacts. Such, according to him, is "*the white man's burden*" (97), but in truth it is not the burden of white men but of people of color and women—those on the lowest echelons of the patriarchal hierarchy.

Patriarchy enslaves and impoverishes one-half of the world so that it can appropriate to itself the fat of the land. "They did eat," Mrs. Lynn Jones comments, observing the vast quantities of food consumed at the Victorian picnic party (101). Most especially, as Woolf saw it, Victorian men consumed meat (ham, grouse, chicken, game pasties), an ecologically expensive foodstuff, the demands of whose production ensure that there cannot be enough food to go around. The surfeit of meat that clings to Mr. Hardcastle's mustache is a comment on the obscenity of a section of society that gorges itself while others starve and then applauds its own moral superiority.

The name Hardcastle, male-identified by its phallic resonance, alludes to defensive embattlement around one's possessions and to the sense of separation from the other that characterizes androcentric systems and enables those within them to exploit that other. The name also suggests a favorite Victorian aphorism: An English*man*'s home is *his* castle. The idea being that man is never at the bottom of the heap, for, be it ever so humble, his "castle" is a realm in which he always holds absolute sway. There, as Woolf knew to her personal cost, he can be a petty tyrant without sanction. Indeed, there is something "'unhygienic' about the home," as Mrs. Lynn Jones points out. This unwholesomeness appears to her like meat that has gone off, an appropriate simile given the centrality of meat in the patriarchal equation. With an unwitting touch of satire, she remembers that the servants' term for rotten meat is "with whiskers" (103), a phrase which strikingly connotes Mr Hardcastle himself, brushing crumbs of meat from his copious facial hair (101).

Mr Hardcastle's prayer of thanks for food, drink, nature, and peace is the ultimate hypocrisy. The Christian God's plenty is the product of enslavement and domination, nature is a force he is bent on suppressing, and peace has never come in his time. By happy accident or intention, a note of protest is introduced at this point, the hindquarters of the donkey, played by Albert the "village idiot," suddenly moving, so that the prayer is drowned out by laughter (102). The small Pagan triumph indicates once again that the victory of Christian church over nature is only Pyrrhic, that connection to ancient holistic forms of spirituality may be mislaid but can never be eradicated. Even Eleanor, devoted servant of patriarchal Christianity, is subconsciously aware of this truth, opening the picnic scene with the observation that the church appears tiny among the trees (99)—an implicit acknowledgment that man-made Christianity remains insignificant in the context of all-encompassing nature.

For a moment at the close of her play, Miss La Trobe thinks that she has failed, that the audience is unable or unwilling to read her covert message. Reality is too strong for them to stomach, she thinks (130). Grating her hands on the bark of a tree, she feels that she is dying, bleeding into the ground—then all at once rain starts to fall. A successful Isis, a fruitful Demeter,[17] she has finally brought about the meteorological and emotional inundation that all are looking for in the hot, dry, wartorn summer; the climax of her play/rite is fructifying rain and cathartic tears. When the rain stops, the smell of fertile earth rises from the ground (107).

Whereas for the male artist in a man's world, artistic success confers personal status, for Miss La Trobe, lesbian, female prehistorian, boundary-dweller, this can never be the case. Nor is it the point of her artistic endeavor. Hers is the Witch's work, of transfiguring the world, and the play is her "cauldron." A true Pagan, she looks to "nature" to complete that art which otherwise remains sterile and meaningless (107). She sees the play as the product of her own submersion in a fertilizing water, in which she seeks the deep underwater roots beneath the net of "conventions" (41). Bart intuits, accurately, that what she wants is the same as the carp in the pond: darkness and mud, a whisky in the pub where simple words sink down like maggots (120). Indeed, in the murk of the pub with its aqueous murmur of voices and its pictures of the cow and the ox, alcohol sinks her into a primitive riverbed consciousness that germinates new ideas, revolutionary phrases, ancient sentences (125).[18]

Throughout Woolf's work food and eating are the focus of a huge amount of loving attention and minute examination. Her novels (as indeed her personal writing) evince a sensual delight in food that is a part of a tremendous passion for life—a passion based on the recognition of what James King calls "sacred beauty" (xv). While one can reject Thakur's speculation that Woolf "had started feeling the need of some type of religious faith" at the time of writing *Between the Acts* (she had always deplored institutional religion and deplored it with a particular fervor in *Between the Acts*), Thakur is not wide of the mark in noticing an attempt on the part of a woman who was indeed "of a mystical bent of mind" (145) to understand and explore the spiritual dimension of human existence. This important shift in orientation in relation to love of life, joy in beauty, and the "moment of being" entailed the sacralization of experiences that Woolf had always recognized as transcendent of rationally defined reality, but that she had not thus far considered in an explicitly spiritual light. That she had not previously made this spiritual connection can be explained by the fact that those experiences which she understood as numinous were often rooted in areas of life that androcentric Judeo-Christianity defines as sensual and thus diametrically opposed to the spiritual. In *Between the Acts* Woolf's concern is to heal this rift, to reclaim and reconsecrate those aspects of human existence that patriarchal religion has condemned and split off from divinity.

The search for the Mother Goddess can be seen as the apotheosis of Woolf's search for a human mother figure. She had always found qualities of fertility and maternity in the women she loved. "Mercifully Nessa is back," she wrote of Vanessa Bell. "My earth is watered again" (*D 3*, 186). "You hang there so fruity so rich," she told Vita Sackville-West (*L 3*, 326), and she described Ethel Smyth's life as "a full moon orange harvest glow" (*L 6*, 404). Concurrently with *Between the Acts*, Woolf was writing, in "A Sketch of the Past," on a deeper level than ever before, and in what are essentially mystical terms, of the numinous presence and emotionally life-sustaining qualities of her mother. Here she describes her childhood as "that great Cathedral space," and her mother as at the "very centre" of it (*MOB*, 81), simply and ineffably, "the whole thing" (83).

The beginning of a reorientation away from human mother figures and toward a transpersonal, spiritual mother suggests a positive development in

Woolf's psychological relationship with her actual childhood deficit in maternal care, for whereas the ongoing need for a mother surrogate evinces a continuing dependence on an extrinsic source of nurturance, relationship with the Goddess may be supposed to embody connection with a distillation of the quality of maternity that can be internalized and owned, and which thus holds the potential for genuine empowerment. In the painful process of unearthing her buried experiences of sexual abuse, Woolf was very much in need of such an internalized mother in order to support and nurture her own awakening child, but in 1942, she was out on a limb not only in her determination to know and speak of her own abuse but also in her quest for the matristic.[19] Only now, more than a half century on, with many women recognizing the absolute necessity of making such spiritual and sexual disinterments in our own lives, can we begin to recognize how truly pioneering was Woolf's endeavor to liberate both Goddess and abused child into personal and cultural consciousness. In her final work, if not ultimately in her life, she succeeded in rejoining body with soul, in celebrating the numinousness of sex, love, food, and nurturance, in asserting that such are essential components of women's spiritual experience.

Notes

Preface

1. Susie Orbach speaks of deciphering the anorexic woman's "text" in a similar way (1986, 102).
2. See Jane Marcus 1984.
3. As Mary Daly notes, given the context of sexual abuse, Bell writes of Woolf's "madness" with "grotesque insensitivity" (1984, 296).
4. Aside from Virginia Woolf herself, Angelica Garnett is, to my knowledge, the only Stephen descendant who has attempted an honest evaluation of the family's dynamics (see *Deceived with Kindness*).
5. Since Woolf stated clearly and categorically that she had been sexually abused when very young by Gerald Duckworth (*MOB*, 69) and also later (in a *possibly* less intrusive manner) by George Duckworth ("22 Hyde Park Gate," *MOB*), I do not think it justifiable to regard this abuse as other than fact.
6. Kamiya's letter and article are held in the Monk's House Papers at the University of Sussex.
7. See, for example, Hilde Bruch, whose work was central to the subsequent revision in psychoanalytical thinking about anorexia:

   In 1940 Walker and his co-workers . . . [related] eating to the symbolization of pregnancy fantasies. This theory of the fear of oral impregnation was considered the cornerstone in the psychodynamics of anorexia nervosa. I approached my first anorexic patients under this orientation, and was puzzled that I observed this morbid preoccupation with sex and pregnancy only in exceptional cases. Subsequently I have come to rate patients with this preoccupation as *atypical*. (*Eating Disorders,* 1974, 238)

8. As Orbach notes, for the anorexic woman food is "an ongoing preoccupation" (1986, 102).
9. The glib and belittling view of anorexia as a body fixation—thus an extreme form of a culturally assigned "female vanity"—is popularly purveyed by the patriarchal media.

Introduction

1. According to Louie Mayer, cook to the Woolfs, Virginia was fond of pheasant (Noble, 157–158).
2. Mayer, who was taught the art by Virginia, recalled that "she could make beautiful bread": "I was surprised at how complicated the process was and how accurately Mrs Woolf carried it out. She showed me how to make the dough with the right quantities of yeast and flour, and then how to knead it. She returned three or four times during the morning to knead it again. Finally she made the dough into the shape of a cottage loaf and baked it at just the right temperature" (Noble, 157).
3. See also *D 6*, 106, and *L 5*, 226.
4. In *The Collected Shorter Fiction*.
5. Given that Virginia and Leonard were in permanent conflict over how much and what Virginia ought to eat, the usefulness of Mayer's account in an evaluation of Virginia's relationship with food is mitigated by its reference to the Woolfs as an entity.
6. ". . . there has been an increasing incidence in anorexia nervosa over time. Jones et al. (1980) in the USA found that the number of diagnosed cases almost doubled from 0.35 (1960–69) to 0.64 per 100,000 (1970–76). This increase occurred solely in the female population" (West, 13–14). For an overview, see Naomi Wolf (148–152)—according to whom, "The anorexic patient herself is thinner now than were previous generations of patients" (150). Because anorexia is a condition of denial, and anorexic women do not readily present themselves to the medical establishment, most statistics on anorexia in the population account for only the tip of the iceberg. I have also encountered very many women in deep but "subclinical" degrees of distress.

Chapter 1

1. Because 90 percent of those diagnosed with an eating disorder are female, I have opted (not without some unease) to use the words "woman," "she," and the like to refer to the person in eating distress. It is not my wish to deny the real pain of men with food problems, and I am aware that the difficulties for these men are often compounded by the fact that anorexia, bulimia, and compulsive eating are regarded as "women's problems." I believe, however, that eating distress is fundamentally a feminist issue, and that to suggest otherwise is to collude with patriarchy in concealing the real significance of eating disorders.
2. Anorexia was extant before the industrial age but not in the epidemic proportions of today. See Joan Jacobs Brumberg, *Fasting Girls,* for a history.
3. Nor would I wish to exaggerate them. With the possible exception of osteoporosis, all of the biological symptoms contingent on anorexia are reversible. The mortality rate is given by Hsu et al. as 2 per cent, by Isager et al. as 8.2 percent, and by Patton as 3.3 percent (West, 18). Suzanne Abraham and

Derek Llewellyn-Jones suggest a figure in the range 2 to 6 percent (128) and Richard Gordon in the range 5 to 10 percent (18). It is important to note that these figures relate to *diagnosed* anorexia, in which emaciation tends to be more extreme and the prognosis poor. In my opinion the prognosis is made poorer by the hospital refeeding "treatments" that those diagnosed anorexic are often subjected to.

4. Marion Woodman writes, "Increasingly, I see the food complex as a neurosis compelling intelligent women toward consciousness" (1982, 22), a statement that I would echo (although I would question the elitist assumption that this kind of consciousness is available only to women who are "intelligent").

5. However, anorexia is not rigidly bound to these religio-cultural origins. Advanced capitalism in Japan, for example, has produced a high incidence of eating disorders (R. Gordon, 35–36). In Britain, several studies have found eating distress to be most prevalent (and, sadly, most invisible) among ethnic Indian Asian women (Waller, Coakley, and Richards, 25).

6. See, for example, Merlin Stone 1975.

7. Annie Fursland makes this point in "Eve Was Framed" (in Lawrence 1987, 23).

8. Anorexic women themselves report that self-starvation is a response to a sense of impotence. Frances says: "I needed to have something in my life that I was in control of . . . I felt that by limiting my food intake I was gaining a sense of power" (MacSween, 203; ellipses in original). Another anorexic woman writes: "I started to feel that I had no power in the world—even eating was for others, not for me. I had to find something that was mine. I learned that I could control what I ate, how much—that's all I had, the only thing that was mine" (Maine, 81–82).

9. The experience of Martha, a formerly anorexic woman interviewed by Éve Székely, illustrates this movement (Székely, 171).

10. Marilyn Lawrence also points out that hospital treatment is "potentially destructive and . . . can create as many difficulties as it solves" (1984, 90). Roger Slade observes: "Experience shows that when an increase in weight is forced upon an anorexic she will comply until she can escape from hospital; but then she will immediately set about losing the weight she has gained. There is a very real danger at this point that she will change to vomiting or laxative abuse" (86).

11. As Denise Connors notes, "women's sickness can be seen as a means of channeling women's potential deviance away from a collective, system-destructive route and into a more privatized and self-destructive path . . . the sick role has served to neutralize and contain women's rage, their subversive force and potential to envision and create a new way of life" (quoted in Daly 1984, 358n).

12. Abraham and Llewellyn-Jones allege that "The problem is that patients with eating disorders tend to 'play games' and to manipulate the therapist" (68). Gordon writes, "Anorexics are notorious among hospital staff for their deceitful and manipulative behaviour" (133).

13. Described in Peter Dally and Joan Gomez 1979, 109.

14. As Margot Maine observes: "The fields of child development, abnormal psychology, and personality development overflow with theories about the negative impact of mothers on their children. The eating disorders literature is no exception to this" (17). See also Ann Erickson for a mother's first-person account.
15. Although, obviously, not all fathers abuse, and fathers are not the only abusers.
16. According to feminist psychotherapist Susan Wooley "the institution of psychotherapy . . . [has] changed radically in the last 20 years; where once it helped the powerless to 'adjust' to their condition, now it [has] spawned first one advocacy movement, then another, creating a shift in power relations certain to be opposed by many" (in Schwartz and Cohn, 195).

Chapter 2

1. Suzanne Henig sees her in this latter way, commenting in the introduction to the two stories, "Harriet, one can easily observe, has been portrayed in the role of a maternal parental figure rather than of a wife" (CFE/EPF, iv).
2. For example, Rachel in *The Voyage Out,* the Ramsay children in *To the Lighthouse,* Rhoda in *The Waves,* and George in *Between the Acts.*
3. The illness leading up to Julia's death was diagnosed as influenza, which began in mid-February 1895, remitted, worsened, and, at the end of April, gave way to rheumatic fever. She died on May 5 (King, 52). According to Virginia, Stella had observed that Julia's health was failing and grew increasingly fearful for her; however, she was unable to communicate to Leslie how overworked and tired Julia was (*MOB,* 43).
4. Leslie's desire for separation is remembered in *To the Lighthouse* (see p. 66).
5. Hilde Bruch ascribes anorexia to a "continuously inappropriate"—perhaps neglectful—parental response to an infant's signals of need. This gives rise to "a perplexing confusion" manifesting as the inability to identify correctly and respond appropriately to hunger (*Eating Disorders,* 56).
6. For example, Johan Vanderlinden and Walter Vandereycken write, "sexual and/or physical abuse in childhood place adults at special risk for developing psychological crises and even psychiatric disorders, including anorexia nervosa and bulimia nervosa" (in Schwartz and Cohn, 20).
7. Leonard Woolf states that Virginia suffered a third "minor breakdown" in childhood (1963, 76) but does not specify what or when he is referring to.
8. The passage is partially quoted by Hermione Lee in *Virginia Woolf* (178).
9. Reproof rather than reassurance seems an inappropriate response on Leslie's part. Interestingly, in Woolf's description of the episode, her father evinces the same anxiety that he rebukes his daughter for.
10. Family patterns die hard. In *Deceived with Kindness* Angelica Garnett writes of her mother, Vanessa Bell: "For many years I was so much a part of Vanessa, and she of me, that I could not have attempted to describe her with detachment" (15).

11. An anorexic woman's sense of dependence on her mother can be devastating. Catherine Dunbar, who starved herself to death, wrote:

GOD IM HUMAN AND HELPLESS
JUST HELP I CANNOT GO ON
AWAY FROM MUMMY SAVE ME, HELP
MUMMY YOU ARE MY SAVIOUR MY LIFE
I CANNOT LIVE WITHOUT YOU
(Dunbar, 93)

12. She asks Clive in a letter to "Kiss her [Vanessa], most passionately, in all my private places" and tell her "how fond I am of her husband?" (*L 1*, 325).
13. Abuse survivors who have been forced to perform fellatio often make a connection between eating and choking. For example, Debbie, who is anorexic and bulimic, describes how "Some forms of abuse made me scared of eating, scared of putting anything into my mouth, swallowing the food and feeling I would be sick" (*Signpost*, the Newsletter for the EDA, February 1996).
14. So great was her shame that, as she told Mary Hutchinson, for ten years she had been too embarrassed to ask in a shop for sanitary towels and had made her own out of kapok. She was, however, at this point (1924) unable to connect with the reason for her shame, which she put down to an "inexplicable . . . prudery" (*L 6*, 505).
15. It is possible that menstruation also put her at greater risk of sexual abuse. According to The Women's Research Centre, some abusers are "excited" when their victims reach menarche, seeing "the onset of menstruation as an excuse for having intercourse with them" (93).
16. Her periods continued to be erratic up until the menopause.
17. Of all the Stephen/Duckworth children, Laura was the most cruelly treated and the most seriously damaged by her upbringing. She has been regarded as mentally deficient, backward, or, in Virginia's terms, "an idiot" (*MOB*, 83), but as Louise DeSalvo points out, there is little evidence that this was the case. Her behavior suggests suppressed hurt and fury: she could read, but was often too nervous or too angry to do so; she stammered and developed a nervous tic, and had tantrums (Desalvo 1989, 26 and 28). Although she was slow to speak and teethe, her mother, Minny, did not regard her as a backward or difficult child, and "It was only after Minny's death, when Laura was five, that Leslie began to be anxious" (Lee 1996, 101). The early loss of her mother led to severe deprivation of care and contact for the rest of her childhood. A major regression in her development took place around the time of Leslie's remarriage (DeSalvo 1989, 32), and she was sequestered in a separate part of the house. At the age of twenty she was institutionalized.
18. In interviews carried out by The Women's Research Centre, women frequently described their abusers as "particularly concerned about upholding a positive public image. They sought to be perceived as good neighbours,

family men, good with children. In some cases these men held positions of leadership in the community . . . Others were active in their churches" (30).
19. As Susie Orbach comments, Weir Mitchell's "prescriptive measures would not be out of place in a large number of hospital divisions dedicated to the treatment of anorexia today: a rich diet, attention from the doctor, and the acceptance of the wisdom of the doctor's interventions" (1986, 26).
20. The words in quotation marks are Vanessa's but are clearly paraphrases of Madge's remarks in a previous letter.
21. Vanessa's statement evinces a double-think: In the same breath that she says Virginia *had* suffered from an "illness" she also claims, contradictorily, that her own action had *prevented* Virginia from becoming ill.
22. See, for example, p. 19.
23. She later described what it felt like to be a young woman struggling for identity in the context of such a patriarchal family past in *Night and Day*.
24. For Salvador Minuchin, Bernice Rosman, and Lester Baker, "enmeshment" denotes "an extreme form of proximity and intensity in family interactions." In an enmeshed family "changes within one family member or between two members reverberate throughout the system," and "subsystem boundaries . . . are poorly differentiated, weak, and easily crossed" (30). This kind of family system is, according to Minuchin et al, conducive to creating anorexia in a child striving to achieve autonomy within it.
25. "Can one ever satisfy father?" was the question that dominated the life of one of Bruch's anorexic clients (*Eating Disorders,* 1974, 84). "I never felt that I was enough," says anorexic Patricia of her father; "there was no room for failure for me" (Maine 90–91). Former ballerina Gelsey Kirkland, who has performed an intricate *pas de deux* with anorexia, writes of the first—belated—time her father saw her on stage: "For me to realize that he was there induced emotional terror that went beyond stage fright. I knew I would be judged by the only person other than myself whom it was impossible to please" (45).
26. Many anorexic women's fathers share this sense of having not achieved and the tendency to project it onto their daughters. Patricia writes, "My father felt he was a failure. I think he looked to me to fill some of his own hopes" (Maine, 90). In Bruch's sample of fifty-one families producing an anorexic child, there was a pronounced tendency for fathers to feel "in some sense second best" (*Eating Disorders,* 1974, 82).
27. This was a tactic that Virginia also used—in a semi-ironic way. In 1926, for instance, she told Vita Sackville-West that she was suffering from a headache: "I lie in a chair. It isn't bad: but I tell you, to get your sympathy: to make you protective" (*L 3,* 302).
28. Though, oddly, he thinks that this relationship was "not significant at all" (50).
29. This incident, which took place a year after Virginia had written "The Experiences of a Paterfamilias," is suggestive of the passage in the story in which the cockney spills the baby's milk in the cab. Virginia was clearly accurate in

her observation that even when food had been provided and prepared by her mother it was unlikely to find its way into the children's mouths in a fit state for consumption if her father was in charge of getting it there.
30. Jane Dunn notes that she would always endeavor "to control her feelings with a code of reasonableness so rigidly adhered to in her daily life that she could only learn to absorb her own suffering" (243–244).
31. For example, the father of Catherine Dunbar, who is described by her mother as "a disciplinarian; he expected his children to be models of good behaviour, especially at mealtimes, and to speak only when spoken to . . . He never actually pressurized them to work hard, but made it clear he expected them to give of their best" (Dunbar, 17).
32. Woolf recalled Maria Jackson as beautiful and sweet-smelling but emotionally clinging; "one had to take a deep breath before one kissed her," she wrote, "or one would be suffocated—she held one so long in her arms" (quoted in Lee 1996, 92).

Chapter 3

1. Wooley observes: "Before the 1970s . . . Childhood sexual abuse was regarded by most clinicians as rare and had been characterized in the well-known Kinsey report as essentially harmless" (in Schwartz and Cohn, 193).
2. Now subsumed into the Eating Disorders Association.
3. Peter Alexander suggests that Mr. Ramsay is partially modeled on Leonard Woolf (151).
4. Marlene Boskind-White and William C. White, Jr. comment that many of the women in their bulimarexic therapy groups "were nutrition majors who were obviously aware of the basics of good nutrition but failed to adhere to them" (156).
5. Mainstream therapists frequently react with ill-concealed outrage to their anorexic clients' preference for such symbolic thought structures over patriarchally approved, scientific cause-and-effect relationships. Hilde Bruch writes, "the clinging to . . . abnormal imagery is amazing. They are aware that their ideas do not coincide with what they have learned, but their reactions and behaviour are dominated by fantastic notions about what happens to food" (1978, 83). Mara Selvini-Palazzoli describes "with utter astonishment" an anorexic client who was also a doctor, yet who "nevertheless treated her own body in the most absurd and anti-scientific, and sometimes even magical way, thus ignoring the most elementary tenets of medical science" (82).
6. Cf Susan Griffin's feminist prose poem *Woman and Nature:* "She [woman] can even, yes, even hear what the birds say. (And the birds bring messages from the dead, and the dead bring messages from the universe.) This cleanness of her ears accounts for her wisdom . . . We would think her raving, but she speaks to us so sweetly of what she says can be, that we too begin to see these things. We know her clarity for her own . . ." (180–181)

7. He may have been influenced by Savage's description of what he termed "moral insanity" and illustrated with the case of a girl who, according to her father (himself a bluffly honest man with four "normal minded" sons), was a congenital liar and would—apparently quite ingenuously—regale her parents with fantastic stories about the extraordinary things that had happened to her, all entirely fictional (quoted in Trombley, 117).
8. For example, in 1928 Vanessa Bell wrote of a visit to the asylum in St. Rémy where Van Gogh had been incarcerated: "It's a wonderful place and Virginia hoped she'd be shut up there next time she went cracked" (V. Bell, 332).
9. Gerald Brenan notes this intense sexuality (L. Woolf 1990, 162).
10. The ambiguity of "lived" as a euphemism for "fucked" is interesting, suggesting as it does that Virginia's entire *life* with Leonard was in some sense a failure.
11. Una, who was hospitalized when her weight dropped to 5 stone 4 pounds (74 pounds), writes of her experience: "Words just cannot convey my bitterness over what happened there . . . They forced food down me . . . They told me I could leave when I reached 6½ st [91 pounds]. So, I behaved like an angel, soon reached 6½ st and was allowed to leave . . . Of course, the only reason I wanted to leave was so that I could lose all this unwanted weight—and yet I felt *so* guilty, so out of control, so confused" (Quoted in MacSween, 245).
12. The British psychiatrist R. D. Laing observes: "what is called psychosis is sometimes simply the sudden removal of the veil of the false self, which had been serving to maintain an outer behavioural normality that may, long ago, have failed to be any reflection of the state of affairs in the secret self. Then the self will pour out accusations of persecution at the hands of that person with whom the false self has been complying for years" (99).
13. Roger Poole estimates that 9 stone (126 pounds) was a usual weight for Virginia (154) (who was a tall woman). Virginia herself gives at this time both 9 stone (*L 2*, 67) and 9 stone 7 pounds (133 pounds) (169–170) as her normal weight.
14. Angelica Garnett felt that had Leonard been her father, she would have been like "one of his dogs, never beaten but always intimidated by the force of his personality" (108).
15. In August 1926 Vita told Harold Nicolson that she had slept with Virginia twice (Sackville-West and Nicolson, 159).
16. It seems very likely that early on in her life Virginia had also been sexually involved with Violet Dickinson, to whom she wrote in 1903, "It is astonishing what depths—hot volcano depths—your finger has stirred in Sparroy [Violet's nickname for Virginia]" (*L 1*, 85).
17. In 1917 Leonard judged Charleston too far for Virginia to cycle from Asheham. Virginia found this "absurd" and "quite unreasonable," but she felt that she could not countermand Leonard's orders because then *he* would get in a state (*L 2*, 171).
18. In 1918 Virginia explained to Vanessa that she would like to stay with her for a night but she was expecting her period and had promised to spend it

lying down in future (*L 2*, 218). In 1921 a doctor was called when she menstruated (*D 2*, 131).
19. Inasmuch as an anorexic binge is experienced definitively as outside the eater's control, this episode of eating is clearly something different; Virginia describes having made a conscious decision to eat gluttonously. Inasmuch, too, as a binge is usually secret and always productive of intense guilt, neither again does Virginia's experience on this occasion seem to fit the picture. On the other hand, however, if a binge is also defined as an episode of eating not in response to hunger but to emotional or ontological cues, and one that is solitary rather than social, the dinner in Buzards does have characteristics of such a compulsive use of food.
20. Freud's suppression of this information was publicized by Florence Rush (*The Best Kept Secret,* 1980) and Jeffrey Masson (*The Assault on Truth,* 1984).
21. Woolf uses the expression "finger on lips" twice in the very short section of "A Sketch of the Past" dealing with the time of her mother's death and her own exposure to the Duckworth brothers (*MOB,* 93–94).
22. This letter may relate to a suicide attempt some days earlier. For the dating see *L 6,* 489.
23. As Mary Daly puts it, "Had there been available to her a community of Tidal Musing Women, she most probably would not have needed the 'tidy cure of death'" (1984, 297).

Chapter 4

1. June Cummins notes that his name suggests terra firma (in Daugherty and Barrett, 206).
2. Hewet's objection may reflect an undercurrent of jealousy. Phyllis Rose makes the point that "What Terence describes would sound to a man, I venture to guess, like a splendid marriage" (84).
3. According to Mitchell Leaska, "the olive is an ancient symbol of fertility. Ironically, however, the cultivated olive cannot breed: it must be grafted on to a wild olive tree" (*PH,* 193).
4. As Helen also notes, while politicians shout and rail, those who are really working to improve human society are left "to starve" (86).
5. Lucy Goodison points out that in modern Western culture, women are routinely identified with the cat (6).
6. Dalloway's surrender to the asparagus probably derives from an experience of Leonard's on a squally Channel crossing during the Woolfs' honeymoon, in which "an enormous gherkin swimming in oil and vinegar" appeared for breakfast, along with fried eggs, bacon, rolls, and coffee. Leonard reflected that eating the breakfast, with the French coast rising and falling before his eyes, was one of his most courageous deeds (L. Woolf, 1963, 83). Dalloway's precision regarding facts and his valorization of self-control appear to be modeled on traits of Leonard's.

7. Woolf described Gerald Duckworth similarly, referring to him when she went to tea in 1936 as "an obese and obsolete alligator" (*D 5*, 21 and *L 6*, 28).
8. Barbara Walker points out that "A world-wide symbol of the Great Mother was the pointed oval sign of the yoni, known as *vesica piscis*, vessel of the fish" (313), and that "The fish symbol of the yonic Goddess was so revered throughout the Roman Empire that Christian authorities insisted on taking it over, with extensive revision of myths to deny its earlier female-genital meanings" (314).
9. Hirst is based on Lytton Strachey, who was, according to Jane Dunn, like Woolf "uneasy" with his "corporeity" (167). She writes, "Burdened with an implacable self-disgust, . . . Lytton Strachey deplored his own ugliness, fearing that he was as unattractive to others as he was to himself" (165).
10. This identification may allude to Samuel Richardson's *Clarissa*, which contains the line "Daughters are chickens brought up for the tables of other men" (77). Clarissa's death (by self-starvation) is linked like Rachel's to sexual duress within an abusive phallocentric social system.
11. Hewet innocently suspects that marriage is harder on women than on men (228).

Chapter 5

1. As critics have noted as early on as Winifred Holtby in 1932.
2. What Rachel calls her room is in fact hers only by default, being officially a kind of sitting room for elderly ladies. She appropriates it when the *Euphrosyne* is not full (*TVO*, 25–26).
3. Carol Ohmann regards Jacob's journey as a failed quest, an unsuccessful attempt to bring about the revitalization of Western culture.
4. Woolf's diaries contain several records of such inspirational dinners. In 1917, for instance, she dined with Roger Fry and Clive Bell at a bandanna-covered table, where they "eat out of dishes each holding a different bean or lettuce"; "delicious food for a change," she remarked. They drank wine and finished the meal with "soft white cheese" and sugar. After dinner, Woolf reports, "taking a splendid flight above personalities we discussed literature and aesthetics." She comments that she enjoyed the conversation, because "the atmosphere puts ideas into one's head, and instead of having to curtail them, or expatiate, one can speak them straight out & be understood—indeed disagreed with" (*D 1*, 80).
5. Woolf satirized such ceremonial dress in *Three Guineas* (see p. 23–25).
6. Wordsworth's "phantom of delight" is a paragon of traditional feminine virtues, "A perfect woman" and "A creature not too bright or good/For human nature's daily food." I would like to thank Isobel Grundy for pointing out this reference.
7. A sideline on the women's college meal is provided by E. E. Duncan-Jones, a student at Newnham College when Woolf visited. She writes: "It was dis-

quieting to learn later . . . that Mrs Woolf had brought out a book (*A Room of One's Own*) describing her Newnham dinner. Her purpose was, of course, to evoke pity for the poverty of the women's colleges, but at the time it made us, her hosts, decidedly uncomfortable" (Stape, 14).

8. According to some writers, Jacob's own social class is not necessarily superior to Plumer's. Shirley Panken sees Jacob's social status as "indeterminate" (11), arguing that he is neither particularly privileged nor especially self-assured. A. Zwerdling, on the other hand, asserts that Jacob is "well-connected if not rich, his credentials impeccable and his future course apparently secure" and that "everything in his life [is] a traditional step to establishing success" (33). Sarah Ruddick describes Jacob as an "inheritor" in a "world governed by divisions of class and sex" (in Marcus 1981, 193).

9. Woolf shared Jacob's distaste for such writers (see "Modern Fiction," *The Common Reader One*, 147). The Plumers are apparently modeled partly on Sidney and Beatrice Webb—whose virtues Woolf was compelled to acknowledge but could not admire. On a Sunday visit to the Webbs' in 1920, she ate the same meal—mutton, cabbage, and apple tart—that Jacob eats at the Plumers'—and with the same sense of dismal depression: "all adequate but joyless," she recorded (*D 2*, 20).

10. As Makiko Minow-Pinkney notes, Jacob himself remains oblivious to all this female distress: "[He] enacts a repressive blindness in relation to the women in the novel . . . This groundswell of female suffering articulates a deepseated critique of Jacob as a representative upper middle-class man" (48–49).

11. Such poverty is sexually determined. Fanny wonders at how young men's pockets are filled with silver coins, whereas she, a young woman, has only a limited supply in her purse (102).

12. Something of Fanny's helpless distraction with regard to food is shared by Betty Flanders. Preoccupied by the apparently irresolvable dilemma of her love life, Betty forgets the meat (7) and loses track of the cheese (15).

13. I would strongly take issue with Pamela Transue's view: "Florinda has no patronymic, which suggests that she has in some sense freed herself from patriarchy at the same time that she makes her living off it" (56).

14. The source for this episode seems to be an argument that Woolf witnessed while with Clive Bell at the Café Royal in 1919, in which a woman dining with a man threw her glass on the floor, rattled the knives and plates, overturned the mustard pot, and marched out (*D 1*, 251).

15. Beverly Schlack infers that the work in Jacob's room is *Heroes and Hero Worship*, in which "the question that serves as the title of Jacob's essay was answered in the affirmative by Carlyle, who declared, 'the History of the world is but the Biography of great men'" (42).

Chapter 6

1. Makiko Minow-Pinkney comments on "how obsessive she [Clarissa] is about shoes and gloves . . . It is as if without this minute 'passionate' attention the

extremities of the body cannot be trusted not to fly asunder, acting out the physical dissociation their owner so often experiences" (62).
2. Contrary to Peter's assertion that no woman, particularly Clarissa, can understand a man's sexual feelings for women (133).
3. Patricia Cranmer discusses the match in the crocus and other images of female sexual arousal in Woolf's work in "Notes from Underground: Lesbian Ritual in the Writings of Virginia Woolf" (in Hussey and Neverow-Turk 1991).
4. Beverly Schlack writes of the memoir, "soldiers died of exposure to the freezing cold or of starvation, despite eating their horses" (62).
5. Emily Jensen, for instance, considers Clarissa's party-giving to be a concession to the shallow socializing demanded of a politician's wife and a betrayal of a nonconformist lesbian past ("Clarissa Dalloway's Respectable Suicide," in Marcus 1984). Schlack writes, "Clarissa embodies . . . [the] social order in all its superficiality and substitution of mere vivacity for intensity and death" (64).
6. Hugh, generously talking to old ladies and recalling great desserts of the past, is apparently modeled on George and Gerald Duckworth.
7. Roger Poole observes that these weights approximate to Woolf's own before and after the bedrest cures of 1913 to 1915 (154–155). Woolf originally gave her own maiden name, Stephen, to the character that became Septimus.
8. Stephen Trombley deals in detail with the correspondences between Holmes and Bradshaw and Woolf's own doctors.
9. In a working notebook she envisaged the novel's structure:

Suppose it to be connected in this way:
Sanity and insanity.
Mrs D. seeing the truth. S.S. seeing the insane truth . . .
(quoted in King, 354)

10. Hilde Bruch observes comparable instances of what she refers to as "psychotic disorganization" (1978, 11)—the effect of acute or chronic starvation, she believes—in anorexic women, explaining that "They will speak of the world as gloriously, or unbearably vivid, or say that all their senses are keener" (13).
11. Schlack traces allusions to Ceres/Demeter in *Mrs. Dalloway* (in Bloom). Elizabeth Abel (in Bloom) and Maria DiBattista explore references to Demeter and Persephone in the novel.
12. There is a parallel here with bulimic behavior as explicated by Mira Dana and Marilyn Lawrence: "Symbolically it is as though she [the bulimic woman] wants to possess, consume and control the person she desires . . . Not being able to do so, she consumes the food instead . . . Her attitude is *incorporative* in that her aim is to get something inside herself where she cannot be robbed of it; she has no confidence about being given enough" (81).
13. Kim Chernin describes such an emotional dependency on food in *Womansize:* "what I was feeling was not hunger at all . . . I had awakened feeling

lonely... and I was frightened... What I wanted from food was companionship, comfort, reassurance, a sense of warmth and well-being that was hard for me to find in my own life... I was hungering, it was true; but food apparently was not what I was hungering for" (11).
14. The distasteful nature of her corporeity is possibly related to her German connections. In Bayreuth in 1909, Woolf described the Germans as "hideous" and as "monster men and women." She was appalled by their proclivity for "great joints covered with fat" and huge jugs of beer, and saw the women's faces as "puddings of red dough" (*L 1*, 403, 407).

Chapter 7

1. These feelings are similar to Sheila MacLeod's toward her father when she was anorexic. She recalls perceiving him as a tyrant who prohibited the ordinary games and pleasures that other children enjoyed. She was furious with him and at times hated him (40–41).
2. The Eating Disorders Association describes the conflicting messages that anorexia expresses as "Leave me alone, let me live my own life, I hate you/Don't ever leave me, I can't cope on my own, I love you" (leaflet, "Help for Family and Friends").
3. As Ellen Rosenman comments, "the mother's influence may be so pervasive that her daughters cannot find their own voices but can only contemplate their separate identities covertly" (1986, 47).
4. Inanna, Ishtar, and Asherah are associated with the holy tree—probably a fig (Sjöö and Mor, 269; Stone 1975, 175). Demeter is linked with the olive and the fig (Stone 1990, 369). According to J. Frazer, she sits under an olive tree at Eleusis to mourn the abduction of Persephone (518).
5. Sjöö and Mor, 103.
6. James King notes the connection between Mrs. Ramsay's artistic success with the Boeuf en Daube and Woolf's sense that her origins as a writer stemmed to a large degree from her mother's French blood (384).
7. See, for example, Mary Beth Pringle, "Killing the Angel of the House: Spatial Poetics in Woolf's *To the Lighthouse*" (in Hussey and Neverow, 310).
8. She contrasted this "succulence" with the "commendable" and "public spirited" but desiccated company of the Arnold Forsters, whose "very mangy meals" and "despising the flesh" depressed her (*Congenial Spirits*, 373).
9. Jane Lilienfeld discusses domestic violence and Mr. Ramsay as an abuser in "Like a Lion Seeking Whom he Could Devour" (in Hussey and Neverow-Turk).
10. Woolf wrote similarly of Julia Stephen as having become convinced of the "futility of... effort" (*MOB*, 36) and as having finally sunk "like an exhausted swimmer" (39).
11. For example, "it was beloved Au Set [Isis] who first understood the ways of the seeds and the planting, bringing the abundance of the stalks of wheat and barley which were so proudly carried at Her sacred festivals, in honour

and commemoration of what She so ingeniously discovered in the beginning" (Stone 1990, 277).
12. In this respect he fits neatly into the paternal paradigm constructed by MacLeod as anorexia-genic (176).
13. Woolf understood the pleasure of such an empty space in which to work. She described a solitary stay at Giggleswick in 1906: "my solitude has been exquisite . . . When will I dine? When will I breakfast? I settle precisely according to my own taste, and then the door is shut on me, & I may read for two hours peacefully if I like" (*APA,* 301).

Chapter 8

1. Some of Rhoda's signature statements find an almost uncanny echo in the words of anorexic Catherine Dunbar: "Anna [her sister] is strong, intelligent and sensible, but me, I have no confidence and am just a little helpless baby. All I can do is cry and cry Help me, save me, help me please" (quoted in Dunbar, 92).
2. Rhoda's failure of identity at the puddle is based on one of Woolf's own childhood experiences. See *MOB,* 78, and *D 3,* 113.
3. A (male) anorexic client of Michael Strober and Joel Yager's describes a similar terror of being "faceless" (in Garfinkel and Garner 1985, 368).
4. In the café Louis must resort to imitating the other diners to order his beef (69).
5. In *The Years,* Sara also holds her knife and fork like weapons (219).
6. Images of omnipotent control over a microcosm recur in Woolf's fiction. In *The Voyage Out,* the picnic party shifts the contours of the ant world (133), and in *To the Lighthouse* Minta casts clouds with her hand over the rock-pool "like God himself" (82–83).
7. Likewise, as various writers have pointed out (Bruch, *Eating Disorders,* 1974, 269; Garfinkel and Garner 1982, 10), anorexia is not a death wish; rather it is a solution—or pseudosolution—to the "problem" of biological mortality. (See Mara Selvini-Palazzoli, 81).
8. Hilde Bruch observes that such a temporal lurch is felt by many anorexic women. A client, Vicky, for example, experienced movement through time and constant confrontation with an unknowable future as destabilizing. Unstructured time filled her with a sense of "emptiness or discontinuity" that she found "threatening and ominous," and against which she defended with a rigid system of eating rituals (1978, 87–88). Formerly anorexic Martha also describes how an approaching weekend appeared "like a black abyss," in the face of which "I had to have every moment planned because unstructured time meant terror" (Székely, 154).
9. See also Peter Dally and Joan Gomez 1979, 50, and Selvini-Palazzoli, 74.
10. Whereas Rhoda regards *en*gorgement as the worst possible fate, *dis*gorgement is Neville's greatest horror (137).

11. Dabbling in his tea and digging out his crumpet, Bernard indeed does not resemble Byron, who has been described, controversially, as anorexic (see, for example, Margolis [99] and Schwartz [38]), and was, at the least, particular with regard to eating behavior.
12. Louis is also described as having "snail-green eyes" (18).
13. In her diary for 1897 Virginia Stephen writes, "Life is a hard business—one needs a rhinirocerous [sic] skin—& that one has not got" (*APA*, 132).
14. The ships also link Louis with Rhoda's ontological problems, with her petal fleet and her fantasy of suicide in the sea.
15. The waitresses suggest one of Rhoda's images. She compares the mean and hostile faces on the street to soup plates served by scullions (121).
16. Another of Bruch's clients reported that she "felt so little differentiated from others that she would assume the identity of whomever she was around" (*Eating Disorders*, 1974, 93).
17. "Palatable" is taken from the version of the text used by Triad Panther Books (London, 1985). The Penguin edition uses "palpable."
18. Bernard experiences the same sense of stabilizing immortality when he thinks of having children (85–86)
19. Woolf uses the image of children netted into cots in *To the Lighthouse*, in reference to Mrs. Ramsay's desire to retain her children (66).
20. In earlier drafts of the novel, Bernard's prototype, John, was more emphatically gluttonous: "He would talk, . . . thickly smearing his bread with anchovy paste. He ate in great mouthfuls; often absent mindedly; but he was not by any means oblivious to the pleasures of the flesh. He was fond of rich food; {fond of} would rub a piece of bread round and round a plate" (*TW:Hol*, 30). Later, as Bernard, he declares, "I am going to help myself to some of that delicious cold herring although the others have not yet come" (ibid., 215).

Chapter 9

1. Woolf describes the etiquette of the tea table as she learned it in "A Sketch of the Past." Although the teatable manner had, she said, inhibited her early writing, she recognized that it also had some merits, being based upon such "civilized qualities" as "restraint, sympathy, unselfishness," which enabled one "to say a great many things which would be inaudible if one marched straight up and spoke out" (*MOB*, 150).
2. Virginia Stephen's diary entry for June 10, 1897, describes a tea at which such a kettle refused to boil (*APA*, 102)
3. Mark Girouard describes the nineteenth-century sexing of the female-identified drawing room (where tea was taken) and the masculine dining room (233, 292).
4. The dining room at Abercorn Terrace is clearly a version of that at 22 Hyde Park Gate, which according to Woolf, "smelt slightly of wine, cigars, food

{had a suppressed food smell} . . . It was a very Victorian dining room; with a complete set of chairs carved in oak; high backed; with red plush panels. At dinner time with all its silver candles, silver dishes, knives and forks and napkins, the dinner table looked very festive" (Add Ms 61973).

5. In *The Waves,* as in *The Years,* the pillar-box is an image for confrontation with the body as a source of humiliation and pain. Bernard, filled suddenly with disgust at his corporeality, feels that he has walked into a pillar-box, banging his head and making a fool of himself (225).
6. Jane Marcus suggests that Rose's feminism is modeled on Ethel Smyth's (1987, 51–52).
7. In "A Sketch of the Past," Woolf associates Julia Stephen with the strains of distant music. She is described in her daughter's imagination as stepping through a window into a garden with a plate of strawberries and cream while music drifts out of the house (*MOB,* 87).
8. Troy Cooper has used *Antigone* to explicate anorexia: "The power that the anorexic takes is used by Antigone in Greek tragedy. It is the power of saying no to the demands or impositions of others" (in Lawrence 1987, 186).
9. Woolf referred to Milton as "the last of the masculinists" (*D1,* 193).
10. Hilde Bruch notes that women may adopt anorexia as a symbolic gesture of dissociation from oppressive sectors of society. An anorexic client from an upper-class family explains her thinness as a coded message that she is not wealthy and her life not one of ease. Fatness for her connotes historical kings who are "just rich and powerful and do nothing and everybody works for them" (*Eating Disorders,* 1974, 95).
11. A feature of the professional world, the chop-house was alien territory to women in 1914. Reay Tannahill explains that when the middle-class woman's "husband ate out it was likely to be at a chop-house . . . ; she herself rarely, if ever, dined out except at the homes of friends or sometimes at a tea shop or tea garden" (327).
12. Sara Pargiter is also linked to the biblical Sarah by her characteristic and disturbing laughter: "And Sarah said, God hath made me to laugh, so that all that hear will laugh with me" (Genesis 21:6). It has been argued that Sarah, who spent much of her life in a sacred grove of terebinth trees in Mamre, was in fact a priestess of the Goddess Asherah (see Orenstein, 148–149).
13. As Louise DeSalvo notes, "For Woolf, there was something utterly bizarre about asking women to join with men in resisting tyranny abroad, while requesting that women submit to the tyranny of their fathers and brothers at home" (1989, 191).
14. This view of Vanessa Bell was clearly idealistic. Angelica Garnett's memoir, France Spalding's biography of Bell, and Jane Dunn's work on Bell and Woolf have gone some way to exploding Woolf's myth.
15. The excised passage is given in full in an appendix to Grace Radin's *Virginia Woolf's The Years: The Evolution of a Novel* (pages unnumbered), from which all the following references are taken.

16. Given Woolf's abuse by George Duckworth, it is significant that in this earlier draft of the novel Peggy describes her brother, here called George, as "all sex," explicitly contrasting her own sexual suppression with his sexual excess (quoted in King, 513).
17. Richard Kennedy, in 1928 an employee of the Hogarth Press, describes in his diary a supper at which Virginia recounted how "she had been to a nightclub the night before and how marvellous it was inventing new foxtrot steps" (in Stape, 119).

Chapter 10

1. Writers who have contributed to the uncovering of *Between the Acts*' subtext of matristic Goddesshood include: Eileen Barrett ("Matriarchal Myth on a Patriarchal Stage," in Marcus 1984), Evelyn Haller ("Isis Unveiled," in Marcus 1984); Judy Little ("Festive Comedy in Woolf's *Between the Acts*"), Madeline Moore (*The Short Season Between Two Silences*), and Sandra Shuttuck ("The Stage of Scholarship: Crossing the Bridge from Harrison to Woolf," in Marcus 1987).
2. The first patriarchal invasions of matristic Europe (by a people known variously as the Indo-Europeans, Indo-Aryans, Aryans, or Kurgans) occurred around 2400 to 3000 BCE (Gimbutas 1991, 436; Stone 1975, 63). In the earliest historical records, these people are portrayed as "aggressive warriors riding two abreast in horse-drawn war chariots" (Stone 1975, 62).
3. According to Monica Sjöö and Barbara Mor, in Neolithic Egypt and Mesopotamia "the horned cow appears with a significance going back to the Old Stone Age." Hathor was a Cow Goddess, and Isis wore cows' horns. In dynastic Egypt the cow continued to be "She who gives you blessings from Heaven above and from the Abyss below, blessings of Mother-Life." On her milk the sacred kings and queens were ritually fed (161).
4. Haller connects this ritual with a Greco-Alexandrian rite for the night when Isis's star, Sothis, rose. According to Haller, "The rising marked three events simultaneously: the birth of a new year, the summer solstice, and the beginning of the inundation" (in Marcus 1984, 116).
5. George's experience clearly derives from two interconnected childhood moments of being described by Woolf in "A Sketch of the Past." In the first she is fighting with Thoby in the garden at St. Ives when suddenly she questions the desire to hurt another person and, dropping her fists, allows him to beat her. In the second she is looking at a flower bed when she is struck with a sense of the mystical interconnection of parts—how plant, flower, and leaf are not really things in themselves but part of the greater wholeness of the Earth (*MOB*, 71).
6. Horses are connected historically with the coming of the patriarchal invaders in their horse-drawn war chariots. According to Marija Gimbutas:

> Horse riding changed the course of European prehistory. Coupled with the use of weapons, the mounted warrior became a deadly

menace to the peaceful, unarmed agriculturalists... If we look back at European history, at the routine massacres by horse-riding Scythians, Sarmatians, Huns, Avars, Romans, Slavs and Vikings and the horse-drawn chariots of the Celts and those described by Homer— even the Christian Crusaders—we see how violence, abetted by the rise of the swift horse, became a dominant aspect of life. (1991, 354)

This (pre)historical context explains Mrs. Haines's comment that as a child she never feared cows, only horses (7).

7. For example, Susan in *The Waves* and Milly in *The Years*.
8. Alice Miller echoes Isa's words: "Today I know that we cannot be free if we forget, relativize, or forgive the crimes committed in childhood... I want to fight against forgetting... I want to remember what I was forced to forget and know why I had to do so" (*Banished Knowledge*, 1991, 33).
9. Woolf retained a similar personal association of incest with a dying fish on a hook and a brother's act of brutality. In "A Sketch of the Past" (written contemporaneously with *Between the Acts*), she recounts a memory—perhaps real, perhaps imagined, she says—of Gerald Duckworth in the larder using a broom to beat to death a live fish wriggling on a hook (*MOB*, 132).
10. The swallow imagery is pertinent also to the Isis myth; Isis turns herself into a swallow in order to go in search of the body of Osiris.
11. Lucy's memory derives from one of Woolf's own. She recalled that at St. Ives a woman called Mrs Adams delivered the fish. The lobsters in her basket were still alive and would open and close their claws on the kitchen table (*MOB*, 132).
12. "Lady" is the title—or, often, translation of the name—of the Goddess in cultures around the world.
13. The name Oliver, on the other hand, evokes Cromwell and seventeenth-century Puritanism. The enforcement of this rigorously prohibitive creed with its New Model Army may be seen as another reflection of the prehistoric suppression of the matristic by the new patriarchal religion. Many of the traditional festivities that the Puritans attempted stamp out (such as the May Pole) are Pagan in origin.
14. After his death, Swithin was buried at his own request under the cathedral eaves so that rainwater might fall on his grave. When his body was exhumed and reinterred inside the cathedral, violent storms broke, giving rise to the belief that rain on St. Swithin's day will continue for forty days.
15. Eileen Barrett sees the name "Manresa" as made up of "man" plus *res* (Latin for "thing"). For Barrett, this naming "emphasizes her [Mrs Manresa's] allegiances and establishes her as the image of the [pseudo] goddess in the male imagination" (24).
16. Rose Collis points to lesbian producer/director Edy Craig as a model for Miss La Trobe (66). As she notes, Woolf met Craig through Vita Sackville-West on an occasion in 1932 when Vita gave a reading of her poem "The Land" at Craig's rural Barn Theatre (65).

17. "At the Eleusinian Mysteries, sacred to Demeter and her daughter, the worshippers at the conclusion of the ceremonies would look up to heaven and cry 'Rain!' then to Earth and cry 'Be fruitful!'" (Jones and Pennick, 17).
18. Her use of alcohol to generate words suggests a practice of ancient seeresses. At the Delphic Oracle, the Pythoness drank Kassotis, a liquid from an underground fountain in order to become possessed of the spirit of prophecy (Shepsut, 206).
19. Important work had been done before and during Woolf's life-time on uncovering our matristic past, for example, Bachofen's *Das Mutterrecht,* 1861; Morgan's *Ancient Society,* 1877; Briffault's *The Mothers,* 1927; and Jane Harrison's work, especially *Prolegomena to the Study of Greek Religion,* 1903. However, the feminist task of synthesizing these new writings into a consistent understanding of the pre-patriarchal era and of reowning that past had not largely been undertaken when Woolf was alive.

Texts Cited in Abbreviation

Add Ms 61973: Original typescript held in the British Museum.
APA: A Passionate Apprentice: The Early Journals 1897–1909 (ed. Mitchell A. Leaska), The Hogarth Press, London, 1990.
AROOO: A Room of One's Own, The Hogarth Press, London, 1929; Penguin, Harmondsworth, Middlesex, 1945.
BTA: Between the Acts (ed. Stella McNichol; introduced and annotated by Gillian Beer), The Hogarth Press, London, 1941; Penguin, Harmondsworth, Middlesex, 1992.
CFE/EPF: A Cockney's Farming Experiences and The Experiences of a Pater-familias (ed. Suzanne Henig), San Diego State University Press, San Diego, 1972.
D: Diary (5 vols.) (ed. Ann Olivier Bell and Andrew McNeillie), The Hogarth Press, London, 1977–84.
JR: Jacob's Room (ed. Sue Rowe), The Hogarth Press, London 1922; Penguin, Harmondsworth, Middlesex, 1992.
L: Letters (6 vols.) (ed. Nigel Nicolson and Joanne Trautman), The Hogarth Press, London, 1975–80.
MD: Mrs. Dalloway (ed. Stella McNichol; introduced and annotated by Elaine Showalter), The Hogarth Press, London, 1925; Penguin, Harmondsworth, Middlesex, 1992.
MHP: Monks House Papers, held at the University of Sussex.
MOB: Moments of Being (ed. Jeanne Schulkind), The Hogarth Press, London, 1976, 1985.
PH: Pointz Hall: The Earlier and Later Typescripts of Between the Acts (ed. Mitchell A. Leaska), University Publications, New York, 1983.
TP: The Pargiters: The Novel-Essay Portion of The Years (ed. Mitchell A. Leaska), The Hogarth Press, London, 1978.
TTL: To the Lighthouse (ed. Stella McNichol; introduced and annotated by Hermione Lee), The Hogarth Press, London, 1927; Penguin, Harmondsworth, Middlesex, 1992.
TVO: The Voyage Out (ed. Jane Wheare), The Hogarth Press, London, 1915; Penguin, Harmondsworth, Middlesex, 1992.
TW: The Waves (ed. Kate Flint), The Hogarth Press, London, 1931; Penguin, Harmondsworth, Middlesex, 1992.

TW:Hol: The Waves: The Two Holograph Drafts (ed. J. W. Graham), The Hogarth Press, London, 1976.

TY: The Years, The Hogarth Press, London, 1937; Penguin, Harmondsworth, Middlesex, 1968.

Bibliography

Abraham, Suzanne, and Llewellyn-Jones, Derek, *Eating Disorders: The Facts,* Oxford University Press, Oxford, 1997.
Alexander, Peter, *Leonard and Virginia Woolf: A Literary Partnership,* Harvester Wheatsheaf, London, 1992.
Allison, E. (ed.) *Handbook of Assessment Methods for Eating Behaviors and Weight-Related Problems,* Sage Publications, London, 1995.
Annan, Noel, *Leslie Stephen: The Godless Victorian,* Weidenfeld and Nicolson, London, 1984.
Barrett, Eileen, "Matriarchal myth on a patriarchal stage: Virginia Woolf's Between the Acts," *Twentieth Century Literature,* 33, no. 1, 1987, pp. 18–37.
Bass, Ellen, and Davis, Laura, *The Courage to Heal: A Guide for Women Survivors of Child Sexual Abuse,* Vermilion, London, 1989.
Batchelor, John, *Virginia Woolf: The Major Novels,* Cambridge University Press, Cambridge, UK, 1991.
Beja, Morris (ed.), *Virginia Woolf: To the Lighthouse: A Casebook,* Macmillan, London, 1970.
Bell, Clive, *Old Friends: Personal Recollections,* Cassell, London, 1988.
Bell, Quentin, *Virginia Woolf: A Biography* (2 vols.), The Hogarth Press, London, 1982.
Bell, Vanessa (ed. Regina Marler), *Selected Letters of Vanessa Bell,* Bloomsbury, London, 1993.
Beumont, Pierre J. V., Burrows, Graham D., and Casper, Regina C. (eds.) *Handbook of Eating Disorders Part 1: Anorexia and Bulimia Nervosa,* Elsevier, Oxford, 1987.
Bishop, Edward, *Virginia Woolf,* Macmillan, London, 1991.
Blinder, Barton J., Chaitin, Barry F., and Goldstein, Renee S. (eds.) *The Eating Disorders: Medical and Psychological Bases of Diagnosis and Treatment,* PMA Publishing Group, New York, 1988.
Bloom, Harold (ed.), *Virginia Woolf,* Chelsea House, New York, 1986.
Blume, E. Sue, *Secret Survivors: Uncovering Incest and Its After-Effects in Women,* John Wiley & Sons, London, 1990.
Bond, Alma, *Who Killed Virginia Woolf? A Psychobiography,* Insight Books, New York, 1989.
Boskind-White, Marlene, and White, William C. Jr., *Bulimarexia: The Binge/Purge Cycle,* W. W. Norton and Co., New York, 1987.

Bovey, Shelley, *The Forbidden Body: Why Being Fat Is Not a Sin,* Pandora, London, 1989.
Bowlby, Rachel, *Virginia Woolf: Feminist Destinations,* Basil Blackwell, Oxford, 1988.
Bowlby, Rachel (ed.), *Virginia Woolf,* Longman, Harlow, Essex, 1992.
van den Brouche, Stephen, Vandereycken, Walter, and Norré, Jan, *Eating Disorders and Marital Relationships,* Routledge, London, 1997.
Bruch, Hilde, *Eating Disorders: Obesity, Anorexia Nervosa and the Person Within,* Routledge and Kegan Paul, London, 1974.
Bruch, Hilde, *The Golden Cage: The Enigma of Anorexia Nervosa,* Open Books, Somerset, 1978.
Bruch, Hilde, "The perils of behavior modification in the treatment of anorexia nervosa," *Journal of the American Medical Association,* 230, 1974, pp. 1419–1422.
Brumberg, Joan Jacobs, *Fasting Girls: The Emergence of Anorexia Nervosa as a Modern Disease,* Harvard University Press, Cambridge, MA, 1988.
Buckroyd, Julia, *Eating Your Heart Out: Understanding and Overcoming Eating Disorders,* Optima, London, 1994.
Caramagno, Thomas, *The Flight of the Mind: Virginia Woolf's Art and Manic Depressive Illness,* University of California Press, Berkeley, 1992.
Caws, Mary Ann, *Women of Bloomsbury: Virginia, Vanessa and Carrington,* Routledge, New York, 1990.
Chernin, Kim, *The Hungry Self: Women, Eating and Identity,* Virago Press, London, 1986.
Chernin, *Womansize: The Tyranny of Slenderness,* The Women's Press, London, 1983.
Chesler, Phyllis, *Women and Madness,* Avon, New York, 1972.
Clements, Patricia, and Grundy, Isobel (eds.), *Virginia Woolf: New Critical Essays,* Vision Barnes and Noble, London, 1983.
Collis, Rose, *Portraits to the Wall: Lesbian Lives Unveiled,* Cassell, London, 1994.
Cooper, Charlotte, *Fat and Proud: The Politics of Size,* The Women's Press, London, 1998.
Crisp, A., *Anorexia Nervosa: Let Me Be,* Academic Press, London, 1980.
Dally, Peter, and Gomez, Joan, *Anorexia Nervosa,* Heinemann, London, 1979.
Dally, Peter, and Gomez, Joan, *Obesity and Anorexia Nervosa: A Question of Shape,* Faber, London, 1980.
Daly, Mary, *Beyond God the Father: Towards a Philosophy of Women's Liberation,* The Women's Press, London, 1986.
Daly, Mary, *Outercourse: The Be-Dazzling Voyage,* The Women's Press, London, 1993.
Daly, Mary, *Pure Lust: Elemental Feminist Philosophy,* The Women's Press, London, 1984.
Dana, Mira, and Lawrence, Marilyn, *Women's Secret Disorder: A New Understanding of Bulimia,* Grafton, London, 1988.
Daugherty, Beth Rigel and Barrett, Eileen (eds.), *Virginia Woolf: Texts and Contexts: Selected Papers from the Fifth Annual Conference on Virginia Woolf,* Pace University Press, New York, 1996.

Davis, Vanessa, Andrew, Hilary, and Pearce, Carole, *Betrayal of Trust: Women Understanding and Overcoming Their Experience of Childhood Sexual Abuse,* Ashgrove Press, 1995.

DeSalvo, Louise, *Virginia Woolf: The Impact of Child Sexual Abuse on Her Life and Work,* The Women's Press, London, 1989.

DeSalvo, Louise, *Virginia Woolf's First Voyage: A Novel in the Making,* Hutchinson, London, 1980.

DiBattista, Maria, *Virginia Woolf's Major Novels: The Fables of Anon,* Yale University Press, New Haven, CT, 1980.

Dolan, Bridget, and Gitzinger, Inez (eds.) *Why Women? Gender Issues and Eating Disorders,* European Council on Eating Disorders, London, 1991; The Athlone Press, London, 1995.

Dresser, Rebecca, "Feeding the hunger artists: Legal issues in treating anorexia nervosa," *Wisconsin Law Review,* 2, 1984, pp. 297–384.

Dunbar, Maureen, *Catherine: A Tragic Life,* Penguin, Harmondsworth, Middlesex, 1987.

Dunn, Jane, *A Very Close Conspiracy: Vanessa Bell and Virginia Woolf,* Jonathan Cape, London, 1990.

Edel, Leon, *Bloomsbury: A House of Lions,* The Hogarth Press, London, 1979.

Ehrenreich, Barbara, and English, Deirdre, *Complaints and Disorders: The Sexual Politics of Sickness,* Writers and Readers Publishing Cooperative, New York, 1976.

Ehrenreich, Barbara and English, Deirdre, *For Her Own Good, One Hundred and Fifty Years of Experts' Advice to Women,* Pluto Press, London, 1979.

Ellman, Maud, *The Hunger Artists: Starving, Writing and Imprisonment,* Virago Press, London, 1993.

Erickson, Ann, *Anorexia Nervosa: The Broken Circle,* Faber, London, 1985.

Faller, Kathleen Coulburn, *Child Sexual Abuse: An Interdisciplinary Manual for Diagnosis, Case Management and Treatment,* Macmillan Education, London, 1989.

Ferrer, Daniel, *Virginia Woolf and the Madness of Language,* Routledge, London, 1990.

Fleischman, Avrom, *Virginia Woolf: A Critical Reading,* The John Hopkins University Press, Baltimore, 1975.

Fraser, Sylvia, *My Mother's House: A Memory of Incest and Healing,* Virago Press, London, 1989.

Frazer, J., *The Golden Bough: A Study in Magic and Religion,* Macmillan, London, 1971.

Friedrich, William, *Psychotherapy of Sexually Abused Children and their Families,* W. W. Norton and Co., New York, 1990.

Garfinkel, Paul E., and Garner, David M., *Anorexia Nervosa: A Multidimensional Perspective,* Brunner-Mazel, New York, 1982.

Garfinkel, Paul E., and Garner, David M. (eds.) *Handbook of Psychotherapy for Anorexia Nervosa and Bulimia,* Guilford Press, New York, 1985.

Garnett, Angelica, *Deceived with Kindness: A Bloomsbury Childhood,* Oxford University Press, Oxford, 1984.

Gilbert, Sandra, and Gubar, Susan, *The Madwoman in the Attic: The Woman Writer and Nineteenth Century Literary Imagination,* Yale University Press, New Haven, CT, 1980.

Gillespie, Diane Filby, *The Sisters' Arts: The Writing and Painting of Virginia Woolf and Vanessa Bell,* Syracuse University Press, Syracuse, NY, 1988.

Gimbutas, Marija, *The Civilization of the Goddess: The World of Old Europe,* Harper Collins, San Francisco, 1991.

Gimbutas, Marija, *The Gods and Goddessses of Old Europe: 7000 to 3500 BC, Myths, Legends and Cult Images,* Thames and Hudson, London, 1974.

Girouard, Mark, *Life in the English Country House,* Penguin, Harmondsworth, Middlesex, 1980.

Glendinning, Victoria, *Vita: The Life of Vita Sackville-West,* Weidenfeld and Nicolson, London, 1983.

Goodison, Lucy, *Moving Heaven and Earth: Sexuality, Spirituality and Social Change,* Pandora Press, London, 1992.

Gordon, Lyndall, *Virginia Woolf: A Writer's Life,* Oxford University Press and W. W. Norton, New York, 1984.

Gordon, Richard A., *Anorexia and Bulimia: Anatomy of a Social Epidemic,* Basil Blackwell, Oxford, 1990.

Gorsky, Susan Rubinow, *Virginia Woolf,* George Prior Publishers, London, 1978.

Griffin, Susan, *Woman and Nature: The Roaring Inside Her,* The Women's Press, London, 1984.

Griffiths, Rosayn A., Beumont, Pierre J. V., Beumont, Daphne, Touyz, Stephen W., Williams, Hazel, and Lowinger, Kitty, "Anorexie à deux: An ominous sign for recovery," European Eating Disorders Review, 3, no. 1, March 1995, pp. 2–14.

Guiguet, Jean, *Virginia Woolf and Her Works,* Harcourt Brace Jovanovich, New York, 1962.

Hafley, James, *The Glass Roof: Virginia Woolf as Novelist,* University of California Press, Berkeley, 1954.

Hall, Liz, and Lloyd, Siobhan, *Surviving Childhood Sexual Abuse: A Handbook for Helping Women Challenge their Past,* The Falmer Press, London, 1993.

Harding, Esther, *Woman's Mysteries,* Century, London, 1989.

Harrison, Jane Ellen, Prolegomena to the Study of Greek Religion, Cambridge University Press, Cambridge, UK, 1903; Princeton University Press, Princeton, NJ, 1991.

Heilbrun, Carolyn, *Towards a Recognition of Androgyny: Aspects of Male and Female in Literature,* Alfred A. Knopf, New York, 1973.

Heilbrun, Carolyn, *Writing a Woman's Life,* The Women's Press, London, 1989.

Hesse-Biber, Sharlene, *Am I Thin Enough Yet?: The Cult of Thinness and the Commercialization of Identity,* Oxford University Press, Oxford, 1997.

Holtby, Winifred, *Virginia Woolf,* Wishart and Co., London, 1932.

Homans, Margaret (ed.), *Virginia Woolf: A Collection of Critical Essays,* Prentice Hall, New York, 1993.

Hussey, Mark, and Neverow, Vara (eds.), *Virginia Woolf: Emerging Perspectives: Selected Papers from the Third Annual Conference on Virginia Woolf, Lincoln University, Jefferson City, MS, June 10–13, 1993,* Pace University Press, New York, 1994.

Hussey, Mark, and Neverow-Turk, Vara (eds.), *Virginia Woolf Miscellanies: Proceedings of the First Annual Conference on Virginia Woolf, Pace University, New York, June 7–9, 1992,* Pace University Press, New York, 1991.

Hyman, Virginia R., *To the Lighthouse and Beyond: Transformations in the Narratives of Virginia Woolf,* Peter Lang, New York, 1988.

Jalland, Pat (ed.) *Octavia Wilberforce: The Autobiography of a Pioneer Woman Doctor,* Cassell, London, 1989.

Johnson, Craig (ed.) *Psychodynamic Treatment of Anorexia Nervosa and Bulimia,* Guilford Press, New York, 1991.

Jones, Prudence, and Pennick, Nigel, *A History of Pagan Europe,* Routledge, London, 1995.

Kelley, Alice van Buren, *The Novels of Virginia Woolf: Fact and Fiction,* University of Chicago Press, Chicago, 1971.

Kenney, Susan, "Two endings: Virginia Woolf's suicide and Between the Acts," *University of Toronto Quarterly,* 44, 1975, pp. 265–289.

King, James, *Virginia Woolf,* Hamish Hamilton, London, 1994.

Kirkland, Gelsey (with Greg Lawrence), *Dancing on My Grave,* Jove Books, New York, 1987.

Kurtz, Marilyn, *Virginia Woolf: Reflections and Reverberations,* Peter Lang, New York 1990.

Laing, R. D., *The Divided Self,* Penguin, Harmondsworth, Middlesex, 1964.

Lawrence, Marilyn, *The Anorexic Experience,* The Women's Press, London, 1984.

Lawrence, Marilyn (ed.), *Fed Up and Hungry: Women, Oppression and Food,* The Women's Press, London, 1987.

Leaska, Mitchell A., *The Novels of Virginia Woolf from Beginning to End,* Weidenfeld and Nicolson, London, 1977.

Leaska, Mitchell A., *Virginia Woolf's To the Lighthouse: A Study in Critical Method,* The Hogarth Press, London, 1970.

Lee, Hermione, *The Novels of Virginia Woolf,* Methuen, London, 1977.

Lee, Hermione, *Virginia Woolf,* Chatto and Windus, London, 1996.

Levens, Mary, *Eating Disorders and Magical Control of the Body: Treatment through Art Therapy,* Routledge, London, 1995.

Levenkrom, S., *Treating and Overcoming Anorexia Nervosa,* Scribner's Sons, New York, 1982.

Lilienfeld, Jane, "The deceptiveness of beauty: Mother love and mother hate in *To the Lighthouse,*" *Twentieth Century Literature,* 23, 1977, pp. 345–76.

Little, Judy, *Comedy and the Woman Writer,* University of Nebraska Press, Lincoln, 1983.

Little, Judy, "Festive comedy in Woolf's Between the Acts," *Women and Literature,* Spring, 1977, pp. 26–37.

Logue, A. W., *The Psychology of Eating and Drinking,* W. H. Freeman and Co., New York, 1986.
Love, Jean O., *Virginia Woolf: Sources of Madness and Art,* University of California Press, Berkeley, 1977.
Love, Jean O., *Worlds in Consciousness: Mythopoetic Thought in the Novels of Virginia Woolf,* University of California Press, Berkeley, 1970.
MacLeod, Sheila, *The Art of Starvation,* Virago Press, London, 1981.
MacSween, Morag, *Anorexic Bodies: A Feminist and Sociological Perspective on Anorexia Nervosa,* Routledge, London, 1993.
Marcus, Jane (ed.), *New Feminist Essays on Virginia Woolf,* Macmillan, London, 1981.
Marcus, Jane (ed.), *Virginia Woolf: A Feminist Slant,* University of Nebraska Press, Lincoln, 1984.
Marcus, Jane (ed.), *Virginia Woolf and Bloomsbury,* Macmillan, London, 1987.
Marcus, Jane, *Virginia Woolf and the Languages of Patriarchy,* Indiana University Press, Bloomington, 1987.
Marder, Herbert, *Feminism and Art: A Study of Virginia Woolf,* University of Chicago Press, Chicago, 1968.
Maine, Margot, *Father Hunger: Fathers, Daughters and Food,* Simon and Schuster, London, 1993.
Malson, Helen, *The Thin Woman: Feminism, Post-Structuralism and the Social Psychology of Anorexia Nervosa,* Routledge, London, 1998.
Margolis, K., *To Eat or Not to Eat,* Camden Press, 1988.
Masson, Jeffrey, *The Assault on Truth: Freud's Suppression of the Seduction Theory,* Farrar, Strauss and Giroux, New York, 1984.
May, Keith M., "Proust, Virginia Woolf and the neo-Freudians," *Out of the Maelstrom: Psychology and the Novel in the Twentieth Century,* Elek Books, London, 1977, pp. 67–71.
McLaurin, Allen, *Virginia Woolf: The Echoes Enslaved,* Cambridge University Press, 1973.
McNichol, Stella, *Virginia Woolf and the Poetry of Fiction,* Routledge, London, 1990.
Meisl, Perry, *The Absent Father: Virginia Woolf and Walter Pater,* Yale University Press, New Haven, CT, 1980.
Mephane, John, *Virginia Woolf: A Literary Life,* Macmillan, London, 1991.
Meyorowitz, Selma S., *Leonard Woolf,* Twayne Publishers, Boston, 1982.
Miller, Alice, *Banished Knowledge: Facing Childhood Injuries,* Virago Press, London, 1991.
Miller, Alice, *Breaking Down the Wall of Silence to Join the Waiting Child,* Virago Press, London, 1991.
Miller, Alice, *Thou Shalt Not Be Aware: Society's Betrayal of the Child,* Pluto Press, London, 1991.
Miller, C. Ruth, *Virginia Woolf: The Frames of Life,* Macmillan, London, 1988.
Millett, Kate, *The Loony Bin Trip,* Virago Press, London, 1991.
Minow-Pinkney, Makiko, *Virginia Woolf and the Problem of the Subjective,* Harvester Press, Brighton, 1987.

Minuchin, Salvador, Rosman, Bernice, and Baker, Lester, *Psychosomatic Families: Anorexia Nervosa in Context,* Harvard University Press, Cambridge, MA, 1978.

Moore, Madeline, *The Short Season Between Two Silences: The Mystical and the Political in the Novels of Virginia Woolf,* George Allen and Unwin, London, 1984.

Mott, Alexander, and Lumsden, Barry D., *Understanding Eating Disorders: Anorexia, Bulimia Nervosa and Obesity,* Taylor and Francis, Washington, DC, 1994.

Naremore, James, *The World Without a Self,* Yale University Press, New Haven, CT, 1973.

Nasser, Mervat, *Culture and Weight Consciousness,* Routledge, London, 1997.

Nelson, Sarah, *Incest: Fact and Myth,* Stramullion Co-operative Ltd., Edinburgh, 1987.

Nicolson, Nigel, *Portrait of a Marriage,* Weidenfeld and Nicolson, London, 1973.

Noble, Joan Russell (ed.), *Recollections of Virginia Woolf,* Peter Owen, London, 1972.

Novak, Jane, *The Razor Edge of Balance: A Study of Virginia Woolf,* University of Miami Press, Coral Gables, 1975.

Ohmann, Carol, "Culture and anarchy in *Jacob's Room,*" *Contemporary Literature,* 18, 1977, pp. 180–192.

Orbach, Susie, *Fat Is a Feminist Issue: The Anti-Diet Guide to Permanent Weight Loss,* Paddington Press, London, 1984.

Orbach, Susie, *Hunger Strike: The Anorectic's Struggle as a Metaphor for Our Age,* Faber and Faber, London, 1986.

Orenstein, Gloria, *The Reflowering of the Goddess,* Pergamon Press, New York, 1990.

Palmer, R. L., *Anorexia Nervosa: A Guide for Sufferers and their Families,* Penguin, Harmondsworth, Middlesex, 1984.

Panken, Shirley, *Virginia Woolf and the Lust of Creation: A Psychoanalytic Exploration,* State University of New York Press, Albany, 1987.

Paul, Janis M., *Victorian Heritage of Virginia Woolf: The External World in Her Novels,* Pilgrim Books, Norman, Oklahoma, 1987.

Pederson, Glenn, "Vision in To the Lighthouse," *Publications of the Modern Language Association,* 73, 1958, pp. 585–600.

Phillips, Kathy, *Virginia Woolf Against Empire,* University of Tennessee Press, Knoxville, 1994.

Poole, Roger, *The Unknown Virginia Woolf,* Cambridge University Press, Cambridge, UK, 1978.

Poresky, Louise A., *The Elusive Self: Psyche and Spirit in Virginia Woolf's Novels,* Associated Universities Presses, London, 1981.

Radin, Grace, *Virginia Woolf's The Years: The Evolution of a Novel,* University of Tennessee Press, Knoxville, 1981.

Raitt, Susan, *Virginia Woolf's To the Lighthouse,* Harvester Wheatsheaf, Hemel Hempstead, 1990.

Raitt, Susan, *Vita and Virginia: The Work and Friendship of Vita Sackville-West and Virginia Woolf,* Clarendon Press, Oxford, 1993.

Renvoize, Jean, *Incest: A Family Pattern,* Routledge and Kegan Paul, London, 1982.

Richardson, Samuel, *Clarissa, or the History of a Young Lady,* Penguin, Harmondsworth, Middlesex, 1985.

Richter, Harvena, *Virginia Woolf: The Inward Voyage,* Princeton University Press, Princeton, NJ, 1980.

Rose, Phyllis, *Woman of Letters: A Life of Virginia Woolf,* Routledge and Kegan Paul, London, 1979.

Rosenman, Ellen Bayuk, *A Room of One's Own: Women Writers and the Politics of Creativity,* Twayne Publishers, New York, 1995.

Rosenman, Ellen Bayuk, *The Invisible Presence: Virginia Woolf and the Mother-Daughter Relationship,* Louisiana State University Press, Baton Rouge, 1986.

Rosenthal, Michael, *Virginia Woolf,* Routledge and Kegan Paul, London, 1979.

Ruotolo, Lucio P., *The Interrupted Moment: A View of Virginia Woolf's Novels,* Stanford University Press, Stanford, CA, 1986.

Rush, Florence, *The Best Kept Secret: Sexual Abuse of Children,* McGraw-Hill, New York, 1980.

Sackville-West, Vita (ed. Louise DeSalvo and Mitchell A. Leaska), *The Letters of Vita Sackville-West to Virginia Woolf,* William Morrow, New York, 1985.

Sackville-West, Vita, and Nicolson, Harold (ed. Nigel Nicolson), *Vita and Harold: The Letters of Vita Sackville-West and Harold Nicolson 1910–1962,* Weidenfeld and Nicolson, London, 1992.

Schlack, Beverley Ann, *Continuing Presences: Virginia Woolf's Use of Literary Allusion,* Pennsylvania State University Press, University Park, 1979.

Schmidt, U., Evans, K., Tiller, J., and Treasure, J., "Puberty, sexual milestones and abuse: How are they related in eating disorder patients?" *Psychological Medicine,* 25, 1995, pp. 413–417.

Schwartz, Hillel, *Never Satisfied: A Cultural History of Diets, Fantasies and Fat,* The Free Press, New York 1986.

Schwartz, Mark, and Cohn, Leigh (eds.), *Sexual Abuse and Eating Disorders,* Brunner-Mazel, New York, 1996.

Selvini-Palazzoli, Mara, *Self-Starvation: From the Intrapsychic to the Transpersonal Approach to Anorexia Nervosa,* Human Context Books, Haywards Heath, West Sussex, 1974.

Shanahan, Mary Steussy, "Between the Acts: Virginia Woolf's final endeavor in art," *Texas Studies in Literature and Language,* 14, 1972, pp. 121–138.

Shepsut, Asia, *Journey of the Priestess,* Aquarian Press, London, 1993.

Showalter, Elaine, *The Female Malady: Women, Madness and English Culture, 1830–1980,* Virago Press, London, 1987.

Showalter, Elaine, *A Literature of Their Own: British Women Novelists from Brontë to Lessing,* Virago Press, London, 1982.

Sjöö, Monica, and Mor, Barbara, *The Great Cosmic Mother,* HarperCollins, San Francisco, 1991.

Slade, Roger, *The Anorexia Nervosa Reference Book,* Harper & Row, London, 1984.

Sophocles, (trans. E. F. Watling), *The Theban Plays,* Penguin, Harmondsworth, Middlesex, 1986.

Spalding, Frances, *Vanessa Bell,* Weidenfeld and Nicolson, London, 1983.

Spater, George, and Parsons, Ian, *A Marriage of True Minds: An Intimate Portrait of Leonard and Virginia Woolf,* Jonathan Cape and Hogarth Press, London, 1977.

Spilka, Mark, *Virginia Woolf's Quarrel with Grieving*, University of Nebraska Press, Lincoln, 1980.
Squier, Susan Merill, *Virginia Woolf and London: The Sexual Politics of the City*, University of California Press, Berkeley, 1985.
Stape, J. H. (ed.), *Virginia Woolf: Interviews and Recollections*, Macmillan, London, 1995.
Stephen, Julia Duckworth (ed. Diane F. Gillespie and Elizabeth Steele), *Stories for Children, Essays for Adults*, Syracuse University Press, Syracuse, NY, 1987.
Stephen, Leslie (ed. Alan Bell) *Sir Leslie Stephen's Mausoleum Book*, Clarendon Press, Oxford, 1977.
Stone, Merlin, *Ancient Mirrors of Womanhood*, Beacon Press, Boston, 1990.
Stone, Merlin, *When God Was a Woman*, Harcourt Brace Jovanovich, New York, 1975.
Stunkard, Albert J., and Stellar, Eliot (eds.), *Eating and Its Disorders*, Raven Press, New York, 1984.
Székely, Éve, *Never Too Thin*, The Women's Press, London, 1988.
Szmuckler, George, Dare, Chris, and Treasure, Janet (eds.) *A Handbook of Eating Disorders: Theory, Treatment and Research*, John Wiley & Sons, London, 1995.
Tannahill, Reay, *Food in History*, Penguin, Harmondsworth, Middlesex, 1988.
Thakur, N. C., *The Symbolism of Virginia Woolf*, Oxford University Press, Oxford, 1965.
Thone, Ruth Raymond, *Fat: A Worse Fate than Death*, The Harrington Park Press, Bighampton, NJ, 1997.
Topping, Nancy, *Virginia Woolf and the Androgynous Vision*, Rutgers University Press, 1973.
Transue, Pamela, *Virginia Woolf and the Politics of Style*, State University of New York Press, Albany, 1986.
Trombley, Stephen, *All That Summer She Was Mad: Virginia Woolf and Her Doctors*, Junction Books, London, 1981.
Ussher, Jane, *The Psychology of the Female Body*, Routledge, London, 1989.
Ussher, Jane, *Women's Madness: Misogyny or Mental Illness?* Harvester Wheatsheaf, Hemel Hempstead, 1991.
Vandereycken, Walter, and Meermann, Rolf, *Anorexia Nervosa: A Clinician's Guide to Treatment*, Walter de Gruyter, Berlin, 1984.
Vigersky, R. (ed.), *Anorexia Nervosa*, Raven Press, New York, 1977.
Vincent, L. M., *Competing with the Sylph: Dancers and the Pursuit of the Ideal Body Form*, Andrews and McMeel, New York, 1979.
Walker, Barbara, *The Women's Encyclopedia of Myths and Secrets*, Pandora, London, 1995.
Walker, Moira, *Surviving Secrets*, Open University Press, Buckingham, 1992.
Waller, Glenn (ed.) "Special issue: Dissociation and the eating disorders," *European Eating Disorders Review*, 3, no. 3, 1995.
Waller, Glenn, Coakley, Margaret, and Richards, Lorna, "Bulimic attitudes among Asian and Caucasian schoolgirls," *European Eating Disorders Review*, 3, no. 1, 1995, pp. 24–34.

Walsh, B., *Eating Behavior in Eating Disorders,* American Psychiatric Press, Washington, DC, 1988.

Ward, Elizabeth, *Father Daughter Rape,* The Women's Press, London, 1984.

Warner, Eric (ed.), *Virginia Woolf: A Centenary Perspective,* St. Martin's Press, New York, 1984.

Waskett, Carole, *Counselling People in Eating Distress,* British Association for Counselling, Rugby, Warwickshire, 1993.

West, Richard, *Eating Disorders: Anorexia Nervosa and Bulimia Nervosa,* Office of Health Economics, London, 1994.

Wheare, Jane, *Virginia Woolf: Dramatic Novelist,* Macmillan, London, 1989.

Wilson, Jean Moorcroft, *Virginia Woolf, Life and London: A Biography of Place,* Macmillan, London, 1989.

Wolf, Naomi, *The Beauty Myth,* Chatto and Windus, London, 1990.

Women's Research Centre, *Recollecting Our Lives: Women's Experience of Childhood Sexual Abuse,* Press Gang Publishers, Vancouver, 1989.

Woodman, Marion, *Addiction to Perfection: The Still Unravished Bride,* Inner City Books, Toronto, 1982.

Woodman, Marion, *The Owl Was a Baker's Daughter: Obesity, Anorexia Nervosa and the Repressed Feminine,* Inner City Book, Toronto, 1980.

Woolf, Leonard, *Beginning Again: An Autobiography of the Years 1911–1918,* The Hogarth Press, London, 1963.

Woolf, Leonard, *Downhill All the Way: An Autobiography of the Years 1919–1938,* The Hogarth Press, London, 1967.

Woolf, Leonard, *Growing: An Autobiography of the Years 1904–1911,* The Hogarth Press, London, 1961.

Woolf, Leonard, *The Journey Not the Arrival Matters: An Autobiography of the Years 1939–1969,* The Hogarth Press, 1969.

Woolf, Leonard (ed. Frederic Spotts), *Letters of Leonard Woolf,* Weidenfeld and Nicolson, London, 1990.

Woolf, Leonard, *Sowing: An Autobiography of the Years 1880–1904,* The Hogarth Press, London, 1960.

Woolf, Leonard, *The Wise Virgins,* The Hogarth Press, 1914, 1979.

Woolf, Virginia (ed. Mary Lyon), *Books and Portraits,* The Hogarth Press, London, 1977.

Woolf, Virginia (ed. Leonard Woolf), *The Captain's Death Bed and Other Essays,* The Hogarth Press, London, 1950, 1981.

Woolf, Virginia (ed. Susan Dick), *The Complete Shorter Fiction of Virginia Woolf,* Triad Grafton, London, 1987.

Woolf, Virginia, *The Common Reader: One,* The Hogarth Press, London, 1925, 1984.

Woolf, Virginia, *The Common Reader: Two,* The Hogarth Press, London, 1932, 1986.

Woolf, Virginia (ed. Joanne Trautmann), *Congenial Spirits: The Letters of Virginia Woolf,* The Hogarth Press, London, 1989.

Woolf, Virginia (ed. Leonard Woolf), *The Death of the Moth,* The Hogarth Press, London, 1947, 1981.
Woolf, Virginia, *Flush: A Biography,* The Hogarth Press, London, 1933, 1983.
Woolf, Virginia (ed. Leonard Woolf), *Granite and Rainbow,* The Hogarth Press, London, 1958, 1981.
Woolf, Virginia, *A Haunted House,* The Hogarth Press, London, 1944; Grafton Books, London, 1985.
Woolf, Virginia (ed. Leonard Woolf), *The Moment and Other Essays,* The Hogarth Press, London, 1947, 1981.
Woolf, Virginia (ed. Stella McNichol), *Mrs. Dalloway's Party,* The Hogarth Press, London, 1978.
Woolf, Virginia (ed. Julia Briggs), *Night and Day,* The Hogarth Press, London, 1919; Penguin, Harmondsworth, Middlesex, 1992.
Woolf, Virginia (ed. Brenda Lyons; introduced and annotated by Sandra, M. Gilbert), *Orlando,* The Hogarth Press, London, 1928; Penguin, Harmondsworth, Middlesex, 1993.
Woolf, Virginia, *Three Guineas,* The Hogarth Press, London, 1938, 1986.
Woolf, Virginia (ed. Susan Dick), *To the Lighthouse: The Original Holograph Draft,* The Hogarth Press, London, 1983.
Woolf, Virginia (ed. S. P. Rosenbaum), *Women and Fiction: The Manuscript Versions of A Room of One's Own,* Blackwell Publishers, Oxford, 1992.
Zwerdling, A., *Virginia Woolf and the Real World,* University of California Press, Berkeley, 1986.

Index

Abraham, Suzanne & Llewellyn-Jones, Derek 3, 6, 231 n.12
abuse *see* sexual abuse
Alexander, Peter xii, 55, 64, 235 n. 3
angel, woman as, xiii, 94, 176, 177, 196
anger *see* rage
Annan, Noel 31, 33, 35
anorexia nervosa 1–11
  and the body ix, 4–5, 11, 29, 78, 157, 229 n.9
  conformity and rebellion in 4, 10, 41–2, 60, 78
  as coping strategy 45, 58, 68, 242 n.7
  and denial 4
  and *élan vital* 117–18
  and the family 30, 32–3, 234 n.24
  and fathers 9, 31, 32, 37, 38, 133–4, 234 n.26
  as "illness" 7, 231 n.11
  incidence 11, 230 n.5
  and Judeo-Christianity 2
  as metaphor v, 54, 61
  mortality rates 230–1 n.3
  and mothers 9, 19, 41, 133, 135, 182
  in novels 77, 83–4, 87–8, 118, 121, 133–5, 144, 155, 158–9
  as ontological problem v, ix, 1–5, 157
  and rage 5–7, 31, 134
  and time 242 n. 8
  treatments 6–11, 53, 58–60, 230–1 n.3b, 231 n.10
  and VW v, viii–ix, xiii, xv–xvi, 29, 45, 126
  see also eating disorders; sexual abuse; women, anorexic
asceticism
  of Leslie Stephen 35–6, 46
  of LW 46, 63, 65
  in *Mrs. Dalloway* 120–1, 122, 129–30
  and religion 2, 91
  in *To the Lighthouse* 36, 146–7, 151
  of VW viii, xiii, 35, 65
  in *The Years* 183–4, 197
Ashham (Woolfs' home) 59–60, 63

Barrett, Eileen 204, 235 n.1, 246 n.15

Bell, Angelica, *see* Garnett, Angelica
Bell, Clive (brother-in-law of VW) 51, 59, 239 n.14
  VW's interest in 20, 56, 238 n.4
Bell, Quentin vi–vii, 18, 52, 54, 60–1, 64, 68, 69, 185,
Bell, Vanessa (sister of VW)
  as child 15
  contracts typhoid 28–9
  and daughter 232 n.10
  and LW 65
  and Maggie Pargiter 188, 244 n.14
  marriage to Clive Bell 20
  "Notes on Virginia's Childhood" 16, 17–18
  relationship with father 42
  sensuality 56
  sexual abuse of 20, 22, 24–5, 27, 59
  and VW: begs to eat 23, 73; as caretaker of xiv, 19, 27, 42, 73; maternal protection of 19–20; medical treatment of 26–8; mental health of 60, 236 n.8; sexual relationship with 20, 66, 226
  weight 29–30, 62
Between the Acts 203–27
  and agricultural revolution 204–5
  Albert 225
  barn in 215–16
  Bartholomew Oliver (Bart) 213; destroys George's world 206, 207; as Father God 206–9, 213, 217; and fish 213; and incest 211–12, 216; and India 206–7; as intruder into kitchen 216–17; and Isa 218; and Miss La Trobe 226; and Mrs. Manresa 219–20; and patriarchal family 218; and rationalism 223
  Candish (butler) 217–18
  and challenge to patriarchy 221
  and class system 139, 216, 218
  cow in 204, 205, 245 n.3, 307
  dining room in 217–18
  and Egyptian mythology 205, 210–15, 246 n.10
  Eliza Clark 222

fish and fishing in 208, 211–14, 246 n.9
George Oliver 206, 207, 232 n.2
Giles Oliver 210, 211, 219
Goddess in 205, 207–9, 213–17, 219–26, 246 n.12
greenhouse in 209–10
invasion in 216
Isa Oliver: and barrenness 208; children 207; and gang rape report 208, 217; and greenhouse 209–10; as Ishtar 207; and Isis 210–13, 221, 246 n.10; loathing of domesticity 218; marriage failure 211; and Mrs. Manresa 220, 221; and pear tree 208–9; and Rupert Haines 210; and submerged memory 208, 209, 210, 212; suicide fantasies 210; and thirst 210
Jessie Pook (cook) 217
and Judeo-Christianity 203, 209–10, 214–15, 219, 225–6
kitchen in 216–18, 224
larder in 216
Lucy Swithin: and apricots 209, 220; and the barn 215–16; and Bart 211; and Christianity 214; and fish 213; and incest 212–13; and Isis 215; and the kitchen 216, 218; makes sandwiches 216; and Old Religion 213–16; and St Swithin 214, 246 n.14
Mabel (nurse) 207
Miss La Trobe: and drought 211, 225; and gynecentric revision 205–6, 221, 225–6; as Isis 225; as outsider 221
and mother-child bond 207, 226–7
Mrs. Manresa: and the body 219–20; fortune-telling 221; fruitfulness 220–1; helps herself 219; as Isis 220; and Old Religion 219–20; as outsider 218; as primitive 219, 220; sensuality 219; as teacher of women 220
Mrs. Sands: and the cat 214, 216; as deity 217; and fruit tree 209; and kitchen and larder 216–17; makes sandwiches 216; and Old Religion 213, 214, 216
and patriarchy and history 203, 204–14, 219, 221–5
rape in 208, 212, 216–17, 222–3
Reverend Streatfield 214–15
Rupert Haines, and Isa Oliver 210
sacramental tea 216
Sohrab (dog) 218
Sunny (cat) 214, 216
war in 128–9, 204, 212–13
William Dodge 209–10, 218
binge-eating 69, 237 n.19
bipolar disorder, *see* depression, manic
Bloomsbury group, and rationality 50–1

body
and anorexia ix, 4–5, 11, 229 n.9
and bodilessness xiii, 29, 77–8
body-soul dichotomy xvi, 2–3, 77–8, 102, 104, 111, 129, 156, 203, 227
control over 8–9, 17, 78–9, 81–2
and exercise 35
as sordid ix, 56, 127, 157, 173
in *The Voyage Out* 77–98
VW's relationship with ix, xiii, xvi, 13, 17, 21, 29, 35, 53–4, 56
Bond, Alma vii, 46, 59–60, 61
Brenan, Gerald xiii, 51, 55, 59, 236 n.9
Bruch, Hilde 2, 3, 4–5, 41, 155, 157, 229 n.7, 232 n.5, 234 nn.25.26, 235 n.5, 240 n.10, 242 n.8, 243 n.16, 244 n.10
Buckroyd, Julia 53, 71
bulimia nervosa 232 n.6, 240 n.12
Burley (nursing home) 52, 53–4, 57

Cameron, Julia Margaret 40
Caramagno, Thomas vii
Carlyle, Thomas 112–13, 239 n.15
Case, Janet (teacher) 57, 60, 62
Cecil, David xiii, vx
celibacy, female 119–20
Charleston (sister's country house) xiii, 65, 67
chastity, female 119–20
Chernin, Kim 2, 4, 240–1 n.13
choking, and sexual abuse 21, 23–4
chop-house, and male culture 185, 244 n.11
Christianity, *see* Judeo-Christianity
Clapham Sect 35, 46
class system 86, 88,104, 123, 139, 142, 164–6, 190–2, 195, 199, 216, 218, 239 nn.8,10
"A Cockney's Farming Experiences" 13–16
colonialism 89, 90, 92, 206–7, 224
Congenial Spirits 140
Connolly, Cyril xiii
consciousness, mythopoeic 48–51, 67
conversation, and food vx
Cox, Ka 53, 55, 62
Craig, Maurice, as doctor of VW 46, 50, 52, 60, 61, 62
creativity
  and the body xvi
  of dinner party 121–3, 126, 127, 131
  and domesticity xii, 82
  female 134, 138–9, 145–6, 153
  and food 134
  and madness x, 22
  male 82, 138–9
  and rationality 48, 51

Dalingridge Place (home of George Duckworth) 58

Dalley, Peter xiv, 8–9
Daly, Mary ix, 229 n.3, 237 n.23
Davis, Vanessa, Andrew, Hilary & Pearce, Carole 10
Death of the Moth xiii, xvi, 176
depression, manic, *see* manic depression
DeSalvo, Louise viii, 14, 15, 16–18, 20, 21, 23–4, 27, 33, 42, 56, 70, 72, 208, 209, 244 n.13
DiBattista, Maria 133, 240 n.11
Dickinson, Violet
 and LW's letters 17, 20, 22–3, 27–9, 54, 60–1
 as maternal figure 19
 VW's sexual relationship with 236 n.16
disempowerment
 of anorexic women 2, 4–5, 7, 11, 49, 54, 231 n.8
 and hysteria 21
 and patriarchy 80–1, 83–7, 88, 90–8, 106, 119, 138, 182–4
doctors
 and LW 46–8, 50, 58–62, 73
 in novels 127, 129
 of VW 21, 22, 25, 46, 50, 58, 60, 63, 69–70, 72–3
domesticity, and writing xii, 82
dreams
 in novels 96–7, 162, 179–80, 184
 of VW 53, 96
Dresser, Rebecca 6
Duckworth, George (half brother of VW)
 and childhood 15
 and Dalingridge Place 59
 and greed 17, 240 n.6
 and outings with VW 22, 25
 and sexual abuse of Vanessa Stephen 20, 22, 24–5, 27
 and sexual abuse of VW 17, 20–1, 24–5, 27, 30, 34, 37, 59, 71–2, 245 n.16
 social ambitions 24–5
 social respectability 24
Duckworth, Gerald (half brother of VW) 15
 and greed 17, 238 n.7a, 240 n.6
 and sexual abuse of VW 17, 18, 25, 30, 59, 70–1, 96, 229 n.5, 246 n.9
 weight 29–30
Duckworth, Stella (half sister of VW)
 death 37, 38, 42
 and eating 38
 and Leslie Stephen 30, 42
 marriage to Jack Hills 42
 and mother 15, 40, 232 n.3
 and VW's breakdown 21–2
Dunbar, Maureen 49
Dunn, Jane viii, 27, 29, 235 n.30, 238 n.9, 244 n.14

eating disorders
 and patriarchy 1, 2–5, 7–9, 11, 21, 77, 78, 230 n.1b
 and sexual abuse viii, ix, 9–10, 17, 21, 23–4, 31, 71, 212, 232 n.6
 see also anorexia nervosa
Eating Disorders Association (EDA) v, 235 n.2, 241 n.2
education
 as male privilege 101–2
 university 41, 92, 101–2, 160, 189–92, 195
 of VW 21–2, 31
 of women 26, 41
Ehrenreich, Barbara vi
Eliot, T. S. 67
emotion, suppression xiv, 37, 38, 40, 72
empowerment, female 5, 11, 219, 227
English, Deirdre vi
"The Experiences of a Pater-familias" 13–17, 32, 234–5 n.29

family, and patriarchy xiv, 31, 34, 80–5, 92, 188, 218–19
fantasy
 and control 156–7
 and food 16
 sexual abuse seen as 72
 and suicide 157–8, 210, 243 n.14
fathers/fathering
 and anorexia 9, 31, 32, 37, 38, 133–4, 234 n.26
 in patriarchal society 133–4, 146–53
 and sexual abuse 232 n.15
feminism
 and anorexia 1, 5, 7
 and empowerment 5
 and female madness ix–x
 and interpretation of VW vi
 and LW 64
 in novels 179, 180–1
 and therapy 10
Fleischman, Avrom 137
Flush, and food xi
food
 and ontology ix, xv–xvi
 VW's attitudes to v, viii, xiii–xvi; in childhood 13–14; pleasure in 23, 28, 43, 67, 226, 238 n.4; refusal xiii, 23, 46–9, 58–63
 in writing of VW xi–xii, xvi, 68
force-feeding 6, 7, 10, 61, 185
Forrester, Hilary 7
Freud/Freudianism, viii, 58, 72, 237 n.20
frigidity 26, 56, 120–1
Fry, Roger 25, 58, 60, 70, 238 n.4

Garnett, Angelica (niece of VW) xiv

and LW 51, 61, 64, 65, 236 n.14
memoir of VW 27, 38
and Stephen family 229 n.4
and Vanessa Bell 232 n.10, 244 n.14
Gomez, Joan 7–8
Granite and Rainbow 51
Grant, Duncan (lover of Vanessa Bell) 62
greed xiv–xv, 17, 238 n.7, 240 n.6
Grundy, Isobel 101, 238 n.6
guilt
 and reluctance to eat xiii, 46, 48, 57, 65
 and sexual abuse 10, 17, 26, 71

Hall, Liz & Lloyd, Siobhan 10
Halliday, F. E. 31
Head, Henry, as doctor of VW 46, 58
Hills, Jack (husband of Stella Duckworth) 25, 42
Hills, Stella, *see* Duckworth, Stella
Hogarth Press 70, 72, 245 n.17
homosexuality 128, 160, 210, 218
horses, and patriarchy 245 n.6
Hudson, Nan 71–2
hunger
 acceptance 169
 and cultural disinheritance 101
 elimination 3–4
 existential 81, 108, 136–7, 144
 satisfaction 105, 106, 131
"22 Hyde Park Gate" 17, 24, 25, 71–2
22 Hyde Park Gate (childhood home of VW) vii, 30, 243–4 n.4
Hyslop, T. B., as doctor of VW 46, 50, 52
hysteria, treatment 21

identity
 suppression 3, 5, 79, 81, 111–12, 117
 VW's sense of 22, 28, 29–30, 31, 70
incest 42, 72, 211–12, 216, 237 n.20
 and VW, *see* sexual abuse
insanity, *see* madness
Isherwood, Christopher xiii
Isis 145, 210–13, 220–1, 225, 246 n.10

Jackson, Julia, *see* Stephen, Julia
Jackson, Maria (mother of Julia Stephen) 15, 36, 40
Jacob's Room 99–115
 Betty Flanders 114, 239 n.12
 Bonamy 106
 butterflies in 114
 café in 107, 109–10, 166
 Clara Durrant 99, 111–12, 115
 Cowan 101
 Cruttendon 108, 114
 Curnow 99
 establishment as carnivorous 115

Evan Wentworth-Williams, Greek meal 113
Fanny Elmer 100, 106–9, 112, 118, 157
Florinda 99–100, 108–12
Huxtable 101
Jacob Flanders: and biblical Jacob 99, 101, 111; cadges a meal 106; as Carlylian hero 112–13; and Clara Durrant 111–12; compared with Rachel Vinrace 100, 105–6, 114–15; feast of cherries 114; and Florinda 109, 110–11; and Greece 100, 113; and hunger 105, 106; mediocre food 104–5; more than sufficiency 111; sense of identity 100, 105–7, 111; social class 239 nn.8,10; tragic fate 100, 113–15; view of sexualized women 110–11; voyage around Scilly Isles 106
Jinny Carslake 107–8, 118, 157
Lady Miller's picnic 114
Mother Stuart 109
motherlessness of women in 109, 112
Mr. Clutterbuck 115
Mr. Plumer (don) 104–5
Mrs. Pascoe 99
Mrs. Plumer 104–5, 190
Nick Bramham 107
Sandra Wentworth-Williams 112, 113
Sopwith (don) 101
Stenhouse 101, 104
Timothy Durrant 99, 100, 106, 114
and university as cake 101–2
and *The Voyage Out* 100
and wastage of women's lives 99–100
World War I 99, 113, 114, 115
Joyce, James xii
Judeo-Christianity
 and anorexia 2
 and body-soul dichotomy 203
 and patriarchy 93, 185, 187, 209–10, 214–15, 219, 225–6
Jung, C. G. 137

Kamiya, Miyeko viii
Keats, John, "Ode to a Nightingale" 210
Kenney, Susan 204
Keynes, John Maynard, and LW 49
King, James vii, 20, 22, 34–5, 40, 52, 226, 241 n.6
kitchen xii, 122–3, 163, 169–71, 216–18, 224

Lawrence, Marilyn 7, 19, 166, 231 n.10, 240 n.12
Leaska, Mitchell 79, 191, 211, 212, 237 n.3
Lee, Hermione viii, ix, 25, 232 n.8
lesbianism
 in *Between the Acts* 205, 211, 221, 225
 in *Mrs. Dalloway* 119–20, 128, 129–30, 131
 of VW and Vanessa Bell 20, 55–6, 66

of VW and Violet Dickinson 236 n.16
of VW and Vita Sackville-West xii, 55, 66, 236 n.15
Levens, Mary 133
Lilienfeld, Jane 133, 137, 241 n.9
Little, Judy 209, 216, 235 n.1
Love, Jean O. vii, 23, 32–3, 38, 40–2

MacCarthy, Molly 57, 59
MacLeod, Sheila v, xiv, 30, 31, 121, 158, 241 n.1, 242 n.12
madness
 assumed of VW vi–x, xiii–xiv, 22, 25–8, 45, 46–7, 59, 74
Maine, Margot 10, 32, 232 n.14
manic depression, and VW vi, vii, viii
Marcus, Jane vi, 119, 186–7, 244 n.6
marriage
 and control of women's bodies 79, 81–2, 93
 and patriarchy 81, 93, 95–8, 119, 143–4, 182–4
Martin, Kingsley xiv
matriarchy, in *The Years* 191
matrism 2
 in *Between the Acts* 203–5, 207–9, 212–26, 228, 235 n.1
 in *Mrs. Dalloway* 128–9
 in *To the Lighthouse* 137
 in *The Voyage Out* 91–2, 95
 in *The Years* 183, 185, 203
Mayer, Louie (cook) xii–xiii, xv, 230 nn.1a,2a
meat, and patriarchy 63, 91, 104–5, 185–7, 189, 212, 224–5
Memoir Club 71
memory, submerged xiv, 70–1, 208, 209, 210
menstruation, and sexual abuse 22–3, 233 n.15
milk
 and nurture 14, 16, 94, 144, 149, 232 n.2
 in treatment of VW 46–7, 62, 67, 69, 73
Miller, Alice 209, 246 n.8
Millett, Kate ix–x
Minuchin, Salvador, Rosman, Bernice & Baker, Lester 7–8, 30, 32, 234 n.24
Mitchell, Silas Weir 26, 27, 234 n.19
Moments of Being 16, 17, 19, 20–1, 24–5, 30–2, 35, 38, 40, 42, 71
Monk's House (Woolfs' home) xii, 60, 65
Moore, Madeline viii, 162, 208, 220
Mor, Barbara 205, 245 n.3
Mortimer, Raymond xiii
mothers/mothering
 of anorexic daughters 9, 19, 41, 133, 135, 182
 daughters' ambivalent relationships with 19, 233 n.11
 in patriarchal society 78, 93, 95, 133–7, 143–4

in *To the Lighthouse* 133, 134, 135–8, 140–6, 149
in *The Years* 175–6, 179, 181, 187–9, 191–3, 197–8, 200–2, 203
Mrs. Dalloway 117–32
 and asceticism 120–1, 122, 129–30
 Clarissa Dalloway: and anorexia 118, 121, 127; and asexuality 118–19, 127; and celibacy in marriage 119–20; and Clarissan nuns 119; and class system 123, 139; and creativity 121–3, 126, 127, 131, 139; and dinner party 117, 121–3, 124, 126, 127, 131–2, 139; and Doris Kilman 130–1; exclusion from lunch party 124; 'failure' of Richard 128; and harvest 128; and internal schism 117; and joy in life 117–18, 119, 129, 132; and lesbianism 119–20, 129, 131; sense of identity 118, 120, 129, 131; and servants 122; slightness 118, 125; and withdrawal 127
 Doris Kilman: and Christianity 129; corporeality 129, 241 n.14; emotional deprivation 130, 131; German ancestry 130–1, 241 n.14; insatiability 130; lesbianism 129–30, 131; as scapegoat for Clarissa 131
 Dr. Holmes 126–7, 129, 131
 Elizabeth Dalloway 119, 129–30
 Evans 128
 Evelyn Whitbread 126
 female principle destroyed 128
 Hugh Whitbread 121, 122, 124, 125–6, 130, 131, 198
 kitchen in 122–3
 Lady Bradshaw 126, 211
 Millicent (Lady) Bruton: and lunch party 117, 124–5; and male world 123–4
 Milly Brush 125
 Mrs. Walker (cook) 122–3, 125, 139, 217
 Peter Walsh 120, 122, 124, 125, 126, 128, 132, 240 n.2
 Rezia Warren Smith 128
 Richard Dalloway 120, 121, 122, 124
 Sally Seton, and Clarissa Dalloway 119, 129, 131
 Septimus Warren Smith 126, 127–8, 129
 war in 128–9, 130
 William Bradshaw 126, 127, 129

neurasthenia vi, xiii, 26, 46
"The New Biography" 51
Nicolson, Harold 55
Night and Day 234 n.23
Noble, Joan Russell xiii

Ohmann, Carol 100, 238 n.3

"Old Bloomsbury" 24, 25, 43, 71
Orbach, Susie 4, 8, 9, 10, 11, 49, 68–9, 79, 229 nn.1, 8, 234 n.19
pacifism, and feminism 181
Panken, Shirley viii, 41, 68, 69, 127, 183, 239 n.8
The Pargiters, see *The Years*
Parsons, Trekkie 55, 60
paternalism, and treatment of anorexic women 8–9
Patmore, Coventry 176
patriarchy
  as abusive ix, xiv, 10
  acculturation to ix, 4–5, 91–2, 95
  challenges to xiv, 11, 221
  and disempowerment of women 80–1, 83–7, 88, 90–8, 106, 119, 138, 182–4
  and eating disorders 1, 2–5, 7–9, 11, 21, 77, 78, 230 n.1b
  and the family xiv, 31, 34, 80–5, 92, 188, 218–19
  and fathering 133–4, 146–53
  and history 128, 204–14, 219, 221–5
  and interpretation of VW xvi, 48
  and meat 63, 91, 104–5, 185–7, 189, 212, 224–5
  and mothering 78, 93, 95, 133–7, 143–4
  and religion 2–3, 93, 129, 207–8, 214–17, 219, 226
  and sense of identity 5, 111–12, 117
  and tradition 178
  and violence 181, 186
Pattle, Virginia 40
Paul, Janis M. xii, xiii
pillar-box, as image 179, 244 n.5
Plath, Sylvia ix
play
  and Age of Reason 223
  ascendancy of aggressive young male 222–3
  and cakes 218
  and female disinheritance 223–4
  and matrism 203, 205–6, 221–6
  patriarchal policeman 203, 207, 224
  and rape 222–3
  and Victorian age 224–5
Plomer, William xv
Plough Inn, Holford 57–8, 67
Poole, Roger vii, 52, 55, 61, 236 n.13, 240 n.7
power, *see* disempowerment; empowerment
pregnancy, and anorexia viii, 229 n.7
"Professions for Women" xii, xvi, 176
psychiatry, and treatment of anorexia 6–11
psychoanalysis, and anorexia viii, 10–11, 229 n.7
Puritanism 246 n.13

Radin, Grace 181, 244 n.15

rage
  anorexic 5–7, 31, 134
  of Leslie Stephen 36, 37
  of VW 21, 31, 59, 60–1, 127
rape
  and anorexia 10
  in *Between the Acts* 208, 212, 216–17, 222–3
  treatment as 9, 10
rationality ix, ix–xii, 48, 50, 51
rebellion, in anorexia 4, 10, 41–2
religion
  and patriarchy 2–3, 93, 129, 185, 207–9, 214–17, 219, 226
  see also Judeo-Christianity; matrism
"Reminiscences" 18, 40, 42
Richardson, Samuel, *Clarissa* 118, 238 n.10
Richter, Harvena xi
Robins, Elizabeth 70, 73
A Room of One's Own
  men's college meal in xi, 102–3
  and satiety 159
  and subordination of women 125
  women's college meal in xi, 102, 103–4, 238–9 n.7b
Rose, Phyllis vii, ix, 237 n.2
Rosenman, Ellen xvi, 95, 118, 121, 176, 205, 241 n.3
Rosenthal, Michael vii
Ruotolo, Lucio 77, 121, 140

Sackville-West, Vita
  daring of 66–7
  and food 67, 68
  "The Land" 246 n.16
  and LW 66
  and maternal protection of VW 19, 32, 66
  sexual relationship with VW xii, 55, 66, 226, 236 n.15
  and VW's attitude to food 66
  VW's letters to xii, 63, 65, 70
  and VW's sexual abuse 71–2
St. Ives, *see* Talland House
Sands, Ethel 71–2
Savage, George 24
  knowledge of VW's abuse 27, 59
  and moral insanity 236 n.7
  and rationalism 49–50
  treats Vanessa 29
  treats VW 26, 28, 46, 54, 57
  and VW's desire for children 52
schizophrenia, assumed, of VW viii
Schlack, Beverly 155, 239 n.15, 240 nn.4,5,11
Schwartz, Hillel vi, 26
Selvini-Palazzoli, Mara 2, 37, 68, 117–18, 235 n.5
Seton, David (family doctor) 21, 22, 72
Sexton, Anne ix

sexual abuse
and eating disorders viii, ix, 9–10, 17, 21, 23–4, 53, 71, 212, 232 n.6
as unacknowledged 45, 235 n.1
of VW vi, vii, viii, ix, xiii, 24–5, 32, 229 nn.3.5; and eating disorder 18, 31; and marriage 43, 53, 59; and menstruation 22–3, 233 n.15; recovered memory of xiii, 70–1, 208, 209, 227; and silence 20–1, 27, 31, 35, 73; and suppression of sexuality 20; Vanessa's awareness of 27; writing about 16–17, 34, 71–3, 96, 224, 245 n.16
shame, *see* guilt
Shaw, George Bernard 104
silence
and sexual abuse 20–1, 27, 31, 73
and suppression of emotion xiii, 37, 38, 72
Sjöö, Monica 205, 245 n.3
"A Sketch of the Past"
and childhood sexual abuse 17, 70–3, 246 n.9
and mother 19, 40, 226, 244 n.7
and teatable etiquette 243 n.1
and Thoby 245 n.5
Slade, Roger 1, 231 n.10
Smyth, Ethel
appetite xiv
and fertility 226
heroism 181
VW's letters to 53, 63, 64, 68, 69, 70, 71
Sophie (Stephen family's cook) 28
Sophocles, *Antigone* 183, 185, 189, 244 n.8
Spalding, Frances 27, 244 n.14
Spater, George & Parsons, Ian 49, 61
Spender, Stephen xi
Squier, Susan 131
Stape, J. H. xiii
starvation 15–16, 240 n.10
Stephen, Adrian (brother of VW) 28, 33, 36, 38, 41
Stephen, Ann (niece of VW) xiv
Stephen, Caroline Emilia (aunt of VW) 28, 119
Stephen, James (father of Leslie) vii, 33, 35
Stephen, James Fitzjames, as manic depressive vii
Stephen, Jane (mother of Leslie) 33
Stephen, Judith (niece of VW) xiv
Stephen, Julia (mother of VW)
and birth of VW 15
death vii, 15, 18–21, 30, 37–8, 42, 72
desire for independence 41
and early weaning of VW 14–15
and Leslie Stephen 32, 36–7, 241 n.10
and mother, nursing 15, 36, 40
The Mysterious Voice 38–9
"Notes from Sick Rooms" 40
obedience valued 38–9

praises VW 32
as provider of food 36
relationship with Stella 40
relationship with VW 18–19, 40–1, 154
and response to illness 39–41
and suffrage movement 41
and the tea table 176
VW associates with music 244 n.7
Stephen, Laura (half sister of VW) vii, 15, 23, 31
and food 23–4
and sexual abuse 24
Stephen, Leslie (father of VW)
asceticism 35–6, 46
death 18, 42–3, 53
and family 31, 32, 38
and father 34
final illness 24
and food 36
and Julia Stephen vii, 30, 37–8, 41, 42, 72, 241 n.10
and LW 64
as manic depressive vii
Mausoleum Book 36, 37
and mother 34
and need for wife-surrogate 30, 42
as needy child 32–3, 36, 41
obedience valued 38
and rationalism 32, 37–8
relationship with Vanessa 42
relationship with VW 19, 22, 30–3, 35, 154
sends Thoby to school 34–5
and upbringing of children 14–15
and walking 15, 22, 33, 34, 35, 66
Stephen, Thoby (brother of VW) 15, 20, 245 n.5
death 38
sent to school 22, 34–5
suicidal distress 21–2
Stephen, Vanessa, *see* Bell, Vanessa
Stephen, Virginia, *see* Woolf, Virginia
Strachey, Alix xiii, 64
Strachey, James 67
Strachey, Lytton
and LW 54–5
as St. John Hirst 238 n.9
VW considers marriage to 45
and VW as ratiocinator 48
VW's letters to 56, 57, 62, 67
suffrage movement 41, 86–7
Sunday Tramps 35
Swinburne, A. C., "Itylus" 212
Sydney-Turner, Saxon 62
Szasz, Thomas 78

Talland House, Cornwall vii, 16, 18, 31, 36
Tannahill, Reay 185, 193, 212
Thakur, N. C. 204, 226

Thomas, Jean 52, 53–4
Thompson, William Irwin 204
Three Guineas 101, 187, 238 n.5
    quoted 5
through-sight of VW vi
To the Lighthouse 133–54
    Andrew Ramsay 32, 150
    Cam Ramsay 133–4, 135, 152; eats food of father 150–2
    Charles Tansley 136, 142–3; and work and food 135, 139, 142–3
    and class system 139, 142
    father/fathering in 133–4, 146–53
    and female creativity 134, 138–9, 145–6, 153
    James Ramsay 151, 152
    Lily Briscoe: and anorexia 133, 135, 144; and Charles Tansley 136, 142–3; as child 135, 137; and compositional unity 137–9; and female art 137–9, 152–3; grief and emptiness at loss 136–7; 'hand to mouth' attitude 135; and hunger for nurturance 135–7; and marriage 144; and Mr. Ramsay 144, 145, 146, 149, 153–4; and Mrs. Ramsay 149–50, 153–4, 194; reconciliation with parent figures 135, 152; sense of identity 135, 137–8, 153; slightness 144; as voice of VW 135
    meals of father in 134, 150–3
    meals of mother in 134, 136–47, 151–2, 153
    Mildred (cook) 139, 141
    Minta Doyle 141, 143–4, 242 n.6
    mother/mothering in 133, 134, 135–8, 140–6, 149
    Mr. Carmichael 146, 147, 153
    Mr. Ramsay: as abuser 241 n.9; as adventurer 146, 147, 151; asceticism 36, 146–7, 151; and children 32, 133–5, 148, 150–1; and empty landscape 147, 148–9; and family 148; and fishermen 151, 152; hunger for nurturance 37, 135–6, 144–5, 147–51, 153; as Leslie Stephen 31–2, 36, 37–8, 154, 232 n.4; as LW 48, 235 n.3; rage 147, 149, 150, 152; and scrubbed table 146–7; and sense of erosion 148; and truth 48; and wife 38, 135, 144–5, 147–8, 150, 178; and work and food 134, 135, 139, 142, 148
    Mrs. McNab 144, 145, 149
    Mrs. Ramsay: bee and hive as symbols 136, 137, 170; Boeuf en Daube dinner party 134–153, 179, 194; and children 32, 146; and control of wilderness 145; death 144–5, 149–50, 194; and feminine role 135, 136, 148; as the Goddess 137, 139, 141, 143, 145; as Julia Stephen 41; and marriage 143–4, 149; and meals 134, 136–9; and milk 144, 149; self-sacrifice 144–5, 148; tree as symbol 137, 138, 145
    Nancy Ramsay 150
    Paul Rayley 143–4
    Prue Ramsay 134, 149, 150
    quoted 48
    Ramsay children 143, 232 n.2
    Rose Ramsay 134–5, 145–6
    William Bankes: Boeuf en Daube dinner party 140, 141, 145, 151; and Lily Briscoe 138, 141, 146; and work and food 135, 139, 141–2
Transue, Pamela 157, 239 n.13
Trombley, Stephen viii–ix, 23, 50, 240 n.8

Vaughan, Madge (cousin of VW) 19, 23, 26–8
virginity, and sexual abuse xiv, 55
voices, hearing x, 23, 26, 27–8, 47–8, 74
The Voyage Out 77–98
    Alice Flushing 89, 92, 94
    ants as microcosm 242 n.6
    Arthur Venning 80, 81, 97,
    Aunts Kate and Lucy 94
    Catholicism 90–1
    chickens 93
    Clarissa Dalloway 86, 87–8, 91
    colonialism: cultural theft 89, 92; and food 89, 90
    Eleanor (aunt) 94
    Emma Paley 80–1
    Evelyn Murgatroyd 93
    fish in 81, 91–2
    Grice (steward) 91
    Helen Ambrose 79, 83, 88, 237 n.4; as caretaker of Ridley Ambrose 82, 84; conflict in relationship with Rachel 95–6; as mother figure 94–5; and St. John Hirst 92; as teacher-liberator 95, 100
    hotel 82, 88–9, 90–3, 97–8, 158, 199
    and Indian culture 88–90, 94–5, 97
    and *Jacob's Room* 100
    and Leslie Stephen 32
    Miss Allan: androgynous identity 85; and fear of contamination 90; and gift of preserved ginger 84–5; as single working woman 84, 85, 87
    Mrs. Chailey 83
    Mrs. Elliot 81–2, 84, 90
    Mrs. Thornbury 84, 98
    and patriarchy as predatory 88–9, 91–2, 95, 98
    Rachel Vinrace: anorexic characteristics 77, 83–4, 87–8; and bodilessness 77–8, 96; and Catholicism 91; child identity 77, 78, 94; compared with Jacob Flanders 100, 104–6, 114–15; death 81, 83–5, 97–8,

100, 114–15; as helper of father 79; and Hewet 83, 90, 93; and Hirst 92–3; and Indian culture 89–90; as livestock 93; and marriage 81, 93; and maternal deprivation 77, 94, 95, 97; and mealtimes 82–3, 88; and milk 94, 232 n.2; and patriarchy 77–9, 80–1, 83–5, 86, 87, 88, 90–8, 100, 106; and politics and women's rights 86; repression of volition 78, 79, 100; and selfhood 95, 104; sexual desire for Helen Ambrose 95–6
Richard Dalloway: and Catholicism 91; and LW 237 n.6; and Rachel Vinrace 96; and seasickness 87; and women's rights 86–7
Ridley Ambrose 79, 82, 83–4, 94
St. John Hirst 88, 92, 238 n.9
and seasickness 87
Signor Rodriguez 91
starving cat story 86–7
Susan Warrington 79–80, 81
Terence Hewet: and bodilessness 78; and food 81; and Helen Ambrose 82, 96; and Rachel Vinrace 83, 90, 95, 96, 97, 100
Theresa Vinrace 94, 95
Wilfred Flushing 89, 92, 97–8
William Pepper 79, 98
Willoughby Vinrace 79, 87, 100
walking
  enjoyed by Leslie Stephen 15, 22, 33, 34, 35, 66
  enjoyed by VW xv, 22, 34, 35, 70
  in novels 146, 147, 148
Waskett, Carole 10, 20, 54
"The Watering Place" xv
The Waves 155–73
  Bernard 155; appetite and fullness 159, 172, 243 n.20; and body 156, 172–3, 244 n.5; bread-pellet-making 161–2; breakdown 156, 171–3; as Byron 161, 243 n.11; and death 172–3; and eating xi; effectiveness 156; sense of identity 171–3; slovenliness 160–1; and sociability 159, 161–2, 165, 167, 172; and Susan 170, 171; and time 243 n.18
  birds in 162, 163
  café in 165–6
  community in 140, 159, 161, 168, 196
  Jinny 155, 202; and age 169; and bodily secretions 168; and communality 168; as force for form and harmony 168; and orgasm 168–9; sense of identity 168–9, 171; and time 168–9
  and kitchen rubbish heap 162–3, 165
  Louis 155; and body 163; as counterpart of Rhoda 156, 161, 164; and imitation 156, 167–8, 242 n.4; as immigrant 164; and

poetic order 165–6; and working-class people 164–6
  Neville 155; and fullness xi, 159–60; homosexuality 160; and intimacy 161; and Percival 167; tidiness and order 160–1; and the university 160
  Percival 167
  quoted xi
  Rhoda: and anorexia 155, 158–9; and body 77, 155–9, 162–3, 168, 172–3; and communality 140, 161, 168; control fantasies 156–7; crossing the puddle 155, 156, 171; disintegration fears 157; exclusion from university 160; and gluttony 158; and imitation 167–8; ineffectiveness 156; and milk 232 n.2; and pellet image 162; regressive introspection 162; sense of identity 155–6, 157, 161, 163, 167, 171; suicide fantasies 157–8, 243 n.14; and time 158, 168
  snails in 162–3
  Susan 155, 156, 246 n.7; bread-making xi, 169–70; and child-bearing 169–71; entrapment 171; and Jinny 168; and kitchen 163, 169–71; and possession 171; preserve-making 170; sense of identity 169, 171; and time 169
  and the university 160
Webb, Sidney & Beatrice 239 n.9
weight
  and female empowerment 219
  gain and loss 29–30, 43, 60, 61–3, 67, 92
  as mark of mental stability 126, 127
  recording 45, 59
Wells, H. G. 104
Wilberforce, Octavia (doctor of VW) 63, 69, 70, 72–4
women, anorexic
  and access to food 68
  and attitudes to food v, viii, 3–4
  and attitudes to self xiii, 3
  defense mechanisms 118
  and disempowerment 2, 4–5, 7, 11, 21, 49, 54, 231 n.8
  hospital treatment of 1, 6–11, 53, 231 n.10
  and imitation of others 166
  as "manipulative", 8, 54
  and mind trapped in body 3, 158–9
  and nurturance 41
  and persuasion to eat 49
  as text v
Women's Research Centre 17, 233 nn.15,18
Woodman, Marion 2–3, 5, 231 n.4
Wooley, Susan 232 n.16, 235 n.1
Woolf, Leonard

character: asceticism 46, 63, 65; jealousy 66; and rationality 47–9, 63; strength of personality 61, 64, 236 n.14; tightness with money 45, 64; and truth 47, 49, 51 and doctors of VW 46–8, 50, 58–9, 60–2, 73 enjoyment of solitude 242 n.13
and feminism 64
and food 57–8, 65–6, 230 n.5, 237 n. 6
and guilt 46
and sexuality 54–6
and VW: and anorexia viii; awareness of her illness 52; breakdowns 52, 232 n.7; as caretaker of VW v, xiv, 42, 45–7, 54–64, 73–4, 120; and children 52–3; control of social life 45, 63–7, 236 n.17; engagement 20, 53, 54; and manic depression vi; marriage 45–75; maternal protection of 19; and neurasthenia vi, 46; and record-keeping 46–7, 59–60; refusal to eat xiv, 46–9, 58–63; rejection by VW 60–1; walking 35; in World War II 69; writing 32
weight 62–3
writings: *The Journey Not the Arrival Matters* 69; *Sowing* 46, 55; *The Wise Virgins* 51
Woolf, Virginia
appearance: elegance 18, 65; thinness 18, 69, 73
and body, *see* body
character: asceticism viii, xiii, 35, 65; desire for approval 32; feelings of failure 53, 57, 59; pleasure in life 74–5, 117, 226; practicality xiii; sociability 63–4, 65, 66, 140, 167; and spirituality 226; and truth 49, 51, 75
childhood and adolescence 13–43; anxiety attack 21–2; appetite 17–18; birth 15; early weaning 14–15; and food fantasies 16; and writing 13–17
and cooking xii–xii; bread-making xii, 230 n.2; lessons 60; in World War II 68; and writing xii, 68
and dreams 53, 96
education 21–2, 31
and family: family boundaries 18, 30–1, 33, 56; father 14–15, 19, 22, 30–2, 35, 154, 232 n.9; and manic depression vii; mother as carer 14–15; mother's death vii, 18–21; mother, relationship with 18–19, 40–1, 154; and patriarchy xiv, 188; relationship with Vanessa Bell 19–20, 29, 42, 55–6, 66, 226; as scapegoat 31
food and eating: attitudes to v, viii, xi–xvi, 45, 65–6; binge-eating 69, 237 n.19; disgust at eating ix, xiv–xv; dislike of overeating xiv, xv, 67, 88–9; dislike of poverty in food xv; enjoyment of 16, 23, 28, 43, 67, 226, 238 n.4; and guilt xiii, 46, 57, 65; as life-enhancing xv; metaphorical meanings 48; refusal xiii, 23, 46–9, 58–63; and simplicity 66; as treatment 21, 26–8, 46–9, 53–4, 57–63, 73–4, 127; wartime preoccupation with 68–9; and wartime rationing xiii, 67–8; weight 29–30, 43, 45, 59, 60, 61–3, 67; and work 65; in writing viii, xi–xii, xvi, 13–17, 88–9, 226
marriage 45–75; ambivalence about LW 57, 65, 74; desire for children 52–3, 74; engagement to LW 20, 53, 54; honeymoon 55–7; and LW as caretaker v, xiv, 42, 45–6, 54–64, 73–4, 120; and LW's control of money 45, 64; quarrels with LW 49, 60–1, 63; and sexuality 43, 53, 54–6, 59
mental health: anorexia, *see* anorexia nervosa; attitude to carers 41–2; breakdowns and treatment vii, xiii, 18–25, 26–8, 46–7, 52, 57–62, 73–4, 127; in Burley nursing home 52, 53–4, 57; depression vii, 27, 59, 69–70; loss of emotion xiv, 37, 70, 72; manic depression diagnosis vi, vii–viii; neurasthenia diagnosis vi, xiv, 46; and nurture deficit 14, 19, 41–2; presumed madness vi–x, xiii–xiv, 25–8, 45, 74; sanity vi; and sense of identity 22, 28, 29–30, 31, 70
and mother-figure, need for 19–20, 38, 41–2, 226–7
and patriarchy xvi, 5, 48
physical health: fainting fits 64; menstruation 22, 45, 59, 67, 236–7 n.18; and psychological distress vi, 54; thinness 18, 69, 73; whooping cough 18
pleasures: walking xv, 22, 34, 35, 70
rage: at treatment 59, 127; with father 21, 31; with George Duckworth 21; with LW 60–1
and rationality 48–9, 51, 63
and sexual abuse, *see* sexual abuse
suicide 26, 31, 46, 58, 59, 74–5, 127
writing: and breakdowns 22, 54; in childhood 13–17; diaries xii, xv, 21–2, 69–70, 243 n.2, 243 n.13; and father 32–3; and food xi–xii, xvi, 68; and French inheritance 241 n.6; inability during war 70; and Leslie Stephen 32–3; as lifeline 70; prohibited 22, 54, 73–4; and sexual abuse 16–17, 34, 71–3, 96
Wordsworth, William 104, 238 n.6
World War I
and cannon fodder 113, 114
and guilt felt by women 115

and *Jacob's Room* 99, 113
and *The Years* 186, 187–9, 199
World War II
    and *Between the Acts* 204, 212–13
    and food rationing 67–8
    and VW's depression 69–70
    and VW's inability of write 70
    and VW's preoccupation with food xv, 68–9
Wright, Maurice, as doctor of VW 46
writing, and domesticity xii, 82

The Years 43, 175–202
    Abel Pargiter: and daughters 192; death 196–7; and dinner 178–9, 185; and Eugenie 181–2; and Martin's food 176–7, 195; and tea-table culture 176, 178–9, 182; and wife 178, 179
    Abrahamson 186–7, 188
    Bigge (cook) 189
    Crosby 177, 178, 195
    Delia Pargiter: and breaking down of social barriers 199; dancing 200–1; and father 178, 179; and flowers 200; party 175, 196, 199–202; as rebel 177, 178; reconciliation with mother 202; resentment of mother 177–8, 200
    Digby Pargiter 183, 185, 192
    Edward Pargiter 183, 189
    Eleanor Pargiter: and Abel 185, 195, 196–7; and afternoon tea as roll call 177; chain restaurant meal 193–6, 200; and domestic revolution 188; embraces change 192, 197, 201–2; and male tyranny 195, 196; and oppression of working-class women 195; and Rose (younger) 180, 181
    Eugenie Pargiter 181–2, 194, 196, 200
    fathers/fatherhood in 176
    history of women and food in 175–6
    Hugh Gibbs 198–9
    Kitty Malone/Lasswade 177, 196, 201; as Antigone 189; ice cream with Mrs. Fripp 190–1; lunch with Mrs. Malone 190; and Oxford university 189–92, 195; size 189; tea with the Hughes/Robsons 191–2; working-class sympathies 190–2, 199
    Lucy Craddock 190, 191, 192
    Maggie Pargiter: bohemianism 187; and dirt 188; and feminism 181; and flowers 202; and food 189; iconoclasm 187–8; possessiveness 198; rebellion against patriarchy 187–8; relative liberty 175; and Vanessa Bell 188; and World War I 188–9
    Martin Pargiter 176–7, 184–5, 195
    Milly Pargiter/Gibbs 177, 198–9, 246 n.7
    mother/mothering in 175–6, 179, 181, 187–9, 191–3, 197–8, 200–2, 203
    Mrs. Carter 191
    Mrs. Fripp 190–1
    Mrs. Hughes 191–2
    Mrs. Malone xi, 190
    mutton in 185–7, 189
    Nicholas Pargiter 184, 188, 195, 201–2
    North Pargiter: and militarism 184, 186, 189; and Milly 198, 199; as mutton-fed man 186; and Peggy 186, 198, 199; as rebel 186; and Sara 183–4, 185–6, 187, 199
    Old Chuffy 190
    and Oxford university 189–92, 195
    Peggy Pargiter 181, 186, 197–8, 199, 200
    Renny 187–8, 189, 202
    Rose Pargiter (elder) 177–8, 179, 180, 200
    Rose Pargiter (younger) 175; and body 179, 180; and cake 179–80; and dirt and shame 188; and flasher 179–80, 185; force-feeding 185; masculine identity 180–1; and women's rights activism 179, 180–1, 183, 185
    Sam Robson 192
    Sara Pargiter: and Abrahamson 186–7, 188; and alcohol 184; as Antigone 183, 184, 185; ascetic separateness 183–4; as child-like 182, 184; chop-house meal 184–5; cooks dinner for North 185–6; and dirt 188; and feminism 181; and meals 242 n.5; and mother's waltz 182, 183, 194; physical deformity 182–4; relative liberty 175; sense of identity 105; sleep 184; and smell of food xi; stain on 188; thinness 182
    and tea-table culture 176–9, 180–2, 192, 200
    and war 186, 187–9, 199